THE
TWO-YEAR-OLD
GUIDE 2021

DAN BRIDEN

Marten Julian (Publisher) 2021 ©
69 Highgate, Kendal,
Cumbria, LA9 4ED

01539 741 007
rebecca@martenjulian.com
www.martenjulian.com

First published in Great Britain in 2021 by Marten Julian

A CIP catalogue record of this book is available from the British Library.

ISBN 978-1-8382317-2-9

Photography
Francesca Altoft Photography
www.francescaaltoft.co.uk

Layout:
Steve Dixon

Proof reading:
Ian Greensill (Marten's chapter and Stallion chapter)
Richard Grummitt (Dan's writing)

Published by:
Marten Julian, 69 Highgate, Kendal, Cumbria LA9 4ED
Tel: 01539 741 007 www.martenjulian.com

CONTENTS

FOREWORD

Producing a book of this quality takes a lot of time and trouble and Dan has managed to ensure that much of the two-year-old population of 2021 is covered in this edition.

There are promising two-year-olds everywhere and they can come from varying sources. Any trainer can find an above-average two-year-old and seemingly any stallion can produce a good one, so Dan and Marten have tried to point us all in the right direction to find the real ones.

This is clearly a labour of love and a book that is appreciated by the purists, but all practitioners in racing – whether they be owners, breeders, trainers or jockeys – will continually reflect on the contents and refer to them throughout the next two years.

Marten's racing knowledge knows no bounds and he has been studying form and writing about racing for as long as I have been training, and that seems to be a long time. Dan is relatively new to the business but no less keen and his knowledge and groundwork have produced a book of great quality.

I hope you enjoy it as much as I will and I look forward to it landing on my desk in the weeks to come.

William Haggas

William Haggas (Racing Post)

INTRODUCTION

Welcome to the second edition of the Two-Year-Old Guide. I am delighted to have been asked to do the book again by Marten Julian after the positive sales figures and response to the 2020 version.

To say it was a Herculean effort from all involved to get last year's book out in good time would be an understatement. It was certainly a unique set of circumstances under which to embark upon such a project.

It simply wouldn't have happened without Rebecca Julian and Steve Dixon putting it all together, Richard Grummitt's tireless proofreading (and correction of my mistakes!), Francesca Altoft's wonderful photography, and of course the owners, trainers and breeders who all so generously gave their time despite all the uncertainty around last spring.

It is never easy to know the ideal time to publish such a publication. I feel that March is a little too soon to be asking people about young horses, but any later than April or May and you run the risk of missing too much of the season and indeed run a bit close to Royal Ascot.

Therefore, some trainers either couldn't offer quite as much as they'd have liked in terms of input, or simply didn't want to contribute full stop - which I quite understand.

However, the response overall has been phenomenal. To a woman and man, every trainer I asked to feature in the book got back to me in good time. I managed to complete the interview process in little more than a week thanks to the co-operation of all those who feature in the book.

As you will see, there are some new names in this year's edition, including Sean Woods after two decades spent in Hong Kong. Rather aptly for the subject matter of this book, his final big-race winner in the UK had been Atlantis Prince in the Royal Lodge Stakes back in 2000. With his first two-year-old runners finishing first and a very close second, he is a trainer to follow this year.

Kevin Philippart de Foy is a new name to both the book and indeed the training ranks. The Belgian gained his racing education under the likes of John Oxx, Criquette Head, Christophe Clement and James Fanshawe, with the latter another new name to the book this year.

With such an education, it is easy to understand why he has made such a swift and pronounced impact as a trainer. He was insightful, professional and incredibly helpful when putting forward his two-year-olds for the book.

Another new name to be featured is bloodstock analyst, Michelle Kinane. As befitting such a surname, her knowledge of horses and their pedigrees is second to none. Her article on this year's first-season sires is a most welcome addition.

It is also a privilege to have the likes of John Warren, Chris Richardson and Richard Ryan appear this year for the first time. Teddy Grimthorpe once again proved how generous he is with his time when supplying me with ten Juddmonte Farms two-year-olds in the very same week he stepped down from his role as their racing manager after over two decades in the role. I wish him well for the future.

I know some people baulk at the idea of contributing to publications such as this for fear of "making a perfect fool one of oneself," as one prominent owner/breeder who politely declined the chance to appear put it to me! I can assure everyone that their thoughts are always welcome - win, lose or draw.

That said, I must congratulate Eve Johnston Houghton on her contribution last season. All bar two of her two-year-olds from the book that raced went on to win at least once. Having already won the Brocklesby Stakes with Chipotle, Eve has certainly set the bar very high for 2021!

I have also taken an in-depth look at two-year-olds from some of the bigger stables who couldn't contribute, including 50 of John and Thady Gosden's two-year-olds. I felt it was important to cover their crop in as much detail as possible, given they won't be readily available elsewhere.

Thanks to all of you for your support, whether you have contributed to the book or taken the trouble of buying a copy. Hopefully it proves both an enjoyable and informative read.

Dan Briden

HOW TO GUIDE

AEROSPACE (IRE)
15/4 b c Sea The Stars - Talent (New Approach)
Owner: Godolphin Sales price: 300,000gns (Stroud Coleman Bloodstock)

This is what each part means:

Horse name - AEROSPACE
(IRE) - Country of birth
15/4 - Date of birth
B - Bay
C - Colt
Sea The Stars - Sire
Talent - Dam
(New Approach) - Sire of Dam
After sales price in brackets is the name of the purchaser.

Please note that the information in the main body of the book, including names and pedigrees, was correct up to April 12. After this point we continued checking for names to amend the index.

This means some horses appear as unnamed in the book yet in the index appear with their name. Consequently if you look up a horse in the index it may state a page number yet when you go to the page it will show as unnamed. This is because some horses were named after the layout was complete and because they are in alphabetical order we could not move them within the book.

Horses that this relates to have a (N) next to their name to help identify them and serve as a reminder.

Clients who buy the book direct from us, the publisher, will receive updates on horse names. If you have bought the book from a book shop please contact us for details on how to subscribe to our enhanced service. Proof of purchase will be required.

The book is split into three sections.

Section 1 covers trainers who spoke with Dan and shared their opinions and views on the two-year-olds they consider to be of particular interest.

Section 2 features a selection of owners, breeders, syndicate managers and bloodstock agents who spoke with Dan and shared their thoughts on the two-year-olds they consider to be of particular interest.

Section 3 relates to interesting two-year-olds that are with stables who were not able to speak with us.

Please note that there are four indexes; Horse, Sire, Dam and Trainer. Please note the index lists the main reference point, not every mention. For example, if a sire is mentioned as being the sire of a horse, it is listed in the sire index but if it is mentioned again within the write-up this second reference will not appear.

ANDREW BALDING

ANGEL'S POINT
11/4 b/gr f Dark Angel - Madonna Dell'orto (Montjeu)
Owner: Sheikh Mohammed Obaid Al Maktoum Sales price: 260,000gns
(Andrew Balding)

Half-sister to Group 1-placed 7f-1m winner (including at Group 2/Listed
level) I Can Fly, Group 3-placed UK/French 6-7.5f winner (including at Listed
level) Viscount Barfield and two other winners. Dam a maiden half-sister to
Poule d'Essai des Poulains winner Landseer, Group 1-placed 8-10f winner
(including at Listed level) Ikhtyar and the dam of 8/10f 3yo Listed winner
Moneycantbuymelove (herself later dam of Japanese 10f Grade 1 winner
Mikki Love).

*"A daughter of Dark Angel, who is related to a nice horse we trained called
Viscount Barfield, while I Can Fly was a smart filly for Aidan O'Brien. This is a
filly we very much liked at the sales, and she is a quality individual who is one
for the summer onwards."*

ANTIPHON (IRE)
8/2 b c Kodiac - Freedom's Light (Galileo)
Owner: George Strawbridge Sales price: n/a

Half-brother to useful dual 6f 2yo winner Firelight and French 9.5f 3yo winner
Lauderdale. Dam a Group 3-placed dual 12f winner (including at Listed level)
who was a full sister to French 12.5f 3yo Listed winner Oh Beautiful and a
three-parts sister to 2m 3yo Listed winner Face The Facts.

*"A small but strong colt, who will likely be one of our first two-year-old runners.
He will obviously be quick enough to begin over 5f but is ultimately one for 6f
in time."*

ATTACHE (IRE)
26/2 b c Declaration of War - Go Kart (Intense Focus)
Owner: Kennet Valley Thoroughbreds VII Sales price: £42,000 (Kern/Lillingston
Association)

First foal of a Listed-placed triple Irish 5f winner who was a half-sister to useful
Irish dual 5f 2yo winner Dream Kart and fairly useful Irish 8-12f winner Muzbid
out of an unraced daughter of a French 1m 3yo Listed winner.

"This colt is a forward going individual and very much a two-year-old type. He will want 6f to begin with, and holds entries in all the sales events this summer."

BERKSHIRE PHOENIX (IRE)
25/3 b c Bungle Inthejungle - Scarlet Wings (Sir Percy)
Owner: Berkshire Parts & Panels Ltd Sales price: £18,000 (Andrew Balding)

Second foal of a once-raced maiden half-sister to Group 1-placed 6-10.5f winner (including at Group 2/3 level) Sri Putra and useful 11.5f 3yo Flat/2m Grade 3 hurdle winner Duty out of an unraced half-sister to Prix de Diane winner Caerlina (later dam of 7f 2yo winner/Irish 1000 Guineas and Poule d'Essai des Pouliches third La Nuit Rose, herself the dam of US 1m Grade 2 winner Tam Lin).

"This colt goes along nicely at this stage and would be another of our sharper two-year-olds. There is some stamina in his pedigree, but the sire has imparted plenty of speed and precocity."

BERKSHIRE SHADOW
12/3 gr c Dark Angel - Angel Vision (Oasis Dream)
Owner: Berkshire Parts & Panels Ltd Sales price: 40,000gns (Andrew Balding)

Second foal of a 7f-1m 3yo winner who was a half-sister to UK/US 8.5-12f winner Bohemian Dance Angel Vision out of a four-time 10/12f Group 1 winner (including the Breeders' Cup Filly & Mare Turf) who was a full sister to German 10f Group 1 winner Greek Dance and 10f Group 3 winner New Morning and a half-sister to French 12f Group 1 winner Mountain High.

"A nice, strong colt who moves well at this stage. He is another one who is pretty sharp and will start at 5f in April, but he will probably be happier over 6f in the long run."

CRUCIAL CHOICE
29/3 b c Siyouni - Prefer (Galileo)
Owner: Sheikh Mohammed Obaid Al Maktoum Sales price: 120,000gns (Andrew Balding)

Second foal of a once-raced maiden sister to French 12.5f 3yo Listed winner Dirgam, Irish 7f 3yo winner/1000 Guineas third Moth and Group 3/Listed-placed 1m 2yo winner Spin, a three-parts sister to Group 1-placed 8-10f winner (including at Listed level) Rave Reviews, 12f 3yo Listed winner Fermion (later dam of 6f 2yo winner/Coventry Stakes runner-up Roman Soldier) and Cheshire Oaks winner Sail and half-sister to smart 8-10f winner (including at Group 3/Listed level) Hearthstead Maison.

"A horse with a bit of quality about him. The Siyouni/Galileo cross is a good one, and I would expect him to be running from July onwards. He will start over 7f but will want 1m before long."

FRANKLIN WILLIAM
24/4 b c Frankel - Kiyoshi (Dubawi)
Owner: Sheikha Melissa Al Fahad Sales price: n/a

Half-brother to 8-12f Flat/2m hurdle winner Iron Heart. Dam a smart 6-7f winner (including twice at Group 3 level) who was the daughter of a Listed-placed 8-10f winning half-sister to useful 6f 2yo winner Cosmo.

"A fine, big colt who is a half-brother to a winner we trained and out of a classy two-year-old who won at Royal Ascot. He is a really nice type for the 7f races from June onwards."

HARROW (IRE)
19/3 gr c El Kabeir - School Run (Invincible Spirit)
Owner: Highclere Thoroughbred Racing - Wisteria Sales price: 85,000gns
(John & Jake Warren)

Second foal of a 5f 3yo winner who was a half-sister to French 1m 3yo Listed winner Noor Sahara out of a 6f 3yo winning half-sister to Flying Childers Stakes winner Land of Dreams (later dam of five-time 6/7f Group 1 winner Dream Ahead and grandam of Cheveley Park Stakes winner Fairyland) and the maiden dam of 6f 2yo Group 3 winner/Cheveley Park Stakes runner-up Princess Noor.

"A nice, athletic son of one of the more interesting first-season sires about. He does it all very nicely at this stage and should be running over 6f in May. We like him."

IMMINENT
10/5 b f Dubawi - Enticement (Montjeu)
Owner: The Queen Sales price: n/a

Full sister to smart 7-10.5f winner (including at Listed level) Diploma and a half-sister to useful 7f-1m winner Pick Your Choice and useful 7-9f winner Elector. Dam a 1m 2yo Listed winner who was a half-sister to French 7f 3yo Group 3 winner Surfrider and Group 3/Listed-placed 2020 Irish 7f 3yo winner Soul Search.

"A lovely filly owned and bred by Her Majesty. She is a strong, attractive filly who is incredibly straightforward to deal with. I can see her having quite an active two-year-old campaign, which will probably begin in June."

LUNAR GAZE
8/4 b f Sea The Moon - Lady Brora (Dashing Blade)
Owner: Kingsclere Racing Club Sales price: n/a

Half-sister to Racing Post Trophy winner Elm Park, Group 2/3-placed 9-10f winner Brorocco and three other winners. Dam a 1m 3yo winner who was a half-sister to 11-12f Flat/very useful 2m 5f-3m 1f hurdle (including at Listed level) winner Tweedledrum.

"She isn't here yet. We have had all the family, and she looks a nice autumn/ three-year-old project."

MR ZIPPI
28/4 b c Intello - Izzi Top (Pivotal)
Owner: Castle Down Racing Sales price: 100,000gns (Vendor)

Half-brother to Group 3-placed 7f 2yo winner Prince Eiji, Listed-placed 7-10f winner Willie John, very useful 6-7f winner Dreamfield and 2020 8-8.5f 3yo winner Bizzi Lizzi. Dam a dual 10f Group 1 winner who was a half-sister to Group 1-placed 8-10f winner (including at Group 2/Listed level) Jazzi Top.

"Another who is not in yet. He is from a very good family, and all the reports from the pre-trainer suggest he is a very nice horse."

NOBEL (IRE)
20/3 ch c Lope de Vega - Starlet (Sea The Stars)
Owner: Qatar Racing Limited Sales price: 825,000gns (David Redvers Bloodstock)

Half-brother to 2020 Irish 7f 3yo Group 3 winner Love Locket and 11.5f 3yo Listed winner Raakib Alhawa. Dam an Irish 12f 3yo winner who was the daughter of a Listed-placed Irish 7f 2yo winning half-sister to six-time 7-12f Group/Grade 1 winner High Chaparral, Dante Stakes winner Black Bear Island and the dam of 2020 Prix de Diane/Nassau Stakes winner Fancy Blue.

"I loved this colt at the sales, and I was delighted that Qatar Racing decided to send him our way. He is a gorgeous horse with plenty of quality and is one who will be running over 7f to begin with from the middle of the season."

NYMPHADORA
6/4 b f No Nay Never - Bewitchment (Pivotal)
Owner: St Albans Bloodstock Limited Sales price: 185,000gns (Blandford Bloodstock)

Half-sister to useful multiple 5f winner Laith Alareen. Dam a maiden sister to 6f 2yo winner Hip and half-sister to Cheveley Park Stakes winner Hooray,

French 1m 2yo Listed winner Hypnotic and Listed-placed 6f-1m winner Mazyoun out of a 7f 2yo Listed-winning half-sister to Cherry Hinton Stakes winner/1000 Guineas third Dazzle and the dam of high-class sprinter Danehurst.

"This is a quality filly, who is well forward and very much a two-year-old type. She is bred to sprint and looks like following suit. I can see her be ready enough to run at something like the Craven meeting."

OASIS GIFT
16/2 b c Oasis Dream - Siren's Gift (Cadeaux Genereux)
Owner: J C Smith Sales price: n/a

Half-brother to Group 3-placed triple 6f winner Rebel Streak and very useful 5-6f winner Merdon Castle. Dam a Listed-placed triple 5f winner who was a full sister to Group 2/3-placed triple 5f winner (including at Listed level) Speed Cop.

"He didn't come in until fairly late but is a nice, strong two-year-old type who should make his mark at some point this season."

SCHMILSSON
22/4 b c Muhaarar - Zee Zee Top (Zafonic)
Owner: Mick and Janice Mariscotti Sales price: 75,000gns (Andrew Balding)

Half-brother to dual 10f Group 1 winner Izzi Top, French 10f 3yo Group 2 winner/Prix de l'Opera runner-up Jazzi Top, very useful UK/US 7-8.5f winner Emaraaty, very useful UK/UAE 8-11f winner Rock N Roll Ransom and 2020 dual 1m 3yo winner Flyin' High. Dam a Prix de l'Opera winner who was a half-sister to Eclipse Stakes/King George VI And Queen Elizabeth Stakes winner Opera House and dual Ascot Gold Cup/Irish St Leger winner Kayf Tara.

"These owners have had plenty of joy with horses bought from Meon Valley Stud. This colt was purchased when his year-older half-brother, Flyin' High, was still a maiden but has since won both starts for us and looks a good prospect. This would be a similar sort in that he will be starting off in midsummer over 7f but will stay further in time."

SILVER DAWN
7/5 gr f Dark Angel - Strictly Dancing (Danehill Dancer)
Owner: J C Smith Sales price: n/a

Half-sister to smart multiple 6-7f winner (including at Group 3 level) Dancing Star, 2020 7f Group 3 winner Foxtrot Lady, useful 8-10f winner Dance of Fire and two other winners. Dam a useful 6f 3yo winning daughter of Nunthorpe Stakes winner Lochangel, herself a half-sister to Nunthorpe Stakes/dual Prix de l'Abbaye winner Lochsong.

"We have enjoyed lots of success with the female members of this family. She is a nice type, but like most of them, will get better and better with age."

SIXTIES LOOK
17/3 b c Sixties Icon - Averami (Averti)
Owner: Kingsclere Racing Club Sales price: n/a

Half-brother to Australian 10f Group 1 winner Side Glance, Listed-placed 8.5-14f winner Rawaki, useful 7f-1m winner Spirit Warning and three other winners including 3m Grade 3 hurdle winner Taglietelle. Dam a 7f 3yo winner who was a full sister to fairly useful 7-8.5f winner Amica.

"He is a nice colt, who is another Kingsclere Racing Club horse from a family well known to us. He has done a fair bit of work already and goes nicely. I think he has the requisite speed to kick off over 6f in June."

SOUL STOPPER
11/2 b c Postponed - Perfect Spirit (Invincible Spirit)
Owner: Sheikh Mohammed Obaid Al Maktoum Sales price: 140,000gns (Not Sold)

Closely related to smart 5-7f winner (including at Group 3/Listed level) Perfect Tribute (by Dubawi), 10-12f 3yo Flat/2m hurdle winner Al Kherb (by Al Kazeem) and 7f 2yo winner Tadqeeq (by Makfi). Dam an unraced close relation to 13.5f Listed winner Swift Tango out of a once-raced maiden three-parts sister to 7f Group 3/Listed winner/2000 Guineas runner-up Enrique.

"A fine, big colt who we like. He is a middle-distance project for next year and beyond, but has got plenty of quality and can hopefully achieve something this backend."

TACK (FR)
15/2 b c Iffraaj - Make Fast (Makfi)
Owner: The Queen Sales price: n/a

Half-brother to 2020 Windsor Castle Stakes/July Stakes winner, Tactical. Dam a Listed-placed 6f 2yo winner who was the daughter of a 7f 2yo Group 3-winning half-sister to useful 8.5f 2yo winner Big Challenge and useful 11.5f 3yo winner Hikari (later dam of 10f 3yo Listed winner Raise You and Listed-placed 2020 12f 3yo winner Lady G).

"A half-brother to our Royal Ascot and July Stakes winner Tactical. This colt wouldn't be quite as sharp as him and will almost certainly need 6f from the get-go. He is a nice horse in his own right and should make his first appearance sometime in June or July."

Tactical

WAR IN HEAVEN (IRE)
14/2 b c Exceed And Excel - Burma Sun (Rip Van Winkle)
Owner: Michael Blencowe Sales price: 50,000gns (Andrew Balding)

First foal of a German 10f 3yo winner who was a half-sister to St Leger Italiano winner Burma Gold, Listed-placed French 7.5f 2yo winner Burma Sea (later dam of French 6f 2yo Group 3 winner Devil) and the dams of Irish 7f 2yo Group 3 winner Blue de Vega and French 1m 1f 3yo Listed winner Bay of Poets.

"A nice type who has done a few bits upsides and goes well. I hope he will be ready to run at the end of May over 6f."

WOLSEY (USA)
9/3 b/br c Kitten's Joy - Justaroundmidnight (Danehill Dancer)
Owner: Qatar Racing Limited Sales price: $275,000 (Fergus Galvin)

Half-brother to 2020 US 10f 3yo Grade 1 winner Duopoly. Dam a US 8.5f Grade 3 winner who was a full sister to useful 8-11f winner Towerlands Park and a half-sister to Group 2-placed 12f-2m winner Aircraft Carrier and Listed-placed dual 5f winner Boris Grigoriev.

"A nice colt who is essentially a middle-distance horse for next year so won't be hurried. He should make it out at some point this backend over 7f/1m."

UNNAMED
23/1 ch c Frankel - Mix And Mingle (Exceed And Excel)
Owner: King Power Racing Co Ltd Sales price: 300,000gns (SackvilleDonald)

First foal of a 7f Group 3 winner who was a full sister to useful 2020 dual 7f 3yo winner Double Or Bubble and a half-sister to UK/Qatari 9-10f winner May Queen out of a 12f 3yo winning close relation to Group 1-placed 7-12f winner (including at Group 2/3 level)/St Leger runner-up High Accolade.

"A gorgeous colt with a lot of quality about him. He will probably be one for the middle of the season over 7f+ and is one we particularly like."

UNNAMED (IRE)
10/4 ch c Lope de Vega - Princess Serena (Unbridled's Song)
Owner: King Power Racing Co Ltd Sales price: 230,000gns (SackvilleDonald)

Full brother to high-class multiple 8-9f winner (including at Group 1 level) Zabeel Prince, a three-parts brother to Australian 7f/1m Group 2 winner Puissance de Lune and 10f 3yo Listed winner Queen Power (both by Shamardal) and a half-brother to the dam of Coronation Stakes winner Rizeena and 2021 UAE 1m 1f Group 2 winner Summer Romance. Dam a US 1m winner who was a half-sister to US 8.5f 3yo Grade 2 winner Doubles Partner.

"A very athletic colt with lots of natural ability, but he is going to be a longer-term project who will do better as a three-year-old."

UNNAMED
21/3 b c Nathaniel - Robema (Cadeaux Genereux)
Owner: King Power Racing Co Ltd Sales price: 200,000gns (SackvilleDonald)

Closely related to 1m 2yo Listed winner Connect and Listed-placed 7-8.5f winner Atlantic Sun (both by Roderic O'Connor) and a half-brother to useful dual 6f 2yo winner Leontes. Dam a 7.5f-1m winner who was a full sister to Listed-placed 8-8.5f winner Granted (later dam of 10f Listed winner Rewarded and 1m 3yo Listed winner Perfect Star (herself dam of 7f 2yo Group 3 winner Kilmah)).

"We had his half-brother, Leontes, a few years back who won a couple of times for us as a two-year-old. This colt is more precocious than your typical Nathaniel and will be ready to go as soon as the 7f races are here. It is still very early days, but we will see if he can put his hand up for something like the Chesham Stakes on that first outing."

UNNAMED
9/3 b c Frankel - Sharp Susan (Touch Gold)
Owner: Cayton Park Stud Sales price: n/a

Half-brother to South African four-time 9/10f Group 1 winner Oh Susanna and Australian triple 6f Listed winner Signore Fox. Dam a Grade 1-placed US 8.5-9f winner (including at Grade 2/3 level) who was closely related to US 1m 1f Grade 1 winner Spring At Last and a half-sister to US 1m Grade 1 winner Sharp Lisa (later dam of Australian 12f Group 1 winner Foundry and 13f 3yo Group 3 winner/St Leger third Housesofparliament).

"A fine, big horse with a fantastic pedigree. Frankels seem to come in two moulds and he falls into the potential middle-distance three-year-old category."

UNNAMED (IRE)
28/2 b c Galileo Gold - Silk Fan (Unfuwain)
Owner: Al Shaqab Racing Sales price: 80,000gns (C Gordon Watson Bloodstock/Al Shaqab)

Half-brother to Group 3/Listed-placed 5-6f 2yo winner Haikbidiac, useful 6-7f 2yo winner Dance Fever and four other winners. Dam a useful triple 7f winner who was a half-sister to Group 1-placed 5-6f 2yo winner (including twice at Group 2 level) Gutaifan; family of Lockinge Stakes winner Mustashry and French 5f 3yo Listed winner/Queen Mary Stakes third Shades of Blue.

"A medium-sized, athletic colt who goes very well. He has had a small setback but should still be capable of doing something as a two-year-old."

UNNAMED
23/1 ch c Lope de Vega - Stone Roses (Rip Van Winkle)
Owner: Apollo Racing & SRB Equine Sales price: 130,000gns (Andrew Balding)

Second foal of a French 10f 3yo Listed winner who was a half-sister to Group 3-placed French/UK 6f-1m winner (including at Listed level) Straight Right out of a French 7.5f 2yo winning half-sister to French 10f 3yo Group 3/Listed winner Sersia (later dam of Australian 8/10f Group 1 winner Contributer) and French 7f 3yo Listed winner Mayyadah.

"A lovely colt by Lope de Vega, who is related to a nice horse we trained called Straight Right. I can see him being in action from the middle of summer onwards over 7f."

RALPH BECKETT

CONVECTION
9/2 b f Oasis Dream - Mechanism (Zamindar)
Owner: Juddmonte Sales price: n/a

Second foal of a French 8.5f 3yo winner who was a full sister to Falmouth Stakes winner Timepiece and a half-sister to French 10f 2yo Group 1 winner Passage of Time (later dam of 8/10.5f Group 2 winner Time Test) and King Edward VII Stakes winner/St Leger fourth Father Time.

"She is quite a backward filly, who hasn't been here all that long. Her sister had plenty of ability, so this filly ought to be able to go a bit, but we will be taking our time with her given that she's not long arrived."

CRESTA DE VEGA (IRE)
8/5 b c Lope de Vega - Bibury (Royal Applause)
Owner: Marc Chan Sales price: 170,000gns (McCalmont Bloodstock)

Full brother to smart 6-10f winner (including at Group 3/Listed level) Steel of Madrid. Dam an Irish 7f 3yo winner who was a half-sister to Ascot Gold Cup winner Rite of Passage out of a useful US 7-8.5f winning granddaughter of top-class racemare Dahlia.

"This is a grand colt, who is growing and changing all the time. Therefore, I suspect we won't see him until the autumn, which is in line with what his pedigree tells us."

DAIQUIRI DREAM
4/4 b f Dubawi - Cocktail Queen (Motivator)
Owner: J C Smith Sales price: n/a

Full sister to useful 7f-1m winner Tom Collins. Dam a smart UK/French 8.5-12.5f winner (including at Group 2/3 level) who was a half-sister to useful dual 1m winner Gold Prince, 7f-1m 3yo winner Hidden Fire (later dam of 1m 3yo Listed winner Sea of Flames) and the unraced dam of 2020 Italian 2000 Guineas winner Cima Emergency.

"A big, tall filly who will take a bit of time but is a lovely individual who I am looking forward to seeing in action during the autumn. Her dam handled cut very well."

DEODAR
27/2 br c Bated Breath - Tested (Selkirk)
Owner: Juddmonte Sales price: n/a

Third foal of a smart Irish 7-7.5f winner (including at Group 3/Listed level) who was closely related to 7f 2yo winner Escape Proof out of a French 10f 3yo Group 3-winning sister to smart prolific 7-8.5f winner (including at Group 3/ Listed level) Vortex and French 12f 3yo Group 3 winner Danefair (later dam of four-time 7f Group 3/Listed winner Trade Fair) and a half-sister to Listed-placed French 1m 1f 2yo winner Estala (later dam of four-time 7f/1m Grade 1 winner Ventura).

"He looks like a two-year-old type but hasn't really switched on mentally, so we haven't cracked on with him just yet. The little bit he has done so far has pleased us though."

ELECTRESS
8/3 b f Galileo - Just The Judge (Lawman)
Owner: Qatar Racing Limited Sales price: n/a

Half-sister to 2021 Irish 12f winner Swift Verdict and 2020 1m 2yo winner Nash Nasha. Dam a high-class 7-10f winner (including the Irish 1000 Guineas)/1000 Guineas runner-up who was a half-sister to Listed-placed Irish 1m 2yo winner Obliterator out of a maiden half-sister to 12f 3yo Group 3 winner/Oaks third High Heeled.

"She has a good way of going and moves very well. I am mindful of the fact the dam was a good juvenile, and I can certainly see this filly making a two-year-old at some point this year. I expect her to kick off in the middle of the summer."

ELENA'S GIFT
14/2 ch f Frankel - Sant Elena (Efisio)
Owner: The Eclipse Partnership Sales price: n/a

Closely related to Japanese 12f Listed winner Best Approach (by New Approach) and a half-sister to Prix Morny/Middle Park Stakes winner Reckless Abandon, 2020 French 7f 2yo Listed winner Erasmo and the dam of 7f 2yo Group 3 winner West End Girl. Dam a Listed-placed UK/Canadian 6f-1m winner who was a half-sister to Prix Maurice de Gheest winner Brando and US 9/10f Grade 1 winner Ticker Tape.

"This is a backward filly, who isn't at all like her half-brother, Reckless Abandon, who was obviously a very good juvenile. She is another who is growing and changing all the time - very much a work in progress. Another one who you won't see until later on."

HELLO YOU (IRE)
1/3 b f Invincible Spirit - Lucrece (Pivotal)
Owner: Amo Racing Limited Sales price: €350,000 (Robson Aguiar)

Three-parts sister to useful 2020 7-8.5f 3yo winner Ajyaall (by Invincible Spirit) and a half-sister to 5f 3yo winner Lufricia. Dam a French 7-7.5f winner who was a half-sister to high-class multiple French 5-6.5f winner (including the Prix Maurice de Gheest) Signs of Blessing.

"She cost plenty at auction and certainly moves like a nice horse. She could be ready to get going by May and we like her."

LOVELY MANA (IRE)
15/4 b f Dabirsim - Enraptured (Oasis Dream)
Owner: Amo Racing Limited Sales price: 115,000gns (A C Elliott, Agent/R Beckett)

Half-sister to Listed-placed 2020 6f 2yo winner Meu Amor. Dam a 7f 2yo winner who was closely related to Irish 1m Group 3 winner Pincheck and a half-sister to 2020 Irish 7f 3yo Group 3 winner Valeria Messalina out of a 10-12f winning sister to US 11f Grade 1 winner Prince Arch and half-sister to Irish 7f 2yo Group 1 winner Kingsfort.

"This filly has done a lot of growing recently so won't be appearing imminently. However, she moves well, and if she is as hardy as her year-older sibling, we'll be having plenty of fun with her this year."

PUFFING (IRE)
24/1 b f Kingman - Puff (Camacho)
Owner: Mr & Mrs David Aykroyd Sales price: n/a

Half-sister to UK/Saudi Arabian 7f-1m winner Mesquite and two other winners. Dam a Fred Darling Stakes winner/Cheveley Park Stakes fourth who was a half-sister to Group 1-placed prolific 6-8.5f winner (including at Group 2/3 level) Sovereign Debt.

"We trained the mare to win the Fred Darling, but she's been pretty disappointing so far as a broodmare, but I'm hanging my hat on the fact the lesser types were colts and this is a filly. Hopefully she has inherited her dam's resilience because, if she has, we should have some sport with her this season. She is a little behind the others at present and won't be overly early but we do like her."

RECHERCHER
11/3 b f Nathaniel - Regardez (Champs Elysees)
Owner: J H Richmond-Watson Sales price: n/a

Half-sister to useful 7f-1m winner Impatient. Dam a Group 3-placed 8-10f winner (including at Listed level) who was closely related to French 9.5f 3yo Listed winner Glance and a half-sister to Listed-placed 6-7f winner Compton and once-raced 2020 1m 2yo winner Scope out of a 7f-1m winning half-sister to Oaks winner/St Leger third Look Here.

"Quite a waspish sort of filly, but she is a much better model than her year-older sister who didn't make it out as a two-year-old. I would hope this filly will do, although I doubt she will be appearing this side of August. I should imagine she will begin over 7f - though will likely want 1m before too long."

RICH RHYTHM
26/1 b c Profitable - Gift of Music (Cadeaux Genereux)
Owner: J C Smith Sales price: n/a

Half-brother to Group 3-placed dual 6f winner No Nonsense. Dam a 6f 2yo winner who was the daughter of a 5f Listed-winning sister to useful 5-6f winner Swan Song and half-sister to Group 2/3-placed multiple 6-7f winner (including at Listed level) Lochridge.

"A big, backward homebred of Jeff Smith's, who is going to need some juice in the ground. I doubt we will be seeing him in action until the autumn when the ground should be in his favour at least."

SEATTLE KING
3/3 b c Kingman - Snoqualmie Star (Galileo)
Owner: J C Smith Sales price: n/a

Half-brother to useful 10-12f winner Tribal Craft. Dam an 8-10f winner who was closely related to Group 2-placed 7-12.5f winner (including twice at Listed level) Snoqualmie Girl and 10f 3yo Listed winner Snoqualmie Boy and a half-sister to very useful 8-8.5f winner Merlin Magic out of a maiden sister to Racing Post Trophy winner Seattle Rhyme.

"This is quite a light-framed colt who wouldn't be the biggest, but I like the way he goes about things. He is progressing all the time and I hope that he could see action during the early part of the summer."

SHOUTOUT
23/4 ch f Havana Gold - Lady Dragon (Galileo)
Owner: Qatar Racing Limited Sales price: n/a

Half-sister to useful triple 7f winner Afraid of Nothing and once-raced 2020 8.5f 2yo winner Twisted Reality. Dam a Listed-placed French 12-13f winner who was a half-sister to Swedish 12f Group 3 winner Dorcia and French 1m 2yo Listed winner Kirkinola out of a Cherry Hinton Stakes-winning half-sister to 1m Group 3 winner Shot To Fame.

"She hasn't been here long but has thrived in the time she has - putting on plenty of weight and condition. I can see her making the track some time during the latter part of the summer. She is an entirely different type to her half-sister, Afraid of Nothing, and I can see her making up into a nice filly at some point this season."

UMAX (IRE)
8/3 b c Kingman - Bella Nostalgia (Raven's Pass)
Owner: Amo Racing Limited & Arjun Waney Sales price: 300,000gns (Aguiar Bloodstock)

Half-brother to 6f-1m 2yo winner Incinerator. Dam a Listed-placed 1m 3yo winner who was a half-sister to Group 3-placed multiple 5-7f winner (including at Listed level) Pretend and 14f Listed winner Fiulin out of an Italian 8.5-10f winning half-sister to eight-time 9-12f Group/Grade 1 winner Falbrav.

"An enormous colt but strong with it. His half-brother was a good two-year-old for Hugo Palmer last year, and I am hopeful this colt can follow suit from midsummer onwards."

UNSPOKEN (IRE)
19/2 b c Territories - Silent Secret (Dubai Destination)
Owner: The Audax Partnership Sales price: 65,000gns (Vendor)

Half-brother to Irish 7f 2yo Listed winner Sparkle'n'joy and four other winners. Dam a 7.5f 2yo winner who was a half-sister to Irish 7f/1m Group 3 winner Cheyenne Star (grandam of four-time 8-10f Group 1 winner Barney Roy) and the unraced dam of high-class prolific 6f-1m winner (including at Group 1 level) Gordon Lord Byron.

"A pretty forward individual who goes well. I suspect he will be one my earlier two-year-old runners and is one that I particularly like at this moment in time."

VEE SIGHT
10/5 b c Churchill - Look So (Efisio)
Owner: J H Richmond-Watson Sales price: n/a

Closely related to once-raced 2020 1m 2yo winner Scope (by Teofilo) and a half-brother to Group 3-placed 8-10f winner (including at Listed level) Regardez, French 9.5f 3yo Listed winner Glance and Listed-placed 6-7f winner Compton. Dam a 7f-1m winner who was a half-sister to Oaks winner/St Leger third Look Here (later dam of 14f Listed winner Hereby).

"I wasn't mad on him as a yearling, but he has positively thrived ever since and really got his act together. The dam's progeny all made two-year-olds at some point, and I can see this colt figuring during the second half of the summer. I like the way he goes."

Scope (left)

WESTOVER
24/4 b c Frankel - Mirabilis (Lear Fan)
Owner: Juddmonte Sales price: n/a

Full brother to smart UK/US 8.5-11f winner (including at Group 3/Listed level) Monarchs Glen and useful 2020 7-8.5f 2yo winner Fabilis and a half-brother to useful 5-6f winner Cordial. Dam a Group 1-placed French/US 7f-1m winner (including at Grade 3/Listed level) who was a half-sister to Prix de Diane winner Nebraska Tornado and 10f 3yo Group 2/Listed winner Burning Sun.

"The polar opposite of his year-older brother, Fabilis. He is a tall, sizeable individual who finds things easy at this stage, though I don't imagine we will be galloping him properly until the summer. That said, I can see him doing something at two."

UNNAMED (IRE)
12/3 b f Lope de Vega - Witches Brew (Duke of Marmalade)
Owner: RFZ Technology & Apollo Racing Sales price: £150,000 (Ralph Beckett)

Full sister to smart 7-12f winner (including at Group 3/Listed level) Antonia de Vega. Dam a Listed-placed Irish 7f 3yo winner who was a half-sister to Prix Jacques le Marois winner/2000 Guineas third Al Wukair and Group 3-placed 6-7f winner Dream Today.

"A sweet filly with more size about her than Antonia de Vega, who we obviously enjoyed plenty of success with. She has found the spring tough, so we have been minding her. I should think she's some way off fast work still, but we like her and hopefully she can appear at some point during the summer."

MICHAEL BELL

ADJUVANT (IRE)
25/4 b c New Bay - Levanto (Lawman)
Owner: A C Bound Sales price: £16,000 (MLW Bell Racing)

Half-brother to 2020 Irish 1m 1f 3yo winner Silvertown. Dam a useful Irish 8-12f winner who was the daughter of a thrice-raced maiden half-sister to St Leger winner/Derby runner-up Rule of Law, Grade 2-placed US 8-9f winner Dame Marie (dam of Grade 2-placed 2020 US 8.5f 2yo winner Abarta) and Listed-placed Irish 8.5f 3yo winner Totally Devoted (later dam of 7f Group 3 winner Tomyris).

"The dam was pretty useful in Ireland, and I thought he was well bought at 16k. He goes along nicely enough, and I am hopeful he will give us some fun this season."

AT LIBERTY (IRE)
6/4 b c Muhaarar - Federation (Motivator)
Owner: David Fish & Partner Sales price: 50,000gns (A C Elliott, Agent/M L W Bell)

Half-brother to 2020 Japanese 6f 2yo winner Hitoyogiri. Dam a Grade 3/ Listed-placed UK/US 8-8.5f winner who was closely related to 8.5f 3yo winner Titivation (later dam of 12f Listed winner Titi Makfi) and a half-sister to five-time 1m Group 1 winner (including the 1000 Guineas) Attraction (later dam of 10.5f Group 2 winner Elarqam).

"We liked him a lot as a yearling. I feel that Muhaarar is bubbling under as a sire. He had a good autumn just after we bought this colt, and the year-older sibling won a race in Japan before placing at a good level next time, so the mare can do it too. I like him and hope to have him out in June over 6f."

BALTIMORE BOY (IRE)
20/4 b c Starspangledbanner - Biaraafa (Araafa)
Owner: The Hawtin Family & Mrs I Corbani Sales price: £85,000 (A C Elliott, Agent)

Half-brother to useful dual 7f 2yo winner Doublet. Dam a 6-7f winner who was a half-sister to Listed-placed 13f 3yo winner Bite of The Cherry, Listed-placed 8-8.5f winner Bighearted, Listed-placed Irish 7f 2yo winner Pietra Dura (later dam of US 10f Grade 3 winner Turning Top) and the dam of four-time 10.5/12f Group 1 winner Postponed and Italian 10f Group 1 winner God Given.

"An easy-moving colt, who we liked as a yearling and like even more now. I obviously know this family well, having trained some nice fillies from it including the dam, while the sire can produce good horses. He covers the ground well and I can see him making an appearance over 6f in June."

BETWEEN THE SHEETS (IRE)
25/4 gr f El Kabeir - Shena's Dream (Oasis Dream)
Owner: Christopher Wright Sales price: 45,000gns (Nick Bell For M Bell)

Half-sister to Group 1-placed 2020 5-6f 2yo winner (including at Group 2/ Listed level) Miss Amulet and two other winners. Dam a 6f-1m winner who was a half-sister to useful 10f 3yo winner Leningrad and 1m 2yo winner Shooting Gallery.

"Her half-sister was one of the better two-year-olds around in 2020 and reached the frame at the highest level soon after we bought this filly. She skips along really nicely and looks a precocious sort."

CAIO SHARK (IRE)
7/2 b c Kodi Bear - Liel (Pivotal)
Owner: Amo Racing Limited Sales price: 55,000gns (Nick Bell)

Fifth foal of a maiden half-sister to Group 2-placed UK/Australian 8.5-13f winner (including twice at Listed level) Tall Ship, useful multiple 6-8.5f winner Chevalier, useful multiple 7f winners Aflame and Yellowhammer and the dam of Prix de Diane winner Channel out of a Cheveley Park Stakes winner.

"A big, strong, well-made colt, who is from a fast family. He should be relatively early and looks to have enough boot to start off over five furlongs."

GREAT MAX (IRE)
6/3 b c Wootton Bassett - Teeslemee (Youmzain)
Owner: Amo Racing Limited Sales price: 260,000gns (Robson Aguiar)

First foal of a French 11.5f 3yo winner who was a full sister to Chesham Stakes winner Suits You and French 1m 2yo winner Carnival Zain out of an Irish dual 7f 3yo winner; family of US 8.5/9f Grade 3 winner Pachattack, herself the dam of Irish 1m 2yo Group 3 winner Liquid Amber.

"A particularly nice horse, who is a strong, easy-moving individual. The dam's brother won the Chesham Stakes in 2015 and, given what we are seeing of him to this point, I can see that race being a realistic target for this colt."

HAARAR
30/3 b c Muhaarar - Interchange (Montjeu)
Owner: D W & L Y Payne and G & T Blackiston Sales price: 50,000gns (Richard Frisby)

Three-parts brother to useful Irish 7-7.5f 3yo winner Bronte (by Oasis Dream) and a half-brother to Listed-placed 6f 2yo winner Tiburtina and useful 2020 multiple 11.5-14f 3yo winner Prince Alex. Dam a 12f 3yo winner who was a half-sister to Listed-placed Irish 1m 3yo winner Sandtime and 12f 3yo winner Carenage (grandam of dual 12f Group 3 winner Cubanita).

"His half-brother, Prince Alex, was a slow-maturing type who got better with racing last season, but I can see this colt coming to hand much earlier. He gets up Warren Hill easily and I can see him making up into a summer two-year-old over 7f."

HEATHERDOWN HERO
11/2 b c Sea The Moon - Mariee (Archipenko)
Owner: The Heatherdonians 1 Sales price: 22,000gns (MLW Bell Racing)

First foal of a dual 7f 3yo winner who was out of a 10-12f 3yo winning daughter of an unraced half-sister to July Cup winner Polish Patriot and the unraced dam of high-class multiple 7-11f winner (including at Group 1 level) Lady Jane Digby and Group 1-placed multiple 6-9f winner (including at Group 3/Listed level) Gateman.

"I thought he was well bought at 22,000gns. His dam won her first two races and was useful enough, and though the immediate pedigree isn't overly strong, it goes back to some smart horses. Sea The Moon tends to upgrade his mares, and this colt looks talented on what we see. I am hoping to have him out towards the backend of the summer."

IMPROVISE (FR)
3/4 b f Iffraaj - Set To Music (Danehill Dancer)
Owner: The Queen Sales price: n/a

Full sister to Listed-placed 8.5-10f winner Eightsome Reel. Dam a Group 2/3-placed 10-12f winner (including twice at Listed level) who was a half-sister to Listed-placed Irish 10f 3yo winner Zarafsha, useful UK/Australian 8.5-11f winner Mr Reckless and the unraced dam of Group 3-placed 2020 French 7f 2yo winner La Gioiosa.

"We trained both the brother and the dam, who improved significantly with time and distance. I suspect this filly will come to hand a good bit earlier than either of those, and everyone that has ridden work on her has been complimentary. She will begin over 7f in the summer and we like her."

KICKBOX
13/2 b/br c Dabirsim - Rich Legacy (Holy Roman Emperor)
Owner: Qatar Racing Limited Sales price: n/a

First foal of a May Hill Stakes winner who was the daughter of a twice-raced maiden sister to Deutsches Derby winner Borgia and half-sister to Deutsches Derby/Coronation Cup winner Boreal and the dam of St Leger Italiano winner Burma Gold out of a Deutsches St Leger winner.

"The dam was a good two-year-old for Ralph Beckett and the owners. This colt is a first foal and isn't overly big, but he has good bone and is a strong, well-made individual. We will be pressing on with him soon in an attempt to make him into a summer two-year-old."

MISS HARMONY
25/4 ch f Tamayuz - Muaamara (Bahamian Bounty)
Owner: Mr C Philipps, Mr T Redman & Mr T Trotter Sales price: 47,000gns (Richard Frisby)

Half-sister to useful 2020 5-6f 2yo winner Showalong. Dam a useful dual 6f winner who was a full sister to useful 8-8.5f winner Rampant Lion and a half-sister to Group 2-placed UK/UAE 6f-1m winner (including at Listed level) Master of War.

"This filly is a particularly good mover - very light on her feet. She covers the ground well and should make a useful mid-season two-year-old over seven furlongs on what we see."

MOONLIT WARRIOR
29/3 ch g Sea The Moon - Claiomh Solais (Galileo)
Owner: Sarah and Wayne Dale and Mr David Fish Sales price: £28,000 (R Frisby BS)

Half-brother to useful Irish/Hong Kong 7-9f winner Proud Sky. Dam an Irish 1m 3yo winner/Irish 1000 Guineas fourth who was a full sister to dual 6f 2yo Group 3 winner/1000 Guineas runner-up Cuis Ghaire, Irish 1m 1f 3yo Group 3 winner/Moyglare Stud Stakes runner-up Scintillula, Irish 12f 3yo Listed winner The Major General and Irish 7f 2yo winner/1000 Guineas third Gile Na Greine.

"He was very heavy as a yearling and we struggled to get the weight off so decided to geld him. He is a strong, well-made type and he could pretty much end up anywhere with a pedigree like his - other than at Epsom next June, that is!"

SPRING IS SPRUNG (FR)
21/2 b c Oasis Dream - Kinematic (Kyllachy)
Owner: The Queen Sales price: n/a

Half-brother to 2020 Italian 7.5f 2yo Listed winner Collinsbay and useful 6.5f 2yo winner King's Lynn. Dam a 5.5f 2yo winner who was a half-sister to 6f 3yo Listed winner Musical Comedy and six other winners including 6f 2yo winners Otago and Ring of Truth out of a Listed-placed 10f 3yo winner.

"A strong, powerful colt, who has a good mind and works well. He made his debut at Windsor on April 12 and showed plenty of toe until fitness appeared to fail him at the business end of matters. He will probably reappear in the first week of May, and we are still hopeful that he can develop into a nice two-year-old this season."

Spring Is Sprung

UNNAMED (IRE)
30/4 b f Gleneagles - All's Forgotten (Darshaan)
Owner: Lady Bamford Sales price: n/a

Full sister to 2020 14f 3yo winner Immortal Beloved and a three-parts sister to 13f 3yo Group 3 winner Shantaram, 12f 3yo Listed winner To Eternity, 14f 3yo Listed winner Forever Now and Irish 7f 2yo winner/2000 Guineas third Gan Amhras (all by Galileo). Dam an Irish 8.5f 3yo winner who was a half-sister to UAE 1m Listed winner Parole Board.

"She is a strong, deep-girthed filly, who is well-made and already quite mature. Although there's plenty of stamina on the page, I could see her making up into a summer or early autumn two-year-old over 7f. We are happy with everything she has done to this point."

UNNAMED (IRE)
24/3 ch f Lope de Vega - Bristol Bay (Montjeu)
Owner: The Hawtin Family & Partners Sales price: 60,000gns (MLW Bell Racing)

Full sister to Group 2-placed 8-9f winner (including at Listed level) Bay of Poets. Dam a German 11f 3yo winner who was a half-sister to St Leger Italiano winner Burma Gold, Listed-placed French 7.5f 2yo winner Burma Sea (later dam of French 6f 2yo Group 3 winner Devil) and the dam of Irish 7f 2yo Group 3 winner Blue de Vega (all by Lope de Vega) out of a maiden sister to Deutsches Derby winner Borgia and half-sister to Deutsches Derby/Coronation Cup winner Boreal.

"By an excellent sire, she is a full sister to a good one and looks to find everything very easy at this stage. She is keen to get on with things so will need minding, but we very much like what we see."

UNNAMED
2/4 b c Invincible Spirit - Sariska (Pivotal)
Owner: Lady Bamford Sales price: n/a

Three-parts brother to useful 8.5f 3yo winner Snow Moon (by Oasis Dream) and a half-brother to useful 12.5-14f winner Surya. Dam a very smart 7-12f winner (including the Oaks and Irish Oaks) who was a half-sister to 14f Listed winner Gull Wing (later dam of smart middle-distance performers Eagle Top, The Lark and Wings of Desire).

"We obviously trained the mare to win the Oaks and Irish Oaks, and this colt would be by far the most precocious of her progeny to date. He's an absolute tank physically and is the first one out of Sariska I have trained that has got me excited."

UNNAMED (IRE)
27/4 ch c Frankel - The Lark (Pivotal)
Owner: Lady Bamford Sales price: n/a

Half-brother to very useful 2020 dual 1m 3yo winner Magical Morning. Dam a Park Hill Stakes winner/Oaks third who was a full sister to King Edward VII Stakes winner/King George VI And Queen Elizabeth Stakes runner-up Eagle Top and Dante Stakes winner/Derby fourth Wings of Desire and a half-sister to Group 2/3-placed 8.5-10f winner Crowned Eagle.

"Still in pre-training but will be arriving soon. He will obviously take time and likely be a middle-distance prospect for next year, but it's good to have another one out of a mare that we trained to a good level for Lady Bamford."

ED BETHELL

CHICANERY
17/1 b f Aclaim - Feint (Teofilo)
Owner: Paul G Jacobs Sales price: 5,000gns (Vendor)

First foal of a 10f 3yo winner who was a half-sister to Listed-placed French 1m 2yo winner Rowan Brae, useful 5-6f winner Alkhor and useful 7f-1m 3yo winner Flying Hammer out of a maiden half-sister to 7f Group 3/Listed winner Ardkinglass, the dam of Listed winners Succession (1m) and Succinct (10f) and the grandam of Gimcrack Stakes winner Sir Gerry.

"She is very sharp and, all being well, will be our first two-year-old runner of the year at Beverley on April 22. Whilst not very big, she is definitely up to winning a race or two this season."

CHILLINGHAM (IRE)
24/2 b c Ulysses - Last Jewel (Invincible Spirit)
Owner: Mr J Carrick & Mr S Taylor Sales price: 40,000gns (James & Edward Bethell)

Second foal of an unraced half-sister to high-class Irish multiple 10-14f winner (including at Group 3/Listed level)/Irish St Leger runner-up Profound Beauty (later dam of Irish 1m Listed winner Rose De Pierre), Listed-placed 8-10f Flat/dual 2m hurdle winner Rock Critic and the unraced dam of Irish 1m 1f dual Group 3 winner Carla Bianca out of an Irish 10f 3yo Listed-winning half-sister to Ribblesdale Stakes winner Irresistible Jewel (later dam of smart trio Mad About You, Princess Highway and Royal Diamond).

"A lovely, big horse who moves really well. Given his size and pedigree he won't be out earlier than the autumn and is essentially one for next year, but we like him a fair bit."

EMILY POST
6/3 b f Charming Thought - Mary Read (Bahamian Bounty)
Owner: Hot To Trot Racing 2 & Mrs F Denniff Sales price: n/a

Half-sister to 6-7f winner Jacquotte Delahaye and 8.5-12.5f winner Dubai Bounty (later dam of smart sprinter Kachy). Dam a Group 3/Listed-placed dual 5f 2yo winner who was a half-sister to Listed-placed 6f-1m winner Above N Beyond and Listed-placed 6f 2yo winner Tiana (later dam of five-time 1m Group 2 winner Beat The Bank and smart sprinter Salt Island).

"She hasn't been with us all that long but is a good mover who is progressing

well. It's too early to know much yet but we're happy with how it has gone to this point."

EXMINSTER (IRE)
24/4 b c Ribchester - Surface of Earth (Empire Maker)
Owner: Clarendon Thoroughbred Racing Sales price: £22,000 (James & Edward Bethell)

Fourth foal of a maiden close relation to US 8.5f Grade 2 winner Surya (later dam of US 1m 1f Grade 1 winner Aruna and US 1m 1f Grade 2 winner Hoop of Colour) and the dam of 1m 3yo Listed winner Consort and a half-sister to French 1m 2yo winner Wind Silence (later dam of Irish 7f 3yo Listed winner/ Poule d'Essai des Poulains third Honoured Guest).

"A big, leggy colt, who has been doing all that has been asked of him easily. He is a late-maturing type who won't be seen until August but we really like him."

FEARBY (IRE)
9/2 b c Havana Gold - Coolminx (One Cool Cat)
Owner: Clarendon Thoroughbred Racing Sales price: 21,000gns (Edward Bethell/Blandford Bloodstock)

Half-brother to UK/Hong Kong 7f-1m winner Cool Team. Dam a Listed-placed 5-7f winner who was a full sister to useful dual 5f 2yo winner Baycat and a half-sister to Grade 1-placed Irish/US multiple 7.5-8.5f winner (including four times at Grade 2 level) Beau Recall.

"An unassuming little colt, who is fast and very straightforward. He is both mentally and physically mature so should be making his debut before May, possibly at Ripon on April 24."

KHURUMBI (IRE)
12/3 b f The Gurkha - Sharaarah (Oasis Dream)
Owner: Geoffrey van Cutsem & Partners Sales price: £25,000 (James Bethell)

Half-sister to Group 1-placed multiple 5f winner (including at Listed level) Moss Gill, useful 6f-1m winner Ulshaw Bridge and 7f 2yo winner Surrajah. Dam a useful 5-6f winner who was a full sister to 5-6f 2yo winner Sadafiya and a half-sister to Group 2/3-placed 5f 2yo winner Burwaaz out of a 6f 2yo Listed winner.

"She was small as a yearling but has done a huge of amount of growing since then and is coming along nicely. Like her siblings she has a good character and a bit of about her - big shoulders and a backside to match. We are very happy with her at the moment, though it's too early to know how she compares to her aforementioned siblings in terms of ability."

RICH KING
11/3 b c Gleneagles - Hairspray (Bahamian Bounty)
Owner: Vickers Racing Sales price: 45,000gns (James & Edward Bethell)

Closely related to smart 7-8.5f winner (including at Group 3/Listed level) Epsom Icon and Listed-placed 6f 2yo winner Modern Millie (both by Sixties Icon) and a half-brother to 2020 7f 2yo winner Barber of Seville. Dam a useful multiple 6f winner who was a half-sister to Listed-placed 6-8.5f winner Medieval.

"A very nice colt who is thriving physically at present. He has a good middle to him and is growing all the time. The family all seem to be 6/7f two-year-olds and I suspect he will fall into that category too. We really like him."

YOUNG WINSTON
14/2 b c Churchill - Come With Me (Dansili)
Owner: Geoffrey van Cutsem & Partners Sales price: 32,000gns (James & Edward Bethell)

First foal of a maiden sister to 2020 10f 3yo Group 3 winner Berlin Tango and half-sister to useful 7-10f winner Jupiter Light and useful US triple 8.5f winner Tasit out of a Group/Grade 1-placed 6-9.5f winner (including at Group/Grade 3 level)/Poule d'Essai des Pouliches third who was closely related to Irish 12f Group 3 winner Pink Symphony.

"He is a bull of a colt - not the biggest but very strong. He has a great character and is very professional, though we will take our time and wait for the six-furlong races to begin in May. Another we really like."

UNNAMED
19/4 ch f Garswood - Highleaf (Pivotal)
Owner: David W Armstrong Sales price: n/a

Half-sister to dual 7f 2yo winner Borsdane Wood. Dam an unraced sister to the unraced dam of July Cup winner Mayson and half-sister to 6f 2yo Listed winner Bathwick Bear, Group 3-placed multiple 5-10f winner Folio and useful dual 6f winner Heath Charnock.

"A very well put together filly, who goes along nicely and is coming along well. She is likely to appear towards the end of May or beginning of June. I imagine she will start off over 5f but is likely to want another furlong before long."

UNNAMED
3/4 ch f Garswood - Winter's Night (Night Shift)
Owner: David W Armstrong Sales price: n/a

Half-sister to 5-6f winner Melrose Way. Dam a Listed-placed 6-7f winner who was the daughter of a maiden half-sister to Group 1-placed 5-6f winner (including the Norfolk Stakes) Baron's Pit, Listed-placed multiple 6-7f winner Ice Age and the dam of dual 1m Listed winner Bravo Zolo.

"A lovely filly who is progressing really well. She is as strong as any two-year-old colt here, and will be one to watch out for in June/July if she continues to show what she does at present."

KARL BURKE

AASSER (FR)
19/2 bl c Dabirsim - Iffraja (Iffraaj)
Owner: Mohamed Saeed Al Shahi Sales price: €35,000 (Federico Barberini)

Half-brother to French 6f 2yo Listed winner Abama. Dam a maiden half-sister to smart Irish 5-6f winner (including twice at Listed level) Great Minds out of a useful Irish/French 5.5-6f winning half-sister to 6f Group 1 winner Pipalong (later dam of Irish 6.5f 2yo Group 3 winner Walk On Bye), 6f 2yo Listed winner Out of Africa, 5f 2yo winner/Flying Childers Stakes runner-up China Eyes and Group 3/Listed-placed Irish 7f 3yo winner Silver Shoon.

"A big, strong colt who we like a lot. He won't be overly early but everything he has done so far has pleased us."

ATTAGIRL
15/3 br f Wootton Bassett - Catalina Bay (Pastoral Pursuits)
Owner: Clipper Logistics Sales price: £90,000 (Jill Lamb Bloodstock)

Second foal of an Italian 6f 2yo Listed winner who was a half-sister to very useful Irish 5f 2yo winner Mr Scarlet out of an unraced daughter of a 6f 2yo winning half-sister to Italian 12f 3yo Listed winner Green Room and useful dual 5f 2yo winner In Uniform.

"She has only arrived recently but is a lovely filly with a good bit of size about her. She will likely do better at three but should be seen this summer and can hopefully achieve something at two."

DIAMOND PEARL
21/2 b f Ardad - On Her Way (Medicean)
Owner: Amo Racing Limited Sales price: 52,000gns (Robson Aguiar)

Half-sister to 7f 3yo Listed winner/Coventry Stakes runner-up Headway and very useful UK/Hong Kong triple 7f winner Awe. Dam a 10-11f 3yo winner who was a half-sister to Group 1-placed UK/Hong Kong 7f-1m winner Chater Way and useful UK/Hong Kong 7f-1m winner Beauty Prince.

"She wasn't with us during the winter and only entered training in March, but we had liked her as a yearling. She is a sharp little filly who should make a two-year-old, though she's been a bit under the weather so we've had to back off her for the time being."

FRISKY
18/3 ch f Bated Breath - Thrill (Pivotal)
Owner: Cheveley Park Stud Sales price: n/a

Half-sister to 5-6f winners Effusive and Hollander. Dam a useful dual 7f winner who was a full sister to Nell Gwyn Stakes winner/1000 Guineas fourth Infallible (later dam of Falmouth Stakes winner Veracious and high-class miler Mutakayyef), 6f 3yo Listed winner Remarkable, Group 3/Listed-placed multiple 5-6f winner Watchable and a three-parts sister to the unraced dam of Prix Maurice de Gheest winner Garswood.

"A lovely daughter of Bated Breath who looks fairly sharp. She will certainly have enough speed for five furlongs but I doubt she will be appearing until May at the earliest."

GIFTED GOLD (IRE)
24/3 ch f Galileo Gold - Flare of Firelight (Birdstone)
Owner: Carl Waters & Mrs E Burke Sales price: 82,000gns (Kelly Burke/Carl Waters)

Half-sister to Gimcrack Stakes/Champagne Stakes winner Threat. Dam a maiden half-sister to Group 2-placed French 9-10.5f winner (including at Listed level) That Which Is Not and the dam of 6f 2yo winner/Coventry Stakes third Eltezam out of an Irish 10.5f Group 1-winning half-sister to the dam of Oaks winner Light Shift (herself dam of Eclipse Stakes and Juddmonte International Stakes winner Ulysses).

"A half-sister to a smart two-year-old in Threat and by one of the more exciting first-season sires. She won't be ready for action until May or June when the six-furlong races begin. She looks nice."

GIRIA (IRE)
13/3 ch f Exceed And Excel - Silent Confession (Mr Greeley)
Owner: AlMohamediya Racing Sales price: n/a

Half-sister to Italian 6-7f winner Galador and Hungarian 1m 2yo winner Sea My Soul. Dam an unraced daughter of a US 11f Listed-winning half-sister to Irish 12f 3yo Group 3 winner/Irish Derby third Stellar Mass and Listed-placed UK/UAE 10-11.5f winner Fairmile.

"A lovely filly with plenty of size and scope about her. Unsurprisingly, she has been a little weak and will certainly be one for later on, but we like the look her."

HONEY SWEET (IRE)
16/2 b f Adaay - Sweet Sienna (Harbour Watch)
Owner: Nick Bradley Racing 14 & Mrs E Burke Sales price: 50,000gns (Karl Burke/Nick Bradley Racing)

First foal of a maiden half-sister to Group 1-placed 5-6f winner (including at Listed level) Keep Busy and Listed-placed 5f 2yo winner Looks A Million out of a smart prolific 5-6f winner (including at Group 2/3 level) who was a half-sister to Prix Morny winner Unfortunately.

"She is a lovely filly, who we really liked as a yearling and ended up paying a fair amount for. I'd hope she will be ready to start off sometime in May. I am really keen on her prospects."

HOOKED ON YOU (IRE)
7/4 b f Starspangledbanner - Plying (Hard Spun)
Owner: John & Jess Dance Sales price: 130,000gns (Creighton Schwartz Bloodstock)

Half-sister to 2020 Cheveley Park Stakes winner Alcohol Free and French 1m 1f 3yo Listed winner Alexander James. Dam a French 6.5-7f 3yo winner who was a half-sister to Group 2-placed 5f 2yo winner Kissing Lights and the dam of Group 3-placed 6f 2yo winner Zifena out of a useful 5f 2yo winning half-sister to Solario Stakes winner Raise A Grand.

"A half-sister to last year's Cheveley Park Stakes winner, Alcohol Free. She has only just arrived and will take a bit of time. I suspect she'll be one for the middle of the summer onwards."

Alcohol Free

JAKKS GROOVE (IRE)
5/3 ch c Profitable - By The Edge (Shinko Forest)
Owner: John & Jess Dance Sales price: 37,000gns (Karl Burke)

Half-brother to useful 5-6f winner Astro Jakk. Dam a multiple 5f winner who was a full sister to Listed-placed multiple 5f winner How's She Cuttin' (later dam of Group 1-placed 5-7f winner (including at Group 3/Listed level) Washington DC) out of a 5-6f winning half-sister to the unraced dam of 6f 2yo Group 3 winner/Cheveley Park Stakes runner-up Aspen Darlin.

"A half-brother to a solid handicapper called Astro Jakk, who we train for John Dance's syndicate, Titanium Racing. I have got four two-year-olds by Profitable and none of them are especially forward, but, like the other three, this is a nice colt who should be in action by the summer. He looks an out-and-out sprinter, as per his page."

KORKER (IRE)
19/3 b c Dandy Man - Adaptation (Spectrum)
Owner: Fine Claret Racing & More Turf Racing Sales price: £50,000 (Karl Burke)

Full brother to 2020 Irish 1m winner Adapt To Dan and a half-brother to useful 6-7f winner Parnassian and 2020 7f 2yo winner Elakazaam. Dam a dual 6f 2yo winner who the daughter of a Listed-placed UK/US 11.5-12f winning half-sister to US 9/10f Grade 1 winner Squeak and Listed-placed 7f 3yo winner Mystify; family of smart sprinters Mr Lupton, Sir Maximilian and Tipsy Creek.

"A very sharp colt, who would have been one of our first two-year-old runners had he not got a touch of sore shins. He is back working now and should be in action by the end of April. I have trained two of his siblings to win at two and this colt would be as sharp, if not sharper, than them."

LULLABY BAY
31/1 b f Profitable - Dubai Affair (Dubawi)
Owner: Bearstone Stud Limited Sales price: 35,000gns (Vendor)

Half-sister to 5f 2yo winner Raasel and once-raced 7f 2yo winner Star Jewel. Dam a 5f 2yo winner who was a half-sister to 6f 2yo Listed winner Queen's Grace, useful 7-10f winner Poet's Prince and useful 6f 2yo winner Poet's Princess out of a five-time 5-7f Listed-winning half-sister to July Cup winner Sakhee's Secret and 6f Listed winner Palace Moon.

"A nice filly, who is back with her owners having a little break at present but is due back in soon. She is another one by Profitable who will be one for the summer onwards."

SHERDIL (IRE)
8/4 b c Dandy Man - Chicago Fall (Dark Angel)
Owner: Khalifa Dasmal Sales price: £40,000 (Federico Barberini)

First foal of an Irish 7f 3yo winner who was a half-sister to Listed-placed dual 6f winner Antica and the dam of Irish 1m Listed winner Lily's Rainbow and Listed-placed Irish 5-6f winner Julia's Magic (by Dandy Man) out of a once-raced maiden half-sister to the unraced dam of Hong Kong 6f Group 1 winner Peniaphobia, French 5f 2yo Listed winner Rapacity Alexander (both by Dandy Man) and Group 3/Listed-placed 5f 2yo winner Safari Sunset.

"A very sharp sort, who has had a little holdup but should be ready to go by the end of April. He is from a speedy family and will begin over five furlongs."

SNOOZE N YOU LOSE (FR)
9/4 b f Ribchester - Wake Up Call (Noverre)
Owner: Mrs Melba Bryce Sales price: £60,000 (Vendor)

Half-sister to Group 2-placed UK/UAE 6f-1m winner (including at Listed level) Zaman and two other winners. Dam a Listed-placed 6-7f winner who was a half-sister to UAE Oaks winner Tamarillo (later dam of 7f 3yo Group 3 winner Summer Fete, herself dam of 5/6f 2yo Group 2 winner/Cheveley Park Stakes runner-up Raffle Prize) and the dam of smart UK/US 6f-1m winner (including at Grade 2/3 level) Up In Time.

"A nice filly who needs to strengthen up and fill her frame. I imagine she will be ready to start in May or June over six furlongs."

TEDDY'S PROFIT (IRE)
1/4 b c Profitable - Newsroom (Manduro)
Owner: C Hirst & Mrs E Burke Sales price: 37,000gns (Karl & Kelly Burke)

Third foal of a useful French 10f 3yo winner who was a half-sister to Group 1-placed multiple 5-5.5f 2yo winner (including at Group 2/Listed level) Signora Cabello, Listed-placed 6f 2yo winner La Presse and Listed-placed French 1m 3yo winner Emirates Girl (later dam of UAE 2000 Guineas winner Fly At Dawn) out of a Group 3-placed 6f 2yo winning half-sister to Flying Childers Stakes winner Sheer Viking.

"A big, strong colt, who still has a bit of filling out and growing to do. He won't be an early five- furlong type of two-year-old but is a nice horse with a bit of scope who should do well this season."

UNNAMED
8/2 b c Invincible Spirit - Bruni Heinke (Dutch Art)
Owner: David W Armstrong Sales price: n/a

Three-parts brother to very useful 5-6f winner Ainsdale (by Mayson) and
a half-brother to fairly useful triple 6f winner Cale Lane and 2020 triple 5f
winner Lyons Lane. Dam a once-raced sister to Prix Maurice de Gheest winner
Garswood and half-sister to Group 2-placed Irish 1m 2yo winner Zagitova out
of an unraced close relation to Nell Gwyn Stakes winner/1000 Guineas fourth
Infallible.

*"His three-parts brother, Ainsdale, is a horse who is ground-dependent but one
that we really rate. This colt would be stronger than he was at this stage. He
has had a touch of sore shins but is back in work now. Whilst he hasn't done
anything serious yet, he has looked the part in all that he has done."*

UNNAMED
6/2 b c Profitable - La Roumegue (Henrythenavigator)
Owner: AlMohamediya Racing Sales price: £58,000 (Karl & Kelly Burke)

Half-brother to 8.5-9.5f 2yo winner Locked N' Loaded. Dam a maiden half-
sister to stakes-placed US 5f-1m winner Activity Report out of an unraced
half-sister to German 7f 2yo Listed winner Winter Quarters, Listed-placed 6f
2yo winner Jumilla (grandam of high-class sprinters Caspian Prince and Spirit
Quartz and great-grandam of Hong Kong five-time 10-12f Group 1 winner
Exultant) and Listed-placed 7f 2yo winner Spurned (later dam of German 1m
Group 2 winner Passing Glance).

*"A nice colt, who we've just backed off from at present as he's going through a
growing phase. He will be one for the summer onwards and is a horse that we
like."*

OWEN BURROWS

ANNAF (IRE)
22/5 br c Muhaarar - Shimah (Storm Cat)
Owner: Shadwell Estate Co Sales price: n/a

Full brother to once-raced 5.5f 2yo winner Raheeq, a three-parts brother to smart UK/UAE 5-7f winner (including at Listed level) Mushir (by Oasis Dream) and a half-brother to useful Irish 1m 2yo winner Moghamarah. Dam a Group 1-placed Irish dual 6f 2yo winner (including at Listed level) who was a half-sister to 6f 3yo Group 2 winner Haatef, smart Irish 6-7f winner (including at Group 3/Listed level) Walayef and Irish dual 6f 3yo Listed winner Ulfah.

"A late May foal but quite small. It is a sharp family, and we won't be wasting much time in pressing on with him unless he tells us otherwise. His year-older half-sister was speedy but hot with it. Thankfully, this colt is much sharper mentally."

EKLIL
16/3 b c Invincible Spirit - Raaqy (Dubawi)
Owner: Shadwell Estate Co Sales price: n/a

Second foal of a useful 6.5f 2yo winner who was a half-sister to 7f Listed winner Mankib and 6f 2yo winner Rayaheen (later dam of 7f 2yo Group 3/Listed winner Tajaanus and very useful UK/UAE 5-7.5f winner Motafaawit) out of a Cheveley Park Stakes/1000 Guineas winner.

"We know the family quite well and this is a strong colt who is a nice size. He is doing absolutely everything right at present and will be debuting in late May or June over 6f should he continue to please us."

UNNAMED
5/4 b f Intello - Aghareed (Kingmambo)
Owner: Shadwell Estate Co Sales price: n/a

Half-sister to 2020 Geoffrey Freer, Stakes winner Hukum and useful 8-10f winner Kasbaan. Dam a French 10.5f 3yo Listed-winning daughter of a US 10/11f Grade 1 winner from the excellent family of Nashwan, Nayef, Ghanaati etc.

"A half-sister to our Royal Ascot and Geoffrey Freer winner Hukum. She is a lovely filly who looks nice from what little work we've done with her but is very much one for the backend."

Hukum

UNNAMED (IRE)
8/3 b f Ribchester - Aneedah (Invincible Spirit)
Owner: Sheikh Ahmed Al Maktoum Sales price: 110,000gns (Shadwell Estate Company)

Half-sister to 5f Listed winner Gorgeous Noora. Dam a Listed-placed 1m 2yo winner who was a full sister to Group 1-placed multiple 5-6f winner (including at Group 2/Listed level) Muthmir and a half-sister to Irish 7f 2yo Group 3 winner My Titania (dam of Group 3-placed 2020 1m 3yo winner My Oberon).

"A strong filly who is shaping up to follow her pedigree, inasmuch as she is looking speedy without necessarily being precocious. She is cantering away at present and doing everything right."

UNNAMED
17/2 ch c Lope de Vega - Ashaaqah (Dansili)
Owner: Shadwell Estate Co Sales price: n/a

Half-brother to 1m 3yo winners Areehaa and Mahaarat. Dam a maiden half-sister to useful 1m 3yo winner Ehtiraas out of a French 10f 3yo Listed-winning half-sister to US 10/11f Grade 1 winner Lahudood (later dam of French 10f 3yo Listed winner Aghareed, herself dam of 2020 Geoffrey Freer Stakes winner Hukum).

"A nice type for the backend. He moves nicely and is currently cantering away third lot."

UNNAMED (IRE)
24/2 ch f Profitable - Bold Assumption (Observatory)
Owner: Shadwell Estate Co Sales price: 150,000gns (Shadwell Estate Company)

Half-sister to 1m 2yo Listed winner/Poule d'Essai des Pouliches runner-up Irish Rookie and three other winners. Dam an unraced half-sister to Listed-placed French 11f 3yo winner Well Dressed and Listed-placed French 12f 3yo winner Tsar's Pride (later dam of Italian 10/12f Group 3 winner Exhibit One and 3yo Listed winners Pavlosk (1m) and Rostova (1m 1f)).

"A nice, neat filly, who is currently doing a couple of canters a day. She is doing everything right and should be one of our earlier two-year-old runners all being well."

UNNAMED (IRE)
28/3 b/br c Aclaim - Kendal Mint (Kyllachy)
Owner: Shadwell Estate Co Sales price: 145,000gns (Shadwell Estate Company)

Half-brother to useful 2020 6f 3yo winner Fresh. Dam a 6f 2yo winner who was a half-sister to Listed-placed Italian 5f 2yo winner Lady Ro and useful 12f-2m winner Monsieur Lambrays out of a dual 7f 3yo winning sister to Listed-placed 5-6f winner Woodnook and half-sister to 6f 2yo Group 2 winner Nevisian Lad.

"A big, strong horse who is cantering away at present. He has been a touch immature mentally but is steadily getting there and should make up into a summer two-year-old. I imagine he will begin over 6f."

UNNAMED (IRE)
23/5 b c Invincible Spirit - Mejala (Red Ransom)
Owner: Shadwell Estate Co Sales price: n/a

Full brother to Listed-placed 6f 2yo winner Mutaaqeb. Dam a 10f 3yo winner who was a half-sister to Group 3/Listed-placed dual 7f winner/Poule d'Essai des Poulains fourth Muwaary, 6f 3yo Listed winner Ethaara (later dam of 1m 3yo Listed winner Etaab) and 7f 2yo Listed winners Mudaaraah and Sudoor (later dam of French 10.5f 3yo Group 3 winner Raseed) out of an unraced sister to Champagne Stakes winner Bahhare and half-sister to very smart miler Bahri.

"His brother was a decent horse for us a couple of seasons ago. This colt is a

bit smaller than him and also fairly weak at this stage. He needs to strengthen up and hasn't done anything serious in terms of work, but I hope to see him on the track come the late summer or early autumn."

UNNAMED
16/4 b f Muhaarar - Moonlit Garden (Exceed And Excel)
Owner: Sheikh Ahmed Al Maktoum Sales price: 110,000gns (Shadwell Estate Company)

Half-sister to Group 3-placed 5-6f winner Mokaatil and Listed-placed French triple 1m winner Dan. Dam a Listed-placed Irish 6f 2yo winner who was closely related to useful multiple 5-6f winner Profile Star out of an Irish 6-7f winner; family of Chesham Stakes/Mill Reef Stakes winner Red Cross.

"A half-sister to Mokaatil, who placed in a Cornwallis and also finished fourth in the Windsor Castle at Royal Ascot for us as a two-year-old. This filly looks a sharp, early type herself, though still needs to come her in coat. She has done absolutely everything right to this point, and we will be increasing her workload fairly shortly. Muhaarars haven't always proved to be early, but being a half-sister to Mokaatil and out of an Exceed And Excel mare, you'd expect this filly to be pretty precocious."

UNNAMED
5/2 br c Awtaad - Mudawanah (Dansili)
Owner: Shadwell Estate Co Sales price: n/a

Second foal of an unraced sister to 7f 3yo Group 3 winner Talaayeb and half-sister to UAE dual 1m Group 3 winner Muntazah, 1m 3yo Listed winner Wadilsafa and Listed-placed dual 10f 3yo winner Ojooba out of a 1m 1f 3yo Listed winner/Oaks third who was a half-sister to 1000 Guineas winner Ghanaati and 12f Group 3 winner/Champion Stakes runner-up Mawatheeq.

"This colt is from one of Sheikh Hamdan's best families. He has only just arrived from Dubai, and they reportedly quite liked him over there. He had his first hack canter recently and is a strong horse who will be one for later on."

UNNAMED
7/3 ch f Lope de Vega - Mutebah (Marju)
Owner: Shadwell Estate Co Sales price: n/a

Three-parts sister to 2020 7f 2yo winner/Champagne Stakes runner-up Albasheer (by Shamardal). Dam a French 10.5f winner who was a full sister to useful 9.5-12f 3yo winner Estedaama out of a 10f 3yo winning three-parts sister to very useful 10-12f winner Ezdiyaad and half-sister to US 10f Grade 2 winner Makderah and Italian 1m 3yo Group 2 winner Oriental Fashion.

"A three-parts sister to our good two-year-old of last season, Albasheer. This filly is a lovely, scopey sort who is thriving at present, but she will be more of a backend type than her half-brother."

UNNAMED (IRE)
20/4 b c Dark Angel - Soraaya (Elnadim)
Owner: Sheikh Ahmed Al Maktoum Sales price: n/a

Half-brother to very useful 8.5-11.5f winner Mannaal. Dam a Group 2-placed dual 6f 2yo winner (including at Group 3 level) who was a half-sister to Group 1-placed dual 6f 2yo winner (including at Listed level) Declaration of War; family of Queen Mary Stakes winner Shining Hour.

"A really nice colt who is a good mover. You would look at him standing in his box and think that he wants time, but he really catches the eye in his work. We won't be pressing any buttons with him just yet, but he should make a nice two-year-old from the summer onwards."

JULIE CAMACHO

BOASTED
21/1 b f Showcasing - Tinted (Galileo)
Owner: Martin Hughes Sales price: n/a

First foal of a once-raced half-sister to Listed-placed UK/US 6f-1m winner Royal Banker, useful 5-6f winner Regal Royale, useful 7f-1m winner Bobby Wheeler and the dam of dual 7f Group 3 winner Regal Realm (herself the dam of triple 8/10f Group 3 winner/Eclipse Stakes third Regal Reality) out of a Cheveley Park Stakes-winning half-sister to Listed-placed 8-14f winner/St Leger fourth Regal Flush.

"She was homebred by Martin Hughes, who is a new owner to the yard. We are pleased with her attitude towards her work, but she has some size and scope so we won't be in any rush with her. However, we like everything we've seen so far and are looking forward to seeing her in action."

BURNING EMOTION
10/2 b f Mondialiste - Flame Out (Excelebration)
Owner: Exors of The Late Mr G Turnbull Sales price: £7,000 (Nick Turnbull)

First foal of an unraced half-sister to very useful 7f-1m winner (including at Listed level) Sea of Flames out of a 7f-1m 3yo winner who was a half-sister to smart 8.5-12.5f winner (including at Group 2/3 level) Cocktail Queen, useful dual 1m winner Gold Prince and the unraced dam of 2020 Italian 2000 Guineas winner Cima Emergency.

"She has been a consummate professional in her early work and looks promising at this stage. She has the scope to improve physically but is coping well with everything at the moment. We are looking forward to pushing on with her in the coming weeks."

ENRAGED
1/3 b f Adaay - Little Lady Katie (Lord Shanakill)
Owner: A Barnes & Cliff Stud Sales price: £29,000 (Andrew Barnes)

First foal of a fairly useful 6f-1m winner who was a half-sister to five winners out of a Listed-placed 7.5f 3yo winning half-sister to 1m Group 2 winner Safawan, Group 3/Listed-placed 5f 2yo winner Safka (later dam of 1m 3yo Listed winner Speedfit Too) and several other winners including the dam of French 11f 3yo Group 2/US 11f Grade 2 winner Sayarshan.

"She is a sharp-looking type who really enjoys her exercise and gives us the impression that she will come to hand nicely in the first half of the year. It is still early days, but she has created a favourable impression on everyone and hopefully that remains the case."

ROSHAMBO
31/3 b f Due Diligence - Horsforth (Kyllachy)
Owner: Morecool Racing Sales price: £8,000 (Julie Camacho)

Half-sister to 2020 5f 2yo winner Lazyitis. Dam a multiple 5f winner who was a half-sister to useful 7f-1m winner Glengarry and useful French 6.5-7f winner Secret Lady out of an unraced half-sister to Group 3-placed 5-6f winner Bonnie Charlie and fairly useful UK/Irish 6-7.5f winner Angel Palanas.

"A strong-looking half-sister to Lazyitis, who won on her final start at two last season for us. She improved with every run, and Roshambo compares favourably to her year-older sibling at this stage. We are extremely pleased with her so far."

HENRY CANDY

BRUSH CREEK
19/2 b f Twilight Son - Resort (Oasis Dream)
Owner: Cheveley Park Stud Sales price: n/a

Full sister to 2020 7f 2yo winner In Paradise, a three-parts sister to Listed-placed 5f 2yo winner Secret Venture (by Kyllachy) and a half-sister to useful multiple 7-8.5f winner Supersta. Dam a 7f-1m 3yo winner who was a three-parts sister to high-class 6-7f winner (including twice at Group 2 level) Byron and a half-sister to five winners and Cheshire Oaks runner-up Gay Heroine out of a Cheveley Park Stakes winner.

"An early foal who is unsurprisingly mature physically, but she just needs grow up a bit mentally. I suspect she will be nice in time and ought to be in action by June. She looks to be a pure sprinter."

BUSSELTON
9/4 b c Dark Angel - Pirouette (Pivotal)
Owner: The Earl Cadogan Sales price: 48,000gns (Henry Candy)

First foal of a German 7f Listed winner who was a half-sister to Grade 1-placed UK/US 6f-1m winner (including at Grade 2/Listed level) Passified, very useful prolific 6-7f winner Zomerlust and dual 6f 2yo winner Bond Royale (later dam of Listed-placed triple 5f winner Lady Royale) out of a 6f 2yo winning half-sister to 6f Group 2 winner Harmonic Way.

"A nice, big colt who is going nicely so far, though is only doing sensible work upsides. Dark Angels are inclined to need a little bit of time, and I can see him being ready to run in June or July over 6f."

CENTRE DRIVE
14/4 b f Iffraaj - Upper Street (Dansili)
Owner: Major M G Wyatt Sales price: n/a

Fourth foal of a 10f 3yo winner who was a full sister to UK/US 8.5-12f winner Bohemian Dance and a half-sister to useful 7f-1m 3yo winner Angel Vision and four other winners out of a four-time 10/12f Group 1 winner (including the Breeders' Cup Filly & Mare Turf) who was a full sister to German 10f Group 1 winner Greek Dance and 10f Group 3 winner New Morning and a half-sister to French 12f Group 1 winner Mountain High.

"She has grown an enormous amount and would be getting up to 16.2hh now. Given she is a mid-April foal, you'd assume she would have gone weak by now but she actually carries herself very well. All the work riders seem to like her a lot and she will be a nice filly in time, but her size means we will take our time. One for the autumn over 7f/1m."

HEARTBREAK LASS
24/3 b f Cotai Glory - Motion Lass (Motivator)
Owner: A Davis Sales price: £150,000 (Vendor)

Half-sister to high-class 5-5.5f winner (at Group 2/3 level, including the Norfolk Stakes and Flying Childers Stakes) A'Ali. Dam a maiden half-sister to 1m 1f 3yo Group 3 winner Enforcer, useful UK/UAE 5-7f winner Zalzilah, useful dual 5f 2yo winner Lord of The Inn and seven other winners.

"Obviously speedily-bred being a half-sister to A'Ali. She just needs to settle down a bit as she wants to do everything in a terrible hurry. Although she was very small when she came in, I am delighted to say that she is growing and developing all the time and there is a lot more scope about her now. I am just going along quietly with her at present, and I am sure she'll take very little training when the time comes. I imagine she will be running around May or June time."

JACK LESLIE
6/4 b g Twilight Son - Fenella Rose (Compton Place)
Owner: Paul G Jacobs Sales price: 34,000gns (Henry Candy)

Three-parts brother to Irish dual 5f 3yo winner Enough Said (by Kyllachy). Dam a 6f 2yo winner who was a half-sister to useful 7-8.5f winner Arigato, useful triple 6f winner Twilight Heir (by Twilight Son), useful 5-6f 2yo winners Tassel and Tishtar and three other winners out of a useful 6f 2yo winner.

"He was recently gelded and is a very strong horse who is a lovely mover. Most of the Twilight Sons I've trained have seemingly needed 6f but he may well begin over 5f. I like him a lot and can see him being a nice summer two-year-old."

NIARBYL BAY
14/3 b g Nayef - Danae (Dansili)
Owner: Girsonfield Ltd Sales price: n/a

Full brother to 2020 9.5f winner Maiden Castle. Dam a useful 7f 3yo winner who was a half-sister to Group 1-placed multiple 6f winner (including at Group 3/Listed level) Gorse and useful dual 7f winner Puya (later dam of 10f Group 3 winner Chain of Daisies).

"He had a few issues and didn't thrive at stud, but he has blossomed into a nice horse since being here. He is a beautiful mover like the rest of the family and has a lovely character. Given he had a troubled start to life, I doubt he will be in action much before the autumn. He will want at least 7f."

PENGUIN ISLAND
8/3 b f The Gurkha - In Secret (Dalakhani)
Owner: The Earl Cadogan Sales price: n/a

Half-sister to useful 13f 3yo winner Mt Augustus and 1m 3yo winner Canal Rocks. Dam a maiden half-sister to Group 2-placed multiple 7f winner (including at Group 3 level) Jedburgh, Listed-placed 7f 2yo winner Presbyterian Nun, useful 6-7f winner Yair Hill, useful 10-11.5f 3yo winner In Disguise and useful 10-12f winner Warlu Way out of a 5f 2yo Listed winner.

"Another who had a few problems growing up and she wasn't much to look at when she first came in. However, she has done very well in a short space of time and we now like her a lot. She moves well and is a great enthusiast. I doubt she will make it to the track until the latter part of the year."

TWILIGHT MISCHIEF
10/1 b f Twilight Son - Cardrona (Selkirk)
Owner: Candy, Pritchard & Thomas Sales price: 5,000gns (Henry Candy)

Half-sister to Irish 1m winner Treble Cone. Dam a maiden sister to smart 6f-1m winner (including twice at Listed level) Selinka (later dam of Irish dual 5f Group 3 winner Hit The Bid) out of a dual 6f Listed-winning half-sister to Group 3-placed 6f 2yo winner Umniya and the dam of 6f 2yo Listed winner/Norfolk Stakes runner-up Log Out Island and 6f 3yo Listed winner Khaadem.

"This is a big, strong filly who we particularly like. She has coped really well with her work, and I could see her being a middle-of-the-season two-year-old over sprint trips. It's true to say that she was given away at auction, but she was well worth a punt given the depth to her pedigree."

ROGER CHARLTON

ANNIE'S SONG (IRE)
9/4 b f Camacho - Dutch Treaty (Dutch Art)
Owner: Philip Newton and Elizabeth Railton Sales price: £50,000 (Vendor)

Third foal of a twice-raced maiden sister to 6f Listed winner Exhort and half-sister to 2020 Commonwealth Cup winner Golden Horde and very useful 2020 6-6.5f 2yo winner Line Of Departure out of a 9.5f 3yo winner who was a half-sister to smart multiple 7f-1m winner (including at Group 2/3 level) Producer.

"She comes from the good and very active family of Golden Horde. She is a tough, strong filly, who ought to make a two-year-old over 6f this year."

CHEF DE PARTIE
10/4 b c Siyouni - Nessina (Hennessy)
Owner: Brook Farm Bloodstock Sales price: 95,000gns (Vendor)

Half-brother to Gimcrack Stakes winner Ajaya and smart 8-12f winner (including twice at Group 3 level) Extra Elusive. Dam an unraced half-sister to dual 7f 3yo Listed winner Tantina (later dam of UAE 1m 1f Group 1 winner Cityscape, high-class sprinter Bated Breath and grandam of St Leger winner Logician and high-class sprinter Equilateral).

"A half-brother to a Gimcrack winner and also our smart horse, Extra Elusive. This is a strong, good-moving colt who is forward going. I can see him running over 6/7f from June onwards."

FOZZIE BEAR (IRE)
1/3 b g Kodiac - Dabtiyra (Dr Devious)
Owner: de Zoete, Inglett & Jones Sales price: 75,000gns (Amanda Skiffington for Roger Charlton)

Full brother to 7f/1m 2yo Listed winner Washaar and closely related to two winners including 2020 12.5f 3yo winner Roman's Empress (by Holy Roman Emperor). Dam a once-raced half-sister to Listed-placed Irish 12-14f 3yo winner Dibiya (later dam of dual 7f Listed winner Di Fede and Irish 11f 3yo Listed winner Dibayani); family of Darshaan and Dar Re Mi.

"A strong, powerful individual by a prolific producer of two-year-old winners. He is similar to the same owners' Smokey Bear in terms of pedigree and profile. This gelding is quite speedy and should make a two-year-old at some point."

FRESH FANCY (IRE)
15/2 b f New Approach - Pure Fantasy (Fastnet Rock)
Owner: The Queen Sales price: n/a

Full sister to 2020 10f 2yo winner Pied Piper. Dam a dual 10f 3yo winner who was closely related to Listed-placed 6f-1m winner Quadrille and useful 6-7f winner Free Verse out of a 10f 3yo Listed-winning sister to Ribblesdale Stakes winner Phantom Gold (later dam of dual 7f Listed winner Golden Stream and 7f 2yo winner/Oaks runner-up Flight of Fancy).

"A strong, attractive filly who moves well. Both the year-older brother and dam won over 10f and there's stamina in the pedigree. She should be running over 7f+ from midsummer onwards."

GOLDEN SHEEN
3/3 ch f Frankel - Yellow Band (Dalakhani)
Owner: Merry Fox Stud Limited Sales price: 100,000gns (Vendor)

First foal of an unraced sister to high-class multiple 10-12f winner (including at Group 1 level) Second Step out of a maiden sister to Irish 7f 2yo Group 2 winner/Poule d'Essai des Pouliches fourth Silk And Scarlet (later dam of US 10f 3yo Grade 1 winner Minorette, Japanese 1m Grade 1 winner Eishin Apollon and UAE 1m 1f Group 1 winner Master of Hounds) and half-sister to French 6f 3yo Group 3 winner Danger Over.

"This filly is out of a half-sister to our good middle-distance performer, Second Step. She is a strong filly, who is quite together and moves well. There is speed in the pedigree and she shows some of that, so should be in action over 6/7f in the first part of the summer."

GRAPH
30/3 b f Frankel - Photographic (Oasis Dream)
Owner: Juddmonte Sales price: n/a

Full sister to 2020 9.5f 2yo winner Side Shot and a half-sister to smart 8-10.5f winner (including the Musidora Stakes)/Prix de Diane fourth Shutter Speed. Dam a useful dual 1m 3yo winner who was a half-sister to Australian triple 8-10f Group 1 winner Foreteller, French 7f 2yo Group 2 winner/Poule d'Essai des Pouliches fourth Modern Look (later dam of US 8.5f Grade 3 winner Grand Jete) and 6f 3yo Listed winner Arabesque (later dam of Gimcrack Stakes winner Showcasing).

"A neat, attractive filly who moves nicely and shows promise. With the likes of Camacho and Showcasing on the page, you would hope she could be running over 6/7f in midsummer."

HONKY TONK MAN (IRE)
22/1 b c Tamayuz - Dance Hall Girl (Dansili)
Owner: de Zoete, Inglett & Jones Sales price: 68,000gns (Amanda Skiffington)

Half-brother to 7f 2yo Listed winner Tashweeq, useful UK/Irish 5-6f winner
Kasbah, useful 6-7f winner Highlight Reel, useful 5-6f 2yo winner Celebrity
Dancer and useful 1m 2yo winner HMS President. Dam an Irish 6.5f 3yo
winner who was closely related to very useful 7-9.5f winner (including at
Listed level) Solar Deity out of an Irish 7f 3yo winning half-sister to Irish 2000
Guineas/Poule d'Essai des Pouliches winner Bachir and Acomb Stakes winner
Elliots World.

"A strong, attractive half-brother to a two-year-old Listed winner and a five-time winner. He is a laid-back individual who should be seen in action over 6/7f from July onwards."

JUMBLY
23/4 b f Gleneagles - Thistle Bird (Selkirk)
Owner: Emmy Rothschild Sales price: n/a

Half-sister to useful 7f-1m winner Bullfinch and 7.5f 2yo winner Thorn. Dam
a high-class multiple 8-10f winner (including at Group 1 level) who was a
half-sister to Group 1-placed UK/Australian 6.5-10f winner (including twice at
Group 3 level) McCreery, 2m 1f/2m 3f Grade 2 hurdle winner Old Guard and 6f
2yo winner Don Marco.

"This filly isn't in training yet but is due come in shortly. She is quite a neat type who is a half-sister to Bullfinch, who enjoyed a very productive campaign last year, while the dam was obviously a Group 1 winner in Ireland for us. This filly should improve with time and will probably be one for the autumn."

LEAF MOTIF
18/4 ch f Bated Breath - Palmette (Oasis Dream)
Owner: Juddmonte Sales price: n/a

Full sister to useful dual 6f 2yo winner Partitia and a half-sister to 2020 Irish 7f
2yo winner Angel Palm. Dam a 6f 3yo winner who was a full sister to Gimcrack
Stakes winner Showcasing, Group 3/Listed-placed 6f 2yo winner Tendu and
Listed-placed dual 6f 3yo winner Bouvardia and half-sister to 6f 3yo Listed
winner/Jersey Stakes runner-up Camacho.

"A very strong and mature-looking filly who hasn't been here that long. She has got quite a speedy pedigree, and I can see her being out in the summer over 6f."

MAJESTIC FIGHTER (IRE)

2/2 ch c Teofilo - Majestic Manner (Dubawi)
Owner: Saeed Jaber Sales price: n/a

Third foal of a 7f 2yo winner who was closely related to high-class multiple 7.5-12f winner (including at Group 3/Listed level) Noor Al Hawa and a half-sister to German 9.5f Listed winner Majestic Jasmine out of a Sun Chariot Stakes-winning half-sister to 11f Group 3 winner Black Spirit, Grade 3-placed US 8.5f 2yo winner Heza Gone West and Listed-placed 7f 2yo winner Hiddnah.

"His close relation won an extremely valuable race in Qatar back in February. This colt hasn't done as much as we would've liked, but he moves well and looks a forward going individual. There's something about him."

MARS MAGIC (IRE)

28/4 b c Magician - Celerina (Choisir)
Owner: Ms Linda Mars Sales price: €7,500 (Culworth Grounds Farm)

Half-brother to useful 2020 Irish multiple 5-6f winner A Step Too Far. Dam a Listed-placed Irish triple 5f winner who was a full sister to useful Irish 5f 2yo winner Another Express and 5-6f winner Gottardo and a half-sister to US dual 1m 2yo stakes winner Clenor; family of Breeders' Cup Juvenile Turf winner Line of Duty.

"The sire has been a little disappointing and this colt was picked up cheaply as a foal. As it turns out, he was exceptionally well bought at 7.5k given the exploits of his half-brother in Ireland last year, who won six races and improved to the tune of 43lbs. This colt looked immature initially but has come together quite well and looks a speedy sort with a sound temperament. He will be one of our first two-year-old runners."

MR WHITE SOCKS

7/3 b c Frankel - Hana Lina (Oasis Dream)
Owner: Saeed Jaber Sales price: n/a

Half-brother to useful 7f 2yo winner Canton Queen. Dam a maiden half-sister to Group 1-placed 5-6f winner (including at Group 2/3 level) Lady of The Desert (later dam of Lowther Stakes winner Queen Kindly (by Frankel)), Listed-placed German/UK multiple 9-14f winner Kings Advice (by Frankel) and very useful UK/German multiple 5-7f winner Sanaadh out of a Cheveley Park Stakes winner.

"A strong, deep-girthed colt, who has Queen's Logic in his pedigree and is out of an Oasis Dream mare, so I doubt he'll stay much beyond 7f. He is a powerful individual who should be in action during the second half of the year."

NOISY NIGHT
26/2 b c Night of Thunder - Ya Hajar (Lycius)
Owner: Saeed Jaber Sales price: n/a

Half-brother to Irish 7f 3yo Listed winner Prince of All, useful Irish 6-7f 3yo winner English Deer, six other winners and the maiden dam of 2021 Champion Bumper winner Sir Gerhard. Dam a French 6f 2yo Group 3 winner who was closely related to 7f 3yo Listed winner Atlantic Sport and a half-sister to St James's Palace Stakes winner/2000 Guineas runner-up Zafeen and UAE 7f Listed winner Akeed Champion.

"A neat horse with a very nice temperament who goes quite nicely. He will be one for the latter half of the season over 7f."

OUT FROM UNDER
20/3 b c Dubawi - Koora (Pivotal)
Owner: White Birch Farm and Fittocks Stud Sales price: 120,000gns (Vendor)

Second foal of a Group 2-placed 10-12f 3yo winner (including at Group 3 level) who was a half-sister to St Leger winner/Breeders' Cup Turf runner-up Milan, Group 3-placed Irish 7f 2yo winner Go For Gold, Listed-placed 10-14f 3yo winner Kahara (later dam of Mehl-Mulhens Rennen winner Karpino) and 11.5f 3yo winner Kibara (later dam of US 8.5f Stakes winner Dubara (by Dubawi)) out of a 12f 3yo Group 3 winner.

"A strong, attractive colt who was retained in part by Fittocks Stud, having not met his reserve at auction. He looks quite forward considering his pedigree is that of a future middle-distance performer. I can see him starting off over 1m in the autumn."

SWEET WILLIAM (IRE)
24/3 b c Sea The Stars - Gale Force (Shirocco)
Owner: Normandie Stud Ltd Sales price: n/a

Half-brother to Listed-placed 8-12f winner Frankel's Storm and once-raced 2020 1m 2yo winner Hurricane Lane. Dam a French 15.5f Listed winner who was a half-sister to 12f Group 1 winner Seal of Approval and Group 3-placed 6-7f winner Instance; family of Derby winner Harzand (by Sea The Stars).

"A good-looking, well-grown colt who hasn't done anything so far. There is plenty of stamina in his pedigree, and it's more about next year with him. I hope to give him a run before the end of the year."

THESIS
2/5 b c Kingman - Nimble Thimble (Mizzen Mast)
Owner: Juddmonte Sales price: n/a

Full brother to French 1m 2yo winner Boardman and a half-brother to Fillies'
Mile winner/1000 Guineas third Quadrilateral. Dam a 9.5f 3yo winner who
was a half-sister to Group/Grade 1-placed UK/US 6-8.5f winner (including at
Grade 2/Group 3 level) Three Valleys and six other winners; exceptional family
of Banks Hill, Cacique, Intercontinental, Champs Elysees, Dansili etc.

*"A half-brother to our good filly, Quadrilateral. We don't know too much about
him at this stage, but he's an attractive colt who moves well and has a good
temperament."*

Quadrilateral

WONDERFUL TIMES (IRE)
11/3 b f Golden Horn - Wonderfully (Galileo)
Owner: Normandie Stud Ltd Sales price: 350,000gns (Stroud Coleman
Bloodstock)

Fourth foal of an Irish 7f 2yo Group 3 winner who was a full sister to 7f 2yo
Group 2 winner/Irish 2000 Guineas runner-up Gustav Klimt, Irish 6f 2yo
Listed winner Cuff, Irish 7f 2yo Listed winner Blissful and Irish 7f 2yo winner/
St James's Palace Stakes third Mars and a half-sister to Italian 1m 2yo Group

1 winner Nayarra and the dams of Ribblesdale Stakes winner Hertford Dancer and Lingfield Derby Trial winner Kilimanjaro.

"This filly has only just arrived and is a strong, attractive individual. We don't really know much more about her at this stage, but I hope she can have a run or two in the autumn."

UNNAMED
3/2 b f Kingman - Choumicha (Paco Boy)
Owner: Mohammed Jaber Sales price: n/a

First foal of a 7f 2yo winner who was a full sister to 2000 Guineas/St James's Palace Stakes winner Galileo Gold and a half-sister to useful dual 7f winner Eshaasy out of a twice-raced maiden half-sister to King's Stand Stakes/Prix de l'Abbaye winner Goldream; family of top-class middle-distance performer Montjeu and Irish 1000 Guineas winner Again.

"This filly has a nice pedigree as the first foal of a sister to Galileo Gold. She is attractive with a good nature and will be one for the autumn starting at 7f."

UNNAMED
6/2 b f Oasis Dream - Dhan Dhana (Dubawi)
Owner: Mohammed Jaber Sales price: n/a

Three-parts sister to Listed-placed 8-10f winner Singyoursong (by Aqlaam). Dam a 9.5-10f 3yo winner who was a half-sister to Group 3-placed 8-10f winner (including at Listed level) Annabelle's Charm (later dam of Middle Park Stakes winner Charming Thought (by Oasis Dream)) and Listed-placed 7f 2yo winner Purple Sage out of a maiden sister to Racing Post Trophy winner Aristotle and half-sister to St James's Palace Stakes winner Starborough.

"An athletic filly who finds it all very easy at this stage. I would expect to see her out sometime during the midsummer over 6/7f."

UNNAMED
17/3 b f Kingman - Langlauf (Raven's Pass)
Owner: Tony Bloom Sales price: n/a

First foal of a useful French/UK 9-14f winner who was a half-sister to Listed-placed UK/UAE 6f-1m winner Fly At Dawn out of a Listed-placed French 1m 3yo winning half-sister to Queen Mary Stakes/Prix Robert Papin winner Signora Cabello and Listed-placed 6f 2yo winner La Presse.

"An attractive filly who hasn't been here very long. It is a mainly middle-distance pedigree and she will probably be one for the end of the summer or autumn."

UNNAMED
25/3 b f Kingman - Lustrous (Champs Elysees)
Owner: St Albans Bloodstock Limited Sales price: 310,000gns (Blandford Bloodstock)

Second foal of a Group 2-placed 7f-1m winner (including at Listed level) who was a half-sister to 6f 2yo Group 3 winner Melody of Love and useful 6-7f winner Nobleman's Nest out of an unraced half-sister to Group 2-placed multiple 7f-1m winner (including at Group 3/Listed level) Ordnance Row; family of Duke Of York Stakes winner/2000 Guineas runner-up Delegator.

"This is a well grown, strong filly with a very good pedigree. She has just gone out for a break, but will hopefully be ready in time to make an appearance at the backend of the season."

UNNAMED
22/2 b c Churchill - Materialistic (Oasis Dream)
Owner: Mohammed Jaber Sales price: 100,000gns (Rabbah Bloodstock)

First foal of a Listed-placed 7f-1m winner who was a half-sister to Group 3-placed 8-14f winner (including at Listed level) Pinzolo and Australian 8/10f Listed winner Dr Drill out of a Lancashire Oaks-winning close relation to 12/14f Listed winner Lion Sands and half-sister to the dam of 2020 Lingfield Derby Trial winner English King and French 11f 3yo Listed winner Prudenzia (herself dam of Irish Oaks winner Chicquita and Australian 10f Group 1 winner Magic Wand).

"A big, powerful colt, who is from the first crop of Churchill and out of an Oasis Dream mare. Therefore, it's perhaps not a surprise that he shows some speed, and I could see him beginning over 6f sometime in June or July."

UNNAMED (IRE)
2/4 b c Kodiac - Nijah (Pivotal)
Owner: Mohammed Jaber Sales price: £75,000 (Rabbah Bloodstock)

Second foal of a French 1m winner who was a half-sister to useful 5-6.5f 2yo winner Prairie Spy out of a 1m 3yo Listed winner/1000 Guineas third; family of five-time 12f-2m Group 2 winner Enbihaar.

"A nice horse who is tough, like most from this sire, and requires plenty of exercise. He shows promise and could be in action by May time."

UNNAMED
21/4 gr f Time Test - Sell Out (Act One)
Owner: Paul & Clare Rooney Sales price: 60,000gns (Kevin Ross Bloodstock)

Half-sister to French 6f 2yo Listed winner Showout, very useful 7f-1m winner Bella Ragazza and useful 10-11f winner Landwade Lad. Dam a French 12f Listed winner who was a half-sister to Fred Darling Stakes winner/Oaks fourth Sueboog (later dam of French 1m 1f Group 1 winner/Derby fourth Best of The Bests and grandam of Australian 12/12.5f Group 3 winner/Melbourne Cup runner-up Prince of Arran) and 6f Listed winner Marika (later dam of triple 8/9f Group 3 winner Kick On).

"This is a neat filly that comes from a good family that is something of a mixture in terms of optimum distance. She is a good-moving, top-of-the-ground sort who shows a bit of zip and ought to be running by the summertime."

UNNAMED (IRE)
26/2 ch f Postponed - Starscape (Cape Cross)
Owner: Mohammed Jaber Sales price: 75,000gns (Rabbah Bloodstock)

First foal of an unraced half-sister to 6f 2yo winner/Acomb Stakes third Zumbi and Listed-placed 8.5f 3yo winner Say No Now out of an unraced sister to Flying Childers Stakes winner Land of Dreams (later dam of five-time 6/7f Group 1 winner Dream Ahead and grandam of Cheveley Park Stakes winner Fairyland).

"A very strong, professional filly, who has speed on the dam's side of the pedigree but is by Postponed, though he did reach a useful level as a two-year-old before going on to become a top-class middle-distance horse. She is an unknown in terms of ability at this stage and only does want you want her to. I like the pedigree and hope that she will be out in July over 7f."

TOM CLOVER

ANJALA (IRE)
28/4 ch f Anjaal - Dreaming Lady (Dream Ahead)
Owner: The Rogues Gallery & Partners Sales price: n/a

Half-sister to Listed-placed 2020 6f 2yo winner Fairy Dust. Dam a maiden half-sister to Listed-placed 5-6f winner Ballymore Castle out of a US 8.5f Grade 3 winner who was a half-sister to US 6.5f 2yo Grade 3 winner Sunray Spirit and useful US 5.5-8.5f winner Dehere of The Dog.

"A half-sister to Fairy Dust, who finished second in the Listed St Hugh's Stakes for us last season. She is a nice little filly who shows speed and goes ok. I can see her being out over 5f in May time."

Fairy Dust

LADY FANFARE (IRE)
15/2 gr f Gutaifan - Secret Key (Key of Luck)
Owner: The Shimplingthorne Syndicate Sales price: 17,000gns (T Clover/J S Bloodstock)

Three-parts sister to Irish 6f 2yo Group 3 winner Exogenesis (by Dark Angel). Dam an Irish 7f winner who was a half-sister to UK/US 5.5-6.5f winner Royal

Highlander; family of Irish 1000 Guineas winner More So and Premio Parioli winner Candy Glen.

"A nice enough filly, who goes nicely enough and is looking well bought at 17k at this stage. She is entered in the Super Sprint and should be out sooner rather than later."

LUMBERJACK
25/4 gr c Mastercraftsman - Wood Chorus (Singspiel)
Owner: The Rogues Gallery & Partners Sales price: 20,000gns (T Clover/J S Bloodstock)

Half-brother to useful multiple 8-10f winner Sands Chorus and four other winners including 2020 7f 2yo winner Sugauli. Dam a Listed-placed 10f 3yo winner who was a half-sister to Yorkshire Cup winner Franklins Gardens and 7f/1m Group 3 winner Polar Ben.

"Medium-sized colt who is a half-brother to Sugauli, who won on debut before being colty beforehand and not running his race next time in a Listed race at Salisbury last season. I hope to see him in action during high summer and I like him."

MR BEAUFORT
24/4 b c Cable Bay - Tan Tan (King's Best)
Owner: The Mr Beaufort Syndicate Sales price: 12,000gns (T Clover/J S Bloodstock)

Half-brother to useful 2020 dual 6f 2yo winner Tanfantic, fairly useful 2020 11-12f 3yo winner Brooklyn Boy, fairly useful dual 5f winner Revived and two other winners. Dam a French 6.5f 3yo winner who was a half-sister to Flying Childers Stakes winner Sahara Star (later dam of five-time 6/7f Group 1 winner Dream Ahead and grandam of Cheveley Park Stakes winner Fairyland).

"An attractive colt, who is a solid, hardy type and very straightforward to deal with. He has done some nice work, and we will look to have him running by May, probably over 6f. The Book 3 sales race at Newmarket in the autumn is hopefully something we can have a look at nearer the time. He will want some ease in the ground."

PAPA COCKTAIL (IRE)
12/3 b c Churchill - Anklet (Acclamation)
Owner: Khalifa Dasmal Sales price: 40,000gns (Federico Barberini)

Three-parts brother to 2021 US 8.5f Grade 3 winner Counterparty Risk (by Australia) and a half-brother to Irish 7f 2yo winner Tonkin. Dam a twice-raced maiden half-sister to Canadian International winner Sarah Lynx, smart 7.5-10f winner (including at Group 3/Listed level) Sugar Boy, 2020 Geelong Cup winner Steel Prince and Group 2-placed 2020 French 12f 3yo winner Influx out of a French 10.5f 3yo Group 3 winner.

"This is a very nice colt who I like quite a bit. He looks a lot like his sire, and I expect to see him starting off over 6f in the summer."

SANFELICE (IRE)
3/3 b f Acclamation - Mickleberry (Desert Style)
Owner: Halcyon Thoroughbreds Sales price: 30,000gns (T Clover/J S Bloodstock)

Half-sister to useful multiple 6f winner Aplomb. Dam a 5f 3yo winner who was a half-sister to 6f 2yo Group 2 winner Alhebayeb, Group 1-placed multiple 5-6f winner (including at Listed level) Humidor, very useful UK/UAE 7f-1m winner Azmaam and the unraced dam of very useful 2020 6f 2yo winner Royal Scimitar.

"This filly was shaping up well until meeting with a small setback. She is still a little immature in any case, and I don't expect to see her out until September/ October time."

ZAIN SARINDA (IRE)
18/2 b c Churchill - Sarinda (Dubawi)
Owner: Elbashir Elhrari Sales price: 62,000gns (Global Equine Group)

Half-brother to useful 5-7f winner Indian Sounds. Dam a German 1m 3yo Listed winner who was a full sister to useful 6-7f winner Bowmaker and a half-sister to Hong Kong 1m 1f Listed winner Pleasure Gains; family of top-class miler Rock of Gibraltar and Moyglare Stud Stakes winner Intricately.

"I have got three by the sire and, like the other two, he has a good temperament. This is a big, athletic sort who has got a nice way of going and I quite like him. He won't be overly early."

UNNAMED
4/4 b c Muhaarar - Primo Lady (Lucky Story)
Owner: The Rogues Gallery & Partners Sales price: 28,000gns (T Clover/J S Bloodstock)

Closely related to Group 2-placed UK/US 5-6f winner (including at stakes level) Out of The Flames (by Showcasing) and a half-brother to French 5f 2yo Group 3 winner Little Kim and useful triple 6f 2yo winner War Storm. Dam a 5f 2yo Listed winner who was a half-sister to useful triple 6f winner Zhiggy's Stardust.

"The mare was good and has done well at stud so far too. Muhaarars tend to need time so he won't be early, but he is training well and I suspect that he will be a sprinter like the majority of the family."

UNNAMED
28/3 b c New Approach - Sharnberry (Shamardal)
Owner: The Rogues Gallery & Partners Sales price: 35,000gns (T Clover/J S Bloodstock)

Half-brother to useful 6f 2yo winner Coase and two other winners. Dam a Group 3/Listed-placed UK/US 6f-1m winner who was a full sister to useful triple 1m winner Margaret's Mission and a half-sister to useful 5-6f winner Master Rooney out of a Listed-placed 5-6f 2yo winner.

"A medium-sized, athletic colt, who is one for the backend and essentially more of a three-year-old type. Nice horse but very much a longer-term prospect."

ED DUNLOP

Thanks to Ed's assistant *Jack Morland* for putting forward the following six two-year-olds from La Grange Stables.

CITIZEN GENERAL (IRE)
1/3 b c Camelot - Capriole (Noverre)
Owner: Paul Turner Sales price: 150,000gns (BBA Ireland/Ed Dunlop Racing)

Half-brother to very useful multiple 5-7f winner (including at Group 3 level) Arnold Lane, useful 2020 Irish 1m 3yo winner Frank Arthur and 2020 Irish 5f 2yo winner Sloane Peterson. Dam an unraced half-sister to Listed-placed UK/UAE 6f-1m winner/2000 Guineas fourth Zoning and useful 7f-1m 3yo winner Lady Zonda (later dam of Fillies' Mile/Yellow Ribbon Stakes winner Hibaayeb, herself the dam of Prix Marcel Boussac/Breeders' Cup Filly & Mare Turf winner Wuheida).

"A scopey, good-looking two-year-old, who has done everything that has been asked of him so far. He will take time but looks like he'll furnish into a lovely horse."

DRAWING CLOCKS
31/3 b c Time Test - Lynnwood Chase (Horse Chestnut)
Owner: Paul Turner Sales price: 150,000gns (Blandford Bloodstock)

Half-brother to triple 11.5-12f 3yo Group 1 winner, (including the Irish Oaks)
Star Catcher, high-class 10-12f winner (including the Canadian International)
Cannock Chase, 10f 3yo Group 2/3 winner Pisco Sour and two other winners.
Dam a maiden half-sister to high-class Irish/UAE 7-9f winner (including at
Group 2/3 level) Lord Admiral.

*"A good-looking son of Time Test, who is a half-brother to Irish Oaks winner
Star Catcher. He has been going well at home and though he'll take time, he
should hopefully make it out before the end of the year."*

FEARLESS BAY (IRE)
3/3 b c Siyouni - Monroe Bay (Makfi)
Owner: Paul Turner Sales price: 230,000gns (Blandford Bloodstock)

First foal of a Group 3-placed French 8-9f winner, (including at Listed level)
who was a full sister to Group 3/Listed-placed UK/Saudi Arabian 7-10f winner
Persian Moon out of a Listed-placed French 11f 3yo winning half-sister to
Group 2-placed French 8-10.5f winner (including twice at Group 3 level)/
Prix de Diane fourth Celimene, French 7f 2yo Listed winner Lunaska and the
grandam of US 1m 1f Grade 1 winner Ana Luna.

*"A racy-looking colt out of Listed winner Monroe Bay. The sire has had another
incredible year at stud, highlighted by the Arc winner, Sottsass, and Dewhurst
Stakes winner, St Mark's Basilica. He is a good-looking, well-built sort who
looks an exciting prospect at this stage."*

TADITA TWITCH
15/2 b f Siyouni - Twitch (Azamour)
Owner: Paul Turner Sales price: 90,000gns (BBA Ireland/Ed Dunlop Racing)

First foal of a 14f Listed winner who was a half-sister to useful 1m 2yo winner
Kaloor, 10f 3yo winners Maracuja and Myopic and the unraced dam of German
7.5f 2yo Listed winner Romsey out of an unraced sister to very smart 6-12f
winner (including eight times at Group 1 level) Viva Pataca and half-sister to
high-class Irish/US 8-11f winner (including twice at Grade 1 level) Laughing.

*"This strong, well-built filly was purchased at Book 1 of the Tattersalls October
Yearling Sale for 90,000gns. As discussed, her sire had another phenomenal
year in 2020, and his daughter looks an early type who has done a few half
speeds so far."*

UNNAMED
5/3 ch f Night of Thunder - Harlequin Girl (Where Or When)
Owner: Shadwell Estate Co Sales price: 110,000gns (Shadwell Estate Company)

Third foal of a maiden half-sister to Gimcrack Stakes winner Blaine, 6f 2yo Listed winner Bogart, Group 3-placed 2020 6f 2yo winner Legal Attack, useful UK/Bahraini 6f-1m winner Byline and the unraced dam of Group 2-placed 2020 7f 2yo winner Youth Spirit.

"This daughter of Night of Thunder is a racy-looking filly with a strong page. She has started to do a few half speeds and will hopefully be ready to run when the six-furlong races begin."

UNNAMED (FR)
19/2 ch c New Bay - Louve Rare (Rock of Gibraltar)
Owner: Shadwell Estate Co Sales price: 205,000gns (Shadwell Estate Company)

Half-brother to French 1m 3yo winner Lamu. Dam a Listed-placed French 1m 1f 2yo winner who was a half-sister to Group/Grade 1-placed French/US 9-10f winner (including at Grade 2/Group 3 level) Loup Breton, French 10.5f 3yo Group 3 winner Lil'Wing and US 12f Listed winner Louve Royale out of a French 10.5f 3yo Group 3-winning half-sister to Prix d'Ispahan winner/Poule d'Essai des Poulains runner-up/Irish Derby third Loup Sauvage and French 1m 2yo Group 1 winner Loup Solitaire.

"This smashing colt was purchased for 205,000gns at Book 2 of the Tattersalls October Yearling Sale. Out of the Listed-placed mare Louve Rare - herself the producer of black type performer Lamu - this colt looks every bit a runner in the making. He is by the Classic winner, New Bay, who had a fantastic first season at stud in 2020, highlighted by Group winners, New Mandate and Saffron Beach. He has done everything that has been asked of him so far and looks to be going well."

HARRY EUSTACE

BE GLORIOUS
4/1 b f Kodiac - Spirit Raiser (Invincible Spirit)
Owner: Glentree Pastoral Pty Ltd Sales price: 80,000gns (Badgers Bloodstock)

Second foal of a 1m Listed winner who was closely related to useful 7f 2yo winner Kona Coast and a half-sister to Group 3-placed UK/UAE 6f-1m winner (including at Listed level) Lovely Pass and useful UK/UAE 7f-1m winner Almoreb out of a Falmouth Stakes-winning half-sister to Swedish 6f Group 3 winner Pistachio and 1m Listed winner Captivator.

"A strong, compact daughter of Kodiac. She is bred to be good and has done a couple of bits of work already, but I don't want to get her revved up and going too quickly as she's got a nice pedigree and won't be all about this year. We will see how she takes the next couple of weeks, and if she does grow we can give her some more time; otherwise you might see her start off over 5f fairly soon. I suspect she'll want 6f before long. A nice filly."

BELHAVEN (IRE)
9/3 ch f Belardo - Park Haven (Marju)
Owner: A M Mitchell Sales price: 17,000gns (Highflyer Bloodstock/H Eustace)

Half-sister to useful UK/US 5.5-6f winner Promote, fairly useful 6f-1m winner Tadaany and 7f-1m 2yo winner Quick Bite. Dam a maiden half-sister to Gordon Stakes winner Rebel Soldier out of a 5.5f 2yo winning half-sister to Queen Elizabeth II Stakes winner Observatory and smart 7-12f winner (including at Group 2/3 level) High Praise.

"She has grown a fair bit since we bought her as a yearling. She did a couple of bits of bridle work and has now gone out for a small break. We will look to get her out sometime in the summer over 6f, though I am mindful of the fact that Belardos seem to want some cut in the ground. A nice filly who will probably prove best over 7f/1m eventually."

CHASING APHRODITE
15/2 b c Profitable - Tutti Frutti (Teofilo)
Owner: Gullwing Enterprises W. L. L. Sales price: 60,000gns (De Burgh Equine)

Third foal of a maiden close relation to Nassau Stakes winner Sultanina and 1m 3yo winners Croque Monsieur and Rum Baba and half-sister to Listed-placed 10f 3yo winner Coconut Creme out of a 10f 3yo Listed winner who was a half-sister to US 12f 3yo Grade 3 winner Dalvina and 10.5f 3yo Listed winner French Dressing.

"He would be the nicest two-year-old here in terms of physique. He is fairly big but not backward and is now back cantering after a small break. We will work him soon and see where we are, but he is a horse who will do even better at three so we'll do right by him this year and run him sparingly."

CLARITUDO
20/3 b c Nathaniel - Clarentine (Dalakhani)
Owner: Jackson XV Sales price: 21,000gns (Highflyer Bloodstock/H Eustace)

Third foal of a Listed-placed dual 1m 3yo winner who was a half-sister to Lingfield Oaks Trial winner Perfect Clarity (by Nathaniel) and Italian 10f Listed winner Law Power out of a Listed-placed dual 7f 2yo winning half-sister to Group 1-placed UK/US 7-11.5f winner (including at Grade 3/Listed level) Cassydora (later dam of smart trio Ernest Hemingway, South Sea Pearl and Toulifaut) and 10f 3yo Listed winner Classic Remark.

"The brief was to buy a backend two-year-old type with a view to a three-year-old campaign, but this colt hasn't grown much since we bought him. He has taken everything we have asked of him in his stride, and we'll be aiming him at one of the earlier 7f races. The big hope is the Chesham and though that's perhaps fanciful, he is owned by some good guys who can at least have a dream for the time being. He will get one shot at it and, unless he wins first time out, we will give him a holiday and bring him back for the latter stages of the season."

FIRST VIOLIN
10/3 b c Norse Dancer - Opera Queen (Nathaniel)
Owner: J C Smith Sales price: n/a

First foal of a thrice-raced maiden sister to useful 2020 11.5-12f 3yo winner Opera Gift and three-parts sister to Group 3-placed 10-11.5f winner (including at Listed level) Opera Gal out of an 8.5f 3yo winning sister to Solario Stakes winner/Dewhurst Stakes third Opera Cape and half-sister to Goodwood Cup winner Grey Shot and the dam of German 1m Group 2 winner Highland Knight.

"A good-looking horse but big and backward with it. I suspect we will geld him fairly soon and he might not even run this year."

FLAMING LORD
4/3 ch c Zarak - Elusive Flame (Elusive City)
Owner: J C Smith Sales price: n/a

Fourth foal of a useful 6-7f winner who was a half-sister to fairly useful 7-14f Flat/Listed-placed 2m hurdle winner Odin out of a maiden half-sister to Group 1-placed UK/French 6f-1m winner (including at Group 3/Listed level) Guys And Dolls, triple 8-11f Listed winner Pawn Broker and Group 3/Listed-placed dual 7f 2yo winner Blushing Bride.

"A really nice colt, who is belying his pedigree in many ways as he is looking quite a forward type at the moment. It is entirely possible that he will grow or not take the training when we increase his workload, but he looks pretty set at this stage so we'll see how we go. I imagine he will start off in late May or June over 6f as things stand."

FOSHAN (IRE)
23/2 b c The Last Lion - China In My Hands (Dark Angel)
Owner: The MacDougall Two Sales price: 30,000gns (Highflyer Bloodstock/H Eustace)

Half-brother to Irish 1m 2yo winner Lafayette Hill. Dam a maiden half-sister to useful 5-6f winner Expensive Date and 2020 Irish 6f 2yo winner Shalaalaa out of a useful 6-7f 3yo winning half-sister to UAE 6f Group 1 winner Muarrab and Molecomb Stakes/Cornwallis Stakes winner Bungle Inthejungle.

"Having initially looked quite a forward type, he has grown and therefore gone a bit weak, so we've backed off him a little. I imagine he will start off over 6f in May/June time. A very nice horse."

J'ADORE (IRE)
3/3 b f Australia - Dillydallydo (Holy Roman Emperor)
Owner: Gullwing Enterprises W. L. L. Sales price: £68,000 (De Burgh Equine)

First foal of an unraced close relation to Group 2/Listed-placed 10-12f Flat/2m-2m 4f hurdle winner Drill Sergeant, Group 3-placed French 10.5f 3yo winner Nobilis and useful 7f 2yo winner Sergeant Ablett; family of 7f 2yo Group 1 winners Intense Focus and Skitter Scatter and Irish Derby winner Solider of Fortune.

"A very attractive filly. Looking at the pedigree you might expect to see a big, backward filly but she doesn't look it, although she does train that way. She has been in since December and has done plenty of groundwork so has now gone out for a break. I am sure she will do well for the time off, and we will be in no hurry with her. Maybe one run this year, but it's all about her three-year-old career and beyond, so she'll require a bit of patience."

LATIN LOVER (IRE)
23/4 b c Starspangledbanner - Blue Dahlia (Shamardal)
Owner: Candour House And Partner Sales price: £21,000 (De Burgh Equine)

Three-parts brother to Irish 5f 3yo winner Court Queen (by Choisir) and a half-brother to Irish 7f-1m winner Gatsby Cap. Dam a useful Irish 5-6f winner who was the daughter of an unraced half-sister to Italian 12f Listed winner River Jig (later dam of Queen Mary Stakes winner Dance Parade, herself the dam of St Leger/Ascot Gold Cup winner Leading Light).

"A very solid colt, who will be one of my earlier two-year-old runners. He is a relaxed character at home but takes an interest in everything around him and doesn't concentrate a huge amount, but when he does he looks a nice horse. I suspect he will run over 5f in April but won't be long in tackling 6f. I am sure he will improve as he gains experience."

REGIMENTAL GENT
20/3 b c The Gurkha - City Girl (Elusive City)
Owner: J C Smith Sales price: n/a

Half-brother to 2020 5f 2yo winner City Code and UK/Spanish 6-7f winner City Gent. Dam a Listed-placed dual 6f winner/Lowther Stakes fourth who was a half-sister to dual 5f winner Olympic Runner and 6f 2yo winner Echo Ridge out of a Group 2/3-placed multiple 6-7f winner (including at Listed level) who was a half-sister to 5f Listed winner Loch Verdi.

"He's not a bad type and could be ready to start racing in the summer over 6/7f. I haven't done a huge amount with him yet to so it's too early to say exactly what he is all about."

JAMES FANSHAWE

ANNIE GALE (IRE)
26/4 b f No Nay Never - Double Fantasy (Indian Ridge)
Owner: Fred Archer Racing - Minting Sales price: £32,000 (Stroud Coleman BS/Fred Archer)

Half-sister to French 6f Listed winner Magical Dreamer, 5f 2yo Listed winner Piece of Paradise, useful 6-7f winner George Rooke and useful dual 6f 2yo winner Ginbar. Dam a German 1m 3yo winner who was a half-sister to Group 3-placed UAE triple 1m winner Zafeen Speed out of a German 1000 Guineas-winning sister to US 8.5f 2yo Grade 1 winner Creaking Board and French/German dual 6f Group 3 winner Dyhim Diamond.

"We are quite familiar with the pedigree having trained the half-sister, Magical Diamond, who improved as she got older and ended up winning five races for us. This filly changed quite a bit physically in the spring and is now a nice, strong sort. She is just cantering away at the moment and will be one for the later in the year."

BIG NEWS (IRE)
24/2 b f Dubawi - Biz Bar (Tobougg)
Owner: Qatar Racing Limited Sales price: €120,000 (Private Sale)

Half-sister to Italian 12f 3yo Group 1 winner Biz The Nurse, Italian 1m 2yo Group 2 winner Biz Heart, Italian 1m 1f 2yo Group 3 winner Misterious Boy, Italian 7.5f 2yo Listed winner Biz Power and very useful 10-12f winner Alfaatik. Dam an Italian 7.5f 2yo Listed winner.

"We were lucky to be sent this filly by Qatar Racing. She is a strong, attractive filly who has been doing plenty of cantering up Warren Hill. Given the distaff side of her pedigree, she will be waiting for the 7f/1m races during the second half of the season but is a nice filly."

BLUEBIRD
17/3 b f Acclamation - Blues Sister (Compton Place)
Owner: Michelle Morris & Jan & Peter Hopper Sales price: n/a

First foal of an unraced sister to very smart multiple 5-6f winner (including at Group 2/3 level) Deacon Blues and a half-sister to very smart multiple 6f winner (including three times at Group 1 level) The Tin Man, Listed-placed multiple 5f winner Holley Shiftwell and four other winners out of a 6-7f winning sister to very useful 6f-1m winner Heretic and half-sister to triple 7f Group 3 winner Warningford.

"A filly bred by the Morrises and Hoppers, she is related to our good sprinters, Deacon Blues and The Tin Man. Like most of the family, she isn't the biggest and will take a bit of time but should be a nice filly for the latter part of the season. She began the breaking in process later than most and is only cantering away steadily at present, but she certainly catches the eye in all that she does."

CITRUS GROVE (IRE)
11/3 b f Oasis Dream - Zest (Duke of Marmalade)
Owner: Elite Racing Club Sales price: n/a

First foal of a Listed-placed 8-10f winner who was a half-sister to Listed-placed 8-8.5f 3yo winner Harmonica out of a 12f 3yo winning close relation to useful 5-6f winner Baralinka (grandam of Nunthorpe Stakes/Prix de l'Abbaye winner Marsha and dual 5f Group 3 winner Judicial) and half-sister to five-time 1m Group 1 winner Soviet Song and the dam of French 10f Group 1 winner Ribbons and Group 2-placed 7f-1m winner Tribute Act.

"This is a strong, compact filly, who hails from one of Elite Racing's best families. I trained the dam who was useful but never quite achieved what I thought she might have been capable of at one point. This would be a more laid-back individual, and she looks a nice prospect for the 7f/1m races a bit later on."

CLIPPER CLASS
17/3 b f Frankel - Speedy Boarding (Shamardal)
Owner: Helena Springfield Ltd Sales price: n/a

Second foal of a high-class 10-10.5f winner (including twice at Group 1 level) who was a half-sister to very useful dual 10f 3yo winner Elwazir (by Frankel), useful dual 1m winner Next Stage and three other winners including the dam of Queen's Vase winner Dashing Willoughby out of an 11f Listed-winning half-sister to Group 1-placed 8-10f winner (including at Listed level) Dash To The Top (later dam of Oaks winner Anapurna (by Frankel)).

"She isn't here yet, but I've seen her a few times at the stud, and she has a similar physique to her mother. Time will tell whether that means anything, but she will be an exciting prospect to have in the yard."

COMPLIANT
14/3 b f Pivotal - Royal Seal (Dansili)
Owner: Cheveley Park Stud Sales price: n/a

Half-sister to 2020 7f 2yo winner Sealed Offer. Dam a useful dual 7f 3yo winner who was a full sister to Breeders' Cup Filly & Mare Turf winner Queen's Trust out of Group 2-placed 6-12f winner (including at Group 3/Listed level) who was a half-sister to French 12f Listed winner Reverie Solitaire (later dam of German 1m Group 2 winner Royal Solitaire), 13f Listed winner Urban Castle and the dam of Group 1-placed triple 7f winner (including at Group 3 level) Dabyah.

"Her dam is a full sister to Queen's Trust, who won at the Breeders Cup meeting for Sir Michael Stoute. This filly goes nicely and is worth a mention despite being one for later on."

EURAQUILO
30/3 b c Raven's Pass - Air Kiss (Red Ransom)
Owner: Dr Catherine Wills Sales price: n/a

Half-brother to Group 2/Listed-placed 14f-2m winner Selino, 10f 3yo winner Airway and three other winners. Dam an unraced half-sister to Prix du Cadran winner/Ascot Gold Cup second Invermark, Princess of Wales's Stakes winner Craigsteel, Swedish 12f Group 3 winner Inchrory and Listed-placed 12f 3yo winner Anniversary out of a Group 2/3-placed 10-13.5f 3yo winner.

"He is owned and bred by one of our longest standing owners, Catherine Wills, and it's therefore a family we know extremely well. His half-brother made up into a good stayer last year and is now in Australia. This colt isn't nearly as backward as some in the family and is a different type, which perhaps isn't a surprise given he's a son of Raven's Pass. He is one I hope to start in the summer over 7f."

ISCHIA
10/5 ch f Equiano - Isola Verde (Oasis Dream)
Owner: Fred Archer Racing - Lady Golightly Sales price: 29,000gns (James Fanshawe/Fred Archer)

Half-sister to useful multiple 5f winner Glory Fighter, useful triple 1m winner Merchant of Venice and 2020 7f 2yo winner Isola Rossa. Dam a 6f 3yo winner who was a half-sister to smart UK/Irish multiple 5-7f winner (including at Listed level) Harry's Bar and Group 3-placed UK/UAE multiple 5-6f winner Mazzini out of a dual 6f Listed-winning sister to July Cup winner Frizzante and half-sister to Group 3-placed multiple 6f winner (including at Listed level) Zidane.

"Another family we know inside out given the dam's a half-sister to a couple of good sprinters we have trained in recent times called Harry's Bar and Mazzini, and you've got Frizzante and Firenze in the pedigree as well. The year-older half-sister won second time out for us last season and looks decent. This is a strong filly who ought to sprint, given she's a daughter of Equiano, but you won't be seeing her until the latter part of the season."

LIBERTUS
21/3 b c Equiano - Italian Connection (Cadeaux Genereux)
Owner: Fred Archer Racing - Peeping Tom Sales price: 42,000gns (Fred Archer Racing/Stroud Coleman Bloodstock)

Full brother to stakes-placed UK/US 5-6.5f winner Lajatico and a half-brother to useful 8-9f 3yo winner Talyani and 2020 7f 3yo winner Elmetto. Dam an unraced sister to Listed-placed Irish 7f 2yo winner Pietra Dura (later dam of US 10f Grade 3 winner Turning Top) and half-sister to Listed-placed winners Bighearted (8-8.5f) and Bite of The Cherry (13f) and the dam of four-time 10.5/12f Group 1 winner Postponed and Italian 10f Group 1 winner God Given.

"This colt was bred by Meon Valley Stud and is an attractive sort who moves well. He has just gone through a growing phase so won't be particularly early. Being by Equiano and out of a Cadeaux Genereux mare, I imagine he will be quick enough to begin over six furlongs. Obviously, this sire with these owners gave us The Tin Man, so hopefully this colt can be yet another success story."

ROYAL SCANDAL
28/2 ch f Dubawi - Seal of Approval (Authorized)
Owner: T R G Vestey Sales price: 120,000gns (James Fanshawe)

Full sister to Group 3-placed 12f 3yo winner Promissory. Dam a 12f Group 1 winner who was a half-sister to French 15.5f Listed winner Gale Force and Listed-placed 6-7f winner Instance out of an Irish 10f 3yo winning half-sister to Irish 3yo Group 3 winners Hamairi (7f) and Hanabad (6f) and the dam of 1m Group 3 winners Hamariyna and Hunaina.

"A tall, rangy filly who is an excellent mover. She is only doing steady work at the moment but finds it all easy and carries herself really nicely. The family can take time but she wouldn't be as immature as her four-year-old half-sister or indeed the dam, which I guess is the Dubawi influence coming through. She might be able to get going at some point during the second half of the season."

WANDERING ROCKS
16/2 ch c Ulysses - West of The Moon (Pivotal)
Owner: Cheveley Park Stud Sales price: 90,000gns (James Fanshawe)

Half-brother to fairly useful 2020 8-8.5f 3yo winner Flying West, fairly useful
dual 6f 3yo winner Moon Song and 7f 2yo winner Constant. Dam a twice-raced
maiden sister to the dam of 2020 Jersey Stakes winner Molatham and 6f Listed
winner Perfection and a half-sister to French 7f 2yo Group 3 winner Moon
Driver and the Listed-placed maiden dam of Group 3 winners Autocratic (10f,
twice) and Evasive (7f).

*"Mr Thompson was keen that I trained some of Ulysses' first crop for Cheveley
Park and I have got three of his progeny in training. This is a colt who is
improving all the time, and his half-sister, Flying West, did well for us last
season, winning on three occasions. It is a lovely Niarchos family that has done
well for Cheveley Park in recent times."*

WILLEM TWEE
29/4 b c Ribchester - Paulinie (Royal Applause)
Owner: Chris van Hoorn Racing Sales price: 37,000gns (Stroud Coleman
Bloodstock)

Second foal of an unraced half-sister to Grade 1-placed US 6-8.5f winner
(including at Grade 2 level) Three Degrees and Group 3-placed 6-7f winner
(including at Listed level) Mehronissa out of a maiden half-sister to US dual 6f
3yo Stakes winner Reissaurus and the dam of US triple 6f Listed winner Vicki
Vallencourt.

*"This colt didn't make his reserve at Book 1 of the Tattersalls October Yearling
Sale, and John Troy kindly phoned me and suggested I should have a good look
at him at the Tattersalls December Yearling Sale. He is a great mover with a
lovely attitude who really catches eye at the moment, and I hope he can give
owner, Chris van Hoorn, plenty of fun. While his pedigree isn't short of speed, I
suspect he will be out over 7f in midsummer."*

CHARLIE FELLOWES

ATRIUM
21/4 b c Holy Roman Emperor - Hail Shower (Red Clubs)
Owner: Highclere Thoroughbred Racing - Pergola Sales price: 60,000gns (John & Jake Warren)

Half-brother to very useful 6-7f 2yo winner (including at Listed level) Milltown Star. Dam an Irish 6.5-7f winner who was the daughter of a maiden close relation to Group 2/3-placed 7-12f winner Raincoat and half-sister to 12f 3yo Listed winner Quenched (later dam of Australian 7.5/12.5f Group 3 winner Excess Knowledge).

"A strong colt from a speedy and precocious family and he certainly fits that mould at the moment. He has done a couple of easy pieces of work and all has gone to plan at this stage. We couldn't be happier with him and hope to have him out over 6f during the first half of the season."

CASSIEL (IRE)
19/4 b c Dark Angel - Masaya (Dansili)
Owner: Dahab Racing Sales price: 38,000gns (C Gordon Watson Bloodstock)

Full brother to 2020 5f 2yo Listed winner Gussy Mac and a half-brother to useful 5-6f winner Shamsaya and 7f 2yo winner Perfect Thought. Dam a very useful 5-7f winner who was the daughter of a French 7f 2yo Listed-winning half-sister to Prix de l'Opera winner Satwa Queen (grandam of 2020 Phoenix Stakes winner Lucky Vega) and French 10f 2yo Group 1 winner Spadoun.

"He is a forward type, who had done a couple of pieces of work and looked very early. In fact, I was aiming him at the Brocklesby until he had a dodgy scope about three weeks prior which put paid to that plan. He is back in full work now and should be in action before May."

Gussy Mac

COOKIES AND CREME
25/3 ch f Siyouni - Coconut Creme (Cape Cross)
Owner: Normandie Stud Ltd Sales price: n/a

First foal of a Listed-placed 10f 3yo winner who was a half-sister to Nassau Stakes winner Sultanina out of a 10f 3yo Listed-winning half-sister to US 12f 3yo Grade 3 winner Dalvina (later dam of 12/14f Listed winner Dal Harraild), 10.5f 3yo Listed winner French Dressing and Listed-placed 7f-1m winner Pretzel.

"A good-looking filly, who looks an unusually early two-year-old for a Normandie-bred horse. She hasn't done anything serious yet as she came in quite late, but she has found things coming pretty easily in the bits of work she has done. I would hope to have her out in June/July and hopefully she can make up into a nice mid-season two-year-old performer. She could be sharp enough to begin over 6f but will ultimately prove best suited by 7f/1m."

DOROTHEE
3/5 b f Equiano - Persario (Bishop of Cashel)
Owner: Hot to Trot Racing 2 and Mrs E Grundy Sales price: n/a

Full sister to very smart multiple 6f winner (including three times at Group 1 level) The Tin Man and a half-sister to very smart multiple 5-6f winner (including at Group 2/3 level) Deacon Blues, Listed-placed multiple 5f winner

Holley Shiftwell and four other winners out of a 6-7f winning half-sister to triple 7f Group 3 winner/Lockinge Stakes runner-up Warningford.

"It is a family I know well from my time at James Fanshawe's yard. She wouldn't be the biggest but then that's a trait of the family, which also tends to require a bit of time and patience. She has done all I have needed of her, so is now out in the paddock for a couple of months. We will bring her back in June and prepare her for a run or two at the backend of the season."

EVE LODGE
18/4 b f Ardad - Sandy Times (Footstepsinthesand)
Owner: Offthebridle Podcast II Sales price: 12,500gns (C Gordon Watson Bloodstock)

Half-sister to 2020 5f 2yo winner Mirror Kisses and Italian 7.5-11.5f winner Twin Grey. Dam a maiden half-sister to Listed-placed 5f 2yo winner Pearl Diva out of an unraced half-sister to five-time US 8-10f Grade 1 winner (including the Belmont Stakes) Lemon Drop Kid and Coventry Stakes winner/Sussex Stakes runner-up Statue of Liberty.

"Ardad was obviously a very sharp son of Kodiac and this filly looks pretty forward herself. She didn't cost much but is a good-looking, strong type who is doing everything nicely so far. I imagine she will be ready to rock and roll come the end of May/beginning of June."

FRESH HOPE
25/3 b f New Approach - Wiener Valkyrie (Shamardal)
Owner: The Eclipse Partnership Sales price: n/a

Half-sister to useful 2020 8-10f 3yo winner Declared Interest. Dam a Grade 3/ Listed-placed 7f 2yo winner who was a half-sister to Racing Post Trophy winner Crowded House, French 10.5f Listed winner On Reflection, Listed-placed 6-8.5f winner Forest Crown (dam of 2021 Lingfield Winter Derby winner Forest of Dean) and the dam of Prix Maurice de Gheest winner Brando and grandam of Prix Morny/Middle Park Stakes winner Reckless Abandon.

"A big, scopey filly and very good-looking with it. She is straightforward and has done everything that I require of her for the time being so, like Dorothee, is now having a couple of months in the paddock. I hope to have her ready for a run or two at the backend of the season. Although she hasn't been asked any serious questions, she looks to have a bit of quality about her and should be a nice horse one day. I like her."

GRAND ALLIANCE (IRE)
31/3 b c Churchill - Endless Love (Dubai Destination)
Owner: Mrs Susan Roy Sales price: n/a

Half-brother to Group 1-placed multiple 7f winner (including at Group 2/3 level) Dutch Connection and Listed-placed 7f 2yo winner Dutch Romance. Dam an unraced half-sister to Listed-placed US 8-8.5f winner Wittgenstein and useful triple 7f 3yo winner Aimez La Vie out of a 1m 2yo Listed-winning half-sister to dual 5f 2yo Listed winner Bella Tusa and the dam of 2020 6f 2yo Listed winner Method.

"A homebred of the Roy's, who is a half-brother to their good horse, Dutch Connection, and from the first crop of Churchill. He is quite immature and a bit narrow and still has plenty of developing to do. However, he is also very straightforward and easy to deal with - you'd barely notice that he is here as he just goes about his own business quietly. He should be a late-summer two-year-old who will have a run or two to see whether he could be one for some of the nicer races in the autumn."

INCHBAE
22/3 b f Golden Horn - Inchina (Montjeu)
Owner: A E Oppenheimer Sales price: n/a

Half-sister to Listed-placed 2020 1m 3yo winner Perfect Inch. Dam a 10f 3yo winner who was the daughter of a 10f 3yo Listed-winning sister to Group 3-placed 7f 2yo winner Inchlonaig and half-sister to triple 7f Group 3 winner Inchinor, 1m 3yo Listed winner Ingozi (later dam of Canadian 10f Grade 1 winner Miss Keller and grandam of St Leger winner Harbour Law and 7f 2yo Group 2 winner Hatta Fort) and the grandam of King George VI & Queen Elizabeth Stakes winner Poet's Word.

"None of Mr Oppenheimer's two-year-olds are here yet. This is a half-sister to our good four-year-old, Perfect Inch, and the reports from pre-trainer, Malcolm Bastard, have been favourable."

MARTHA EDLIN
3/4 b f Intello - Tempest Fugit (High Chaparral)
Owner: Middleham Park Racing LXXV Sales price: 38,000gns (C Gordon Watson/Middleham Park Racing)

Half-sister to 1m 2yo winner Tiempo Vuela. Dam a 13f 3yo Listed winner who was a full sister to 5f 2yo winner/Fillies' Mile runner-up Lady Darshaan (later dam of 10f Listed winner Let's Go) and a half-sister to Prix de l'Abbaye winner Total Gallery out of a Greek 12-13f 3yo winning half-sister to Irish 10f Group 1 winner Ambivalent (later dam of French 12f 3yo Group 2 winner Al Hilalee).

"This filly is a real head-scratcher on pedigree because an Intello filly out of a High Chaparral mare would suggest a big, backward three-year-old type, but she is nothing of the sort. I am not saying she will be a 5f runner but she's very forward and finding it all incredibly easy at this stage. She really ought to be heading out for a holiday now, but I'm going to crack on with her instead and prepare her for a race in June time. I can't believe she will want anything other than 7f to start with and is what I would term a precocious stayer. I think she was very well bought at 38k."

QUEEN AMINATU
17/2 br f Muhaarar - Zeb Un Nisa (Iffraaj)
Owner: A E Oppenheimer Sales price: 28,000gns (Not Sold)

Second foal of a 5f 2yo winner who was a half-sister to fairly useful triple 7f winner Ashamaly out of an unraced half-sister to 2000 Guineas winner Footstepsinthesand, Phoenix Stakes winner Pedro The Great, 1m 3yo Listed winner Belle d'Or and the dam of National Stakes/Irish 2000 Guineas winner Power and Ribblesdale Stakes winners Curvy and Thakafaat.

"Again, she isn't here yet. I saw her a couple of times on the stud and she looked quite a sharp type. I imagine she will be one of the first Hascombe horses to come to me."

SAN FRANCISCO BAY (IRE)
10/2 b c Muhaarar - Stor Mo Chroi (Montjeu)
Owner: Graham Smith-Bernal & Alan Dee Sales price: £10,000 (Gordon Watson/Fellowes)

Third foal of an unraced close relation to dual 11.5f Listed winner Cameron Highland and Group 2/Listed-placed 12f 3yo winner Field of Miracles (dam of 2020 Saudi Arabian 12f Listed winner Making Miracles) and half-sister to very useful 7-10f winner Solid Stone and useful dual 10f winner Sour Mash.

"No one wanted the Muhaarars at the sales last year, so we managed to pick him up very cheaply. All being well, he will be my first two-year-old runner as he is a sharp, very straightforward customer. He does have a slightly awkward head carriage, but there are no real quirks to him other than that and he looks well up to winning races this year."

SOUS LES ETOILES
19/3 b f Sea The Stars - Nyarhini (Fantastic Light)
Owner: A E Oppenheimer Sales price: n/a

Full sister to UK/French 8-9.5f winner Sparkle In His Eyes, a three-parts sister to 1m 3yo Listed winner Token of Love (by Cape Cross) and a half-sister to four winners. Dam a Listed-placed 6f 2yo winner who was a half-sister to

Coronation Stakes winner Rebecca Sharp, Cheshire Oaks winner Hidden Hope (dam of 2020 Ribblesdale Stakes winner/Oaks third Frankly Darling) and the unraced dam of top-class middle-distance performer Golden Horn.

"Not here but wouldn't be far off coming in. She isn't the biggest but that wouldn't be untypical of her sire. For all she's on the smaller side, she is quite immature and narrow so there's room for physical improvement."

SUPER CHIEF
12/4 b c Kingman - Eastern Belle (Champs Elysees)
Owner: A E Oppenheimer Sales price: n/a

Full brother to 2021 1m 3yo Listed winner Megallan. Dam a 10f 3yo Listed winner who was a half-sister to Derby, Eclipse Stakes and Prix de l'Arc de Triomphe winner Golden Horn and Group 3/Listed-placed 2020 7f 2yo winner Dhahabi out of an unraced half-sister to Coronation Stakes winner Rebecca Sharp.

"Again, he wouldn't be the biggest and it shouldn't be too much longer before he's here. He obviously has a lovely pedigree, being a brother to recent Burradon Stakes winner, Megallan. Like that colt, I suspect he will be one for the second half of the season."

SURREY KNIGHT (FR)
15/5 b c Le Havre - Millionaia (Peintre Celebre)
Owner: Surrey Racing (SK) Sales price: €38,000 (Stroud Coleman Bloodstock Limited)

Half-brother to French 12.5f 3yo Listed winner Modern Eagle and Group 3-placed French/Irish 12f winner Mighty Blue. Dam a French 10f 3yo winner/Prix de Diane runner-up who was a half-sister to Irish 7f 2yo winner/Dewhurst Stakes runner-up Fencing Master and the dam of French 12f 3yo Group 2 winner Ming Dynasty.

"Inexpensively purchased in France as a yearling by Anthony Stroud. He is very much a late-season two-year-old type who will do even better next year. For a horse who is like that, he actually finds it all remarkably easy and has improved significantly over the past six weeks or so. I can't believe he is anything other than a backend type but he looks a lovely prospect from what we've seen of him so far. When a backward horse shows anything this early, you know you're in business."

UNNAMED (IRE)
12/4 b c Kodiac - Night Queen (Rip Van Winkle)
Owner: Dahab Racing Sales price: £65,000 (Gordon-Watson Bloodstock)

First foal of an unraced half-sister to 6f 2yo Group 3 winner/Cheveley Park Stakes runner-up Princess Noor out of a once-raced maiden half-sister to Flying Childers Stakes winner Land of Dreams (later dam of five-time 6/7f Group 1 winner Dream Ahead and grandam of Cheveley Park Stakes winner Fairyland (by Kodiac)).

"He wouldn't be your typical Kodiac in that he has got plenty of size and scope, which I suspect is the Rip Van Winkle in him coming through. He is very straightforward and has a good mind. While he hasn't galloped yet, he is doing plenty and is a beautiful mover who just finds it all so easy and really catches the eye. I would say he is the pick of my two-year-olds at this stage, and we'll look to have him in action over 6f by the end of May or early June."

UNNAMED (IRE)
2/3 b f Postponed - Strathnaver (Oasis Dream)
Owner: St Albans Bloodstock Limited Sales price: n/a

Half-sister to useful 2020 8-10f 3yo winner Caen Na Coille and fairly useful 2020 dual 12f 3yo winner Kitten's Dream. Dam a Grade 1-placed UK/US 7.5-12f winner (including at Grade 3 level) who was a half-sister to UAE 1000 Guineas winner Siyaadah, useful 7-12f winner Bridle Belle and useful 8-10f winner Middle Kingdom out of a smart UK/US 6f-8.5f winner (including at Grade 2/Group 3 level).

"She isn't here yet but is said to be the nicest of all those coming in from the pre-trainer. She is a half-sister to Caen Na Coille who won three races for us last year. Postponed was very cold at the sales last year, but he was a top-class, good-looking horse and it's remarkable that people don't seem to learn their lesson. Dubawi was written off, as was his son, Night of Thunder, and look what happened there! I imagine she'll be a slow burner like her half-sister and have a run or two at the end of the year."

JAMES FERGUSON

ARISTOBULUS
14/4 b c Adaay - Salome (Fuisse)
Owner: John Ferguson & Walkuptrotback Sales price: 11,000gns (James Ferguson Racing)

Half-brother to 1m 2yo winner Mazikeen. Dam a maiden half-sister to smart French multiple 6f winner (including twice at Listed level) Silva, Group 3-placed French dual 7f winner Sylvestre and the dams of French 11/12f Group 2 winner Silver Pond and French 9.5f 3yo Listed winner Savoie (herself later dam of 10.5/12f Listed winner Fire Fighting).

"A big, rangy colt who is a hardy type. He isn't overly forward, but I am sure he will be nice in time and should be more than capable of winning races."

DEAUVILLE LEGEND (IRE)
16/3 b c Sea The Stars - Soho Rose (Hernando)
Owner: Boniface Ho Ka Kui Sales price: €200,000 (Avenue Bloodstock)

Half-brother to Listed-placed Irish/UK dual 1m winner Dean Street Doll. Dam a German 11f 3yo Listed winner who was a full sister to Irish 10f Group 2 winner Hanami and a half-sister to dual 12f 3yo Listed winner Dubai Rose (later dam of dual Prix de Royallieu winner The Juliet Rose).

"A nice, rangy colt who has got a big frame to fill into. He is very likeable and has trained really well so far, but he is definitely going to be one for the backend. We will look to get him started towards the end of the summer, and he is an exciting prospect for next season."

INVINCIBLE KING (IRE)
16/3 b c Invincible Spirit - Lulawin (Kyllachy)
Owner: Mrs Susan Roy Sales price: 205,000gns (Michael Roy)

Full brother to Irish 5f 2yo winner Invincible Diva and a half-brother to Irish 6f 2yo Group 2 winner Painted Cliffs. Dam an unraced three-parts sister to St James's Palace Stakes winner Excellent Art and half-sister to very useful 7f-2m 4f winner Double Obsession out of a Listed-placed 6f 2yo winner.

"A nice colt of the Roy's bought from Lynn Lodge at Book 1 of the Tattersalls October Yearling Sale. He has got a good pedigree and the physique to match it. I am very much looking forward to getting going with him and I anticipate him starting off over 6f in June or July."

MISE EN SCENE
19/2 b f Siyouni - Gadfly (Galileo)
Owner: Qatar Racing Limited Sales price: n/a

Third foal of an unraced half-sister to 1000 Guineas winner Speciosa, US 12f Grade 3 winner Major Rhythm and Listed winners Liberally (10.5f) and Special Meaning (12f) out of a US 8.5f 2yo winning half-sister to triple 10/12f Group 1 winner Pride (later dam of French dual 12f Group 2 winner One Foot In Heaven) and French 10.5f Group 3 winner Fate.

"A lovely, homebred daughter of Siyouni from Qatar Racing, and it is fantastic to have been sent one by them. This is a sweet, very straightforward filly who is going to get better with time. I hope to see her in action by August time."

UNNAMED (IRE)
26/4 b c Kodiac - Al Andalyya (Kingmambo)
Owner: The 4letterfirstnames Partnership Sales price: 70,000gns (James Ferguson Racing)

Full brother to high-class multiple 6-12f winner (three times at Group 1 level, including the Caulfield Cup) Best Solution. Dam a maiden half-sister to German 7.5f 2yo Listed winner Kosmische out of a Group 3/Listed-placed Irish 12f 3yo winner who was a full sister to Racing Post Trophy/St Leger winner Brian Boru and the unraced dam of Derby/Prix de l'Arc de Triomphe winner Workforce and a three-parts sister to triple 12f Group 2 winner/St Leger third Sea Moon.

"His brother won the Caulfield Cup for Saeed Bin Suroor, and this is quite a forward colt who won't take long to get ready. He is a likeable, cheeky chap who should begin over 6f in June."

UNNAMED (IRE)
21/4 b c New Bay - Lady Penko (Archipenko)
Owner: The 4letterfirstnames & Ballylinch Stud Sales price: 75,000gns (James Ferguson Racing)

Half-brother to Listed-placed 7.5f 2yo winner Golden Lips. Dam a Group 1-placed French 8-10.5f 3yo winner (including at Listed level) who was the daughter of a maiden half-sister to Grand Prix de Paris/Canadian International winner Erupt and 10f 3yo Listed winner Marie de Medici (later dam of 8/9.5f 3yo Group 3 winner Local Time).

"This a compact, good-looking colt, who has a typically solid outlook for one by a son of Dubawi. I haven't done much with him yet as he has taken a bit of time to come to himself. However, he is a thoroughly likeable individual who should provide his owners with a lot of fun once he is ready to get onto the track."

UNNAMED
10/2 b f Territories - Satsuma (Compton Place)
Owner: Racehorse Lotto Sales price: 18,000gns (Vendor)

Half-sister to Group 2-placed triple 5f 2yo winner (including at Group 3/Listed level) Good Vibes and 2020 6f 2yo winner Kohinoor. Dam a useful 5f 2yo winner who was a half-sister to Group 2-placed 5-6f winner Astrophysics out of a maiden sister to Grade 1-placed Irish/US 7-9f winner Sebastian Flyte and half-sister to Irish 6f 3yo Group 3 winner Age of Chivalry.

"This filly is leased to the Racehorse Lotto by Whitsbury Manor. She was raffled off on Christmas Day, and a lovely guy called Tony Wood had the winning ticket. He came in to see her the other day. This is a small, agile filly, who hasn't been here all that long but won't take much time in getting ready."

UNNAMED
5/3 b c Iffraaj - Sloane Square (Teofilo)
Owner: Michael Buckley Sales price: 130,000gns (Michael Buckley)

Full brother to 2020 US dual 8.5f stakes winner Sloane Garden. Dam an unraced sister to 10f Listed winner Miblish and a half-sister to Group 3-placed Irish dual 6.5f 3yo winner Count John out of a useful Irish 5f 2yo winning half-sister to 6f 2yo Group 2/Listed winner Jewel In The Sand.

"A big, rangy colt and son of Iffraaj, who is typical of his sire's progeny. He will need plenty of time but is a strong individual with a good mind who has a lot of potential."

UNNAMED (IRE)
29/3 ch c Frankel - Ventura (Spectrum)
Owner: The 4letterfirstnames Partnership Sales price: £145,000 (Avenue Bloodstock/Ferguson)

Three-parts brother to Grade 2-placed UK/US 11-14f winner (including at Listed level) Cedar Mountain (by Galileo) and a half-brother to French six-time 6f-1m Group 1 winner Moonlight Cloud. Dam a Listed-placed Irish dual 1m 3yo winner who was a half-sister to the dams of Irish 6f 2yo Group 2 winner Probably and Irish 7f 2yo Listed winner Bruges and the grandam of Solario Stakes winner Talwar.

"A very well put together son of Frankel, who I am in absolutely no rush with. He is a half-brother to Moonlight Cloud, so obviously boasts an exceptional pedigree, but he is one who I am very much taking my time with."

Our cover is never off the pace

We offer specialist, impartial advice on your bloodstock insurance and wealth management requirements, in addition to an extensive range of products and service for private clients, estates, farms, equine businesses and commercial enterprises.

Lycetts

CELEBRATING 60 YEARS
1961-2021

Contact: Richard Freeman
Tel: 01638 676 700
Mobile: 07826 301 429
richard.freeman@lycetts.co.uk

WILLIAM HAGGAS

AMANZOE (IRE)
29/4 b f Fastnet Rock - Starship (Galileo)
Owner: The Starship Partnership II Sales price: n/a

Full sister to Racing Post Trophy winner Rivet and Group 2-placed UK/Hong Kong 7-10f winner (including at Group 3 level) Booming Delight and a half-sister to Irish 10f 3yo Group 3 winner Alexander Pope. Dam a 7f-1m winner who was a half-sister to Group 1-placed multiple 5f winner (including at Group 2/3 level) Superstar Leo (later dam of smart pair Enticing and Sentaril and grandam of three-time Prix de la Foret winner One Master (by Fastnet Rock)).

"She is a sister to our Racing Post Trophy winner, Rivet, who is well-grown but not overly big. Hopefully she will be in action in August, probably starting off over 7f."

CANTERBURY BELL (IRE)
1/4 b f Ribchester - Lavender Lane (Shamardal)
Owner: Jon and Julia Aisbitt Sales price: n/a

Half-sister to very useful dual 1m winner/May Hill Stakes fourth Lilac Road. Dam a Listed-placed French 1m 3yo winner who was a half-sister to smart French triple 10f 3yo winner (including at Group 2 level) Sumbal and French 10.5f 3yo Listed winner Lily Passion out of a Group 1-placed French 10-12f winner.

"I like her. She has a lot of quality and moves well. Her year-older half-sister is very useful and she looks a lot like her. I would hope, like Lilac Road, she will be starting off over 7f in the summer."

CLEAR DAY (FR)
19/1 b c Camelot - Dawn Glory (Oasis Dream)
Owner: The Queen Sales price: n/a

Half-brother to 7.5f 3yo winner Break of Day and 6f 2yo winner First Drive. Dam a thrice-raced maiden half-sister to Australian 10f Group 1 winner My Kingdom of Fife, Group 3/Listed-placed 7f-1m winner Four Winds, useful 8-9f winner Awesome Power and the maiden dam of French 6.5f 2yo Listed winner Royal Spring.

"He isn't at all immature despite the bulk of his pedigree suggesting he probably should be. We always try and get one to Ascot for Her Majesty, and although I am not saying he will be a Chesham horse, it isn't impossible he might be."

CRIOLLO
5/2 gr f Dark Angel - La Rioja (Hellvelyn)
Owner: Qatar Racing Limited Sales price: n/a

First foal of a 6f 2yo Group 3 winner who was a half-sister to Group 3/Listed-placed 6f 2yo winner Pastoral Girl (dam of 2020 6f 2yo winner/Prix Morny third Rhythm Master (by Dark Angel)), Listed-placed triple 5f 2yo winner Lilbourne Lass and the dam of Group 1-placed multiple 5-6f winner (including at Group 3/Listed level) Liberty Beach.

"She hasn't been here too long. A very charming filly who will need a bit of time, but she's a good mover and has a lovely attitude."

Rhythm Master

CRYSTAL CAVES (FR)
10/5 b f Almanzor - Vivacity (Trempolino)
Owner: Bermuda Racing Ltd Sales price: 180,000gns (John & Jake Warren)

Half-sister to Irish 1m 1f Listed winner Riven Light, Group 3/Listed-placed Irish 7f 2yo winner Last Waltz and five other winners. Dam a once-raced maiden half-sister to Lockinge Stakes winner Keltos, Group 1-placed French multiple 7-10f winner (including at Group 2/Listed level)/Poule d'Essai des Poulains third Krataios, Group 1-placed French 10-12.5f winner (including at Group 2/Listed level) Loxias and French 1m Group 3 winner Kavafi.

"It is always nice to have one by a first-season sire and this is an attractive filly. I imagine she will be one for later on, probably starting off at the backend of the summer or early part of the autumn."

EDUCATOR
4/2 br c Deep Impact - Diploma (Dubawi)
Owner: The Queen Sales price: n/a

Second foal of a 10.5f 3yo Group 3 winner who was a half-sister to useful 7f-1m winner Pick Your Choice and useful 7-9f winner Elector out of a 1m 2yo Listed-winning half-sister to French 7f 3yo Group 3 winner Surfrider and Group 3/Listed-placed 2020 Irish 7f 3yo winner Soul Search.

"This is a gorgeous horse. He is strong, well made and an extremely good mover. He does absolutely everything right at this stage but will be another for later on in the season."

ENSHRINE
3/4 b f Ulysses - Sacre Caroline (Blame)
Owner: Cheveley Park Stud Sales price: n/a

Half-sister to Group 2-placed 2020 5f 2yo winner Sacred. Dam an unraced half-sister to five-time US 8-10f Grade 1 winner (including the Breeders' Cup Juvenile Fillies Turf) Lady Eli, US 8.5/9f Grade 3 winner Bizzy Caroline and Grade 3-placed US 8.5f 2yo winner Princesa Caroline out of a US 8.5f 2yo winner; family of Racing Post Trophy winner Palace Episode and Canadian 8.5f 2yo Grade 1 winner Spring In The Air.

"I have always thought Sacred would stay further than sprint trips, so it goes without saying a daughter of Ulysses will definitely want further than one by Exceed And Excel. This filly is still a little bit immature and certainly won't be an early one. Probably another for 7f races in the summer."

HELLO SYDNEY (IRE)
26/2 b c Zoffany - Queen of Stars (Green Desert)
Owner: Abdulla Belhabb Sales price: 80,000gns (Rabbah Bloodstock)

Full brother to Group 1-placed 5-6f 2yo winner (including at Group 2/3 level) Illuminate. Dam an unraced half-sister to Italian 1m 2yo Group 3 winner/ Oaks d'Italia runner-up Lady Catherine out of a French 1m 3yo Listed-winning half-sister to the dam of 10/12f Group 1 winner/Prix du Jockey Club Prince Gibraltar.

"A very nice colt. He is out of a good mare and wasn't overly expensive at 80,000gns. He goes well and should be in action over 6f in June/July."

HURRY UP HEDLEY (IRE)
26/3 b c Mehmas - Forevertwentyone (Approve)
Owner: Ian & Christine Beard & Family Sales price: £25,000 (Hurworth Bloodstock)

First foal of a maiden half-sister to 2020 Irish 7f 3yo Group 3 winner With Thanks out of an unraced half-sister to Grade 3-placed French/US 9-12f winner (including twice at Listed level) Briviesca (later dam of Prix de l'Opera winner Villa Marina), useful 8-9f winner Kinsya and useful 9-10f 3yo winner Wee Frankie.

"He is out of a half-sister to a good filly we train called With Thanks and looks an early one. He looks fast and sharp and is one we will utilise the new banded race system with, given he was a relatively cheap purchase at 25k. I could see him ending up in something like the Super Sprint."

KHANJAR (IRE)
23/2 b c Kodiac - Naafer (Oasis Dream)
Owner: Shadwell Estate Co Sales price: n/a

First foal of a 5.5f 2yo winner who was a full sister to Group 1-placed UK/UAE multiple 5-7f winner (including at Group 2/3 level) Ertijaal and a half-sister to Group 3-placed UK/UAE 8.5-10f winner Muzdawaj and Listed-placed UK/UAE 6f winner Odooj out of a Group 3-placed 6f-1m winner (including at Listed level) who was a half-sister to Group 3/Listed-placed 6f 2yo winner Darajaat.

"He has got a sore shin at present which will push him back a bit. He hadn't moved like a typical Kodiac as he has a big, long, raking stride on him, but everything is currently on hold with him."

KING OF ICE
25/3 ch c Ulysses - Queen of Ice (Selkirk)
Owner: Cheveley Park Stud Sales price: 60,000gns (Peter & Ross Doyle Bloodstock)

Half-brother to Listed-placed 2020 10-11.5f 3yo winner Ice Sprite. Dam a smart 7-12f winner (including twice at Listed level) who was a half-sister to Listed-placed dual 7f winner Ice Gala out of a 10f Listed-winning close relation to Listed-placed 7f 2yo winner White Lake and half-sister to 10f 3yo Listed winner Portal (later dam of 14f 3yo Group 2 winner Pilaster) and the dam of dual 1m Group 2 winner/1000 Guineas second Spacious.

"He looks quite a sharp type despite not being bred to be in any way, shape or form. His mother took an age to come to hand, though did win first time out as a two-year-old late in the season. This colt has shown speed and is one I quite like at this stage. He will be out once the 6f races are here."

M'LADY NICOLE (IRE)
29/4 b f Sea The Stars - Angel of The Gwaun (Sadler's Wells)
Owner: Neil Jones Sales price: n/a

Full sister to French 10f 3yo Group 2 winner Knight To Behold, Irish 10f 3yo Group 3 winner Beauty O'Gwaun, Japanese 2m 1f Grade 3 winner Cosmo Meadow and four other winners. Dam an unraced sister to 8-10f winner/ Derby third Let The Lion Roar and half-sister to high-class prolific 11f-2m 2f winner (including the St Leger) Millenary and 12f 3yo Group 3 winner Head In The Clouds (later dam of Irish 13f Listed winner/Irish Oaks runner-up Roses For The Lady).

"This filly is the first one I have trained for her owner/breeder, Neil Jones. She is a neat filly who moves well, though she has gone out for a break and is with the pre-trainer presently. I would still hope she will be an earlier type than her smart brother, Knight To Behold."

NUANCE
25/1 b c Frankel - Intimation (Dubawi)
Owner: Cheveley Park Stud Sales price: n/a

First foal of a smart 8-10.5f winner (including at Group 3/Listed level) who was a half-sister to Falmouth Stakes winner Veracious (by Frankel), Group 1-placed 8-10f winner (including at Group 2/Listed level) Mutakayyef and Stewards' Cup winner Intrinsic out of a Nell Gwyn Stakes/1000 Guineas fourth who was closely related to the unraced dam of Prix Maurice de Gheest winner Garswood.

"A little bit first foaly and has quite the attitude, though that's improved a good bit since he's been here. The smaller two-year-olds always look earlier types than they actually are, and I am not sure he is either despite his size."

PERFECT ALIBI
23/2 b f Le Havre - Daphne (Duke of Marmalade)
Owner: The Queen Sales price: n/a

First foal of a 13f Listed winner who was closely related to 7f 2yo winner Queen's Prize (dam of Listed-placed 2020 10-10.5f 3yo winner Award Scheme) and a half-sister to Listed-placed UK/Australian 10-12f winner Bold Sniper and very useful UK/UAE 10-12f winner Highland Glen out of a 12f 3yo winning half-sister to dual 7f Listed winner Golden Stream and 7f 2yo winner/Oaks runner-up Flight of Fancy.

"A beautiful, big filly with plenty of scope. She is like her mother in that she has got a bit of character about her, but she is lovely and one to look forward to during the second half of the season."

PERSIST
18/1 b f Frankel - Persuasive (Dark Angel)
Owner: Cheveley Park Stud Sales price: n/a

First foal of a high-class multiple 1m winner (including the Queen Elizabeth II Stakes) who was a half-sister to Group 3-placed multiple 1m winner (including at Listed level) Tisbutadream, very useful 6-7f winner Amazour and 2020 6f 2yo winner Creative Force out a Group 2/3-placed Irish 6-10f winner (including at Listed level).

"She had a small break but is back here now. I like her a lot - there's just something about her. She is tough and genuine and could well make her first appearance at the July meeting."

QUEENLET (IRE)
15/3 b f Kingman - Tesoro (Galileo)
Owner: James Wigan Sales price: n/a

Second foal of a 6f 2yo winner who was a full sister to US 8/10f Grade 1 winner Photo Call and a half-sister to Richmond Stakes winner Land Force out of a 6f 3yo Group 3-winning half-sister to triple 8-10f Group 1 winner (including the Irish 1000 Guineas) Halfway To Heaven (later dam of seven-time 10-12f Group 1 winner Magical and triple 8/10f Group 1 winner/1000 Guineas and Oaks runner-up Rhododendron) and 5/6f Group 3 winner Tickled Pink.

"She was due to be here by now but had a minor setback and is still with the pre-trainer. All the reports from there suggest they like her."

SECOND WIND (IRE)
28/1 b c Kodiac - Princess Janie (Elusive Quality)
Owner: Wrigleys and Wyatts Sales price: 75,000gns (Jill Lamb Bloodstock)

Closely related to Listed-placed Irish 6f 2yo winner Lundy (by Exceed And Excel) and two other winners. Dam a Listed-placed US multiple 6f winner who was a half-sister to Canadian 9/11f 3yo Grade 3 winner Raylene out of a very useful Irish 5-6f 2yo winning three-parts sister to Middle Park Stakes/Queen Anne Stakes winner Ad Valorem.

"He is a strong, well-made colt, who looks one of the sharper two-year-olds here. He has looked natural from an early stage and is a typical Kodiac who can run a bit. I imagine he will be one of our first two-year-old runners."

SENSE OF DUTY
5/3 b/br f Showcasing - Margaret's Mission (Shamardal)
Owner: St Albans Bloodstock Limited Sales price: n/a

Second foal of a fairly useful triple 1m winner who was a full sister to Group 3/ Listed-placed UK/US 6f-1m winner Sharnberry and a half-sister to four winners including useful 5-6f winner Master Rooney out of a Listed-placed 5-6f 2yo winner.

"A sizeable filly with a good action and a nice temperament who was looking quite natural. She has just gone a bit weak on us, so will need more time but is a nice horse."

SHIGAR (IRE)
12/4 b c Farhh - Diala (Iffraaj)
Owner: Abdulla Al Khalifa Sales price: n/a

Half-brother to Craven Stakes winner/2000 Guineas third Skardu. Dam a useful 7f 2yo winner who was a half-sister to 1m 2yo winner Matula out of a 7f 3yo winner; family of US triple 9-12f Grade 1 winner Marquetry.

"This colt is a half-brother to our smart miler, Skardu, and is a good-looking individual with a lot of quality about him. He also has a lovely way of going, and I would hope to see him making his debut around July time over 7f, though it's not beyond the realms of possibility that he might begin over 6f."

TIBER FLOW (IRE)
16/4 br/gr c Caravaggio - Malabar (Raven's Pass)
Owner: Jon and Julia Aisbitt Sales price: n/a

First foal of a smart 7f-1m winner (including twice at Group 3 level)/1000 Guineas fourth who was a half-sister to Prince of Wales's Stakes/King George VI And Queen Elizabeth Stakes winner Poet's Word, very useful 10-11.5f winner Clowance Estate, 2020 1m 2yo winner Top of The Pops and the dam of Group 1-placed Irish/US 5-6f winner (including at Group 2 level) Beckford.

"He has had a troubled time of things and has already had a couple of trips to the vet. I suspect he will come to hand quickly once we start him back, and I'd hope he will be in action come July or August time."

VINTAGE CHOICE (IRE)
25/2 ch c Lope de Vega - Effervesce (Galileo)
Owner: Isa Salman Al Khalifa Sales price: 310,000gns (John & Jake Warren)

Half-brother to 7f 2yo Listed winner Cristal Fizz, useful 6-7f winner Qeyaadah and useful 7f 2yo winner Persuasion. Dam a 10.5f 3yo winner who was a half-sister to Group 1-placed multiple 6f winner (including at Group 3/Listed level) Hitchens, Listed-placed Irish 6f 2yo winner Cava and very useful triple 6f winner Tanzeel.

"An expensive yearling who earned rave reviews from the pre-trainer. He is here now and is a nice, uncomplicated colt who will begin over 7f sometime in the summer."

UNNAMED
10/4 b c Kingman - Bargain Buy (Tamayuz)
Owner: Sheikh Rashid Dalmook Al Maktoum Sales price: n/a

Second foal of a useful 7f-1m winner who was the daughter of an unraced half-sister to useful multiple 7-8.5f winner King's Pavilion, seven other winners and the unraced dam of Prix Maurice de Gheest winner King's Apostle; family of smart performers Atlantic Jewel, East and Tarfshi.

"This colt's dam is related to a good horse we used to train called King's Apostle. He is a nice horse who has done really well of late and should make a two-year-old at some point this year."

UNNAMED
10/3 b f Frankel - Besharah (Kodiac)
Owner: Sheikh Rashid Dalmook Al Maktoum Sales price: n/a

Second foal of a high-class 5-6f 2yo winner (including at Group 2/3 level)/ Cheveley Park Stakes third who was the daughter of an unraced half-sister to smart US 6-8.5f winner (including at Grade 3 level) Kiss Moon and Grade 3-placed US multiple 8-8.5f winner (including four times at Listed level) Kiss Mine.

"I cannot believe how much she has grown. Besharah's first foal was tiny, but this filly was medium-sized and is now a big sort who still has a bit of furnishing to do. I had thought she might be one of the earlier Frankel two-year-olds, but now looks to be more one for the backend of the summer."

UNNAMED
9/3 b c Showcasing - Cloud Line (Danehill Dancer)
Owner: Lael Stables Sales price: n/a

Half-brother to useful 2020 7f 3yo winner Cold Front. Dam a 7f 3yo winner who was a full sister to Group 3-placed 7f-1m winner (including at Listed level) Sentaril and a half-sister to seven other winners, most notably high-class multiple 5f winner (including at Group 3/Listed level) Enticing (later dam of three-time Prix de la Foret winner One Master) out of a Group 1-placed multiple 5f winner (including at Group 2/3 level).

"This is a really nice colt, albeit he's still quite immature at present. The dam had her fair share of problems during her racing days and coped with them admirably well. She hasn't made it as a broodmare just yet, but hopefully this colt can rectify that. He should be one for July onwards."

UNNAMED
12/2 b f Iffraaj - Dawn Horizons (New Approach)
Owner: Sheikh Juma Dalmook Al Maktoum Sales price: 90,000gns (Rabbah Bloodstock)

First foal of a useful 11.5-12f winner who was a full sister to Listed-placed 10-14f winner First In Line, a close relation to 2020 Ribblesdale Stakes winner/Oaks third Frankly Darling and a half-sister to 12f 3yo Listed winner Our Obsession out of a Cheshire Oaks-winning half-sister to Coronation Stakes winner Rebecca Sharp and the unraced dam of top-class middle-distance performer Golden Horn.

"We bought this filly from Mr Oppenheimer last autumn and she is a lengthy, very attractive filly. She will be one for a bit later on but is nice."

UNNAMED
15/2 ch c Frankel - Muffri'Ha (Iffraaj)
Owner: Sheikh Rashid Dalmook Al Maktoum Sales price: n/a

First foal of a Group 1-placed multiple 7-9f winner (including at Group 3/Listed level) who was the daughter of a Group 2-placed 5f-1m winner (including at Group 3/Listed level) who was a half-sister to smart multiple 5f 2yo winner (including at Group 2/3 level) Wunders Dream (later dam of 6f 3yo Listed winner Inyordreams) and the dam of 5f 3yo Listed winner Fashion Queen.

"He is still with the pre-trainer but I saw him ten days ago and thought he had done really well since the first time I saw him. He has let down into a really nice horse, and though I don't envisage him being an early runner, he should be in action come August time."

UNNAMED (IRE)
24/4 b c Kodiac - Nations Alexander (Dark Angel)
Owner: Shadwell Estate Co Sales price: 300,000gns (Shadwell Estate Company)

Second foal of a 7f 2yo Group 3 winner who was the daughter of a once-raced maiden half-sister to Richmond Stakes winner/Middle Park Stakes third Always Hopeful, Listed-placed 6-7f winner Nacho Libre, very useful multiple 6f-1m winner Extraterrestrial and useful dual 6f 2yo winner Enford Princess.

"A medium-sized colt, who is a lovely mover with a nice nature. He cost plenty of money and looks like being quite an early runner on what he is showing us. I hope to have him ready to run in May and if I have a Royal Ascot two-year-old, this is it."

UNNAMED (IRE)
15/2 ch f Frankel - Remember You (Invincible Spirit)
Owner: Sheikh Juma Dalmook Al Maktoum Sales price: 140,000gns (Rabbah Bloodstock)

Closely related to Windsor Castle Stakes winner Southern Hills (by Gleneagles), very useful Irish 7f 2yo winner I Remember You (by Australia) and useful 2020 Irish 7.5f 2yo winner Toshizou (by Galileo). Dam a Group 3/Listed-placed Irish 6f 2yo winner who was the daughter of a maiden three-parts sister to 7f 2yo Group 3 winner Governor Brown.

"A really nice filly who I like, but she suffered an injury in her box and has had to go out for a break. Although enforced, some time away will probably do her a power of good. Hopefully she will be fine and be able to come back in and do something this season."

UNNAMED
1/2 b f Oasis Dream - Sharqeyih (Shamardal)
Owner: Shadwell Estate Co Sales price: n/a

Closely related to fairly useful dual 5f winner Minhaaj (by Invincible Spirit). Dam a 7.5f 3yo winner who was a half-sister to Group 1-placed UK/UAE multiple 5-7f winner (including at Group 2/3 level) Ertijaal (by Oasis Dream) and a half-sister to Group 3-placed UK/UAE 8.5-10f winner Muzdawaj and Listed-placed UK/UAE 6f winner Odooj out of a Group 3-placed 6f-1m winner (including at Listed level).

"I thought she would be much sharper than she's currently proving to be. She hasn't come to herself at all yet which is surprising given she is by Oasis Dream and bred along similar lines to Ertijaal. The Oasis Dreams are also usually speedy, but it hasn't quite happened for her yet, though hopefully the light will come on for her at some point."

UNNAMED
31/3 b c Siyouni - Wonderstruck (Sea The Stars)
Owner: Lael Stable Sales price: n/a

Half-brother to 2020 7f 2yo winner Ready To Venture. Dam a Group 3-placed 12f 3yo winner who was a half-sister to very smart 6f-1m winner (four times at Group 1 level, including the 2000 Guineas) George Washington, very smart 7-11f winner (including three times at Group 1 level) Grandera, smart 10.5-14f winner (including twice at Listed level) Sun Central and five other winners.

"An elegant, attractive colt who moves nicely. We very much like his half-sister who won over 7f as a two-year-old last summer, and I suspect it will be a similar story with this colt. He has every chance of making it."

MICHAEL HALFORD

ASKARABAD (IRE)
30/1 b c Fast Company - Askeria (Sadler's Wells)
Owner: H H Aga Khan Sales price: n/a

Half-brother to very useful Irish 8-9.5f winner Ashraf and Irish 10f 3yo winner Askerana. Dam a maiden close relation to the dam of Australian five-time 7-10f Group 1 winner The Autumn Sun and a half-sister to top-class 7-12f winner (including four times at Group 1 level)/Irish 2000 Guineas runner-up/2000 Guineas third Azamour and Irish 7f 2yo Group 2 winner Arazan.

"A nice colt, who is very straightforward in all that he does. He has shown pace in his work and looks like he will make a two-year-old, so could run in May or June over 6f."

CEALLACH (IRE)
13/5 ch c Lope de Vega - Alvee (Key of Luck)
Owner: P Rooney Sales price: 25,000gns (BBA Ireland)

Half-brother to fairly useful 8.5-12.5f winner Stoney Broke. Dam a maiden half-sister to Prix Royal-Oak winner Allegretto (dam of 2020 12f 3yo Listed winner Cabaletta) and Listed-placed 10f 3yo winner Capricious Cantor out of a Doncaster Cup-winning half-sister to high-class racemares/broodmares Alouette and Last Second and the maiden dam of Irish 1000 Guineas winner/ Oaks runner-up Yesterday.

"A late foal who will take a little bit of time, but we like him and he has done all that has been asked of him nicely to this point."

CRYSTAL CITY (IRE)
26/2 b c Coulsty - Ranallagh Rocket (Acclamation)
Owner: N Hartley Sales price: n/a

Half-brother to Italian 5-6f winner Francisca Pink. Dam an unraced half-sister to very useful dual 5f 2yo winner Bengali Boys and useful 5f 2yo winner Diable d'Or out of a maiden half-sister to triple 7f/1m Listed winner Dubai's Touch, UAE 7f Listed winner Grantley Adams and Group 3-placed 8-9f winner Wannabe Around.

"A good-looking colt with a lovely action and a great temperament. He works nicely and has some pace. He will be out sometime in the summer and we like him."

MAZIYAR (FR)
18/4 b c Charm Spirit - Masiyma (Dalakhani)
Owner: H H Aga Khan Sales price: n/a

Half-brother to Irish 12f Listed winner Massinga, Group 3-placed Irish 1m 2yo winner Masaff and useful Irish 9.5-12f 3yo winner Massayan. Dam a useful Irish dual 12f 3yo winner who was a half-sister to Irish dual 10f 3yo winner/ Irish St Leger runner-up Massiyn out of a Group 3/Listed-placed Irish 12f-2m winner.

"A lovely, good-looking colt with a solid outlook who is going well at this stage. He looks the type to make his mark at two."

RAZAM (IRE)
15/3 b c Churchill - Raydiya (Marju)
Owner: H H Aga Khan Sales price: n/a

Half-brother to Irish 7f 2yo Group 2 winner Raydara (later dam of Listed-placed Irish 7f 2yo winner Ridenza) and French 1m 3yo Listed winner Rondonia. Dam an Irish 12f 3yo Listed winner who was a half-sister to Group 1-placed 10-10.5f winner Roseburg out of a maiden half-sister to Irish 7f 2yo Group 3 winner Rafayda and the dam of Irish 7f 2yo Group 3 winner/Irish 2000 Guineas runner-up Rayeni.

"A lovely colt who we like a lot. He is so natural in everything he does and has shown up very nicely considering the time of year. I would say he is the most forward of His Highnesses two-year-olds."

RIYAMI (IRE)
27/2 b c Fastnet Rock - Riyaba (Dalakhani)
Owner: H H Aga Khan Sales price: n/a

Half-brother to Irish 7f 2yo Listed winner Riyazan. Dam an unraced half-sister to 10f 3yo Listed winner Riyalma and Irish 6f 2yo winner/Moyglare Stud Stakes fourth Rubina (later dam of US 1m 3yo Listed winner Rubilinda) out of a 12f 3yo Listed winner.

"A good-looking, sizeable colt who has a great way of going. He is lovely and we like him a lot, but he will be one for the second half of the season over 7f."

TURBO TWO (IRE)
12/5 b c Holy Roman Emperor - Swish (Monsun)
Owner: Sammy Hon Kit Ma Sales price: £60,000 (Vendor)

Full brother to Irish 6f 2yo Group 3 winner Roman Turbo and a half-brother to German 11f 3yo Listed winner Swacadelic. Dam an unraced sister to four-time 12f Group 1 winner (including the Deutsches Derby/Breeders' Cup Turf) Shirocco, German 12f Group 2 winner/Deutsches Derby runner-up Subiaco and German 10f 3yo Listed winner/Deutsches Derby third Storm Trooper.

"A brother to Roman Turbo who did very well for us, winning the Anglesey Stakes as a two-year-old. This colt is a May foal and wouldn't be as forward as him. He has also grown a fair bit recently, so we are going to take things steadily, but we like him."

UNCONQUERABLE KEEN (IRE)
17/2 b c Clodovil - Queenie Keen (Refuse To Bend)
Owner: N Hartery Sales price: n/a

Half-brother to UK/Hong Kong 7-9f winner Glorious Artist. Dam an Irish 6-6.5f winner who was a half-sister to Group 3-placed UK/Hong Kong 6f-1m winner Celestial Steel and useful Irish triple 6f winner Wychwood Wanderer out of an Irish dual 1m winning half-sister to 6f 2yo Listed winner Duty Paid.

"A big, strong colt who has a lovely way of going. He would be one of our earlier two-year-old types and I think 6f in May would be a good starting point for him. I like him a lot."

UNNAMED (IRE)
28/4 ch c Profitable - Dancing Years (Iffraaj)
Owner: Castle Beech Partnership Sales price: £46,000 (BBA Ireland)

Second foal of a 5-6f winner who was a half-sister to Irish 1m 1f 2yo Group 3 winner Degraves, useful Irish 5-6f winner Kernoff, useful Irish multiple 7-10.5f winner Akasaka and useful Irish 12-12.5f winner Cape of Good Grace out of an Irish 6f 3yo Listed-winning sister to Irish triple 6f Group 3 winner Snaefell and half-sister to the dam of Group 3/Listed-placed 2020 dual 5f 2yo winner Muker.

"This colt has grown a lot recently so we've backed off him for now, though we got a nice education into him. He has a lovely temperament and this is obviously a family we have enjoyed a good bit of success with."

UNNAMED (IRE)
22/4 b f Camelot - Golden Pearl (Oasis Dream)
Owner: M J Enright Sales price: n/a

First foal of a useful Irish 7f 2yo winner who was a full sister to French 1m
3yo Listed winner Pearly Steph, a three-parts sister to Group 3-placed 2020
Irish dual 7f 3yo winner Pearls Galore and a half-sister to 2020 German 11f
Group 3 winner Lucky Lycra out of a German 11f Group 3-winning half-sister to
French 12f Listed winner Pearls Or Passion (later dam of French 12f 3yo Group
3 winner Pelligrina) and the dam of Group 2/Listed-placed 7f 2yo winner
Shagah.

*"The dam did well for us and this filly is her first foal. She has done well to this
point considering she is by Camelot, but we might give her the May grass given
she has grown some much recently. I think she will be lovely in time."*

JESSICA HARRINGTON

ADONIS (IRE)
5/3 ch c Siyouni - Rajaratna (Galileo)
Owner: Niarchos Family Sales price: n/a

Third foal of a once-raced maiden half-sister to Prix Marcel Boussac winner
Denebola (grandam of Prix de Diane winner Senga), US triple 8.5-11f Grade
3 winner Snake Mountain, French 6f 2yo Group 3 winner Loving Kindness
(later dam of French 5.5f 3yo Listed winner Peace Camp), French 7f 3yo Listed
winner Glia and the unraced dam of Prix de l'Arc de Triomphe winner Bago and
French 8/9f Group 1 winner Maxios.

*"A nice colt who seems to be fairly well forward at this stage. I suspect he will
be ready to run in mid-late May over 6/7f."*

ALIZARINE
15/3 b f Sea The Moon - Alea Iacta (Invincible Spirit)
Owner: Miss K Rausing Sales price: n/a

Half-sister to 2020 dual 1m 2yo winner Aleas. Dam a French 1m 2yo Group
3 winner who was a full sister to 10f 3yo Listed winner Aloe Vera and a half-
sister to smart 12-14.5f winner (including at Group 2/Listed level) Alyssa and
Group 3-placed 2020 10f 3yo winner Albaflora out of a once-raced maiden
half-sister to Irish 10f 3yo Group 3 winner Alla Speranza (later dam of 7f 3yo
Group 2/Listed winner Shine So Bright).

"She isn't overly big but has a bit of quality about her. A lovely filly who looks reasonably well forward at this stage and should be starting off over 7f in the early summer."

Aleas

CORVIGLIA (USA)
13/4 ch f Karakontie - Light Blow (Kingmambo)
Owner: Flaxman Stables Ireland Ltd Sales price: n/a

Full sister to 2020 US 8.5f 3yo Grade 3 winner Sole Volante and a half-sister to Canadian 10f 3yo Grade 3 winner Explode. Dam a 15f 3yo winner who was a sister to Oaks winner Light Shift (later dam of very smart middle-distance performer Ulysses) and a half-sister to Irish 10f Group 1 winner Shiva, French dual 12f Group 2 winner Limnos and French 1m 3yo Listed winner Burning Sunset (grandam of Breeders' Cup Turf winner/Derby runner-up Main Sequence).

"This filly is a bit light-framed which isn't untypical of a Karakontie. She goes along ok at this stage but will probably change a lot physically in the coming weeks, so I doubt she'll be early."

DISCOVERIES (IRE)
29/4 b f Mastercraftsman - Alpha Lupi (Rahy)
Owner: Niarchos Family Sales price: n/a

Full sister to very smart 6f-1m winner (four times at Group 1 level, including the Irish 1000 Guineas) Alpha Centauri and a half-sister to 2020 Coronation Stakes winner/Prix de Diane runner-up Alpine Star and Irish 7f 2yo Listed winner Tenth Star. Dam an unraced half-sister to French 7f 2yo Group 3 winner Moon Driver and the Listed-placed maiden dam of Group 3 winners Autocratic (10f, twice) and Evasive (7f) and grandam of 2020 Jersey Stakes winner Molatham.

"A gorgeous filly who is related to our classy fillies, Alpha Centauri and Alpine Star. She doesn't look as precocious as Alpha Centauri but certainly isn't as late as Alpine Star was. I should think she will begin towards the end of May over 6/7f and is an exciting prospect."

ECOUTEZ (IRE)
9/4 b f Exceed And Excel - Ecoutila (Rahy)
Owner: Wellesley/McCalmont/Nicoll Sales price: n/a

Closely related to French 7f 3yo Group 3 winner Surfrider (by Dansili) and a half-sister to 1m 2yo Listed winner Enticement, Group 3/Listed-placed 2020 Irish 7f 3yo winner Soul Search and Listed-placed prolific 7-10f winner Loyalty. Dam an unraced daughter of a French 1m 3yo Listed winner who was a half-sister to Poule d'Essai des Poulains winner Green Tune, Cheveley Park Stakes winner Pas de Response and Prix Robert Papin winner Didyme.

"A nice filly, who looks quite sharp and ought to be among our early batch of 6f two-year-old runners."

EXQUISITE ACCLAIM (IRE)
24/2 b c Acclamation - Exquisite Ruby (Exceed And Excel)
Owner: Zhang Yuesheng Sales price: £155,000 (BBA Ireland/Yulong Investments)

First foal of a maiden sister to useful 6f-1m winner Mississippi and half-sister to high-class prolific 5-6f winner (including the Prix de l'Abbaye) Maarek out of a Group 3-placed multiple 6f winner (including twice at Listed level) who was a half-sister to Irish 6f 2yo Listed winner Alexander Alliance (dam of Group 3/Listed-placed 2020 5-6f 2yo winner Mystery Smiles) and the dam of Flying Childers Stakes winner Ardad.

"A sizeable colt, who is rather typical of the progeny from the sire that I've dealt with - rangy, lengthy and not sharp. He looks nice and I expect him to be running in June over 7f as he doesn't really look like a sprinter at this stage."

HA HA HA (IRE)
18/3 b f Dark Angel - Fashionable (Nashwan)
Owner: M Aziz Sales price: £400,000 (CBR Bloodstock)

Full sister to 2021 Japanese dual 1m 3yo winner Schwarz Kaiser and a half-sister to Group 1-placed Irish 7-9.5f winner (including at Group 3/Listed level)/Irish Oaks runner-up Jack Naylor. Dam a 10f 3yo Listed winner from the family of Group/Grade 1-placed 6-7f 2yo winner (including at Group 2/3 level) Daahyeh and Group 1-placed Irish 7-10f winner (including at Group 2/3 level) Armory.

"A really nice filly who is certainly bred to do the job, being a half-sister to our good filly Jack Naylor. She should be out in the summer over 6/7f."

IMPEACHD ALEXANDER (IRE)
5/2 b f Starspangledbanner - Pious Alexander (Acclamation)
Owner: Charles O'Callaghan, Noel O'Callaghan & Paul O'Callaghan
Sales price: £12,000 (Vendor)

First foal of an Irish 5f 3yo winner who was a half-sister to Group 1-placed 5-6f winner (including at Group 2/3 level) Anthem Alexander (by Starspangledbanner), Group 1-placed 5-6f winner (including at Group 3/Listed level) Dandy Man and the dams of 6f Group 3 winner Hamza and Irish 7f 3yo Listed winner Alkasser out of a 5/6.5f 2yo Group 3 winner.

"A nice filly who is bred to be sharp. She will be ready to start over 6f sometime in May."

IT'S SNOWING (IRE)
27/4 b f Kodiac - Snow Pixie (Flower Alley)
Owner: Anamoine Limited Sales price: €3,000 (BBA Ireland)

Second foal of a once-raced half-sister to six-time 10-12f Group/Grade 1 winner (including the Oaks and Irish Champion Stakes) Snow Fairy out of an Irish 7f 3yo winning half-sister to 10f 3yo Group 3/Listed winner Big Bad Bob; family of Acomb Stakes/Craven Stakes winner Elusive Pimpernel.

"A nice filly, who is out of a half-sister to Snow Fairy. She is getting stronger all the time and should be ready for when the 6/7f races are in full swing."

LUCKY SAN JORE
12/2 gr c Lope de Vega - Claba di San Jore (Barathea)
Owner: Zhang Yuesheng Sales price: 115,000gns (BBA Ireland/Yulong Investments)

Three-parts brother to Italian 10f Group 1/Derby Italiano winner Crackerjack King and Italian 10f 3yo Listed winner/Oaks d'Italia runner-up Joyful Hope (both by Shamardal) and a half-brother to Italian 12f Group 1 winner/Derby Italiano third Jakkalberry, Derby Italiano winner Awelmarduk and Italian triple 10/12f 3yo Listed winner Kidnapping. Dam an Italian 10f 3yo winner who was a half-sister to the grandam of Derby Italiano winner Keep On Fly.

"A big, strong colt who goes very nicely at the moment. I am extremely happy with him, and he should be ready to get going at the end of June or start of July over 7f."

MAGNIFICENT LADY (IRE)
4/3 b f Galileo - Night Visit (Sinndar)
Owner: Zhang Yuesheng Sales price: £185,000 (BBA Ireland/Yulong Investments)

Three-parts sister to Irish Derby winner/Irish 2000 Guineas third Trading Leather and Listed-placed Irish/Australian 11-12.5f winner Wexford Town (both by Teofilo). Dam an unraced daughter of a French 7f 2yo winner who was a sister to 1000 Guineas/Champion Stakes winner Hatoof and US 1m Grade 1 winner Irish Prize and a half-sister to French dual 10f 3yo Listed winner Insijaam (later dam of 10f Group 3 winner/Oaks third Pictavia).

"A well-bred filly who possesses a lot of quality. She won't be early and is definitely one for the second half of the year, but we are looking forward to seeing what she can do."

PANTELLERIA (USA)
6/4 b f Kitten's Joy - Kyllachy Queen (Kyllachy)
Owner: Kilboy Estate Sales price: n/a

First foal of a triple 7f-1m Listed winner who was the daughter of an Italian 10f 3yo Listed-winning half-sister to Italian 10f Listed winner Queen Sensazione, Listed-placed Italian 6f-1m winner Sensazione World and the dam of Italian 11f Group 3 winner/Oaks d'Italia third Fair Nashwan and Italian 1m 3yo Listed winners Fairy Efisio and Fairy Nayef.

"This is a nice filly who looks fairly well forward, which I would think comes from her mother. She shows speed and should be quick enough to begin over 6f in the early summer, but she'll certainly stay another furlong at least."

PARIS LIGHTS (IRE)
21/3 b c Siyouni - Cabaret (Galileo)
Owner: R A Scarborough Sales price: 650,000gns (Vendor)

Full brother to 2020 Dewhurst Stakes winner St Mark's Basilica and a half-brother to Vertem Futurity Trophy/2000 Guineas winner Magna Grecia and useful Irish triple 7f winner Invincible Ryker. Dam an Irish 7f 2yo Group 3 winner who was a half-sister to several winners including smart 7-10f winner (including at Group 3 level) Drumfire and Group 2-placed UK/Hong Kong 6f-1m winner (including at Listed level) Ho Choi.

"A full brother to last year's Dewhurst winner, St Mark's Basilica, who does everything extremely easily at this early stage. A lovely colt who should make a two-year-old from the summer onwards."

SABLONNE
15/4 b f Dark Angel - Starlit Sands (Oasis Dream)
Owner: Miss K Rausing Sales price: n/a

Half-sister to useful 6-7f winner Seychelloise, 2020 5f 2yo winner Sands Of Time and three other winners. Dam a Group 2-placed 5-5.5f 2yo winner (including at Group 3 level) who was a half-sister to four-time 6f Listed winner Sea Dane, 6f 3yo winner Summer Night (later dam of French 1m 2yo Group 3 winner Songerie and Listed winners Soft Morning (9.5f), Sourire (8.5f) and Souvenance (12f)) and the unraced dam of 1m Group 3 winner Chigun.

"A very nice daughter of Dark Angel, who is just starting to come together and we're very happy with her. She isn't a real speedster like one or two in the family but should be out early and will begin at 6f."

SIERRA NEVADA (USA)
13/2 b f American Pharoah - Visions of Clarity (Sadler's Wells)
Owner: Flaxman Stables Ireland Ltd Sales price: n/a

Half-sister to Preakness Stakes winner War of Will, National Stakes winner Pathfork, US 14f Listed winner Tacticus and the unraced dam of 6f Listed winner Buying Trouble and French 7f 2yo Listed winner Nucifera. Dam a French 1m 3yo Listed winner who was closely related to five-time 1m Group/Grade 1 winner (including the Irish 2000 Guineas and Breeders' Cup Mile) Spinning World.

"A gorgeous, big filly - certainly much bigger than her half-brother, Pathfork, who, of course, is the reason why I now train all these lovely horses for the Niarchos family. She is very laid-back and won't be out until the second half of the season."

TREVAUNANCE (IRE)
13/3 b f Muhaarar - Liber Nauticus (Azamour)
Owner: Moyglare Stud Farm Ltd Sales price: n/a

Half-sister to 2020 7f Listed winner Miss Celestial and 2020 Irish 1m 2yo winner Port Sunlight. Dam a Musidora Stakes winner who was a half-sister to Group 2-placed 7f 2yo winner Thetis out of an unraced half-sister to St Leger/ dual Breeders' Cup Turf winner Conduit, Great Voltigeur Stakes winner Hard Top and the dam of Australian 10f Group 1 winner Glass Harmonium and dual 12f Group 3 winner Arab Spring.

"A big filly who is on the weak side at present. She went to the Curragh recently and went along nicely. I imagine she will be ready for when the 7f races are here."

UPBEAT
7/3 b f Invincible Spirit - Blissful Beat (Beat Hollow)
Owner: R A Scarborough Sales price: n/a

Half-sister to high-class multiple 6-7f winner (including at Group 2/3 level) Home of The Brave and two other winners. Dam an unraced sister to useful 6-7f winner Transcend and half-sister to smart multiple 6f-1m winner (including at Group 3/Listed level) Suggestive and 1m 1f 2yo Group 3 winner Rashbag.

"A forward filly, who will be ready to go in the first 6f race of the season if having a clear run between now and then."

VERLINGA (IRE)
8/2 b f Dubawi - Bocca Baciata (Big Bad Bob)
Owner: Flaxman Stables Ireland Ltd Sales price: n/a

Second foal of a Group 1-placed Irish 8-10f winner (including at Group 2/3 level) who was a half-sister to smart French 7f-1m winner (including at Group 3/Listed level)/Poule d'Essai des Pouliches third Topeka and smart French 7-9f winner (including at Group 3/Listed level) Kalsa out of a Group 3-placed French 12.5f 3yo winning half-sister to French 6.5f 2yo Group 3 winner Perugina and the unraced dam of Canadian 1m 2yo Grade 1 winner La Pelosa.

"A very big lady like her mother - she weighs 650 kilos at present! It almost goes without saying that she is a backward filly who won't be seen until the end of the summer at the earliest as we need to get some strength into her so she can carry her bulk."

UNNAMED (IRE)
28/2 ch c Curlin - An Cailin Orga (Galileo)
Owner: Stonestreet Stables LLC Sales price: 240,000gns (Vendor)

Second foal of a useful Irish 10f 3yo winner who was closely related to Irish 1m 2yo Group 2 winner Ol' Man River and useful 1m winner La Figlia out of a triple 1m Group 1 winner (including the 1000 Guineas) who was a half-sister to Mehl-Mulhens Rennen winner Frozen Power and Listed-placed 7f 3yo winner Musical Bar.

"A fine, big horse for the latter part of the season over 7f/1m. It will be interesting to see how a Curlin goes on turf."

UNNAMED (IRE)
1/3 b f Pivotal - Crystal Diamond (Teofilo)
Owner: Zhang Yuesheng Sales price: 180,000gns (BBA Ireland/Yulong Investments)

Third foal of a French 12.5f 3yo Listed winner who was a half-sister to French 12.5f 3yo Group 2 winner Diamond Tango (later dam of Doncaster Cup winner Desert Skyline) out of a French 10.5f 3yo Group 3/Listed winner; family of Irish Derby/St Leger winner Capri and Geelong Cup winner/Melbourne Cup runner-up Bauer.

"A beautiful daughter of Pivotal who has a lot of stamina in her pedigree, but obviously gets speed from her sire. I would hope she could start off over 7f towards the end of the summer or early in the autumn."

UNNAMED (IRE)
2/4 b f Sea The Stars - Greenisland (Fasliyev)
Owner: Stonethorn Stud Farms Limited Sales price: €350,000 (SackvilleDonald)

Full sister to 2020 UAE 1m Listed winner Boerhan and a half-sister to French 5f 2yo Listed winner Shamson. Dam a useful Irish 1m 3yo winner who was a half-sister to Cheveley Park Stakes winner Millisle and 12f Listed winner Ithoughtitwasover.

"A big, strong filly, who is a good-looking type and from the family of our Cheveley Park winner, Millisle. The penny hasn't quite dropped with her yet and she looks one for the backend of the season at this point in time."

UNNAMED (IRE)
6/5 b f Sea The Stars - Green Room (Theatrical)
Owner: Vimal Khosla Sales price: £775,000 (Vendor)

Full sister to useful 8-10f 3yo winner Signe and a half-sister to Oaks winner Forever Together, Prix Jean Prat winner Lord Shanakill and Fillies' Mile winner Together Forever (dam of 2020 Irish 7f 2yo Group 3 winner Military Style) out of an unraced half-sister to US 10f Grade 1 winner Spanish Fern and the dam of US 10f Grade 1 winner Heatseeker.

"This is a very nice filly with a great temperament and a lot of quality about her. She won't be running until the end of the season, but I'm looking forward to seeing what she can do."

UNNAMED (JPN)
15/3 b f Deep Impact - Unbelievable (Fastnet Rock)
Owner: Jonathan Munz Sales price: n/a

Second foal of an unraced close relation to four-time 10-12f winner (including the Irish Oaks)/Oaks runner-up Peeping Fawn (later dam of Chesham Stakes winner/Fillies' Mile runner-up September (by Deep Impact) and Irish 6f 2yo winner/Coventry Stakes third Sir John Hawkins) and a half-sister to French 1m 2yo Group 1 winner Thewayyouare.

"She wouldn't be the biggest but is a lovely filly who has a good way of going. It's certainly exciting to train a daughter of the late Deep Impact, and she ought to be running when the 7f races are here."

RICHARD HUGHES

APACHE GREY (IRE)

4/3 gr c El Kabeir - Laurelita (High Chaparral)
Owner: K Lawrence, P Merritt & Mrs J Blake Sales price: £50,000 (Richard Hughes Racing)

Half-brother to 2020 7f 2yo Group 2/Listed winner Fev Rover and useful 7f-1m winner Bill The Butcher. Dam a 7f 2yo winner who was the daughter of a 6f 2yo winning three-parts sister to US 10f Grade 1 winner Light Jig (later dam of US 10f Grade 1 winner Seek Again and UAE 1m Group 3 winner Treble Jig) and half-sister to French 1m Listed winners Battle Dore (2yo) and Lynton (3yo).

"This is a half-brother to last year's good two-year-old Fev Rover and, like her, won't be a 5f horse. He is full of energy and should be ready to get started by the end of June."

AUSSIE BANKER

27/3 b c Muhaarar - Aristotelicienne (Acclamation)
Owner: Peter Cook Sales price: £40,000 (Richard Hughes Racing Ltd)

Closely related to 6f 2yo winner Aussie Showstopper (by Showcasing). Dam a useful French 6.5f-1m winner who was a half-sister to 7f Listed winner Ceremonial Jade out of a French 7.5f winning sister to French 1m 2yo Listed winner/Poule d'Essai des Pouliches runner-up Firth of Lorne (dam of 2020 7f 2yo Group 2 winner Master of The Seas) and half-sister to the dam of Mehl-Mulhens Rennen winners Dupont and Pacino.

"This is a very straightforward colt, who has improved a lot during the last six weeks or so. I would hope to have him running in early May and he will need 6f before long. We had his half-brother who got better throughout the year as a two-year-old."

CAVALLUCCIO (IRE)

14/3 br c Caravaggio - Gale Song (Invincible Spirit)
Owner: Cognition Land and Water & M Clarke Sales price: £65,000 (Richard Hughes Racing)

Half-brother to useful 2020 6-7f 2yo winner Jimmy Sparks. Dam a 6f 3yo winner who was a three-parts sister to Grade 3-placed US 8-8.5f winner Good Governance and a half-sister to very useful 6f-1m winner Four Seasons out of a 6f 2yo Group 2-winning half-sister to Group 1-placed 7-10f winner Mountain Song, Group 3/Listed-placed 6f 2yo winner Raindancing (grandam of French

7f 2yo Group 3 winner Great Page) and the dam of Breeders' Cup Turf Sprint winner Belvoir Bay.

"A big, strong horse who just needs to cop on a bit. He doesn't look as quick as his pedigree suggests at this early stage, but that could all change once he grows up."

CHIEF WHITE FACE
3/3 ch c Showcasing - Martha Watson (Dream Ahead)
Owner: Jaber Abdullah Sales price: 45,000gns (Richard Hughes Racing)

Second foal of an unraced half-sister to Group 1-placed 5-6f winner (including at Group 2/3 level) Anthem Alexander, Group 1-placed 5-6f winner (including at Group 3/Listed level) Dandy Man, five other winners including the dam of Irish 7f 3yo Listed winner Alkasser and the maiden dam of 6f Group 3 winner/ Prix de l'Abbaye third Hamza.

"He has a lovely pedigree and we're happy with his progress. I doubt he will be an overly early runner, but that isn't untypical for the family and, like them, he looks a sprinting type."

CRUSH AND RUN (IRE)
4/4 b c Zoffany - Mooching Along (Mujahid)
Owner: Thames Boys Sales price: £44,000 (Richard Hughes Racing Ltd)

Half-brother to very useful Irish multiple 5f winner (including at Listed level) Primo Uomo, Listed-placed UK/Hong Kong 6-7f winner Great Spirit, 5f 2yo winner Falabelle and 6f 2yo winner Walkman. Dam an unraced daughter of a maiden half-sister to triple 5f Group 3 winner (including the Norfolk Stakes) Majestic Missile, Irish 5f Listed winner Santo Padre and the unraced dam of 6f 3yo Listed winner/2021 Jebel Hatta runner-up Eqtiraan.

"A hardy little colt, who would have been one of my earliest two-year-old runners but for getting a knock. That pushed him back a bit, but he's a fast horse who should be out in early May over 5f."

MYTHICAL STAR
11/3 b c Starspangledbanner - Timeless Gift (Camacho)
Owner: Mrs Liz Bailey Sales price: £17,000 (Richard Hughes Racing Ltd)

First foal of a French 7.5f 2yo winner who was a half-sister to Group 1-placed multiple 5-7f winner (including at Group 2/3 level) Balthazaar's Gift out of a maiden half-sister to French 1m 3yo Listed winner Green Lady, useful UK/UAE 6f-1m winner Desert Realm, useful 12f 3yo winner Entisar and French 6f 2yo winner Shambo.

"He was meant to run at Kempton in early April but pulled out lame on the morning of the race. He looks to handle the all-weather surface really well, so it's a shame we didn't get to run. I think he will prove himself really well bought at 17k when tackling those auction events throughout the season."

OLYMPIC DREAM
29/1 b c New Approach - Mazuna (Cape Cross)
Owner: Abdulla Al Mansoori Sales price: n/a

Full brother to Group 1-placed 8-14f winner (including at Group 2/3 level) Beautiful Romance and very useful dual 7f winner Good Fortune and a half-brother to Listed-placed UK/Saudi Arabian 6-12f winner Executive Force. Dam a 12f 3yo Group 3 winner who was a half-sister to the dam of 5f Group 3/Listed winner Beyond Desire (herself later dam 5f Listed winner Queen of Desire).

"A lovely, big colt who weighs over 500 kilos and is already 16.1hh. This is as good a moving horse as I have sat on myself. He just floats over the ground. One for the autumn but I like him."

ONE MORE DREAM
21/3 br c Bated Breath - Gracefilly (Invincible Spirit)
Owner: Bill Bailey Sales price: 45,000gns (Richard Hughes Racing)

Third foal of a dual 1m winner who was the daughter of an unraced sister to Irish 1m 3yo Listed winner In The Limelight and Irish 1m 1f 2yo Listed winner On The Nile (grandam of very useful sprinters Roulston Scar and Special Purpose) and three-parts sister to triple 10-12f Group 1 winner Kutub.

"A nice colt who is still a bit backward at present, but he has blossomed into a beautiful horse and should do something at two. He will be out around July time."

REEM ZABEEL (IRE)
1/4 b f Profitable - Ludynosa (Cadeaux Genereux)
Owner: Jaber Abdullah Sales price: £42,000 (Richard Hughes Racing Ltd)

Half-sister to very useful multiple 5-6f winner (including at Listed level) Out Do and useful multiple 5f winner Outrage. Dam a useful 6-7f 3yo winner who was a half-sister to French 12/12.5f 3yo Group 3 winner Silverskaya (later dam of Australian 12f Group 1 winner/Irish Derby runner-up Seville), French 1m Group 2 winner Daneskaya (later dam of very smart Japanese middle-distance performer Six Sense) and US 8/8.5f Listed winner Mumtaz.

"A very straightforward little filly who gives us no issues. She will be out in May and looks a sprinter."

ZERO CARBON (FR)
19/3 b c Acclamation - Clotilde (Dubawi)
Owner: Cognition Land and Water & M Clarke Sales price: 45,000gns (Richard Hughes Racing)

Second foal of a Listed-placed triple 1m winner who was the daughter of a French 1m 1f 3yo Listed-winning half-sister to very useful multiple 6f winner Kaldoun Kingdom; family of St James's Palace Stakes winner/2000 Guineas runner-up Zafeen.

"A lovely horse, who I am aiming at the nice Goodwood meeting in May. He shows plenty of speed and sprinting will be his game. I'm hoping he could be half decent."

UNNAMED (IRE)
9/4 b f Profitable - Coolnagree (Dark Angel)
Owner: Richard Hughes Sales price: 32,000gns (Richard Hughes Racing)

Closely related to French 6f 3yo winner Cool Esprit (by Invincible Spirit) and a half-sister to useful 2020 dual 12.5f winner Ice Pyramid. Dam a Listed-placed Irish dual 7f winner who was a full sister to useful multiple 7f-1m winner Holiday Magic out of a maiden half-sister to Hong Kong triple 6f Group 1 winner Lucky Nine and Japanese 6f Group 3 winner Teehaff.

"An elegant mover who goes particularly well at this stage. She will probably be one of my earlier two-year-old runners and is very much a two-year-old type."

UNNAMED
29/1 b c Olympic Glory - Velvet Revolver (Mujahid)
Owner: M&O Construction & Civil Engineering Ltd Sales price: £58,000 (Richard Hughes Racing Ltd)

Half-brother to Group 2/3-placed French 5-5.5f winner (including twice at Listed level) Ken Colt and 2020 French 5f 2yo Listed winner/Prix Morny fourth Acapulco Gold. Dam a Group 3/Listed-placed Italian multiple 5f winner who was a half-sister to Listed-placed French 6f-1m winner Nobledil and the dam of Italian 6f 2yo Listed winner Noble Hero.

"This lad got a little bit heavy on us so we are just in the process of getting him trimmed down. He isn't a 5f horse and the family can take a bit of time anyway. I don't expect to see him until the second half of the year but he is a nice horse."

EVE JOHNSON HOUGHTON

BASCINET
11/4 ch c Helmet - Finale (Holy Roman Emperor)
Owner: The Woodway 20 Sales price: 12,000gns (Highflyer Bloodstock/Eve Johnson Houghton)

First foal of an 8-8.5f winner who was closely related to useful 10-11f winner Landwade Lad and a half-sister to French 6f 2yo Listed winner Showout and very useful 7f-1m winner Bella Ragazza out of a French 12f Listed-winning half-sister to Fred Darling Stakes winner/Oaks fourth Sueboog (later dam of French 1m 1f Group 1 winner/Derby fourth Best of The Bests) and 6f Listed winner Marika (later dam of triple 8/9f Group 3 winner Kick On).

"I thought he'd be a little sharper than he is, but he is an April foal so it's understandable he is still a bit backward. I would still hope to have him ready to run by May."

BUCKLEY (IRE)
14/2 b g Kodiac - Partita (Montjeu)
Owner: Aston House Stud & Partner Sales price: n/a

Third foal of an unraced close relation to useful 11f 3yo winner Kiefer and half-sister to Geelong Cup winner/Melbourne Cup runner-up Bauer, useful UK/Italian 10-14f winner Boz and useful 10-12f winner Batik (later dam of Italian 7.5f/1m Listed winner Bezique, herself the dam of 9/11f 3yo Listed winner Khalidi).

"We know this family a little bit having trained Kiefer a couple of seasons ago. He has already been gelded and isn't very big, but nor is he an early type either. He goes ok and we will see where we are with him in a month or two."

CABINET OF CLOWNS (IRE)
5/3 gr/ro c Tamayuz - Silver Games (Verglas)
Owner: The Hon Mrs J M Corbett & Mr C Wright Sales price: n/a

Half-brother to Listed-placed 2020 dual 6f 2yo winner Chocoya and Listed-placed UK/US 6-7.5f winner Chiringuita. Dam a useful 7f-1m winner who was a half-sister to 1m 3yo Group 1 winner Nahoodh (later dam of 1m Listed winner Hawkesbury) and useful 5.5-6f 2yo winner Makyon out of an unraced half-sister to French 12f Group 3 winner Not Just Swing.

"This is a really nice colt, and although the dam is by Verglas whose progeny relished cut, he is a very good mover. I can see him being in action by early May and I am extremely happy with him."

CHIPOTLE
5/4 b c Havana Gold - Lightsome (Makfi)
Owner: The Woodway 20 Sales price: 10,000gns (Highflyer Bloodstock/Eve Johnson Houghton)

Second foal of a maiden sister to 6f 2yo winner Mary McPhee (dam of Group 3-placed 2020 Irish 6f 2yo winner Sussex Garden) and half-sister to Group 3-placed 5-6f 2yo winner Mary's Daughter, useful 6f-1m winner Ertikaan, useful 7-8.5f winner Pride of Kings and useful 5-7.5f Flat/2m 2f hurdle winner King's Bastion out of a 5f 2yo winning half-sister to five-time 1m Group 1 winner Attraction.

"A very nice horse who won the Brocklesby in good style. He does it all so easily at home and we've pretty much left him alone since Doncaster. We are aiming him at the two-year-old race at Ascot on trials day on April 28, and that will tell us whether he can go back there for the Royal meeting. If not, there are good races like the Super Sprint or the Book 3 sales race at Newmarket to aim him at."

DAYEM (IRE)
23/2 b c Acclamation - Slovak (Iffraaj)
Owner: KHK Racing Ltd Sales price: £60,000 (Oliver St Lawrence Bloodstock)

Second foal of a 7f-1m winner who was a half-sister to triple 6f Listed winner Katla, Listed-placed Irish dual 5f 3yo winner Rapid Reaction and four other winners out of a maiden half-sister to Prix Jean-Luc Lagardere winner Wootton Bassett, Listed-placed 5-7f winner Mister Hardy and several other winners.

"A nice, racy colt who shows plenty of speed. He will probably start at Newbury in mid-April and is one we particularly like."

DREAMING
26/3 b c Territories - Kerry's Dream (Tobougg)
Owner: Anthony Pye-Jeary & David Ian Sales price: 40,000gns (Highflyer Bloodstock/Eve Johnson Houghton)

Half-brother to Group 3-placed 5-6f 2yo winner (including at Listed level) Ventura Mist, very useful 5-5.5f winner Maljaa and 2020 Irish 5f 2yo winner Mahaaseel. Dam a useful 5f 2yo winner who was a half-sister to French 10.5/12f 3yo Group 3 winner Lady's Purse and Listed-placed dual 6f 2yo winner Dazilyn Lady.

"He was small when we bought him last summer but has really grown which I guess is the Tobougg in him. He has a lovely way of going and will probably start off over 6f at the backend of May."

FLYING SECRET
18/1 b c Showcasing - Secret Sense (Shamardal)
Owner: Jacobs Construction Holdings Ltd & Mr E Kelly Sales price: 75,000gns (Highflyer Bloodstock/Eve Johnson Houghton)

Second foal of a 10f 3yo winner who was a half-sister to Juddmonte International Stakes winner/Derby third Japan, Hong Kong Vase/Grand Prix de Paris winner Mogul, Musidora Stakes/Oaks runner-up Secret Gesture and Irish 10f Group 3 winner Sir Isaac Newton out of a Listed-placed 12-13f winning half-sister to Prix de l'Arc de Triomphe winner Sagamix.

"A very well-bred colt who finds life quite easy. He has had the odd sore shin but nothing major, and we will wait for the 6/7f races with him in the early summer."

KING OF THE DANCE (IRE)
9/2 b c Havana Gold - Figurante (Excellent Art)
Owner: HP Racing King Of The Dance Sales price: £30,000 (Shefford Bloodstock/Highflyer)

First foal of a 6-7f winner who was a half-sister to Italian 1m Group 2 winner Saint Bernard, Italian 1m Listed winner Momix, very useful 12f-2m 5f Flat/2m Grade 2/Listed hurdle/2m 4f Grade 2 chase winner Who Dares Wins and very useful 7f 2yo winner Whispering Angel out of a French 7f 3yo winning half-sister to Prix de la Foret winner Field of Hope.

"Havana Gold is obviously doing very well and this colt goes very well. He will probably be aimed at a maiden at Salisbury in May."

ME NEXT
30/4 ch f Equiano - Next One (Cape Cross)
Owner: Bloomsbury Stud Sales price: n/a

Third foal of a French 10-12f winner who was the daughter of a French 10f 3yo winning three-parts sister to Australian 12f Group 2 winner Au Revoir and half-sister to 8/10f Listed winner Perfect Stride, French 1m 1f 3yo Listed winner Qazyna and French 6f 2yo Listed winner Law Lord.

"This filly comes from a wonderful family that Dad was associated with back in the day, so it is lovely to be involved with it once again. I like her but she does tend to keep a little bit back for herself, so it is rather difficult to know where we are with her at present. She has done all that's been asked of her but no more."

NUVOLARI
28/2 b c Time Test - Luang Prabang (Invincible Spirit)
Owner: Mick & Janice Mariscotti Sales price: 40,000gns (Highflyer Bloodstock/ Eve Johnson Houghton)

First foal of a 7-8.5f winner who was closely related to useful triple 1m winner Bassara and a half-sister to fairly useful 12-14f winner Follow Intello and 10-11f 3yo winner Posh Boy out of a US 10f Grade 2 winner; family of Poule d'Essai des Poulains winner L'Emigrant and Ribblesdale Stakes winner Sahara Slew.

"I like these Time Tests, but this one is on the grow again at present and will be one for the latter part of the season. A very nice horse though."

SAVUKA
18/3 b f Havana Gold - Lulani (Royal Applause)
Owner: Mr & Mrs James Blythe Currie Sales price: n/a

Half-sister to 2020 6f 2yo winner Bhubezi. Dam an 8-9f winner who was a half-sister to fairly useful 7f-1m winner Caiya and French 6.5f 2yo winner Wedding Present out of an unraced half-sister to 2000 Guineas winner Cockney Rebel.

"Her half-brother won for us last season. This filly is still quite backward and needs to grow, but she should be ok in time."

SHEER ROCKS
9/2 ch c Iffraaj - Paradise Cove (Harbour Watch)
Owner: Anthony Pye-Jeary & David Ian Sales price: 18,000gns (Highflyer Bloodstock/Eve Johnson Houghton)

First foal of a 10f 3yo winner who was a half-sister to useful 7-8.5f winner Mukaabra, useful French dual 1m 1f 2yo winner Plume Rose and the dam of French 10/10.5f 3yo Listed winner La Peinture out of an unraced half-sister to Prix du Jockey Club/Prix de l'Arc de Triomphe winner Peintre Celebre.

"Another one that is backward and still growing. He again will be fine once it all falls into place."

TARATARI
19/4 gr c Caravaggio - Premiere Danseuse (Gold Away)
Owner: Gareth Owen Sales price: 30,000gns (Highflyer Bloodstock/Eve Johnson Houghton)

Half-brother to smart 6-7f winner (including at Group 3/Listed level) Pretty Baby. Dam an unraced half-sister to French 12f 3yo Group 2 winner Pacific Rim (dam of 2020 Australian 10.5f Listed winner Paths of Glory), Group 1-placed French 6-11f winner (including at Group 2/3 level) Prairie Star and Listed-placed French 8-12f winner Prairie Flower.

"This colt has done nothing but grow since we bought him last autumn, but then I suppose Caravaggio was a strapping sort. He is a lovely individual who goes well and I like him, but he just needs to get on top of these growing spells as I would like to have him running by May time."

WILLIAM KNIGHT

ASTRAL BEAT (IRE)
3/2 ch c Cotai Glory - Beat The Stars (Verglas)
Owner: Rathmoy Racing II & G C Stevens Sales price: 35,000gns (Richard Knight BS)

Half-brother to Listed-placed Irish/US 7-8.5f winner True To Herself. Dam a maiden sister to Grade 3-placed Irish/US 7f-1m winner (including at Listed level) Driving Snow and half-sister to Listed-placed Irish 7f 2yo winner Dazzling Day; family of triple 10/12f Group 1 winner/1000 Guineas third/Oaks fourth Petrushka and Irish 2000 Guineas/Champion Stakes winner Spectrum.

"A well-made colt with a good mind on him. All being well, he should be running over 6f in June and has a bit of quality about him."

CHECKANDCHALLENGE
8/2 b/br c Fast Company - Likeable (Dalakhani)
Owner: A Hetherton Sales price: 35,000gns (Richard Knight Bloodstock Agent)

Half-brother to useful dual 6f 2yo winner Phijee, useful 7-12f winner White Shaheen and fairly useful multiple 6f winner Inexes. Dam an unraced half-sister to smart 7-10f winner (including at Group 2/3 level) Alkaadhem, smart 6f-1m winner Raising Sand and the dam of 2020 Australian 9/12.5f 3yo Group 1 winner Russian Camelot.

"A big, scopey colt who goes well at this stage. However, I am just inclined to keep the handbrake on him a bit longer as he has a bit of quality and isn't one to rush. He will probably start over 7f in the summer."

GATECRASHER GIRL
14/2 ch f Lope de Vega - Parsnip (Zebedee)
Owner: Chasemore Farm Sales price: n/a

Second foal of a 6f 2yo winner who was a half-sister to Group 1-placed 7f-1m winner (including at Group 2/3 level) Kodi Bear out of an unraced daughter of a 7f-1m winning half-sister to the maiden dam of Mill Reef Stakes winner Cool Creek and the unraced dam of triple 1m Group 1 winner Esoterique.

"She is all there in terms of her physique but her limbs are still quite immature. Everything she has done to this point has been very pleasing, and I suspect she will kick off sometime in midsummer over 7f if all goes to plan between now and then."

QUEL KAIMA (GER)
13/4 b f Exceed And Excel - Queensberry (Tertullian)
Owner: Badger's Set II Sales price: 40,000gns (Vendor)

Third foal of a German 1m 1f winner who was a half-sister to nine winners, most notably Listed-placed US 5-9f winner Meghan's Joy (later dam of US Grade 2 winners Ironicus (8.5f, twice), Norumbega (12f) and On Leave (1m 1f) and US Grade 3 winners Hunting (1m 1f) and Quiet Harbor (8.5f)); family of US 9/10f Grade 1 winner Elate.

"She goes along quite nicely at this stage but would be one for the middle of the season."

TIMESOFTHEESSENCE (IRE)
22/4 b c Time Test - Alys Love (New Approach)
Owner: Mrs Susie Hartley & A Hetherton Sales price: 18,000gns (Richard Knight Bloodstock)

Half-brother to French 5.5f 2yo winner Cape Florida. Dam a maiden half-sister to useful UK/Italian multiple 6-10.5f winner Justice Well out of a useful triple 1m winning half-sister to 6f 3yo Listed winner Nota Bene, German 7f 3yo Listed winner Raphinae and Group 3-placed 6-7f winner Tarjman.

"A well put together colt, who moves well without being flamboyant. He will need a bit of time and is likely to be out mid-late season over 7f/1m."

UNNAMED

2/3 b f New Approach - Dance Awhile (Kodiac)
Owner: Abdullah Al Mansoori Sales price: n/a

Third foal of an unraced close relation to Nunthorpe Stakes winner Margot Did (dam of 2020 US 10f Grade 1 winner Magic Attitude and French 1m 3yo Group 2 winner Mission Impassible) and half-sister to very useful 7f-1m winner Tricorn; family of Prix de la Foret winner Caradak.

"A medium-sized filly, who we need to keep a lid on as she can be a bit hot. She is likeable and moves well. I can see her being out towards the end of the summer."

UNNAMED

11/3 b f Golden Horn - Deveron (Cozzene)
Owner: Saif Ali Sales price: n/a

Three-parts sister to smart 6-9.5f winner (including at Listed level) Lamar (by Cape Cross) and a half-sister to very useful 5f-1m winner (including at Listed level) Haddaf and 7f 2yo winner Dffar. Dam a Group 1-placed 7f 2yo winner who was a full sister to Canadian dual 1m 1f Grade 2 winner Windward Islands and a half-sister to US 1m 2yo Listed winner Hunter Cruise.

"Another who is just a little on the edge in terms of temperament. She can be a bit fizzy and needs treating with kid gloves, but she is going along well at present for a horse that will probably stay further than 1m eventually. She is from a family her owner/breeder has done well with and they usually do something as two-year-olds. One I particularly like at the moment."

UNNAMED (IRE)

15/3 b f Dubawi - Meeznah (Dynaformer)
Owner: Saif Ali & Saeed H Al-Tayer Sales price: n/a

Sixth foal of a high-class 12-14.5f winner (including at Group 2/3 level) who was a half-sister to Group 2/3-placed 1m 2yo winner Shahin and very useful 7f-2m Flat/Grade 2-placed multiple 2m hurdle winner Mirsaale out of a French 12.5f 3yo Listed winner.

"Meeznah hasn't bred a winner from a handful of foals, and they've come in all shapes and sizes from her so far. This filly is sizeable and has plenty of scope. She actually goes along pretty well given her size and the fact she will need 7f at least."

UNNAMED
20/2 b f Kingman - Oshiponga (Barathea)
Owner: Saif Ali Sales price: 40,000gns (Rabbah Bloodstock)

Half-sister to smart 5-7f winner (including at Group 2/Grade 3 level) Hatta Fort, 12f Group 3 winner Spirit of Appin, 7f 2yo Group 3 winner Blue Bayou and the dam of Geoffrey Freer Stakes winner/Irish St Leger runner-up Agent Murphy. Dam a 1m 1f winner who was a half-sister to Canadian 10f Grade 1 winner Miss Keller, Group 2/Listed-placed 7f 2yo winner Kotsi, Group 3/Listed-placed dual 7f 2yo winner Sir George Turner and the dam of St Leger winner Harbour Law.

"A medium-sized filly who wouldn't be a flamboyant mover but, like the Dubawi filly out of Meeznah, she goes nicely for one that won't be running until the backend of the summer over 7f. We will look after her this year as she can be a little feisty at home."

UNNAMED (IRE)
18/2 b c Oasis Dream - Spirit Of Winning (Invincible Spirit)
Owner: Saif Ali Sales price: n/a

Fourth foal of a twice-raced maiden close relation to Group 2-placed 6f-1m winner (including at Listed level) Nebraas (by Oasis Dream) out of a French 12f 3yo winning sister to dual 10f 3yo Listed winner Foodbroker Fancy (later dam of US 12f 3yo Grade 3 winner Dalvina and 3yo Listed winners French Dressing (10.5f) and Soft Centre (10f)) and half-sister to 6f 2yo Listed winner Femme Fatale.

"A medium-sized, hardy colt, who looks one to make hay with this year. He enjoys his work and goes nicely at this stage. I suspect he will be one of our first two-year-olds in action once the 6f races are here."

UNNAMED
17/2 b c Muhaarar - Sunset Avenue (Street Cry)
Owner: Saif Ali Sales price: n/a

Half-brother to Grade 3-placed US dual 1m winner Excellent Sunset, useful dual 7f 2yo winner Path of Thunder and 7f 2yo winner Sunset Flash. Dam a once-raced 7f 2yo winner who was a half-sister to 1m 2yo Listed winner True Cause and four other winners out of an Irish 10f 3yo Group 3 winner.

"A big, scopey colt who goes really well for one of his size and shape. He should make a nice two-year-old from the middle of the season onwards and will probably require 7f to begin with."

HEATHER MAIN

AGAPANTHER
24/5 b f Outstrip - Byroness (Byron)
Owner: Wetumpka Racing Sales price: n/a

Half-sister to 1m 3yo winner Medoras Childe. Dam a 7f-1m winner who was a full sister to useful 6-7f winner Childesplay out of an unraced half-sister to Listed-placed French 6.5-9f winner Priere and Listed-placed 8-9.5f winner Love Your Looks (later dam of 6/7f Group 3 winner Breathtaking Look).

"She is a late foal, so we are being patient with her and allowing her to grow. Her dam, Byroness, and her dam's sister, Childesplay, won a lot of races between them. They were tough, talented, fast fillies, and it is already apparent that Agapanther has inherited these traits. She is fiery, enjoys her work and is naturally gifted with athleticism - hence her name."

DARK ISLAND STAR (IRE)
26/4 b f Caravaggio - Saturn Girl (Danehill Dancer)
Owner: Donald M Kerr Sales price: £20,000 (James Main)

Closely related to useful dual 7f 3yo winner Make A Wish (by No Nay Never) and a half-sister to once-raced 2020 7f 2yo winner Star Seeking and the dam of Chilean 10f Listed winner Million. Dam a 1m 3yo winner who was a half-sister to Group 1-placed Irish multiple 8-9.5f winner (including three times at Listed level) Livadiya, the dam of 8/10f Group 1 winner Linngari and the grandam of Grand Prix de Paris winner Mont Ormel.

"This is an athletic, graceful filly from a good family and by the first-season sire, Caravaggio. She will not be an early type and should be out by mid-season. She has a strong and friendly character."

DIAMOND GIRL
25/2 b f Profitable - Lady Brigid (Holy Roman Emperor)
Owner: Donald M Kerr Sales price: 25,000gns (Hugo Merry Bloodstock/ Heather Main Racing)

Half-sister to useful 5-7f winner Colonel Whitehead. Dam a dual 6f 3yo winner who was a half-sister to 10f 3yo Listed winner We Are Ninety out of an unraced sister to Fillies' Mile winner Listen and Moyglare Stud Stakes winner Sequoyah (later dam of 2000 Guineas and Sussex Stakes winner Henrythenavigator and Irish 1m 3yo Group 3 winner/Irish 1000 Guineas and Prix de Diane third Queen Cleopatra, herself grandam of Irish 10f Group 2 winner/Derby runner-up Cliffs of Moher).

"She is a half-sister to our talented Colonel Whitehead, who has won five races. She should appear sometime during the middle of the season, and is a strongly-built, willing character."

Colonel Whitehead

ILEACH MATHAN (IRE)
28/2 gr c Kodi Bear - Juliette Fair (Dark Angel)
Owner: Coxwell Partnership Sales price: £25,000 (Heather Main Racing)

First foal of a Listed-placed Irish 6f 2yo winner who was a sister to 7f 2yo Group 2 winner Juliet Capulet and 2020 6f 2yo winner Strike Red out of a useful maiden half-sister to 5f 3yo Listed winner Flanders (later dam of 6f Group 1 winner G Force and US 1m 2yo Grade 3 winner Louvain, herself the dam of Poule d'Essai des Pouliches winner Flotilla), French 7f 2yo Listed winner Ascot Family (later dam of Prix Robert Papin winner Family One) and the dam of July Cup winner Lethal Force.

"This colt is an imposing individual, who will be an eyecatcher once he has had time to mature and strengthen up fully."

SIR RANDOLPH
14/4 b c Churchill - Esteemable (Nayef)
Owner: Llewelyn, Runeckles Sales price: £22,000 (Heather Main Racing Ltd)

Half-brother to 2020 6f 3yo winner Fuchsia. Dam a useful multiple 1m winner who was a half-sister to very useful multiple 9.5-10f winner (including at Listed level) Tinshu, Listed-placed UK/UAE 6-9f winner Montpellier and useful 9.5-12f winner Encircled out of an unraced half-sister to German 12f Group 1 winner Catella and German 10f 3yo Listed winner Lizzey Letti.

"This is a forward, honest and sharp two-year-old from a successful family. His dam, Esteemable, won four races and her half-sister, the incredibly consistent and talented Tinshu, won ten races, including at Listed level. He is actually owned by the owners of the latter. By the exciting first-season sire, Churchill, he is compact, speedy and already mature. He will be our first two-year-old runner at Newbury on April 16."

WIZARDING
24/3 b c Showcasing - Dutch S (Dutch Art)
Owner: Mondial Racing & Robert Haim Sales price: 36,000gns (Jared Bernstein & R Haim)

Second foal of a 6f 2yo winner who was a half-sister to useful 6-7f winner King Ragnar and useful 6f-1m winner Pavillon (by Showcasing) out of a 7f 2yo winning half-sister to Group 2/3-placed 7f 2yo winner Lady High Havens and 6f 2yo winner Apache Dream (later dam of Irish 10f Group 3 winner Hall of Mirrors and Italian 6f 3yo Group 3 winner Nikisophia).

"This is a colt with a large physique and has real presence about him. He is strong-bodied and has an excellent attitude. The family tend to take a bit of time, and I suspect he will be one for the backend of the season."

PHILLIP MAKIN

CHISELED
20/2 b c Adaay - Relaxez Vous (Raven's Pass)
Owner: SYPS & Mrs Wendy Burnett Sales price: £42,000 (Aidan O'Ryan/SYPS Ltd)

Second foal of an unraced half-sister to Group 3/Listed-placed UK/Hong Kong 7f-1m winner California Disegno, useful Irish 1m-2m winner King's Vow, useful 1m 2yo winner Psychometry and 7f 2yo winner Magician's Cape out of a Listed-placed 10f 3yo winning half-sister to 10f 3yo Listed winner/Yorkshire Oaks runner-up Ocean Silk.

"This is a strong colt who is a good physical model. He shows plenty of speed and ability, and I would hope that he will be out sometime in May."

PERFECT GLORY (IRE)
9/4 b c Cotai Glory - Perfect Venture (Bahamian Bounty)
Owner: SYPS & Mrs Wendy Burnett Sales price: 40,000gns (SYPS (UK) Ltd)

Half-brother to Group 3-placed Irish 7f 2yo winner Shalailah. Dam a dual 6f 3yo winner who was the daughter of a thrice-raced maiden half-sister to 6f Listed winner Aahayson, UAE 5f Listed winner Take Ten, very useful 6-7f winner Thebes and Listed-placed 7f 2yo winner Betimes.

"This is a big, good-boned horse who takes the eye. He moves well and is very laid-back in all that he does."

UNNAMED (IRE)
12/4 b c Kodiac - Andry Brusselles (Hurricane Run)
Owner: SYPS & Mrs Wendy Burnett Sales price: £40,000 (Aidan O'Ryan/Phil Makin Racing)

Full brother to useful 2020 7f-1m 2yo winner Lady Hayes and a half-brother to useful 2020 Irish 9.5f 3yo winner Pugin. Dam a French 1m Listed winner who was a half-sister to Australian 1m 1f Group 3 winner Pacodali and Group 3-placed 7f-1m winner (including at Listed level) Mitchum Swagger out of a 1m 3yo Listed winner.

"This is nice horse, though he will take a bit of time. I imagine he will be one for the second half of the year over 7f/1m."

UNNAMED (IRE)
23/2 ch g Cotai Glory - Classy Lassy (Tagula)
Owner: John Thomas Hanbury Sales price: £30,000 (Aidan O'Ryan/Philip Makin)

Third foal of a Listed-placed maiden sister to 8-10f Flat/2m hurdle winner Hefner out of a maiden half-sister to Group 3-placed prolific 6-10f winner Waterside and Listed-placed multiple 5-6f winner Seven No Trumps.

"A big horse who is just starting to fill his frame. We haven't pushed any buttons yet, but he is a nice mover who has found the little bits he has done coming easily to him. I should think he will be starting off in June over 6f."

UNNAMED (IRE)
5/4 b c Zoffany - Leniency (Cape Cross)
Owner: W Dennison Sales price: n/a

Half-brother to 7f-1m winner Prying Pandora and 9-10f winner Parole. Dam an unraced half-sister to Prix de la Foret/Sussex Stakes winner Court Masterpiece, French 5f 3yo Listed winner Maybe Forever and useful 6-7f winner Easy Air; family of Irish 1000 Guineas winner Classic Park.

"This is a big, raw-boned horse, who was moving well in the little bits he had done. Unfortunately, he suffered a setback but is one for the backend in any case. We like him."

UNNAMED (IRE)
14/3 b f Highland Reel - Star of Spring (Iffraaj)
Owner: SYPS & Mrs Wendy Burnett Sales price: £22,000 (Aidan O'Ryan/Phillip Makin)

Second foal of a 1m winner who was a sister to useful 7f 2yo winner Musharakaat out of a maiden half-sister to useful 6-7f 2yo winner Witch Of Fire (later dam of Solario Stakes winner Drumfire and grandam of Vertem Futurity Trophy/2000 Guineas winner Magna Grecia and 2020 Dewhurst Stakes winner St Mark's Basilica) and the unraced dam of Irish 7f 2yo Group 3 winner/Moyglare Stud Stakes runner-up Ugo Fire.

"A sizeable filly who is just ticking over at present. We initially thought she would take an age to come to hand, but she has really pulled herself together and is showing us that she's happy to do more. She has got plenty of scope and moves well. I imagine she will start off over 7f."

DAVID MENUISIER

APPEARING
18/3 b c Oasis Dream - Abbakova (Dandy Man)
Owner: Peter Mitchell & Mrs Susan Davis Sales price: 35,000gns (Vendor)

Half-brother to Listed-placed 5-7f winner Deep Intrigue. Dam a Listed-placed Irish 5f 2yo winner who was the daughter of a maiden half-sister to Group 3-placed 6f-1m winner (including at Listed level) Out of Reach (later dam of US 14f Grade 3 winner Inordinate) and Group 2/3-placed 6f 2yo winner Well Warned (later dam of King's Stand Stakes winner Prohibit (by Oasis Dream)).

"A compact colt by Oasis Dream who won't be overly early. He is a nice mover and I expect he will be running in July."

FALLEN FROM HEAVEN
5/3 b f Postponed - Fallen Star (Brief Truce)
Owner: Normandie Stud Ltd Sales price: n/a

Half-sister to Coronation Stakes winner Fallen For You (later dam of dual 7f Group 2 winner Glorious Journey and 2020 7f 2yo Listed winner Love Is You), smart 7-10f winner (including at Listed level) Fallen Idol, Group 2/Listed-placed 1m 2yo winner Fallen In Love (later dam of French 10.5f Group 3 winner Loving Things) and the maiden dam of 1m 3yo Listed winner Light Up Our World. Dam a 1m Listed winner who was a half-sister to Lockinge Stakes winner Fly to the Stars.

"Still in pre-training. She is the last foal of a great broodmare and is likely to be more of a three-year-old prospect."

Love Is You

FLAMENCO FAN
18/2 b f Dark Angel - Annabelle's Charm (Indian Ridge)
Owner: Merry Fox Stud Limited Sales price: 130,000gns (Vendor)

Half-sister to Middle Park Stakes winner Charming Thought, very useful 5-7f winner Spanish City and two other winners. Dam a Group 3-placed 8-10f winner (including at Listed level) who was a half-sister to Listed-placed 7f 2yo winner Purple Sage out of a twice-raced maiden sister to Racing Post Trophy winner Aristotle and Canadian International winner Ballingarry and half-sister to St James's Palace Stakes winner Starborough and the dam of six-time 8-12f Group 1 winner St Nicholas Abbey.

"Another homebred that is still in pre-training. She is a big, rangy filly who will need plenty of time."

GOLDSMITH (IRE)
18/2 b c Shalaa - Ingot of Gold (Dubawi)
Owner: Gail Brown Racing (XIII) Sales price: 65,000gns (Richard Frisby Bloodstock)

Second foal of a French 8.5f winner who was a half-sister to very useful UK/US 7-10f winner (including at Listed level) Rhagori out of a Listed-placed 11-12f 3yo winning half-sister to 10/10.5f 3yo Group 3 winner African Dream, Listed-placed 6-7f winner Lone Wolfe and Listed-placed Irish 1m 1f 3yo winner Fenella's Link.

"This is a very likeable individual with a classy outlook. He moves very well and should be seen from June/July onwards."

GONNETOT (FR)
9/5 b c Recorder - Gondole (Pivotal)
Owner: Gerard Augustin-Normand & Partner Sales price: €23,000 (David Menuisier)

Half-brother to French 12f 3yo winner Gommerville. Dam a once-raced maiden half-sister to 2020 French 5f 2yo Group 3 winner Kalahara and French 6f 2yo Group 3 winner Sasparella out of a French 5-7.5f winning sister to French dual 5f Group 3 winner Only Answer, close relation to French 1m 3yo Group 2 winner/Poule d'Essai des Pouliches runner-up Impressionnante (later dam of Prix du Jockey Club winner Intello) and half-sister to 8/10f Grade 1 winner Mondialiste.

"A May foal who is big and backward but very attractive. I believe in Recorder a lot and this one has been stamped by him. I don't expect to see him until the autumn."

LIONEL
4/2 ch c Lope de Vega - Gretchen (Galileo)
Owner: Normandie Stud Ltd Sales price: n/a

Second foal of a smart 12-14.5f 3yo winner (including at Group 2/Listed level) who was a half-sister to Irish St Leger winner Duncan, Doncaster Cup winner Samuel, Listed-placed 1m 2yo winner Deirdre, useful 11.5-12f 3yo winner Alexana and 12f 3yo winners Romina and Stella Bellissima out of a Group 1-placed 1m 3yo Listed winner/1000 Guineas fourth.

"This is a lovely, scopey colt from a fantastic family. He is a great mover and would make anybody's heart melt. Bred to get better with age, he won't be seen until the autumn."

SECRET ARMY
7/4 ch c Territories - Secret Insider (Elusive Quality)
Owner: Gail Brown Racing (D) Sales price: 20,000gns (Vendor)

Half-brother to useful triple 7f winner Gypsy Whisper. Dam a 7f 3yo winner who was a half-sister to Group 1-placed UK/Australian 7f-1m winner Buffalo River out of a US 8-8.5f winning sister to US 6f 3yo Grade 2 winner Bwana Charlie and US 1m 1f Grade 2 winner My Pal Charlie and half-sister to US 8.5f 3yo Grade 3 winner Bwana Bull and the dams of US 6f 2yo Grade 3 winner Cinco Charlie and US 1m 1f 3yo Grade 3 winner Fast And Accurate.

"A strong-looking colt who is from a good family we know well. I expect he will take time like most by Territories and is one for the second part of the season."

SOAMES FORSYTE
26/1 b c Siyouni - Fleur Forsyte (Teofilo)
Owner: Normandie Stud Ltd Sales price: n/a

First foal of a 10f 3yo Listed winner who was the daughter of a maiden half-sister to Irish St Leger winner Duncan, Doncaster Cup winner Samuel, Park Hill Stakes winner Gretchen and four other winners out of a 1m 3yo Listed winner/1000 Guineas fourth; family of Dante Stakes winner/Derby third Carlton House and Derby runner-up Tamure.

"This is a compact son of Siyouni - very neat and agile with a long stride despite not being the tallest. He is a very attractive individual and looks to be sharper than most of his family."

UNNAMED (USA)
21/2 b c Constitution - Elegant By Nature (Footstepsinthesand)
Owner: Abdullah Saeed Almaddah Sales price: n/a

First foal of an unraced half-sister to US 1m 2yo stakes winner Royal By Nature out of an unraced half-sister to Group 3-placed French 5f 2yo winner Mister Picnic; extended family of Queen Elizabeth II Stakes winner/2000 Guineas runner-up King Of Change and German dual 12f Group 1 winner Mamool.

"A US-bred colt by a sire who has been a hit in his early days at stud. He is weak and rather backward at the moment, and I'm sure he will improve plenty throughout the year."

UNNAMED (FR)
5/2 b f Iffraaj - Gallifrey (Sir Percy)
Owner: Chasemore Farm Sales price: n/a

First foal of a useful 8-12.5f winner who was a full sister to Listed-placed 13.5f 3yo winner Galmarley out of a 1m Listed-winning daughter of an unraced half-sister to French 1m 2yo winner/Derby runner-up Walk In The Park, Group 3-placed Irish 7-8.5f winner (including at Listed level) Soon and the dam of 2020 6f Group 3 winner Tabdeed.

"This is a nice, strong daughter of Iffraaj who should be a midsummer type of two-year-old."

UNNAMED
10/3 gr c Almanzor - Marie Rossa (Testa Rossa)
Owner: Oliver Harris Sales price: €75,000 (David Menuisier)

Half-brother to Listed-placed French dual 1m winner Zvarov and Listed-placed French 7.5-10.5f winner Recover Me. Dam a French/US 8.5-10f winner who was a half-sister to French 10f Group 2 winner/Prix de Diane runner-up Ana Marie (later dam of French 1m 1f 3yo Listed winner Ana Americana) and US 1m Grade 2 winner Charmo.

"A really eye-catching son of Almanzor. He has a great walk to him and a super attitude. It is a very strong French family and he looks a classy individual."

UNNAMED (FR)
22/2 b c Siyouni - Pacifique (Montjeu)
Owner: Michael H Watt Sales price: €210,000 (David Menuisier)

Half-brother to 2020 French 12-15f 3yo winner (including at Group 3/Listed level) Paix and two other winners. Dam a French 15f 3yo Group 3 winner who was a three-parts sister to 2020 Lingfield Derby Trial winner English King and a half-sister to French 11f 3yo Listed winner Prudenzia (later dam of Irish Oaks winner Chicquita and 2020 Australian 10f Group 1 winner Magic Wand).

"This colt is rather untypical of one by his sire as he is a tall, scopey horse who is still rather babyish. He comes from a great middle-distance family and will obviously take time, but he oozes quality."

UNNAMED (FR)
20/2 b f Holy Roman Emperor - Vezina (Bering)
Owner: Quantum Leap Racing XVI Sales price: €120,000 (Not Sold)

Full sister to French 1m 2yo Group 1 winner/Prix du Jockey Club runner-up Morandi and Listed-placed French 8-10f winner Vita. Dam a maiden sister to Listed-placed US 11f 3yo winner Vezing and half-sister to French 10.5f 3yo Group 3 winner Marie de Ken (later dam of French 10f Group 2 winner/Prix de Diane runner-up Ana Marie) and the grandam of Queen Anne Stakes winner Lord Glitters.

"She is a full sister to a Group 1 winner. This is a classy, elegant and very attractive filly who I hope will be seen out sometime in late summer."

ROD MILLMAN

Thanks to *James Millman* for running me through a handful of the stable's two-year-olds for the season ahead.

AMAZONIAN DREAM (IRE)
16/4 b c Bungle Inthejungle - Grandmas Dream (Kyllachy)
Owner: Great Western Racing Sales price: 35,000gns (Rod Millman Racing)

Half-brother to 5f 2yo winner/Windsor Castle Stakes runner-up Savannah's Dream and 5f 2yo winner Savannah's Show. Dam a 5-6f 3yo winner who was a half-sister to 6f 2yo Group 3 winner Tremar and the dam of a Group 3/Listed-placed 6f 2yo winner Squash out of a 5.5f 2yo winning half-sister to Sun Chariot winner Lady In Waiting and the dam of US 1m 1f Grade 1 winner Lea.

"This colt is a strong individual and by a sire that produces plenty of tough and speedy sorts, whilst the dam was quick and has already produced a Windsor Castle runner-up. He should be in action by the end of April and is one we're particularly looking forward to."

FOREVER DREAMING (IRE)
28/2 ch f Showcasing - Melrose Abbey (Selkirk)
Owner: JPM Racing II Sales price: 6,000gns (Millman Racing)

Third foal of a useful 10-12f 3yo winner who was a full sister to 10f 3yo Listed winner Ceilidh House (dam of 2020 1m 3yo Listed winner Kinross) and a half-sister to useful 12f-2m winner Villa Royale, 8.5f 3yo Flat/Grade 3-placed triple 2m hurdle winner Bothy and the dam of Solario Stakes winner/Poule d'Essai des Poulains runner-up First Selection out of a 10/12f Listed winner.

"This filly isn't bred to be early on the dam's side and is a physically imposing sort, but she had shown some of the speed you'd expect for one by her sire before we turned her out in the field to allow her to strengthen up. I imagine she will be one for the backend of the season and should make an even better three-year-old."

MISS ANACO
12/2 b f Adaay - Sonko (Red Clubs)
Owner: Anaco Racing Partnership Sales price: 6,500gns (Rod Millman Racing)

Full sister to 2021 5f 3yo winner Four Adaay. Dam a fairly useful multiple 5f winner who was a half-sister to Group 3-placed dual 6f 2yo winner (including at Listed level) Terror out of a 7f-1m winning daughter of a maiden half-sister to Group 1-placed multiple 6f winner (including at Group 2/Listed level) Indian Rocket and 6f 2yo Listed winner/Norfolk Stakes runner-up The Bonus King.

"We obviously train her year-older sister who has always shown tremendous speed without quite getting the rewards her efforts have deserved. This filly is a more compact type who would have been our first two-year-old runner but for meeting with a minor setback. She is back cantering and should be in action by the end of April or early May."

SOI DAO (IRE)
17/4 b f Twilight Son - Home Cummins (Rip Van Winkle)
Owner: Daddies Girl Partnership Sales price: £12,000 (Rod Millman)

First foal of a Listed-placed 6.5-8.5f winner who was a half-sister to smart 7-10.5f winner (including at Group 2/3 level) Forest Ranger out of a French 9.5f 3yo Listed-winning daughter of a Listed-placed French dual 1m 3yo winner who was a half-sister to French 10.5f 3yo Group 3 winner Tamise (later dam of Australian 12.5f Group 3 winner Motivado) and French 1m 3yo Listed winner Tarzan Cry.

"Another compact filly who unfortunately suffered an injury in the paddock which has delayed the breaking in process with her. However, she is a hardy sort out of a tough mare who was placed at Listed level, so shouldn't be long in catching up with the rest of them."

TWILIGHT TONE
18/3 b/br g Twilight Son - Bikini (Trans Island)
Owner: Crown Connoisseurs Sales price: 10,000gns (Rod Millman Racing)

Half-brother to useful multiple 5-6f winner John Kirkup, triple 7f 3yo winner Tight Fit, multiple 5-6f winner Kommander Kirkup, 2021 5f 3yo winner Havagomecca and 5f 2yo winner Kolossus. Dam a maiden half-sister UK/Italian 5-7.5f winner Magical Roundabout and Italian 5f 2yo winner Baby Mistrial out of a Listed-placed French 1m 2yo winner.

"This gelding is by a sire who was a slow-maturing type, and his first crop seemed to take after him in that regard. He has enjoyed a good time of things in recent months with his runners. This gelding has a bit of size about him but had shown some speed in his work before we turned him out in the field to allow him to strengthen up and mature. He will be one for the second half of the year and is another who'll do even better at three."

TITANIUM
RACING

A fresh approach
to racehorse
ownership

titanium-racing.co.uk

HUGHIE MORRISON

BANNED
8/5 b f Ulysses - Clarietta (Shamardal)
Owner: Michael Kerr-Dineen & Martin Hughes Sales price: 90,000gns (H Morrison)

Closely related to Lingfield Oaks Trial winner Perfect Clarity (by Nathaniel) and a half-sister to Italian 10f Listed winner Law Power and Listed-placed dual 1m 3yo winner Clarentine. Dam a Listed-placed dual 7f 2yo winner who was a half-sister to Group 1-placed UK/US 7-11.5f winner (including at Grade 3/Listed level) Cassydora (later dam of Irish triple 12/14f Group 3 winner Ernest Hemingway and French 1m 2yo Group 3 winner Toulifaut) and 10f 3yo Listed winner Classic Remark.

"This filly is quite a challenge at the moment as she is rather full of herself. She does have a lot of natural ability to go with it thankfully, and I could see her running in July time."

BUSHFIRE
28/2 ch c Australia - Aflame (Shamardal)
Owner: Martin Hughes & Michael Kerr-Dineen Sales price: 50,000gns (C Gordon Watson Bloodstock)

Second foal of a useful triple 7f 3yo winner who was a half-sister to Group 2-placed UK/Australian 8.5-13f winner (including twice at Listed level) Tall Ship, useful multiple 6-8.5f winner Chevalier, useful multiple 7f winner Yellowhammer and four other winners including the dam of Prix de Diane winner Channel out of a Cheveley Park Stakes-winning three-parts sister to Oaks winner Alexandrova.

"This a nice-going colt with a good temperament who looks to be quite forward for one by his sire. He could be sharp enough to begin over 7f/1m in the second part of the summer."

CANTATA
15/5 b f Oasis Dream - Summer's Eve (Singspiel)
Owner: Wardley Bloodstock Sales price: n/a

Half-sister to Listed-placed 7f-1m winner Early Morning, useful triple 2m winner Aurora Grey and two other winners. Dam a Group 3/Listed-placed 1m 1f 3yo winner who was a full sister to Ascot Gold Cup winner Papineau and a half-sister to triple 12/14.5f Group 1 winner (including the St Leger)/Derby runner-up Silver Patriarch.

"She isn't here yet and is a weak, backward filly who will naturally take time, given there's plenty of stamina in her pedigree. I wouldn't expect to see her here until the middle of the summer, so whether she makes it out before her three-year-old career remains to be seen."

COCONUT BAY
30/1 b f Bated Breath - Tropicana Bay (Oasis Dream)
Owner: Helena Springfield Ltd Sales price: 29,000gns (Not Sold)

Third foal of a maiden half-sister to smart 8-10.5f winner (including twice at Group 3 level) Ballet Concerto and Group 1-placed French 6-7.5f 2yo winner Havane Smoker out of a 10f 3yo winning half-sister to Listed-placed 10f 3yo winner Design Perfection; family of 2020 Australian 9/12.5f 3yo Group 1 winner Russian Camelot, Dante Stakes winner Telecaster and Gimcrack Stakes winner Caspar Netscher.

"She only got broken in last month but is a neat, together sort of filly who shouldn't take too long. I could easily see her running at two."

HAYMAKER
13/3 b c Muhaarar - Squash (Pastoral Pursuits)
Owner: Collett, Morrison & Partners Sales price: 42,000gns (H Morrison)

Second foal of a Group 3/Listed-placed 6f 2yo winner who was a half-sister to dual 6f winner Fivetwoeight and 2020 6f 3yo winner Mount Mogan out of a twice-raced sister to 6f 2yo Group 3 winner Tremar and a half-sister to the dam of 5f 2yo winner/Windsor Castle Stakes runner-up Savannah's Dream.

"A fairly well-set colt, who is still rather green but works nicely and has a forward going action. He is very straightforward to deal with and could well be starting off over 6f in May/June."

LUCROSA (IRE)
8/4 b f Profitable - Opportuna (Rock Hard Ten)
Owner: Thurloe Thoroughbreds L Sales price: 47,000gns (Peter & Ross Doyle Bloodstock)

Half-sister to Grade 3-placed Irish 6f 2yo winner Last Opportunity and 2020 dual 7f 2yo winner Round Six. Dam a maiden half-sister to Group 1-placed 6-7f winner (including at Group 3/Listed level) The Cheka and Grade 2/Listed-placed 9-10.5f winner Wall of Sound (later dam of 7f 2yo Group 3 winner Boomer).

"This filly would be as forward as any two-year-old in the yard and has already done a couple of pieces of work. If everything went to plan, she could be running in the early part of May."

PLAGIARISE
19/3 b f Showcasing - Copy-Cat (Lion Cavern)
Owner: Hot To Trot Racing VI Sales price: 40,000gns (Vendor)

Half-sister to Group 2-placed multiple 6f-1m winner (including at Group 3 level) Pastoral Player, Group 2-placed 7f-1m winner (including at Listed level) Chil The Kite, Group 1-placed UK/Hong Kong triple 7f winner Kings Falcon and five other winners including the dam of Group 3-placed 5-7f winner Lincoln. Dam a maiden half-sister to 5f Group 3 winner/Prix de l'Abbaye runner-up Averti.

"This is a filly who was showing us plenty early on before going through a growing phase. I trained a couple of her siblings. Both of them were talented, but Chil The Kite was an absolute angel to deal with, whereas Pastoral Player was quirky like his mother. This filly has a bit of spirit but nothing more than that at this stage. She just needs to come to herself after that growing spell and though she's by Showcasing, neither of her half-brothers appeared until the backend of the summer and I suspect she'll be the same."

PROMOTING (IRE)
25/3 b c Showcasing - Aqualis (Sea The Stars)
Owner: P C J Dalby & R D Schuster Sales price: 50,000gns (James Toller)

Second foal of a 10f 3yo winner who was a half-sister to smart 7f-1m winner (including at Listed level) Pearl Mix out of a French 7f 2yo winning sister to Group 1-placed French 7f-1m winner (including at Group 2/3 level) Rajsaman and smart French 8-10f winner (including at Listed level) Rosawa (later dam of Prix Marcel Boussac winner/Prix de Diane runner-up Rosanara).

"A big, strong colt, who will take plenty of time and be running sometime in the autumn. A nice horse for the future."

REELEMIN
3/2 ch c Highland Reel - Rainbow's Arch (Dubawi)
Owner: Mr and Mrs M T Bevan Sales price: 18,000gns (H Morrison)

Second foal of an unraced sister to UAE 5f Listed winner Shillong out of a Group 1-placed triple 7f winner (including twice at Group 3 level) who was a half-sister to Listed-placed UK/French 5-10f winner Complicit and 7f 2yo winner Onida.

"He is an uncomplicated, honest colt who will lead the string if required. He is a lovely horse to have around the place and should be making an appearance during the middle of the season."

SHOCKWAVES
29/3 gr c Sea The Moon - Having A Blast (Exchange Rate)
Owner: M Kerr-Dineen, M Hughes & W Eason Sales price: 80,000gns
(SackvilleDonald/H Morrison)

Full brother to Australian 7f-1m winner Succendam. Dam a useful French 1m
3yo winner who was the daughter of a US 8.5f 2yo winning half-sister to Grade
1-placed US/Canadian 6.5-9.5f winner (including at Grade 3 level) Breaking
Lucky and the dam of Kentucky Derby winner Country House.

*"A nice, rangy colt, who has looked comfortable with all that has been asked of
him to this point. He is going to be a staying type, and I wouldn't expect to see
him out before September."*

STAY ALERT
28/2 b f Fastnet Rock - Starfala (Galileo)
Owner: Ben & Sir Martyn Arbib Sales price: n/a

Full sister to Group 2-placed 10-12f winner (including at Listed level) Star
Rock and a half-sister to very useful 2020 14f-2m 2f 3yo winner Stag Horn
and useful 13.5f-2m 4f Flat/2m 3f hurdle winner Star Rider. Dam a useful dual
12f 3yo winner/Park Hill Stakes runner-up who was a half-sister to Group 3/
Listed-placed 12-14f winner Sweeping Up and 1m 2yo Listed winner Under
The Rainbow.

*"A thickset filly who hasn't been in all that long. She is a longer-term/three-
year-old project like most of this family and, though she might suddenly go
forward, we won't risk it and will remain patient."*

TANGO TONIGHT
14/2 ch f Pivotal - Last Tango Inparis (Aqlaam)
Owner: Helena Springfield Ltd Sales price: n/a

Second foal of a Listed-placed 1m 2yo winner who was a half-sister to four
winners out of a maiden half-sister to dual 10f Listed winner Marsh Daisy (by
Pivotal), Listed-placed dual 6f 2yo winner Fontana Amorosa, Group 3/Listed-
placed Irish 11.5f 3yo winner Yankee Doodle and the dam of Group 2/3-placed
7f-2m winner (including twice at Listed level) Mildenberger.

*"The dam showed us absolutely nothing in her work at home prior to running,
but she placed and won from two starts as a two-year-old before placing at
Listed level at three. I quite like this filly and she should be in action come the
early autumn."*

WAGGA WAGGA
10/3 ch c Australia - Quiz Mistress (Doyen)
Owner: The Fairy Story Partnership Sales price: n/a

Half-brother to dual 10f winner Sandyman. Dam a Group 3-placed 9.5-14f winner (including three times at Listed level) who was a half-sister to Lingfield Derby Trial winner Saddler's Quest, French 12.5f Listed winner Seren Hill, the maiden dam of high-class 12-15f winner (including at Group 2/3 level)/ Melbourne Cup runner-up Marmelo and 2m Group 3 winner Vent de Force and the unraced dam of French 1m 2yo Group 3 winner Circumvent.

"We obviously know this family very well. This colt reminds me quite a bit of Vent de Force inasmuch as he looks very backward at this stage but will likely make it out before the end of the year. He is going to make a lovely horse next year and beyond."

UNNAMED
17/1 b c Muhaarar - Permission (Authorized)
Owner: Mrs J Scott, J F Dean & Lady Trenchard Sales price: n/a

First foal of a 1m Listed winner who was a half-sister to Group 1-placed multiple 5-6f winner (including at Group 3/Listed level) Cotai Glory and Listed-placed dual 5f 2yo winner Excel's Beauty out of an unraced sister to 6f 2yo winner/Middle Park Stakes third Huntdown and useful dual 6f winner Wingbeat and half-sister to the dam of 2020 7f 2yo Group 3 winner Saffron Beach.

"This colt had a setback, so didn't make it to the sales and only got broken in at the start of this year. He has made good progress and caught up well since, but we're in no rush with him as he's a nice horse who needs looking after. The dam didn't run until mid-June of her three-year-old career, and although this colt should make it out earlier than that, it won't be until the autumn."

WILLIAM MUIR & CHRIS GRASSICK

GALIAC
17/4 b c Kodiac - Gallipot (Galileo)
Owner: Perspicacious Punters Racing Club Sales price: 30,000gns (William R Muir)

Full brother to useful 8-10f winner Gallic and closely related to 2020 12f 3yo winner Galsworthy (by Dansili). Dam a 12f 3yo Listed winner who was closely related to very useful UK/Australian 8-10f winner (including at Listed level) Trade Commissioner and useful 2020 12f 3yo winner Coconut and a half-sister to useful 7f 2yo winner Peterhof out of a Sun Chariot Stakes winner.

"This is a lovely little horse who has developed and done extremely well of late. He is hard as a bullet and could have run very early if I had wanted him to, but I'm not that sort of trainer and we will wait for the 6f races with him. I imagine he will be out in May and he'll definitely win this year."

KING'S COURSE (IRE)
9/2 b/br c Gleneagles - Desert Run (Desert Prince)
Owner: C L A Edginton Sales price: 50,000gns (William R Muir)

Half-brother to useful 7-12.5f winner Sweet P. Dam an unraced half-sister to Group 2-placed 7f-1m winner (including twice at Group 3 level) Purr Along, 5f Listed winner Katawi and Listed-placed UK/US dual 8.5f winner Lady Francesca out of a 7f 3yo winning half-sister to Falmouth Stakes winner Ronda and 2m Listed winner Silver Gilt.

"I fell in love with him at the sales. I have never had a Gleneagles before, but we obviously know this family well having trained a few of them, notably Purr Along who won a Group 3 in France as a two-year-old. He is a strong colt who we have already galloped and he goes really well. Having done all that we wanted him to do, we will now bring him along gradually and get him out in late-April or May. He's another who will definitely win races this season."

LIKE A LION (IRE)
10/2 b c Kodiac - Termagant (Powerscourt)
Owner: Carmel Stud Sales price: 72,000gns (Carmel Stud)

Third foal of a Moyglare Stud Stakes winner who was a half-sister to Listed-placed 8-12f winner Splinter Cell, useful 7.5f-1m 3yo winner Kohlaan and useful 7f 2yo winner Sultan Baybars out of a maiden sister to high-class French/US 8-10f winner (including at Group/Grade 2 level) Kirkwall; family of Dewhurst Stakes winner Distant Music and Coventry Stakes winner Calyx.

"Carmel Stud bought him as a foal with a view to selling him as a yearling last autumn, but the situation last year meant that they didn't take any of their yearlings to auction, so I have been very fortunate to receive some lovely two-year-olds as a result. This colt isn't overly big but is strong. We've had a look at him a couple of times and liked what we've seen. He is so laid-back - you give him a squeeze and he does all that you want but no more. I won't be rushing him as he's very nice."

MAKING MUSIC (IRE)
26/4 b f Mastercraftsman - Rapacity Alexander (Dandy Man)
Owner: Foursome Thoroughbreds Sales price: 75,000gns (Foursome Thoroughbreds)

Half-sister to Listed-placed 2020 Irish 7.5f 2yo winner No Speak Alexander. Dam a French 5f 2yo Listed winner who was a full sister to high-class UK/Hong Kong 5-6f winner (including at Group 1 level) Peniaphobia and a half-sister to Group 3/Listed-placed 5f 2yo winner Safari Sunset.

"I went out with the intention of buying a Mastercraftsman last autumn, and from a handful shortlisted she was the one we ended up buying. She is another we've already galloped and had a look at. Again, we liked what we saw and Martin (Dwyer) was especially complimentary about her. She is either a sprinting type or just an extremely good 7f horse."

MIGHTY AFRA (IRE)
30/3 b f Zoffany - Sweet Coconut (Bahamian Bounty)
Owner: Khalifa Dasmal Sales price: 34,000gns (Federico Barberini)

Third foal of an unraced sister to 6f 2yo Listed winner Bogart and a half-sister to Gimcrack Stakes winner Blaine, Group 3-placed 2020 6f 2yo winner Legal Attack, useful UK/Bahraini 6f-1m winner Byline, 7f 2yo winner Longton and the unraced dam of Group 2-placed 2020 7f 2yo winner Youth Spirit.

"She is owned by Khalifa Dasmal who is a new client introduced to me by my old assistant, David Simcock. We got chatting one day and he said that he would buy me a yearling - true to his word he did. This is a lovely, big filly, who we've only just started cantering but already like what we see. She won't be as early as some already mentioned but moves well and should be ok in time."

PROFOUND ALEXANDER (IRE)
17/2 gr f Kodiac - Smokey Quartz (Dark Angel)
Owner: Noel O'Callaghan Sales price: £17,000 (Not Sold)

First foal of a maiden half-sister to smart Irish 7f-1m winner (including at Group 3/Listed level) Making Light out of an Irish 12f 3yo winner who was a full sister to Group 1-placed 10-12f 3yo winner (including at Group 2/3 level) Irresistible Jewel (later dam of Irish St Leger winner Royal Diamond, Ribblesdale Stakes winner/Irish Oaks third Princess Highway and Irish 7f Group 3 winner Mad About You).

"Because I had bought Making Music who was bred and consigned by him, Noel O'Callaghan phoned and asked if I would like to train one for him, to which I said that I would love to. This is quite a sharp filly who should be early, though she hasn't yet done a huge amount as it took her a little time to settle in. We like how she goes and will have a proper look at her in a couple of weeks."

RED VINEYARD (IRE)
21/3 ch c Slade Power - Artisia (Peintre Celebre)
Owner: Foursome Thoroughbreds Sales price: €29,000 (Foursome Thoroughbreds)

Half-brother to high-class 12-14f winner (including the Hong Kong Vase)/three-time Melbourne Cup runner-up Red Cadeaux, Spanish 12f Listed winner Amazing Red and four other winners. Dam a thrice-raced maiden close relation to dual 5f 2yo Group 3 winner Almaty and the dam of Ascot Gold Cup winner Big Orange and half-sister to Hong Kong dual 10f Group 1 winner Military Attack and very useful 7-10f winner Impeller.

"This is probably the first time the mare has been back to a sprinting influence since she produced Red Cadeaux (by Cadeaux Genereux). We also trained a lovely horse called Impeller from this family a good few years ago. This is a gorgeous colt, and though not an early two-year-old, he is one I am looking forward to seeing at some point during the second part of the year."

RENEGADE ROSE (IRE)
5/2 b f Slade Power - Three D Alexander (Aqlaam)
Owner: Purple & Lilac Racing Sales price: 10,000gns (Vendor)

Half-sister to UK/Bahraini dual 6f winner Aurag. Dam a useful 5f 3yo winner who was a half-sister to Listed-placed multiple 6-7f winner Accession, very useful multiple 5-6f winner Robot Boy, fairly useful dual 6f winner Turn To Rock and fairly useful 6f-1m winner Yorkee Mo Sabee out of a Listed-placed multiple 5f winner.

"A really nice filly, who I think will prove a really good buy at 10k. She is by a sire who has done well for us, with Jack's Point the best of those we've had by him. This filly will also be a sprinter and should be out before the summer is here."

SALT TREATY (IRE)
22/3 ch c National Defense - Salty Sugar (Oasis Dream)
Owner: Muir Racing Partnership - Flemington Sales price: 22,000gns (William R Muir)

First foal of a maiden half-sister to Listed-placed 2020 Irish 5f 2yo winner Admiral Nelson out of a 6f 2yo Listed-winning half-sister to French 7f 2yo Listed winner Hung Parliament; family of Kentucky Derby winner Authentic, Diamond Jubilee Stakes winner Undrafted and US Grade 1 winners American Gal (7f, twice) and Seventh Street (8.5/9f).

"This colt is by a first-season sire and wasn't on my list at the sales, but I got talked into viewing him. He is a striking individual who has grown quite a lot since coming here. I doubt he will be early, but he has a great way of going and there's just something really nice about him. He could end up being smart and he wouldn't put me off getting another one by the sire."

STOCKPYLE
16/4 b c Oasis Dream - La Pyle (Le Havre)
Owner: La Pyle Partnership Sales price: 120,000gns (Vendor)

Half-brother to 2020 King Edward VII Stakes/Great Voltigeur Stakes winner/ St Leger third Pyledriver. Dam a French 10.5-11.5f 3yo winner who was a full sister to smart French/Irish 7-10f winner (including at Group 3/Listed level) Normandel and a half-sister to Grand Prix de Paris winner Mont Ormel out of an Irish 7f 2yo winning half-sister to 8/10f Group 1 winner Linngari.

"He is more forward than Pyledriver was at this stage. He is built like a sprinter - short-coupled and very strong - whereas Pyledriver is a tall, lengthy sort despite also being by a speed influence in Harbour Watch. I haven't asked him too many questions yet as I know the family takes time, but he is natural in all he does and has sat upsides a couple of times. He will be out earlier than Pyledriver and has enough toe to begin at 6f."

UNNAMED
26/4 b c Dark Angel - Ballymore Celebre (Peintre Celebre)
Owner: Carmel Stud Sales price: n/a

Half-brother to 6f 2yo Group 2 winner Anjaal, useful 5-5.5f winner Awesome, useful 10-12f winner Pintrada and 7f 2yo winner Samharry. Dam a French 11.5-13f 3yo winner who was a half-sister to Irish triple 10f Group 3 winner Nysaean, Irish 7f 2yo winner/National Stakes runner-up Celtic Cavalier and the dam of Italian 6f Group 3 winner Uruk and 12f Listed winner All The Aces.

"He has a lovely pedigree and is a big, strapping colt that has loads of presence and scope. I love the way he strides out and he has a cracking attitude. I really like him and hope to have him in action by the end of May or beginning of June over 6f."

JEDD O'KEEFFE

ELYMAS
21/2 ch c Mondialiste - Moghrama (Harbour Watch)
Owner: Exors of The Late Mr G Turnbull Sales price: 60,000gns (Jedd O'Keeffe)

First foal of an unraced half-sister to smart 6f-1m winner (including at Group 2/Listed level) Mythical Magic, smart UK/US 7-8.5f winner (including at Group 3 level) Esentepe, useful 7-8.5f winner Yojimbo and 6f 2yo winner Versaki out of a French 10.5f 3yo winning half-sister to French 6f 2yo Listed winner Mytographie.

"A strong colt who I like a lot. He shows plenty of speed and could start over 5f if we wanted him to, but I suspect we will just wait for the 6f races in May."

HILTS (IRE)
26/3 b c New Bay - Creme Anglaise (Motivator)
Owner: Ellipsis Sales price: 45,000gns (Ellipsis/Jedd O'Keeffe)

Half-brother to useful multiple 12f winner Point In Time. Dam a Listed-placed dual 10f winner who was a half-sister to Swedish triple 8/10f Listed winner Graffiti, German 10f 3yo Listed winner Reine Magique and 7f 2yo winner Read Federica out of a US 6f Listed winner; family of US six-time 8.5-10f Grade 1 winner Best Pal and US 6f Grade 1 winner Richter Scale.

"An athletic colt, who has a super temperament and is coming along really nicely. We gave him February off as he was very forward and isn't an early type. I wouldn't anticipate him running over anything shorter than 7f, and it's likely he will actually begin over 1m, though that's to be determined."

MYSTIC MOONSHADOW
16/3 b f Showcasing - Dream of Joy (Dream Ahead)
Owner: Bez's Racing Club Sales price: 27,000gns (Jedd O'Keeffe)

First foal of a thrice-raced maiden half-sister to high-class 8-12f winner (including twice at Grade 1 level) Wigmore Hall, German 10f 3yo Group 3 winner Lady Liberty, 2020 7f 3yo winner Long Haired Love and 2020 1m 2yo winner Ocean Road out of a 7f 2yo winning half-sister to French 1m 3yo Listed winner Kissing The Camera.

"I have been really pleased with her to this point, and she would be the most forward of our two-year-olds, though that isn't surprising given her pedigree. It all comes naturally to her and she could even be running at the end of April if all goes to plan. It's difficult to guage what sort of ability she has at this stage as the rest of ours are a little way behind her, but she has gone with a couple of older horses and held her own."

PRINCE ACHILLE
16/2 b c Reliable Man - Halle Bop (Dubai Millennium)
Owner: Normandie Stud Ltd Sales price: n/a

Three-parts brother to French 11f 3yo winner Princess Mathilde (by Dalakhani) and a half-brother to Group 3-placed Irish 9-10f winner (including at Listed level) Panstarr and 7f 3yo winner Highest Level. Dam a 6f 2yo winner who was half-sister to Group 2/Listed-placed 9.5f 3yo winner Queen of Naples out of a 10f 3yo Listed-winning half-sister to Derby winner Oath.

"A medium-sized, well put together colt who hasn't been here all that long, having been carefully broken in by Jane Allison. He won't be rushed given his pedigree but is a likeable individual who we are pleased to have."

ROLLAJAM (IRE)
22/3 ch c Belardo - Papaya (Teofilo)
Owner: John & Jess Dance Sales price: 65,000gns (Creighton Schwarz Bloodstock)

Half-brother to 2020 10f 3yo winner Pawpaw. Dam a maiden half-sister to very smart multiple 6f-1m winner (including at Group 1 level)/2000 Guineas runner-up Lend A Hand and Group 2-placed UK/UAE 8-11f winner Emirates Champion out of a 12f 3yo winner.

"I happened to get lucky with this colt. John Dance and I were recently discussing mating plans for his recently retired filly, Continental, who is off to be covered by Belardo. I told him that I'd seen a stunning yearling by that sire at the December sale, and how he was one of my favourites but that I couldn't recall who had bought him. By sheer luck it turned out to be John, and he kindly sent him to us. This is a beautiful colt with a lovely temperament who only came in at the end of February so won't be rushed. There's some stamina in his pedigree but he will likely begin over 6/7f."

UNNAMED (IRE)
1/5 b c Highland Reel - Destalink (Rail Link)
Owner: Highbeck Racing 5 Sales price: 16,000gns (Arthur Walker)

Third foal of a thrice-raced maiden close relation to Group 3-placed 7-14f winner (including at Listed level) Platitude, useful 7f-1m winner Intense and 2020 1m 2yo winner Surefire and half-sister to US 1m 1f Grade 3 winner Button Down and Group 3-placed UK/Saudi Arabian 8-12f winner Model Pupil out of a 14f 3yo Listed-winning half-sister to Oaks winner Reams of Verse, Eclipse Stakes winner Elmaamul and the dam of six-time 10-12f Group/Grade 1 winner Midday.

"A lovely colt, with a great conformation and a temperament to match. He is another we gave February off as he had coped so well with everything until then and there's no need to rush. We will almost certainly wait for the 1m races later, though it's not impossible he will start over 6f. I think he's an exciting prospect for the future."

UNNAMED (IRE)
24/1 b f Poet's Voice - Future Energy (Frankel)
Owner: B McAllister and A Walker Sales price: 21,000gns (Arthur Walker)

First foal of an unraced sister to French 1m 1f 3yo Listed winner Qazyna and half-sister to Australian 12f Group 2 winner Au Revoir, 8/10f Listed winner Perfect Stride and French 6f 2yo Listed winner Law Lord out of a French 1m 3yo Listed-winning half-sister to triple 6/7.5f Group 3 winner Bluebook and Nell Gwyn Stakes winner Myself.

"A strong-looking filly with a good page who isn't as forward as she perhaps looks. She might start over 6f, but it wouldn't be a surprise were we to just go straight in at 7f with her. She's entered for the Book 3 race at Newmarket in October, but that's over 6f and it remains to be seen if she is still running over that sort of trip by then."

UNNAMED (IRE)
7/3 b c Invincible Spirit - More Mischief (Azamour)
Owner: Caron & Paul Chapman Sales price: n/a

First foal of a 10f Listed winner who was a half-sister to Lancashire Oaks winner/Oaks fourth Horseplay and useful 10-11f Flat/Grade 1-placed triple 2m hurdle winner Devilment out of a Group 3-placed 9.5-13f winner (including at Listed level) who was a half-sister to dual 7f Listed winner That Is The Spirit (by Invincible Spirit) and Irish 6f 3yo Listed winner Khukri.

"A very strong colt, who took everything in his stride when being broken in. He is another we gave time off as he won't be an early type. His mum didn't run at all at two, though I think he almost certainly will. A very likeable individual and hopefully he can prove as good as More Mischief, who incidentally has a yearling filly also by Invincible Spirit."

UNNAMED (IRE)
29/3 ch c Churchill - Organza (Pour Moi)
Owner: Caron & Paul Chapman Sales price: n/a

Second foal of a 1m 3yo winner who was a half-sister to French 1m 3yo Listed winner Arctic Gyr, Group 3-placed 6f-1m winner (including at Listed level) Festivale, Group 3/Listed-placed 6f-1m winner Tell and useful 6f 2yo winner Simple Magic.

"A lovely big colt, with plenty of scope and strong with it. He looks the sort who you could press on with, but I suspect if you did then you'd create problems for him and he'd go weak. It isn't impossible he would have the speed to begin over 6f, though it's more likely he will start over 7f. He has patient owners and hopefully they've got another nice horse in this colt."

UNNAMED
15/2 b f Profitable - Passcode (Camacho)
Owner: The City & Provincial Partnership Sales price: £22,000 (Jedd O'Keeffe)

First foal of a 1m 3yo winner who was a half-sister to German 6f 2yo Group 2 winner Pomellato, St Leger Italiano winner Parivash, useful French 11.5f 3yo winner Pom Pom Pom (later dam of German 7f 2yo Listed winner Paloma Ohe) and useful UK/Saudi Arabian 8-12f winner Unwritten.

"This filly looks a proper two-year-old type. Whilst not overly big, she is a strong and powerfully-built individual who shows pace. I'd like to get her out sometime in May."

HUGO PALMER

ASEAN LEGEND (IRE)
5/3 b c Australia - Queenscliff (Danehill Dancer)
Owner: Boniface Ho Ka Kui Sales price: £78,000 (Avenue Bloodstock)

Full brother to 2020 Irish 7f 2yo winner Ace Aussie and a three-parts brother to Group 2/3-placed Irish 12-13f 3yo winner (including at Listed level) Giuseppe Garibaldi (by Galileo). Dam an Irish 1m 3yo winner who was a full sister to Group/Grade 1-placed Irish/US 7-8.5f winner (including three times at Group 3 level)/Irish 1000 Guineas third Carribean Sunset and Group 3/Listed-placed Irish 6-7f 2yo winner Snow Queen.

"If you'd spoken to me in January, I would have said he was backward and unlikely to run more than once at two. However, he has really started to develop and is now a well-proportioned colt who finds everything coming easily. His brother was a good two-year-old for Jessie Harrington last year, and hopefully he can also do something this year. He will probably begin over 7f in July."

CUBAN BEAT
13/2 b f Havana Gold - Stroll Patrol (Mount Nelson)
Owner: Qatar Racing Limited Sales price: n/a

Half-sister to 6f 2yo winner Hot Touch and 2020 7f 2yo winner Mused. Dam a Group 3-placed 6-6.5f winner who was a full sister to Group 3/Listed-placed UK/UAE 7f-1m winner Hors de Combat and a half-sister to four winners including 6f 2yo Group 3 winner Yourtimeisnow out of a thrice-raced maiden half-sister to US 1m 1f Grade 1 winner Stroll.

"I have trained everything out of the mare so far and though the first two foals weren't at all bad, this filly would easily be the biggest and strongest she has produced so far. She is a very attractive type who goes nicely, and I can see her running over 6/7f from July onwards."

DIG TWO (IRE)
28/3 ch c Cotai Glory - Vulnicura (Frozen Power)
Owner: Lit Lung Lee Sales price: £28,000 (SackvilleDonald)

Second foal of an unraced half-sister to Listed-placed Irish 9-9.5f 3yo winner Shifting out of an Italian 6f 2yo Group 3-winning daughter of a 10-14f winner who was a half-sister to the dam of dual 6f Group 3 winner Needwood Blade and US 1m Grade 3 winner Islay Mist.

"A sharp, forward colt, who is still up behind a little and not just an early two-year-old. It didn't quite go according to plan on his debut at Windsor on April 12. He rather sat back in the stalls and then showed signs of inexperience in the race itself and could never get himself on terms. I'd be hopeful he will improve quite a bit on that initial effort."

Dig Two

DUBAWI LEGEND (IRE)
19/4 b c Dubawi - Lovely Pass (Raven's Pass)
Owner: Dr Ali Ridha Sales price: n/a

Half-brother to useful 2020 10-11.5f 3yo winner Golden Pass and 2020 6f 2yo winner Ahlawi. Dam a Group 3-placed UK/UAE 6f-1m winner (including at Listed level) who was a sister to useful UK/UAE 7f-1m winner Almoreb and half-sister to smart 8-8.5f winner (including at Listed level) Spirit Raiser out of a smart 8-10f winner (including at Group 2/Listed level).

"I am quietly hopeful his dam could have a good year as I love the three and four-year-old siblings. The latter is rated 92 after just four runs and I hope she will be a black type performer this season. This colt is the standout individual the mare has produced to date in terms of physique. He is only doing half speeds at the moment and certainly isn't slow. For all not many Dubawis would begin over 5f, he probably could but I think we'll wait for the 6f races to begin."

EBRO RIVER (IRE)
25/1 ch c Galileo Gold - Soft Power (Balmont)
Owner: Al Shaqab Racing Sales price: 75,000gns (C Gordon Watson Bloodstock/Al Shaqab)

Half-brother to 5-6f winner Strong Power. Dam an Irish 7f 3yo winner who was a half-sister to Listed-placed Irish 6f 2yo winner Key Rose, very useful Irish 6-7.5f winner Empirical Power and the dam of Diamond Jubilee Stakes/July Cup winner Slade Power.

"A well-balanced colt, who looks sharp and has plenty of natural speed. He has already done a few bits of work and it all comes extraordinarily easy to him. It wouldn't surprise me if he started at the Craven meeting."

HERETIC (IRE)
20/2 ch c Galileo Gold - Al Jawza (Nathaniel)
Owner: Highclere Thoroughbred Racing - Lime Tree Sales price: £25,000 (Avenue Bloodstock)

First foal of a maiden sister to useful 2020 dual 10f 3yo winner Papa Power and half-sister to Listed-placed 6f-1m winner Rufus King and 2020 5f 2yo winner Madreselva out of a Listed-placed 1m 3yo winning daughter of a German dual 1m 3yo Listed winner.

"This colt is the image of his father. He has grown a lot recently which is good as there was a brief moment where he worried me in terms of his size, but he has caught up and is well-proportioned now. He has a lovely way of going and will definitely make some sort of impact this season, but he has enough scope to go on and be a nice horse next year as well."

JOKING
1/4 b f Time Test - Comic (Be My Chief)
Owner: Floors Stud Ltd Sales price: 50,000gns (SackvilleDonald)

Three-parts sister to useful UK/UAE 7-10f winner George Villiers and 8.5f 2yo winner Nice Future (both by Dubawi) and a half-sister to very smart UK/Hong Kong 6-12f winner (including eight times at Group 1 level) Viva Pataca, high-class Irish/US 8-11f winner (including twice at Grade 1 level) Laughing, Listed-placed 7f-1m 2yo winner Shambolic and the unraced dam of 14f Listed winner Twitch. Dam a 10-11.5f 3yo winner who was a half-sister to smart UK/US 7-10f winner (including at Grade 2/3 level) Brave Act.

"She has only just arrived from pre-training. An attractive filly, she ought to make a two-year-old despite not necessarily being bred to do so. She is the last foal out of a wonderful broodmare and hopefully she can go out on a high with this filly."

NEPTUNE LEGEND (IRE)
28/2 b c Invincible Spirit - Kate The Great (Xaar)
Owner: Boniface Ho Ka Kui Sales price: £350,000 (Avenue Bloodstock)

Three-parts brother to useful 7-7.5f winner New Strategy (by Lawman) and a half-brother to Group 1-placed 5-6f winner (including at Group 3/Listed level) Eastern Impact, Group 3-placed Irish/Canadian 6-6.5f winner (including at stakes level) Miss Katie Mae and Group 3/Listed-placed multiple 6f winner Summerghand. Dam a 5f 2yo winner who was a half-sister to Group 3/Listed-placed triple 6f winner/2000 Guineas fourth Bossy Guest and the dam of 1m Listed winner Another Touch.

"This a solid, good-sized colt who looks pretty sharp. He finds everything incredibly easy and actually reminds me a lot of Gifted Master at this stage. He is absolutely thriving on his work and it's hard to get to the bottom of him at the moment. I imagine he could easily begin over 5f if we needed him to, but he's not that sort of horse. He will probably kick off in May once the 6f events are here. I've liked everything I have seen from him so far."

NOVA LEGEND (IRE)
9/5 b c Galileo - Ghurra (War Chant)
Owner: Boniface Ho Ka Kui Sales price: 550,000gns (Avenue Bloodstock)

Half-brother to Prix Morny/Middle Park Stakes winner Shalaa. Dam a Grade 3-placed UK/US 6-8.5f winner who was closely related to Middle Park Stakes winner Hayil and useful 6f 2yo winner Farqad and a half-sister to Grade 2/3-placed 6-10f winner Tamhid, Listed-placed 7-7.5f 2yo winner Elnahaar and the grandam of Group 1-placed 6f-1m winner (including at Group 2/3 level) Dragon Pulse.

"He is a May foal by Galileo but is a lot more forward than those two facts would normally suggest. He is a strong, solid colt with a high opinion of himself. It isn't out of the question that he could be a Chesham Stakes horse if he continues to thrive."

NOVEL LEGEND (IRE)
8/3 b c Nathaniel - Majestic Dubawi (Dubawi)
Owner: Boniface Ho Ka Kui Sales price: £100,000 (Avenue Bloodstock)

Half-brother to 2020 7f 2yo Group 2/3 winner Isabella Giles and 2020 German triple 6.5/7f Listed winner Majestic Colt. Dam a 6f 2yo Group 3 winner who was the daughter of a twice-raced maiden half-sister to French 7f 3yo Listed winner South Rock (grandam of 7f/1m Group 2 winner Dark Vision and 6f 2yo Group 3 winner/Irish 2000 Guineas third Lope Y Fernandez).

"He was very backward at the beginning of the year, and I thought we'd be giving him a break about now, but he has thrived in recent weeks. Whilst not in full work, everything he has done to this point has come very easily to him which you wouldn't normally associate with Nathaniels at this stage. His dam won over 6f and had a couple of black type performers over 6/7f last season, so I suspect that's helping him in that regard. Saying that, I would be surprised if he started over shorter than 7f. One that we should see from August onwards."

Isabella Giles

POWER OF BEAUTY (IRE)
4/5 b c Slade Power - Beautiful Filly (Oasis Dream)
Owner: Dr Ali Ridha Sales price: n/a

Full brother to 7f 2yo winner Deira Surprise and a half-brother to 7f-1m winner (including at Group 2/Listed level) Unforgetable Filly, UAE 6f Group 3 winner Raven's Corner and useful UK/UAE 6-7f winner Speedy Move. Dam a 6-7f 3yo winner who was the daughter of a maiden half-sister to US 9.5f Grade 1 winner Fire The Groom (later dam of July Cup/Nunthorpe Stakes winner Stravinsky) and 6f Group 1 winner Dowsing.

"This colt is from a family we know well, having trained his half-sister to win the German 1000 Guineas. He has a lovely way of going and does it all very easily so far. I am hoping he could be another nice one from the mare."

SKY LEGEND
18/3 ch c Galileo - Spectre (Siyouni)
Owner: Boniface Ho Ka Kui Sales price: 450,000gns (Avenue Bloodstock)

First foal of a Group 1-placed French dual 7f winner (including at Group 3 level) who was a half-sister to useful 2020 10-12f 3yo winner Mambo Nights out of a German 1m 3yo winning half-sister to Mehl-Mulhens Rennen winner Irian and Geelong Cup winner Ibicenco; family of Deutsches Derby winner In Swoop and Preis der Diana winner Iota.

"This is a medium-sized, muscular colt. There is some speed in his family and he has the action of a quick horse. I think he could be very smart and will probably kick off over 7f in July."

STAR LEGEND (IRE)
13/4 b c Galileo - Thai Haku (Oasis Dream)
Owner: Boniface Ho Ka Kui Sales price: 450,000gns (Avenue Bloodstock)

Full brother to Irish 1m 3yo Listed winner Sarrocchi. Dam a French 1m 3yo Listed winner who was a full sister to Group 3-placed French 8-9f winner (including at Listed level) Albaraah (later dam of French 6f 2yo Group 3 winner/Prix Morny runner-up Alrahma and French 7f 3yo Group 3 winner Efaadah); family of Prix du Jockey Club winner Hernando.

"For a big colt he finds things very easy at the moment. All being well, he should be forward enough to run over 7f/1m before the end of the season."

SYDNEY STREET
3/3 b c Dark Angel - Minnaloushe (Lawman)
Owner: Chelsea Thoroughbreds Ltd Sales price: 60,000gns (Vendor)

Half-brother to useful 2020 6f 2yo winner She Do. Dam a US 1m 3yo winner who was a half-sister to Listed-placed French 7.5f 3yo winner Roscoff (later dam of 2020 Lancashire Oaks winner Manuela de Vega, Italian 7.5f 2yo Group 2 winner Hero Look, dual 12f Listed winner Isabella de Urbina and very useful multiple 1m winner Auxerre).

"A strong, attractive colt who loves his work and is thriving on it. He is one who we have to keep busy as he is very active. I could easily see him being a late May or June two-year-old and he is another that we like."

UNILATERALISM (IRE)
15/3 ch c Starspangledbanner - Barnet (Manduro)
Owner: Lit Lung Lee Sales price: 65,000gns (SackvilleDonald)

Second foal of an unraced half-sister to six winners out of a Yorkshire Oaks winner/St Leger runner-up who was a full sister to 10f 3yo winner/Chester Vase runner-up Arabian Gulf and Group 3-placed 12f 3yo winner Total Command; family of May Hill Stakes winner Half Glance.

"A very muscular, strong colt who looks sharp. I've only trained two horses by Starspangledbanner - one was multiple Group winner Home of The Brave and the other is The Rosstafarian, who is heading to the Craven having won on debut last year and acquiring a mark of 97. Let's hope lightning can strike thrice! This colt goes very well and would be among my favourites at present."

UNNAMED
22/4 b f Night of Thunder - Best Side (King's Best)
Owner: V I Araci Sales price: 70,000gns (Rob Speers/Old Mill Stud)

Half-sister to smart 7-10f winner (including at Group 3/Listed level) Azmeel, German 1m Listed winner Baisse (later dam of Australian 1m Group 1 winner Best of Days) and the dam of Irish 7f-1m winner/Irish 1000 Guineas third Foxtrot Liv. Dam a Listed-placed Irish 7f-1m winner who was a half-sister to Irish 10f 3yo Group 3 winner Grand Ducal and Listed-placed 6f 2yo winner Hurricane Floyd.

"She was actually the smallest of our two-year-olds but has come to hand very quickly. She is very competitive in her work and has acquitted herself well in the couple of little bits of work that she has done. I would be more than hopeful that she can make it out during the first half of the season."

UNNAMED (IRE)
28/1 b c Frankel - Hyper Dream (Oasis Dream)
Owner: V I Araci Sales price: 190,000gns (Not Sold)

First foal of a twice-raced maiden half-sister to Irish 1m 3yo Listed winner Emperor Claudius and the maiden dam of Irish 1m 1f 3yo Group 3 winner/Irish Oaks runner-up Rain Goddess out of a 1000 Guineas-winning half-sister to Irish 10f 3yo Group 3 winner/Irish Derby runner-up Alexander Of Hales, Group 1-placed Irish 1m 2yo winner Chevalier and the unraced dam of Matron Stakes winner Chachamaidee.

"I trained the dam who had plenty of ability though she had to retire before getting to win a race. This colt is just an average size which can happen with first foals, but he is a muscular individual who has done everything right so far. You don't necessarily associate Frankel with earlier types but I think this horse could be just that."

UNNAMED (IRE)
6/4 b c Dark Angel - Pandora's Box (Galileo)
Owner: Middleham Park Racing XCII Sales price: €85,000 (Avenue Bloodstock/ Middleham Park Racing)

Second foal of an unraced sister to Listed-placed French 12-12.5f winner Shada and half-sister to US 11f Listed winner Cold Cold Woman and the dam of Group 1-placed 6f-1m winner (including at Group 2/Listed level) Aljamaaheer; family of Irish Oaks winner Moonstone.

"A big, rangy colt, who is quite backward and more Galileo than Dark Angel to look at. Unfortunately, he recently required surgery, and though he is now back in the yard I suspect he is one for the backend of the year. He has always moved well."

KEVIN PHILIPPART DE FOY

ADORABLE YOU (IRE)
9/3 b f Zarak - Embraceable You (New Approach)
Owner: Normandie Stud Ltd Sales price: n/a

First foal of an unraced three-parts sister to Group 2/Listed-placed 1m 2yo winner Fallen In Love (later dam of French 10.5f Group 3 winner Loving Things) and half-sister to Coronation Stakes winner Fallen For You (later dam of dual 7f Group 2 winner Glorious Journey and 2020 7f 2yo Listed winner Love Is You) and smart 7-10f winner (including at Listed level) Fallen Idol.

"She is from one of Philippa Cooper's lovely families. It doesn't produce many early types, but they are very often lovely racehorses. Her sire was a beautifully-bred horse, who has everything in his favour to make a good stallion. This is a good-moving filly who is growing all the time and will need time, but she has a great attitude and I like her. She will debut in the summer."

CHIQUEADOR (IRE)
27/3 b f Decorated Knight - Grain de Beaute (Lawman)
Owner: Kevin Philippart de Foy Sales price: £20,000 (Philippa Mains/Kevin Philippart)

Half-sister to Listed-placed 2020 French 1m 3yo winner Beaute Pour Toi and 2020 Italian 6-7.5f 2yo winner Sa Pala Umbrossa. Dam an Italian 6f 2yo winner who was closely related to Group 2-placed 5-6f winner (including at Group 3/Listed level) Beyond Desire (later dam of 5f Listed winner Queen Of Desire); family of Irish 2000 Guineas winner Mastercraftsman.

"She was bought from the Irish National Stud and was my pick of the sale we got her from. She is a well-balanced, easy-moving filly, who'll debut over 6f in late May or June but will stay further than that in time."

NEW PURSUIT (IRE)
3/5 ch c New Bay - Soliza (Intikhab)
Owner: Run Away Racing Quest Syndicate Sales price: 30,000gns (Avenue Bloodstock/Kevin Philippart)

Half-brother to useful 12f-2m 4f Flat/2m-3m hurdle/2m 1f chase winner Domination, useful 8-10.5f winner Nayel and 10f 2yo winner Mahab El Shamaal. Dam an Irish triple 10f 3yo winner who was a half-sister to Hong Kong 8/10f Group 1 winner Helene Mascot, Listed-placed 10-12f winner Ovambo and the maiden dam of six-time 8-10.5f Group 1 winner/1000 Guineas runner-up Laurens.

"New Bay had a great first season as a sire. I liked this colt a lot at the sales and have been very pleased with him. He will probably debut over 6f in May with the idea of stepping up to 7f during the summer. I can see him running only a couple of times at two, and we will train him with a three-year-old career in mind."

NICHOLAS GEORGE
1/4 ch c Reliable Man - Carisolo (Dubai Millennium)
Owner: Normandie Stud Ltd Sales price: n/a

Three-parts brother to very useful 8.5-13f winner Wadi Al Hattawi and French 11f 3yo winner Riva Snows (by Dalakhani) and a half-brother to three winners. Dam a twice-raced maiden half-sister to Irish Oaks winner/Oaks runner-up Moonstone (later dam of Chester Vase winner/Derby runner-up US Army Ranger), Prix Saint-Alary winner Cerulean Sky (later dam of Doncaster Cup winner/St Leger third Honolulu) and Irish 12f 3yo Listed winner/Irish Oaks runner-up L'Ancresse (later dam of Irish 14f Group 3/Listed winner/Ascot Gold Cup third Master of Reality).

"He is not here yet but I saw him last week and he's a big, strong horse. He is growing and developing a lot at the moment and is going to make a nice three-year-old, so he is going to be one for later in the year."

POKHARA (IRE)
6/5 b f The Gurkha - Shagra (Pivotal)
Owner: Run Away Racing Himalayan Syndicate Sales price: £15,000 (Philippa Mains/Kevin Philippart)

Half-sister to once-raced French 9.5f 3yo winner Hayyan. Dam an unraced half-sister to Group 3-placed Italian 9-10f winner Sufranel and Irish dual 5f 2yo winner Natalisa out of an Irish 6/7.5f Group 3-winning sister to very smart 5-6f winner (including at Group 1 level) Namid and a half-sister to Group 3-placed Irish 7f 2yo winner Natalis and Listed-placed Irish 7f 2yo winner Mandama.

"A strong, sharp filly and looks like being an early two-year-old. She will debut over 5f with the idea of stepping her up to 6f. I can see her running before May."

SMOOTH CHARMER
4/2 b c Aclaim - Velvet Charm (Excelebration)
Owner: C J Murfitt Sales price: £9,000 (Not Sold)

First foal of a maiden half-sister to UK/Irish 7f-1m winner The Game of Life out of a maiden half-sister to Dubai World Cup winner Moon Ballad, useful 1m 3yo winner Velvet Lady and the unraced dam of Group 1-placed 8-12f winner (including at Group 2/Listed level) Telescope.

"A well-balanced colt who isn't overly big but is strong. He is showing a great attitude to his work and I can see him doing well this season. I should think he will be out over 5f before May."

UNNAMED (IRE)
19/4 b f Fascinating Rock - Legal Lyric (Lawman)
Owner: A Syndicate Sales price: £15,000 (KPF Racing Ltd)

Half-sister to very useful 7f-1m winner Haqeeqy. Dam an Irish dual 6.5f winner who was a half-sister to German 10f Group 2/3 winner Fight Club, German 10f 3yo Group 3 winner Flambo, useful UK/Swedish 7f-1m winner Bullwhip, useful UK/Australian triple 12f winner Fairlight and 7f 2yo winner Adelasia.

"This filly is a half-sister to Haqeeqy, who obviously won the Lincoln on the first day of the season. She is a lovely filly though one we have to keep a lid on, but then Haqeeqy used to be quite hot early and has settled down a lot now. I hope to see this filly debut in May over 6f, and though she will develop with more time, she is a good mover who shows a great attitude in her work."

UNNAMED (IRE)
21/1 b c Vadamos - Zakyah (Exceed And Excel)
Owner: A Syndicate Sales price: 23,000gns (Kevin Ross Bloodstock)

Half-brother to 5f 2yo winner Gifted Zebedee. Dam a maiden half-sister to once-raced 1m 3yo winner Subaana and the maiden dam of 2020 1m 3yo Listed winner/1000 Guineas runner-up Cloak of Spirits out of an 8.5f 3yo winning close relation to very smart 6f-1m winner (including the Irish 2000 Guineas)/Derby third Dubawi and a half-sister to Lancashire Oaks winner Emirates Queen.

"A very strong colt we bought from Tally-Ho Stud at Book 3 of the Tattersalls October Yearling Sale. He is well-balanced, moves really well and is one that I particularly like at this stage. He will debut sometime in June."

JONATHAN PORTMAN

ARDITA
15/4 b f Ardad - Royal Circles (Royal Applause)
Owner: Berkeley Dollar Powell Sales price: £1,500 (J Portman)

Half-sister to UK/Italian multiple 5f winner Pharaoh. Dam an unraced sister to very useful multiple 6-7f winner Right Touch and a half-sister to very useful multiple 1m winner (including at Listed level) Forgive and useful 5-6f winner Loki's Revenge out of a 5f 3yo winning half-sister to 6f Group 2 winner Acclamation.

"She is tiny and was therefore a very cheap purchase. She comes from the family of Acclamation, and that's about all she has going for her on looks and paper, apart from the fact that the sire could be anything. She has a very workmanlike attitude and can hopefully defy logic and give us some fun."

BABY BAY
30/1 ch f New Bay - Albertine Rose (Namid)
Owner: Jaliza Partnership Sales price: 5,000gns (J Portman)

Half-sister to fairly useful multiple 5f winner Seneca Chief and Irish 5f 2yo winner Paytheprice. Dam a Listed-placed 6f 2yo winner who was a half-sister to useful 8-9.5f winner Anton Chigurh and 7f-1m winner Whitechapel.

"She is not very big but moves well and has a great attitude. I hope she'll give her owners some fun from the early summer over 6f."

BELISA DE VEGA (IRE)
17/3 b f Fascinating Rock - Royal Razalma (Lope de Vega)
Owner: One More Moment of Madness Sales price: £22,000 (Jonathan Portman)

Half-sister to 2020 Irish 7f 3yo winner Royal Pippen. Dam a 5f 2yo Group 3 winner who was a half-sister to Irish/Hong Kong 6f-1m winner Intellectualstride and useful triple 5f 2yo winner Visterre out of a Listed-placed Irish triple 7f winner.

"This filly is growing and strengthening by the day and looks a nice type for later in the summer. We trained the dam to win the Cornwallis Stakes, but this filly has more scope and will want further than five furlongs."

ELITE ETOILE
14/3 br g Vadamos - Way To The Stars (Dansili)
Owner: Mrs Suzanne Williams & Partner Sales price: £16,000 (J Portman)

Half-brother to useful 8-9.5f winner Precision Storm. Dam a maiden half-sister to South African five-time 8-11f Grade 1 winner Dancer's Daughter, 7f 2yo Group 3 winner Diktatorial, 1m 1f 3yo winner Stands To Reason and the dam of South African dual 6f Grade 2 winner Search Party out of a Group 3/Listed-placed 5-5.5f 2yo winner.

"He looks like a three-year-old already so will take some time but is a handsome sort who I really like."

ICKYTOO
3/4 b f Heeraat - Icky Woo (Mark of Esteem)
Owner: Cr Lambourn, M Forbes, D Losse & Partners Sales price: 22,000gns (J Portman)

Half-sister to US 12f Grade 3 winner Ickymasho and Group 2/3-placed Australian 7-10f winner Harbour Views. Dam an unraced half-sister to Group 2-placed 6-7f winner Zilch and useful 5-6f 2yo winner Silca Boo (later dam of 6f Listed winner Lightscameraction) out of a 5/6f Group 3 winner.

"She is a half-sister to our nice handicapper, Ickymasho. She is a big girl who will need plenty of time, but we like her."

INFINITE APPEAL
21/4 b f Equiano - Shy Appeal (Barathea)
Owner: Wood Street Syndicate Sales price: 3,800gns (Not Sold)

Half-sister to useful 6-7f winner Quick Breath and fairly useful 8-12f winners Bold Appeal and Broad Appeal. Dam a maiden half-sister to Italian 6f 3yo Group 3 winner Victory Laurel out of a French 7f 3yo winning half-sister to German 6f 2yo Listed winner Shy Lady (later dam of St James's Palace Stakes winner/2000 Guineas runner-up Zafeen).

"This filly gets a mention because we are pretty married to the family, having had her siblings, Broad Appeal and Quick Breath, win plenty for us. We also have her year-older half-sister, Broadhaven, who will hopefully do the same. This filly is quite small and compact, unlike the others, so might be a little earlier."

MILD REFLECTION
20/2 b f Aclaim - Drift And Dream (Exceed And Excel)
Owner: Berkeley Racing Sales price: 13,000gns (J Portman)

Half-sister to 5f 3yo winner Lucky Charm. Dam a fairly useful 5-6f winner who was a half-sister to useful 7f-1m winner Monsea and fairly useful 6-7f winner Ocean Gift out of a 7f 3yo winning half-sister to Listed-placed 5-6f 2yo winner Vikings Bay and the unraced dam of Middle Park Stakes winner Dark Angel.

"She is a decent size and strong with a great attitude. Whilst not being the best of movers, we are very positive about her at this stage."

NEVER NO TROUBLE
8/2 b f Time Test - Kitba (New Approach)
Owner: A Brooke Rankin Sales price: 6,000gns (Vendor)

Second foal of a maiden half-sister to Group 3-placed 10f-2m winner Aajel and fairly useful 12f-2m 1f winner Lady Hestia out of a 14f 3yo winning sister to the dam of Breeders' Cup Filly & Mare Turf winner Lahudood; family of Nashwan, Nayef, Ghanaati etc.

"She has done really well physically since her appearance at the yearling sales, where we bought her privately. It will say plenty about the prospects of the sire if he can put some quality into the mix here. She will be better over 7f to start with, I imagine, but she should have a chance."

OCEAN POTION
16/4 b c Havana Gold - Sunburnt (Haafhd)
Owner: Absolute Solvents Ltd Sales price: 4,500gns (Not Sold)

Half-brother to Hong Kong multiple 6f winner Speed Vision and fairly useful French/UK multiple 5-6f winner Tan. Dam a maiden half-sister to Group 1-placed UK/Hong Kong 7f-1m winner Chater Way, useful UK/Hong Kong 7f-1m winner Beauty Prince and the dam of 7f 3yo Listed winner/Coventry Stakes runner-up Headway (by Havana Gold).

"He moves well and is a handy-sized, compact colt who is looking an early type."

ROMANTIC MEMORIES
20/4 b f Time Test - Midnight Fling (Groom Dancer)
Owner: S Emmet and Miss R Emmet Sales price: 6,000gns (Vendor)

Half-sister to dual 5f 2yo winner Bridge Night, 6-7f 3yo winner Ivadream and 7f-1m winner Intimately. Dam a maiden half-sister to smart multiple 5-7f winner (including at Group 3/Listed level) Definightly.

"This filly is worth a mention due to Time Test who seems to have stamped some quality on this girl. She comes from a hardy, winning but equally fairly modest family. I saw her as a yearling and then received her in early spring and the difference was amazing, I just have a good feel about her and the sire."

SIENNA BONNIE (IRE)
23/1 b f Kodi Bear - Cucuma (Invincible Spirit)
Owner: Mrs Suzanne Williams & Partner Sales price: 4,000gns (J Portman)

Fourth foal of a French 5f 2yo winner who was a half-sister to US 1m Stakes winner Kencumin out of a Group 3-placed 7f 2yo winning sister to Grade 3/Listed-placed US 5.5f-1m winner Obsequious.

"She is tiny but very tough and has some speed, so could be an early type."

SULEVIA
19/4 b f Pearl Secret - Lightable (Shamardal)
Owner: Chapel Stud & Partners Sales price: Not Sold

Second foal of an unraced three-parts sister to Group 1-placed 8-10f winner Felix out of an unraced close relation to Group 3-placed Irish 7f 2yo winner Devotion (dam of 2020 UAE 1000 Guineas winner Dubai Love); family of Poule d'Essai des Poulains winner Make Believe and 6f Group 1 winner Tante Rose.

"She attracted no interest at Book 4 of the Tattersalls October Yearling Sale, but she is a very likeable individual with a bit of strength and scope."

TIDDLYWINX (IRE)
1/4 b f Fascinating Rock - Deviate (Acclamation)
Owner: Old Stoic Racing Club & Partner Sales price: £4,500 (J Portman)

First foal of a 5f 2yo winner who was a sister to Listed-placed 5f 2yo winner Reroute out of a useful Irish 5f 3yo winning half-sister to Hong Kong 12f Group 2 winner Supreme Rabbit, Listed-placed Irish 7f 3yo winner Dangle, Listed-placed 6f 2yo winner Bahati (later dam of five-time 7f/1m Listed winner Tabarrak) and useful Irish 7f 2yo winner Devious Diva (later dam of triple 7/7.5f Group 3 winner Realtra).

"This filly is another who is quite diminutive. Her dam was similar but tough and speedy with it. The sire might mean she is not quite so precocious and speedy, but she has hinted the ability is there somewhere."

UNNAMED
29/1 gr c Hellvelyn - Rebecca de Winter (Kyllachy)
Owner: Mark & Connie Burton Sales price: n/a

Full brother to smart multiple 5f 2yo winner (including at Group 3/Listed level) Mrs Danvers. Dam a 5f 2yo winner who was a half-sister to 6f 2yo Listed winner Izzthatright; family of 2yo Listed winners Soiree (7.5f) and Solaboy (6f).

"This colt deserves a mention simply for the fact that he's a full brother to our unbeaten 2yo, Mrs Danvers. This chap is bigger and will need more time but has a great attitude."

SIR MARK PRESCOTT

ALPENBLUME
25/2 gr f Kendargent - Alwilda (Hernando)
Owner: Miss K Rausing Sales price: n/a

Half-sister to Group 1-placed 7-10f winner (including at Listed level) Alpinista. Dam a German 2m 3f Listed winner who was a half-sister to 11f 3yo Group 3/Listed winner Algometer, 2020 12.5f Listed winner Alignak, French triple 10/10.5f Listed winner All At Sea and Listed-placed 8.5f 2yo winner Albamara.

"A half-sister to our good filly Alpinista, who finished second to Love in the Yorkshire Oaks last summer and now has an official rating of 113. The mother was an incredibly strong stayer and, like her, this filly isn't overly big but attractive with it at least. I would like to think she will be running in June or July over 7f."

ANATOMIC
10/4 gr c Ulysses - Diagnostic (Dutch Art)
Owner: Cheveley Park Stud Sales price: n/a

First foal of a useful 6-7f winner who was a half-sister to useful dual 7f winner Homeopathic out of an unraced sister to 6f Listed winner Prescription and half-sister to 7f 2yo Group 3 winner Cupid's Glory, smart 7-8.5f winner (including at Group 3/Listed level) Clinical (later dam of 7f 2yo winner/Mehl-

Mulhens Rennen runner-up Lockheed) and 8/10f Listed winner Courting (later dam of 1m Listed winner Fury).

"A big, strong horse from the first crop of Ulysses. William Haggas trained the mother with great success, but I have trained most of this family, from Cupid's Glory, to On Call, to Clinical. It is a marvellous, tough family. I didn't turn him away as I tend to do with a lot of big, backward two-year-olds as I felt he was coming along nicely. He bowls along well and I imagine he will debut over 7f."

ARCADIAN FRIEND
6/2 b c Lope de Vega - Best Friend (Galileo)
Owner: John Pearce Racing Ltd Sales price: n/a

Second foal of an unraced sister to high-class 7-12f winner (including three times at Group 1 level) Lush Lashes and Listed-placed Irish 1m 3yo winner Claudio Monteverdi and half-sister to useful multiple 5f-1m winner Scottish Glen; family of Deutsches Derby winner Buzzword.

"A very big horse who we've turned away. He will come back in mid-May and enter training in mid-June with the view to having a run or two at the backend."

BUTTRESS
2/2 b f Ulysses - Vaulted (Kyllachy)
Owner: Cheveley Park Stud Sales price: n/a

First foal of an 8.5f 3yo winner who was a half-sister to Group 1-placed 7f-1m winner (including twice at Group 2 level)/1000 Guineas runner-up Spacious (later dam of a 10f 3yo Listed winner Gabr), Canadian triple 7f/1m Grade 2 winner Dimension, useful 7f-1m winner Artimino and 7f 2yo winner Verandah.

"This isn't a Cheveley Park family I have had much to do with. She is like a lot of my two-year-olds in that they won't make early two-year-olds but nor will they be overly late either. This filly goes nicely and I should think she will begin around July time over 7f."

DAWAHY (IRE)
9/2 ch f Bated Breath - Rahaala (Indian Ridge)
Owner: H H Shaikh Nasser Al Khalifa & Partner Sales price: £35,000 (Oliver St Lawrence Bloodstock)

Half-sister to Irish 1m 3yo Flat/2m 2f hurdle winner Insane Bolt. Dam a maiden half-sister to smart 6f-1m winner (including at Group 2/Listed level) Mythical Magic, smart UK/US 7-8.5f winner (including at Group 3 level) Esentepe, useful 7-8.5f winner Yojimbo and 6f 2yo winner Versaki.

"A medium-sized, attractive filly with a nice pedigree and a pleasant nature. She had sore shins early on but is over that now. I would imagine she will be running over 7f in the autumn, and I think she could be rather nice though I haven't got any proof of that yet."

DENNING
4/3 ch c Recorder - Undress (Dalakhani)
Owner: B Haggas Sales price: n/a

Fourth foal of a twice-raced maiden half-sister to 7f 2yo winner Colour Party out of a US 8.5f 3yo winning sister to Oaks winner/Irish Oaks third Casual Look (later dam of US 1m 1f Grade 3 winner Casual Smile) and French 10f 3yo Listed winner Shabby Chic (later dam of Oaks d'Italia winner Fashion Statement).

"His sire won the Acomb Stakes for William Haggas as a two-year-old. His father, Brian, bred and owns this horse and certainly wins the award for best-named horse in the yard. The judicial enquiry into the Profumo affair was called the Denning Report and the mare is called Undress! This colt is a thoroughly pleasant individual who has always been entirely straightforward to deal with. Whatever level of ability he may possess, he will fulfil it. He is another who will begin over 7f."

GLENISTER (IRE)
15/3 b c Gleneagles - Sistine (Dubai Destination)
Owner: Elite Racing Club Sales price: n/a

Half-brother to Listed-placed 7f 2yo winner Dark Acclaim, 2020 12f 3yo winner Viola and 13-14f 3yo winner Mon Frere. Dam a 14f winner who was a three-parts sister to 1m 1f Group 3 winner Tarfah (later dam of 2000 Guineas/Derby winner Camelot) and a half-sister to very useful 10-14f winner Nautilus out of a 10f 3yo Listed winner.

"We trained Mon Frere to win a couple of races, and he's now jumping with Paul Nicholls. This colt has a bit more pace and is far more likely to make a two-year-old, given that he is another who we've kept in training for the duration of the spring. He goes along nicely."

NOBLE MARK (IRE)
6/2 ch g Animal Kingdom - Above The Mark (Street Cry)
Owner: Jones, Julian, Lee & Royle Sales price: £37,000 (Barry Lynch)

First foal of a US 1m winner who was a full sister to 2021 UAE 14f Group 3 winner Volcanic Sky and Listed-placed 7f 2yo winner Minidress (dam of 2021 UAE Derby winner Rebel's Romance) out of a 10.5/12f Group 3 winner/Oaks third who was a half-sister to high-class middle-distance performers Little

Rock and Whitewater Affair (later dam of Satsuki Shō/Dubai World Cup winner Victoire Pisa and Yasuda Kinen winner Asakusa Den'en).

"We had to geld him quite early as he was rather full of himself. He is a robust individual who always struck me as the type who would go nicely. Unfortunately, he pulled a muscle a couple of weeks ago and that's held him up, otherwise we would have started working him fairly soon. Therefore, he will be late on parade and begin working sometime in June."

NORTH LINCOLN (IRE)
14/2 b c Acclamation - Molly Dolly (Exceed And Excel)
Owner: Timothy J Rooney Sales price: 40,000gns (Vendor)

Full brother to 2020 7f 2yo winner Il Bandito. Dam a very useful 7-7.5f 3yo winner who was the daughter of a maiden half-sister to Irish 1m 3yo Listed winner Swift Gulliver, US 5/5.5f Listed winner Abderian and Listed-placed Irish 6f 2yo winner Minatonic.

"A very big horse who will be a nice three-year-old. Whatever he does at two is a bonus, but he's one we actually kept in training and I imagine he will be running in July or August."

OMNISCIENT
9/4 b c Mukhadram - Miss Dashwood (Dylan Thomas)
Owner: Ne'er Do Wells VII Sales price: 52,000gns (Barry Lynch/Heath House)

Half-brother to smart 8.5f-2m winner (including at Group 2/3 level) Dashing Willoughby. Dam a useful 8.5-12f winner who was a half-sister to high-class 10-10.5f winner (including twice at Group 1 level) Speedy Boarding, very useful dual 10f 3yo winner Elwazir and useful dual 1m winner Next Stage out of an 11f Listed-winning half-sister to Group 1-placed 8-10f winner (including at Listed level) Dash To The Top (later dam of Oaks winner Anapurna).

"He was a plain old thing at auction, and I think I was the only one bidding against the vendor. He is a big, strong, powerful individual who is very much a three-year-old type, which is what his pedigree suggests he should be."

PRETENDING (IRE)
21/4 gr f Make Believe - Gala (Galileo)
Owner: Denford Stud Sales price: n/a

Half-sister to 2021 9.5f 3yo winner Queen Charlotte. Dam a 12f 3yo winner who was the daughter of a Listed-placed French 9.5-10.5f 3yo winning close relation to the unraced dam of French 7f 2yo Group 3 winner Lixirova and half-sister to Czech Derby winner Gontchar and French 12f Listed winner Mashoor.

"A well-bred filly whose half-sister won earlier in the year for John Gosden. She will be a nice three-year-old but might have come to hand by the late autumn as she goes well enough."

SPECTATRICE
22/4 b f Fast Company - Songerie (Hernando)
Owner: Miss K Rausing Sales price: n/a

Half-sister to very useful 11.5f-2m winner Summer Moon, useful 12-13f winner Hardstone and 1m 2yo winner Valitop. Dam a French 1m 2yo Group 3 winner who was a full sister to German 12f Listed winner Souvenance and a half-sister to French 9.5f 3yo Listed winner Soft Morning and Swedish 8.5f 3yo Listed winner Sourire out of a 6f 3yo winning half-sister to French 5.5f 2yo Group 3 winner/Queen Mary Stakes runner-up Starlit Sands.

"Her mother won the Prix des Reservoirs for us and only just missed out on being a very good filly, having finished fourth behind Alexander Goldrun in the Nassau Stakes. She was tall and narrow, and this filly has inherited those physical traits to an even greater extent if anything. A light, good-actioned filly who will appreciate fast ground, I should think she will be appearing mid-late summer."

UNNAMED (FR)
22/1 b f Muhaarar - Chanterelle (Trempolino)
Owner: KHK Racing Ltd Sales price: €200,000 (Oliver St Lawrence)

Half-sister to Group 1-placed 11f-2m winner (including five times at Group 2 level) Enbihaar, Group 2-placed 7f-1m winner Silent Attack, Listed-placed UK/Bahraini 8.5-12f winner King Bolete and fairly useful 2020 8-10f 3yo winner Motamayiz. Dam a once-raced maiden sister to French 7f Group 3/Listed winner Cox Orange (later dam of 1m 3yo Listed winner/1000 Guineas third Vista Bella) and half-sister to Prix Marcel Boussac winner Amonita.

"This filly possesses a good, long action. She might be sharp enough to achieve something as a two-year-old but will very much come into her own at three. I can't see her running before September but she goes well and I think she is a rather nice filly."

UNNAMED (FR)
10/2 b f Almanzor - Penny Lane (Lord of England)
Owner: H H Shaikh Nasser Al Khalifa & Partner Sales price: €250,000 (Oliver St Lawrence)

First foal of a French 1m 2yo Listed winner who was a three-parts sister to German 1m 3yo Group 3 winner Peaceful Love (dam of 2020 French 1m 1f

3yo Group 3 winner Pao Alto) and half-sister to Group 2-placed German 7f-1m winner (including at Group 3/Listed level) Peace Royale (later dam of German 8.5f Group 3 winner/German 1000 Guineas runner-up Peace In Motion) and Group 2/Listed-placed 13f 3yo winner Phiz.

"She is by a sire whose first crop was very popular at the sales. This filly goes nicely and is another one that will likely start off over 7f around July time."

KEVIN RYAN

Thank you to *Megan Nicholls* for helping to assemble the following list of two-year-olds from Kevin's Hambleton Lodge base.

ALIA CHOICE
1/3 b f Dark Angel - Queen Kindly (Frankel)
Owner: Jaber Abdullah Sales price: n/a

First foal of a Lowther Stakes-winning daughter of a Group 1-placed 5-6f winner (including at Group 2/3 level) who was a half-sister to Listed-placed German/UK multiple 9-14f winner Kings Advice and very useful UK/German multiple 5-7f winner Sanaadh out of a Cheveley Park Stakes winner.

"She hasn't been here long but is a nice size for a first foal and obviously has a lovely pedigree. I am looking forward to seeing what she can do."

ASAAYIL
23/2 ch f Pride of Dubai - Camargue (Invincible Spirit)
Owner: Emirates Park Pty Ltd Sales price: n/a

First foal of a 5f 2yo winner who was a half-sister to Group 1-placed 6f-1m winner (including at Group 2/Listed level) Threading out of an unraced sister to top-class 8-10f winner (including three times at Group 1 level) Dubai Millennium and the unraced dam of Group 1-placed 7f-2m winner (including twice at Group 3 level)/Derby runner-up Dee Ex Bee.

"She is by the same sire as our Sweet Solera winner, Star of Emaraaty, and looks a lot like her at this stage. A compact filly who goes along nicely, she should be out in the early summer."

HELLO JUMBO
4/4 gr c Brazen Beau - Gone Sailing (Mizzen Mast)
Owner: T A Rahman Sales price: £22,000 (Hillen/Ryan)

Half-brother to Group 2/3-placed multiple 5-6f winner (including at Listed level) Major Jumbo, useful 2020 6f 2yo winner Uncle Jumbo and three other winners. Dam an unraced daughter of a 7f 3yo winning half-sister Australian triple 8-10f Group 1 winner Foreteller, French 7f 2yo Group 2 winner/Poule d'Essai des Pouliches fourth Modern Look (later dam of US 8.5f Grade 3 winner Grand Jete) and 6f 3yo Listed winner Arabesque (later dam of Gimcrack Stakes winner Showcasing).

"A big, strong colt, who is very similarly stamped to his classy half-brother, Major Jumbo. We've obviously had plenty of success with the family, and this colt should follow in their footsteps on what we've seen so far."

KING OF YORK (IRE)
8/2 b c Kingman - Archangel Gabriel (Arch)
Owner: Sheikh Mohammed Obaid Al Maktoum Sales price: 350,000gns (Kevin Ryan)

Half-brother to 2020 7f-1m 3yo winner Angel of The Glen and 2020 6f 2yo winner Ville de Grace. Dam an unraced sister to US 11f Grade 1 winner Prince Arch and the dam of Irish 1m Group 3 winner Pincheck and 2020 Irish 7f 3yo Group 3 winner Valeria Messalina and half-sister to Irish 7f 2yo Group 1 winner Kingsfort.

"A sizeable colt who we won't be in any rush with. He has done everything nicely up to now and will be one for the second half of the season."

MELAYU KINGDOM (IRE)
2/3 ch c Mehmas - Lauren's Girl (Bushranger)
Owner: Michael Reilly Sales price: n/a

Half-brother to Canadian 1m 2yo Grade 1 winner La Pelosa. Dam an unraced half-sister to French 6.5f 2yo Group 3 winner Perugina and Group 3-placed French 12.5f 3yo winner Sovana (later dam of Group 1-placed Irish 8-10f winner (including at Group 2/3 level) Bocca Baciata, French 7f 2yo Group 3 winner/Poule d'Essai des Pouliches third Topeka and French 1m Group 3 winner Kalsa).

"A typically sharp and compact son of Mehmas, who has done everything nicely at home. He shows plenty of speed and won't be long in making his first appearance."

MERLIN'S LADY (IRE)
4/2 b f Camelot - Mora Bai (Indian Ridge)
Owner: Sheikh Mohammed Obaid Al Maktoum Sales price: 320,000gns (Kevin Ryan)

Full sister to Grade 1-placed 10-12.5f winner (including at Group 2/3 level) Hunting Horn and a half-sister to Group 1-placed 7-10.5f winner (including at Group 2/3 level) David Livingston. Dam an unraced sister to Listed-placed Irish 7f 2yo winner Treasure The Lady (grandam of 2020 Irish 7f 3yo Group 3 winner Love Locket) and half-sister to six-time 7-12f Group/Grade 1 winner High Chaparral, Dante Stakes winner Black Bear Island and the dam of 2020 Prix de Diane winner Fancy Blue.

"A gorgeous, big filly, who has done everything asked of her to this point, though we're not in any sort of hurry with her. She doesn't lack speed but is very much one for the second half of the season."

RAVENSWING (IRE)
1/3 b c Dark Angel - Future Generation (Hurricane Run)
Owner: Sheikh Mohammed Obaid Al Maktoum Sales price: 180,000gns (Kevin Ryan)

Half-brother to smart 10-15f winner (including at Group 2/Listed level) Brundtland. Dam an Irish 1m 3yo Group 3 winner who was a half-sister to Group 3-placed Irish 7f 2yo winner Rasmeyaa out of an unraced half-sister to French 6f Group 3 winner Do The Honours (grandam of Melbourne Cup winner Cross Counter) and Chesham Stakes winner Seba.

"A really athletic colt, who has a sizeable frame to fill. He is a lovely mover and one we are particularly looking forward to."

SMULLEN (IRE)
26/3 ch c Camacho - Day By Day (Kyllachy)
Owner: Mrs J Ryan Sales price: £40,000 (Hillen/Ryan)

Half-brother to useful multiple 5-6f winner Ginger Jam. Dam a Listed-placed 5-6f winner who was a half-sister to Group 3-placed 7f-1m 2yo winner Day of Conquest, Listed runner-up Thought Is Free and the dams of Italian 1m 2yo Group 1 winner Hearts of Fire and 6f 2yo winner/Solario Stakes third Mr Wizard.

"A compact colt who really enjoys his work. He is incredibly straightforward and takes everything in his stride. He looks pretty sharp and should be in action sooner rather than later."

SPITTING FEATHERS (IRE)
5/2 b c Iffraaj - Yellowhammer (Raven's Pass)
Owner: Steve Ryan Sales price: 190,000gns (Stephen Hillen Bloodstock)

First foal of a useful multiple 7f winner who was a full sister to 7f 2yo winner Wren and a half-sister to Group 2-placed UK/Australian 8.5-13f winner (including twice at Listed level) Tall Ship, useful multiple 6-8.5f winner Chevalier and five other winners including the dam of Prix de Diane winner Channel out of a Cheveley Park Stakes-winning three-parts sister to Oaks winner Alexandrova.

"A nice colt who has done everything pleasingly to this point. He has been a quick learner since arriving and will be the type who tells us when he is ready. I imagine he will be in action by the end of the spring."

THUNDERING
18/4 b c Night of Thunder - Cosmea (Compton Place)
Owner: Steve Ryan Sales price: 180,000gns (Stephen Hillen Bloodstock)

Half-brother to useful 7-12f Flat/2m hurdle winner Cosmeapolitan, useful 11.5-12f winner William Hunter, useful 2020 1m 3yo winner Lord Neidin and 2020 7.5f 2yo winner Dromquinna. Dam a 10-11.5f Flat/dual 2m hurdle winner who was a half-sister to useful multiple 5f winner Master of Disguise and 7f 2yo winner Windscreamer.

"A strong, compact colt who is taking his work well. He is obviously related to horses that have stayed well and gone on to be jumpers for Alan King, but Night of Thunder would be the best, and indeed speediest, sire the mare has visited. That certainly shows through in his work as he doesn't lack for speed. He will be one for the seven-furlong races when they begin in earnest."

TIME TO PARLEY
14/2 b f Invincible Spirit - Ashadihan (Kyllachy)
Owner: T A Rahman Sales price: n/a

First foal of a smart 6-7f winner (including at Group 3 level) who was closely related to useful 8-12f winner Everything For You and a half-sister to very useful 6-7f winner (including at Listed level) Beauty Filly (by Invincible Spirit) and very useful multiple 8-10f winner Mythical Madness out of a twice-raced maiden half-sister to 6f 2yo Group 2/3 winner Sander Camillo.

"She is the first foal of our smart racemare, Ashadihan, and we are delighted with her size. Everything has come easily to her so far, and she should be making an appearance before the end of the spring."

TRIPLE TIME (IRE)
19/3 b c Frankel - Reem Three (Mark of Esteem)
Owner: Sheikh Mohammed Obaid Al Maktoum Sales price: n/a

Closely related to high-class 10-12f winner (including at Group 1 level) Ajman Princess (by Teofilo) and high-class 7f-1m winner (including at Group 2/Listed level) Ostilio (by New Approach) and a half-brother to high-class 6f-1m winner (including at Group 3 level) Cape Byron and 7f 2yo winner/Poule d'Essai des Pouliches fourth Imperial Charm. Dam a Listed-placed 8.5-10.5f 3yo winner who was a half-sister to Group 1-placed 8-10f winner (including at Group 2/3 level) Afsare.

"A gorgeous, big colt who is still growing at present. He is quite athletic with it, though, and has taken his work well to this point. He could well be in action before the turn of the summer."

UNNAMED (FR)
26/2 gr c Caravaggio - Pretty Darling (Le Havre)
Owner: T A Rahman Sales price: £85,000 (Hillen/Ryan)

Second foal of a French 9-10.5f 3yo winner who was a half-sister to Group 2-placed Irish 5-6.5f 2yo winner (including at Group 3/Listed level) Peace Envoy and Norwegian 9/12f Group 3 winner Our Last Summer out of a 10f 3yo winning half-sister to Group 3/Listed-placed 7f 2yo winner Everlasting Love.

"A big, strong colt, who is very athletic and has a great attitude. He is by an exciting first-season sire and looks pretty sharp at this stage. One to look forward to."

GEORGE SCOTT

CHANSON D'AMOUR
11/3 gr f Dark Angel - Coral Mist (Bahamian Bounty)
Owner: The Hon Mrs J M Corbett & C Wright Sales price: 27,000gns (JS
Bloodstock/G Scott Racing)

Third foal of a 6f 2yo Group 3 winner who was a three-parts sister to Prix
de la Foret winner Toylsome and the dam of Irish 10f 3yo Listed winners
Hoarding and Western Australia out of a maiden half-sister to Queen Mary
Stakes winner Dance Parade (later dam of St Leger and Ascot Gold Cup winner
Leading Light).

*"A compact, well put together filly, who is very professional and will likely be
my first two-year-old runner. She has got an excellent attitude, and I think she
should be competitive in maiden/novice company once the penny drops."*

EXCEEDINGLY SONIC
4/4 ch f Exceed And Excel - Modify (New Approach)
Owner: Marc Chan Sales price: 70,000gns (McCalmont Bloodstock)

Three-parts sister to 7f 2yo winner Flint Hill (by Excelebration). Dam a 14f
3yo winner who was a half-sister to Group 3/Listed-placed dual 5f 2yo winner
Mary Read (grandam of smart sprinter Kachy), Listed-placed 6f-1m winner
Above N Beyond (by Exceed And Excel) and Listed-placed 6f 2yo winner Tiana
(later dam of five-time 1m Group 2 winner Beat The Bank and smart sprinter
Salt Island (by Exceed And Excel)).

*"A gorgeous, scopey filly, who should be ready to run in the early part of the
summer. I expect her to improve as the season goes on as she will appreciate
decent ground."*

HIGHLIGHTER (IRE)
19/2 b c Australia - Cosmic Fire (Dalakhani)
Owner: Niarchos Family Sales price: 37,000gns (Not Sold)

Half-brother to Grade 3-placed UK/US 7-9.5f winner Ray's The Bar. Dam a
French 11.5f 3yo winner who was a half-sister to French 10f Group 2 winner
Smoking Sun, French 1m 3yo Listed winner Zhiyi and Group 3/Listed-placed
French 7f 2yo winner Ikat (later dam of Breeders' Cup Turf winner Main
Sequence).

"This a tall, scopey and well-balanced colt with a fantastic attitude. He is quite forward for one by his sire, although I still wouldn't expect to see him on the track until the latter part of the summer."

LOVE NEVER ENDING
5/3 b f Siyouni - Encore L'Amour (Azamour)
Owner: E W B Williams Sales price: 50,000gns (Vendor)

Second foal of a Listed-placed 1m 2yo winner who was the daughter of a 10f 3yo winning sister to US 9/10f Grade 1 winner Ticker Tape and half-sister to Prix Maurice de Gheest winner Brando and the dam of Prix Morny/Middle Park Stakes winner Reckless Abandon and grandam of 7f 2yo Group 3 winner West End Girl.

"A sizeable daughter of Siyouni, who has strengthened a fair amount in recent weeks. I wouldn't expect to see much of her until the autumn, but she looks to have plenty of class about her."

MISTRIX (IRE)
12/3 b f Vadamos - Plus Ca Change (Invincible Spirit)
Owner: Airlie Stud & David McGuinness Sales price: £20,000 (De Burgh Equine)

Third foal of an Irish 7f 2yo winner who was a half-sister to Irish 2yo winners Ard San Aer (6f) and Soaring Sky (1m) out of a Listed-placed 11.5-12f 3yo winning half-sister to South African 14f Group 2 winner Kingston Mines; excellent family of Alborada, Aussie Rules, Yesterday etc.

"A tall, really well-made filly who moves nicely. She won't be ready for a little while yet, but we like her and she should be out sometime in the summer over 7f."

MORAG MCCULLOUGH
29/3 b f Exceed And Excel - Whazzat (Daylami)
Owner: The Gredley Family Sales price: n/a

Full sister to Group 1-placed 6-7f winner (including at Group 2/3 level) James Garfield, a three-parts sister to Listed-placed 7.5f-1m winner The Shrew (by Dansili) and a half-sister to useful 8-10f 3yo winner Eva Maria and useful 2020 7f 2yo winner Great Vibes. Dam a Chesham Stakes winner who was a sister to the dam of 2020 10f Group 3 winner Nkosikazi and a half-sister to smart 7f-1m winner (including at Group 3/Listed level) Whazzis and the dam of 2020 Breeders' Cup Mile winner Uni.

"She is an uncomplicated, well-balanced filly, who is similar to her brother in that she's not overly big but has a wonderful attitude. We are about to move into faster work with her, and she should be ready to run before Royal Ascot."

RUBBELDIEKATZ
18/2 b f Helmet - For Henry (Galileo)
Owner: R A H Evans Sales price: n/a

First foal of an unraced sister to 12f Group 3 winner Klassique out of a high-class 6f-1m winner (including at Group 1 level) who was a sister to high-class 6-7f winner (including twice at Group 3 level) J Wonder, a three-parts sister to smart UK/Hong Kong 6-7f winner (including at Group 3 level) California Whip and a half-sister to the dam of 1m 2yo Listed winner/Racing Post Trophy third Celestial Path.

"A tall, lean filly, who is quite an attractive type. She finds it all relatively easy at this stage but won't be ready to run until the autumn. I think she will get a little further than her pedigree might suggest."

T MAXIE (IRE)
20/4 b f Swiss Spirit - Filatelia (Intikhab)
Owner: D Underwood & L Thornley Sales price: n/a

Full sister to useful 2020 5-6f 2yo winner Charlie Fellowes. Dam a French 1m winner who was a full sister to Listed-placed 7f 2yo winner Swift Campaign and very useful 10-11f winner Expense Claim.

"A full sister to Charlie Fellowes, though she is a different type to him - certainly taller - and we are giving her time to strengthen up. She has done a couple of light pieces of work and, all being well, I expect to her on the track sometime in May."

TIME LAPSE (IRE)
21/5 b f Dark Angel - Synchronic (Dansili)
Owner: Niarchos Family Sales price: n/a

Half-sister to useful French 12-14.5f 3yo Flat/2m hurdle winner Homer. Dam an unraced sister to French 11f 3yo Listed winner Prudenzia (later dam of Irish Oaks winner Chicquita) and a half-sister to French 15f 3yo Group 3 winner Pacifique and Lingfield Derby Trial winner English King.

"A classy, easy-moving filly, who has an excellent attitude. On the weak side currently, she looks a lovely prospect for later in the year."

UNNAMED
10/3 ch c Ulysses - Foundation Filly (Lando)
Owner: M J Lilley Sales price: 30,000gns (Vendor)

Half-brother to useful 11.5-12f winner Infrastructure. Dam a useful French 10-14.5f winner who was a half-sister to Italian 10f Group 1 winner Floriot; family of smart stayer Fun Mac.

"A strong, well-made colt who enjoys his training. Although he has got a late-maturing pedigree, he finds life easy at this stage and could well be ready to run during the early part of the summer."

JAMES TATE

DIVINE RAPTURE (IRE)
27/2 gr f Dark Angel - Titivation (Montjeu)
Owner: Saeed Manana Sales price: 75,000gns (Rabbah Bloodstock)

Half-sister to Group 2-placed 8.5-12f winner (including at Listed level) Titi Makfi and useful Irish 9.5-12f winner War Diary. Dam an 8.5f 3yo winner who was closely related to Grade 3/Listed-placed UK/US 8-8.5f winner Federation and a half-sister to five-time 1m Group 1 winner (including the 1000 Guineas) Attraction (later dam of 10.5f Group 2 winner Elarqam).

"A lovely Dark Angel filly, who is a sister to a Listed winner and out of a sister to Attraction. She goes nicely and is one to look out for during the middle of the season."

EBTSAMA (IRE)
23/2 b f Dark Angel - Roseraie (Lawman)
Owner: Sultan Ali Sales price: 105,000gns (Rabbah Bloodstock)

Full sister to 1m 2yo winner/May Hill Stakes runner-up Dark Rose Angel and a half-sister to 2020 7f 2yo winner Dark Company. Dam a Group 3-placed Irish 6f 2yo winner who was a half-sister to Group 3-placed Irish 5-7f winner (including twice at Listed level) Rose Bonheur (later dam of 12f/2m Group 3 winner/St Leger third Nayef Road).

"This filly was purchased for 105,000gns at Book 2 of the Tattersalls October Yearling Sale. She is a lovely, strong daughter of Dark Angel, who ought to be running quite early but has scope do better over 7f/1m later on."

EL HADEEYAH (IRE)
2/4 b f Invincible Spirit - Blhadawa (Iffraaj)
Owner: Sheikh Juma Dalmook Al Maktoum Sales price: n/a

Closely related to fairly useful triple 5f winner Reassure (by Oasis Dream). Dam a 6f Listed winner who was a half-sister to Listed-placed 6-7f 2yo winner Laurentina out of an unraced half-sister to 10f 3yo Listed winner/Oaks third Mezzogiorno (later dam of Irish 10f Group 2 winner Monturani and Listed winners Mill Springs (14f) and Monnavanna (6/7f)).

"Out of a mare the stable trained to win a 6f Listed race, she is a nice, fast filly who will hopefully start off at the Craven meeting."

KING OF GOLD (IRE)
23/2 b c Kingman - Lamar (Cape Cross)
Owner: Saif Ali Sales price: n/a

Second foal of a smart 6-9.5f winner (including at Listed level) who was a half-sister to very useful 5f-1m winner (including at Listed level) Haddaf and 7f 2yo winner Dffar out of a Group 1-placed 7f 2yo winning sister to Canadian dual 1m 1f Grade 2 winner Windward Islands and a half-sister to US 1m 2yo Listed winner Hunter Cruise.

"Out of a mare the stable trained to win a Listed race, he is a beautiful, big colt, who should start over 6f sometime in May."

SAHARA DESERT (IRE)
12/2 b f Dubawi - Asanta Sana (Galileo)
Owner: Saeed Manana Sales price: n/a

First foal of a twice-raced maiden sister to Group 2-placed Irish 7-12f winner (including at Group 3/Listed level) Pretty Perfect out of an Australian 1m 1f Group 3-winning sister to 6/7f 2yo Group 1 winner Holy Roman Emperor; family of Queen Mary Stakes/Lowther Stakes winner Bint Allayl.

"A very nice filly by Dubawi, who should be running in the second half of the season."

STYLISH ICON (IRE)
2/2 b f Starspangledbanner - Refreshed (Rip Van Winkle)
Owner: Saeed Manana Sales price: 32,000gns (Rabbah Bloodstock)

First foal of an unraced half-sister to French 1m 2yo Group 3 winner Shahah, fairly useful 5-6f winner Royal Guinevere and fairly useful 6f-1m winner Ligeia out of an unraced half-sister to Dewhurst Stakes/St James's Palace Stakes winner/2000 Guineas runner-up Grand Lodge, dual 1m 3yo Listed winner Papabile and dual 10f 3yo Listed winner La Persiana (later dam of US 12f Listed winner Qushchi).

"A big, strong filly, who is showing up nicely and likely to start off over five or six furlongs in May."

TAKE A STAND (IRE)
13/3 b c Invincible Spirit - You're Back (Street Cry)
Owner: Saeed Manana Sales price: n/a

Second foal of a Listed-placed French 7f 3yo winner who was closely related to Group 1-placed 7f-1m winner (including at Group 2/3 level) No Excuse Needed and UAE 10f Group 1 winner Capponi out of a French 6f 3yo winning half-sister to French 10f Group 1 winner/Prix de Diane runner-up Fitnah.

"A big, rangy Invincible Spirit colt for the second half of the season."

THE SKY ABOVE (IRE)
8/4 ch f Sea The Stars - El Manati (Iffraaj)
Owner: Sheikh Rashid Dalmook Al Maktoum Sales price: n/a

Half-sister to French 5f 2yo Listed winner Second Generation. Dam a useful 6f 2yo winner who was the daughter of a 7f 2yo winning half-sister to Listed-placed Irish 1m 3yo Flat/2m hurdle winner Hovering and useful 9.5f 3yo winner Pelican Waters; family of Prix Marcel Boussac winner Amonita.

"Out of a mare the stable trained to be Group-placed and a half-sister to a Listed-winning filly, also trained by the stable. A nice filly by Sea The Stars for the summer onwards."

UNNAMED
16/2 b c Dark Angel - Ceaseless (Iffraaj)
Owner: Sheikh Rashid Dalmook Al Maktoum Sales price: n/a

Second foal of a Listed-placed 7f 3yo winner who was a full sister to useful Irish dual 7f winner When Not Iff out of a 1m 2yo winning close relation to Derby winner Oath and triple 8/10.5f Group 1 winner Pelder and half-sister to

10f 3yo Listed winners Audacious Prince and Napoleon's Sister; family of six-time 10-12f Group/Grade 1 winner Snow Fairy.

"A big, strong Dark Angel colt out of a Listed-placed mare trained by the stable. He is a nice prospect for the middle of the season."

UNNAMED
16/4 b f Invincible Spirit - Dulcet (Halling)
Owner: Sheikh Hamed Dalmook Al Maktoum Sales price: n/a

Third foal of a twice-raced maiden sister to high-class French 10-10.5f winner (including at Group 1 level) Cutlass Bay and King Edward VII Stakes winner Boscobel and a half-sister to Group 1-placed UK/French 7-9f winner (including at Group 3 level) Crown Walk out of a once-raced 1m 3yo winning half-sister to US 1m 1f Grade 2 winner Bayeux and French triple 7f Listed winner Colonial.

"A small Invincible Spirit filly, who looks precocious and will start over six furlongs."

UNNAMED (IRE)
20/2 b f Mehmas - Flat White (Elusive Quality)
Owner: Sheikh Juma Dalmook Al Maktoum Sales price: 140,000gns (Rabbah Bloodstock)

First foal of an unraced half-sister to Group 3-placed 8-10f winner Expresso Star, French 1m 3yo Listed winner Adorable, useful 1m 2yo winner Tarikhi and six other winners out of a US 1m 1f Grade 1-winning half-sister to the grandam of Prix Royal-Oak winner Les Beaufs.

"An imposing filly by Mehmas, who is one to look out for in the second half of the season."

UNNAMED
21/2 b c Frankel - Impala (Oasis Dream)
Owner: Saeed Manana Sales price: n/a

First foal of an unraced half-sister to Grand Prix de Paris winner Zambezi Sun, French 10f 3yo Group 2 winner Kalabar, French 9.5f 3yo Listed winner Zero Gravity and Listed-placed French 10f 3yo winner Shared Account (later dam of French 1m 2yo Group 3 winner Pocket Square).

"A big, rangy colt from a nice middle-distance family, who will appear in the second half of the season."

UNNAMED (IRE)
17/4 b f Shamardal - Jira (Medicean)
Owner: Saeed Manana Sales price: n/a

Half-sister to triple 6f winner Jameerah and 2020 6f 2yo winner Fighter Pilot. Dam a 6f 2yo Listed winner who was closely related to King Edward VII Stakes winner Plea Bargain and a half-sister to Group 2-placed 7-10f winner (including at Group 3/Listed level) Lay Time (later dam of French 5f 2yo Listed winner Beau Ideal) and Group 3-placed 7f 2yo winner Dubai Time.

"A sizeable, homebred filly out of a six-furlong Listed winner. She will be out during the second half of the season."

UNNAMED (IRE)
14/1 gr/ro f Dark Angel - Miss Albane (Choisir)
Owner: Saeed Juma Dalmook Al Maktoum Sales price: £66,000 (Rabbah Bloodstock Ltd)

First foal of a French 10.5f 3yo winner who was a half-sister to useful French 6f 2yo winner Sheistheboss out of a Chesham Stakes-winning half-sister to French 6f Group 3 winner Do The Honours (grandam of Melbourne Cup winner Cross Counter) and the unraced dam of French 1m 3yo Group 3 winner Future Generation.

"A strong filly who is likely to start off over five or six furlongs in May."

UNNAMED
11/3 b f Postponed - Mount Elbrus (Barathea)
Owner: Sultan Ali Sales price: n/a

Three-parts sister to useful French 11-12f 3yo winner Shkhara (by Dubawi) and a half-sister to French 11f 3yo Listed winner Lava Flow (later dam of triple 7f Group 1 winner/2000 Guineas third Pinatubo), Group 1-placed 7f-1m 2yo winner Strobilus, useful 8-12f winner Morning Wonder and 1m 2yo winner Ya Hala. Dam a French 10.5f 3yo Listed winner who was closely related to the dam of French 1m 1f 3yo Group 3 winner Master Carpenter.

"A medium-sized filly, who hails from the family of Pinatubo. She has the requisite speed to begin over six furlongs."

Pinatubo

UNNAMED (IRE)
12/3 b/br f Shamardal - Samdaniya (Machiavellian)
Owner: Saeed Manana Sales price: n/a

Half-sister to Group 1-placed dual 7f winner (including at Group 3 level) Dabyah. Dam a 9.5f 3yo winner who was a half-sister to Group 2-placed 6-12f winner (including at Group 3/Listed level) Queen's Best (later dam of Breeders' Cup Filly & Mare Turf winner Queen's Trust), French 12f Listed winner Reverie Solitaire (later dam of German 1m Group 2 winner Royal Solitaire), 13f Listed winner Urban Castle and the dam of Group 3-placed 2020 7f 2yo winner Wedding Dance.

"A lovely filly, who is a half-sister to the smart Dabyah. She is likely to start off in the middle of the season and has shown plenty of speed."

UNNAMED
4/2 b f Kingman - Uleavemebreathless (Tiger Hill)
Owner: Sheikh Juma Dalmook Al Maktoum Sales price: 85,000gns (Vendor)

First foal of a Group 3/Listed-placed Irish/Qatari 7-11f winner who was closely related to useful Irish 6-10f winner Monthly Medal and a half-sister to Listed-placed 7f-1m winner Tobosa out of a 9.5f winning half-sister to Listed-placed 5-6f winner Espartero.

"A nice filly by Kingman, who will start off over six furlongs in the middle of the season."

UNNAMED
26/2 b/br f Churchill - Wadaa (Dynaformer)
Owner: Saeed Manana Sales price: n/a

Half-sister to Group 3-placed 2020 7f 2yo winner Wedding Dance and very useful 8-9f winner Ibraz. Dam a useful 11f 3yo winner who was a half-sister to Group 2-placed 6-12f winner (including at Group 3/Listed level) Queen's Best (later dam of Breeders' Cup Filly & Mare Turf winner Queen's Trust), Listed winners Reverie Solitaire (12f) and Urban Castle (13f) and the dam of Fred Darling Stakes winner Dabyah.

"A Churchill filly, who is a very nice mover, but she is essentially one for longer distances towards the end of the season."

NIGEL TINKLER

ANOTHER BERTIE (IRE)
18/4 b c Acclamation - Temerity (Zoffany)
Owner: John R Saville Sales price: 48,000gns (Jamie Piggott Bloodstock/Nigel Tinkler)

First foal of a useful 7f 2yo winner who was a half-sister to Group 3-placed 6f 2yo winner Roxan out of a 1m 3yo winning sister to 1m 3yo winner/Irish 1000 Guineas fourth Distant Oasis and the maiden dam of 7f 3yo Group 2 winner Kahal and Irish 7f 2yo Listed winner Sahara Princess and half-sister to 1m Group 2 winner Reprimand and French 10f Group 2 winner Wiorno.

"This colt is just going through a growing spell at the moment. I can see him being out over 6f in mid-June. He is a very nice horse with a smashing temperament, and I hope he's good as he's owned by a nice guy called John Saville."

COZICAN (IRE)
16/4 b g Kodiac - Shared Humor (Distorted Humor)
Owner: Martin Webb Racing Sales price: £40,000 (Hardwood Stud)

Third foal of an unraced sister to Group 2-placed French/Australian 8-12f winner (including at Group 3/Listed level) Slow Pace and US 1m 3yo Grade

3 winner Funny Duck and half-sister to Grade 2/3-placed US 8-10f winner Segway and the dam of 2020 US 8.5f 3yo Grade 2 winner King Guillermo.

"He has been gelded already and looks as though he will be a relatively sharp type. I imagine he will begin sometime in May and looks a nice horse at this stage."

DANDY DINMONT (IRE)
18/4 b g Dandy Man - Coconut Kisses (Bahamian Bounty)
Owner: MPS Racing, The Olliers, S Perkins Sales price: £26,000 (Jamie Piggott)

Full brother to 5f 2yo winner Queenoftheclyde and a half-brother to French 5f 2yo Listed winner Ardenode. Dam a dual 5f 2yo winner who was a half-sister to dual 6f 3yo winner Hysterical Lady and 7f-1m 3yo winner Dutch Mistress out of a Listed-placed French 6f 2yo winner; family of smart sprinters Kachy and Salt Island.

"A tidy little horse who will probably be our first two-year-old runner. He should be a fun horse for his owners this season."

DOUGIES DREAM (IRE)
11/5 b g Fast Company - Sidney Girl (Azamour)
Owner: Martin Webb Racing Sales price: 45,000gns (Nigel Tinkler Bloodstock/ Jamie Piggott)

Half-brother to useful triple 1m winner Hombre Rojo, useful 8-10.5f winner Archie Perkins and 2020 7f 2yo winner Isla Kai, 14f-2m winner Champagne Marengo and 7-10f winner Kilbaha Lady. Dam a French 8-10.5f winner who was the daughter of a Listed-placed 7f 2yo winner.

"We have trained three winners out of the dam, including last year's two-year-old, Isla May. This gelding is an extremely nice individual who we are happy with at this stage. He will want 6/7f and is essentially a miler for later on."

LUCKY LUCKY LUCKY (IRE)
27/4 b g Footstepsinthesand - Lovers Peace (Oratorio)
Owner: G Maidment Racing Sales price: £41,000 (Jamie Piggott)

Full brother to Listed-placed Irish 7-10f winner Beach Wedding. Dam an Irish 12-13f 3yo winner who was closely related to useful multiple 7-8.5f winner Day of The Eagle and a half-sister to Group 2-placed multiple 5f winner (including at Listed level) Emerald Peace (later dam of 6f 2yo Listed winner Vital Statistics, herself the dam of French 7f 2yo Group 3 winner/Breeders' Cup Juvenile Fillies Turf runner-up/Poule d'Essai des Pouliches third East).

"Another who will need a little bit of time, but he is an athletic, easy-moving sort. He has a good attitude and should be in action around July or August time."

PRODIGIOUS BLUE (IRE)
20/2 b c Bated Breath - Hellofahaste (Hellvelyn)
Owner: Mr & Mrs I Bendelow Sales price: £39,000 (Nigel Tinkler)

First foal of a Listed-placed 6f 2yo winner who was a half-sister to useful Irish/US 8-8.5f winner Clutchingatstraws and UK/Hong Kong 5-7f winner Great Run out of a maiden half-sister to smart 7f-1m 2yo winner (including at Group 3/Listed level)/Racing Post Trophy runner-up Fantastic View, Group 2-placed 7f 2yo winner Weald Park and useful 6-7f 2yo winner To The Rescue.

"We have had some trouble with him at the stalls, so he needs to eradicate that. His dam was a good two-year-old, and I can see this colt being out in the middle of May. He will want 6f before long but has enough speed for us to think he can start off over 5f. I think he will be alright."

UWONTBELIEVEIT (IRE)
9/4 b f Galileo Gold - Ladylishandra (Mujadil)
Owner: Hot to Trot Racing 1 - Uwontbelieveit Sales price: £65,000 (Vendor)

Half-sister to high-class 2020 triple 5f 2yo winner (including at Group 2/Listed level) Ubettabelieveit, dual 7f Group 3 winner Tropical Paradise, Italian 5f Group 3 winner Harlem Shake and 1m Listed winner Shenanigans. Dam an Irish 6f 2yo winner who was the daughter of a French 11-12f 3yo winning sister to Irish 12f 3yo Group 3 winner Dancing Sunset (later dam of Irish 6f 2yo Listed winner Lady of Kildare).

"A tall, very athletic filly, who is a lovely mover. She has shown some speed but won't be out until June, which certainly didn't do her year-older half-sister any harm whatsoever!"

Ubettabelieveit

UNNAMED (IRE)
6/5 b f Ribchester - Spirit of Dubai (Cape Cross)
Owner: Harlequin Direct Ltd Sales price: 140,000gns (Nigel Tinkler Racing/
Jamie Piggott)

Half-sister to Gimcrack Stakes winner Emaraaty Ana and useful 7f-1m winner
Weld Al Emarat. Dam a 1m 3yo Listed winner who was a half-sister to French
10/10.5f Group 3 winner Trumbaka and French 1m 1f 3yo Listed winner Arctic
Hunt.

*"Quite a late foal and we won't be overracing her this year. She has a great
attitude, but I don't expect to see her in action until August over 6/7f."*

UNNAMED
12/4 b f Iffraaj - Tropical Paradise (Verglas)
Owner: Harlequin Direct Ltd Sales price: 35,000gns (Jamie Piggott Bloodstock/
Nigel Tinkler)

Half-sister to useful 2020 10f 3yo winner Fiji. Dam a dual 7f Group 3 winner
who was a half-sister to high-class 2020 triple 5f 2yo winner (including at
Group 2/Listed level) Ubettabelieveit, Italian 5f Group 3 winner Harlem Shake
and 1m Listed winner Shenanigans out an Irish 6f 2yo winner.

"She is owned by the same people who had the Oaks third, Harlequeen, a few years ago. The brief was to buy them a couple of yearlings that wouldn't just be precocious two-year-olds. She certainly won't be early as she is a tall filly who has grown quite a bit recently. I imagine she will make an appearance towards the end of the summer."

MARCUS TREGONING

A LA FRANCAISE
8/3 ch f Postponed - Alamode (Sir Percy)
Owner: Miss K Rausing Sales price: 50,000gns (Vendor)

Second foal of a Group 3-placed 6f 2yo winner who was the daughter of a maiden half-sister to Australian 7.5f Group 3 winner My Nordic Hero, French 10.5f 3yo Group 3 winner Alvarita (later dam of Irish 10f 3yo Group 3 winner Alla Speranza and grandam of Park Hill Stakes winner Alyssa) and Group 2/3-placed French 10-10.5f winner Albion out of a dual Champion Stakes winner.

"Obviously, I trained the dam who was useful. This filly is a good mover, who wouldn't be an early type but will be in action around July or August over 7f. The hope is she could be one to aim at Glorious Goodwood. I think she is a bright prospect."

OLIVETTI
4/4 b c Showcasing - Tschierschen (Acclamation)
Owner: Halcyon Thoroughbreds Sales price: £34,000 (Halcyon Thoroughbreds)

Half-brother to useful 2020 5-6f 2yo winner Perotto. Dam a 5f 2yo winner who was a sister to the maiden dam of Listed-placed 2020 6f 2yo winner Imperial Yellow and a half-sister to Group 1-placed 6-7f winner Gallagher, Listed-placed UK/UAE 7-10f winner Quick Wit and Listed-placed 5-7f winner Roodeye (dam of 2020 Sussex Stakes winner Mohaather and US 6.5f/1m Grade 2 winner Prize Exhibit (both by Showcasing) and grandam of Queen Anne Stakes winner Accidental Agent).

"He is a half-brother to Perotto, who did really well for us last season. This colt isn't overly big, but very sharp and I hope he is going to be a nice early-season two-year-old for his owners - like his half-brother. He will probably make an appearance in May and has the basic speed to begin over 5f."

Perotto

UNNAMED (IRE)
30/1 b c Invincible Spirit - Arabian Comet (Dubawi)
Owner: Shadwell Estate Co Sales price: n/a

Second foal of a Group 3/Listed-placed 9.5-12f 3yo winner who was a half-sister to smart 7-9f winner (including at Group 2/3 level) Promising Run and useful 7f 2yo winner Kunooz out of a Brazilian 10f Group 1 winner who was a half-sister to Brazilian 10f Group 2 winner Cerutti, Brazilian 1m Group 3 winner Persane and the dam of Argentinian 1m 2yo Group 1 winner Eddington.

"He is a strong colt and a nice size. I had to back off him a bit, but he's coming again now and should be ready to go in July. He will make a two-year-old and I like him."

UNNAMED
24/4 b c Showcasing - Life of Pi (Sea The Stars)
Owner: Shadwell Estate Co Sales price: 150,000gns (Shadwell Estate Company)

Half-brother to 2020 6f 2yo Listed winner Bahrain Pride. Dam an unraced half-sister to French 7f 2yo Listed winner/Poule d'Essai des Poulains fourth Temps Au Temps and Group 3/Listed-placed Irish 6f 2yo winner After (later dam of Irish 7f 2yo Group 2 winner/Cox Plate runner-up Armory) out of a Grade 1-placed Irish 7-10f winner.

"The Sea The Stars in his pedigree has made him a little more backward than you would perhaps hope. He is a very good-looking horse and a nice size for a Showcasing. He just needs time. There's a chance he might start over 7f, but we'll just see how we go with him."

UNNAMED (IRE)
18/2 b c Dark Angel - Maqaasid (Green Desert)
Owner: Shadwell Estate Co Sales price: n/a

Half-brother to 1m 3yo winner Jadeerah and 7f 2yo winner Nawaasi. Dam a Queen Mary Stakes winner/1000 Guineas third who was a half-sister to the maiden dam of Australian 2m Group 1 winner Shraaoh, 13f 3yo Group 3 winner Raheen House, 2020 French 12f Listed winner Sea of Faith and 1m 2yo Listed winner Born With Pride out of an unraced close relation to 1000 Guineas winner Ghanaati.

"A tall, strong colt who takes after the dam's side in that regard. He has shown some speed in his early work and has a solid temperament. A really nice type who I like."

UNNAMED
22/4 ch f Showcasing - Qawaasem (Shamardal)
Owner: Shadwell Estate Co Sales price: n/a

Half-sister to 6f 3yo winner Nubough and 2021 7f 3yo winner Bakr. Dam a Group 3/Listed-placed 6f 2yo winner who was a half-sister to Listed-placed UK/UAE 7-8.5f winner Mukalal and 7f 2yo winner Taqneyya out of a Group 3-placed 7f 2yo winner.

"She will be one of our earlier two-year-old runners. It is quite a sharp family, and she has definitely followed that trend. I imagine she will be seen as soon as the 6f races are underway."

UNNAMED
9/4 b f Outstrip - Quail Landing (Mark of Esteem)
Owner: M P N Tregoning Sales price: 3,000gns (MP Tregoning)

Half-sister to 2020 1m 3yo winner Naval Commander, US dual 1m 3yo winner Minimambo and two other winners. Dam a maiden half-sister to 1m 1f 3yo Group 3 winner Enforcer, useful UK/UAE 5-7f winner Zalzilah, useful dual 5f 2yo winner Lord of The Inn, seven other winners and the maiden dam of Norfolk Stakes/Flying Childers Stakes winner A'Ali.

"Heather Raw is an owner/breeder of ours who owned the mare when she raced for us and bred this filly. I picked her up very cheaply at auction and turned her away for a bit as I didn't have anyone for her. She has come back in and pleasantly surprised me as she is quite pacey and shows plenty of natural ability. She is eligible for every bonus you can think of, and I hope she can be another one that proves good enough to contest one of those nice fillies' events at Glorious Goodwood."

UNNAMED
20/1 gr c Markaz - Rathaath (Oasis Dream)
Owner: Shadwell Estate Co Sales price: n/a

Third foal of a Listed-placed 5-5.5f winner who was a half-sister to very useful 7f-1m winner Raaeq, 5f 2yo winner Fataawy and 6f 2yo winners Giennah and Mushahadaat out of a Listed-placed Irish 6-7f 2yo winner.

"A thickset colt, and it is hard to tell with such horses whether or not they're going to go backward on you. He has done one or two bits of work and goes ok. Most definitely a two-year-old type."

UNNAMED (IRE)
27/2 gr c Dark Angel - Rihaam (Dansili)
Owner: Shadwell Estate Co Sales price: n/a

Second foal of an unraced half-sister to Group 3/Listed-placed dual 7f winner/ Poule d'Essai des Poulains fourth Muwaary, 6f 3yo Listed winner Ethaara (later dam of 1m 3yo Listed winner Etaab), 7f 2yo Listed winners Mudaaraah and Sudoor (later dam of French 10.5f 3yo Group 3 winner Raseed) and Listed-placed 7f 3yo winner Yasmeen.

"A tall, free-moving horse who would probably go weak if you pushed him too soon. He has done enough to suggest he could win a race this year, but is on the back burner just for now to allow him to strengthen up and mature."

UNNAMED
12/1 b c Bated Breath - Sparkle (Oasis Dream)
Owner: Shadwell Estate Co Sales price: 50,000gns (Shadwell Estate Company)

First foal of a maiden half-sister to 10f 3yo Listed winner UAE Jewel and useful 2020 dual 1m 3yo winner Nugget out of a Group 3-placed Irish 7f-1m 2yo winner (including at Listed level) who was the daughter of a maiden half-sister to Irish 2000 Guineas winner Bachelor Duke and the grandam of 2020 Doncaster Cup winner Spanish Mission and 6f 2yo Listed winner Mokarris.

"He is a little bit difficult in that he can be quite spooky. We got on with him while the ground was perfect, and he showed plenty of pace. He is sharp enough to think he will win a race this year."

UNNAMED
14/4 b c Sea The Stars - Umniyah (Shamardal)
Owner: Shadwell Estate Co Sales price: 625,000gns (Shadwell Estate Company)

Full brother to once-raced US 8.5f 2yo winner The Path Not Taken. Dam a once-raced maiden sister to 7/9f Group 3 winner Dubai Prince and half-sister to Listed-placed Irish 8-12f 3yo winner Jakarta Jade, useful 8-10f 2yo winner Mojave Moon and the unraced dam of US 1m 1f Grade 2 winner Tuttipaesi out of an 11-13f 3yo winning half-sister to triple 10f Group/Grade 1 winner Storming Home.

"I felt this was one of the best horses at Book 1 of the Tattersalls October Yearling Sale. He is 16hh already and has a lovely temperament, which isn't always the case with horses by these top stallions. We have had a smooth run with him so far, and although he is very much a second-half-of-the-season two-year-old, he has the ability to be a nice horse one day."

ROGER VARIAN

AIMERIC
16/2 b c Frankel - Aris (Danroad)
Owner: Sheikh Mohammed Obaid Al Maktoum Sales price: 360,000gns (Roger P Varian)

Half-brother to high-class 6f-1m winner (including at Group 1 level) Aclaim and useful 2020 7f 3yo winner Additional. Dam a Listed-placed Irish 7f 3yo winner who was closely related to Moyglare Stud Stakes/Irish 1000 Guineas winner Again (later dam of Listed winners Delphina (13f) and Indian Maharaja (7.5f)) and Group 3/Listed-placed Irish 9.5f 3yo winner Arkadina (later dam of US 11f Grade 3 winner Guilty Twelve).

"A lovely-looking colt who is still immature. He hasn't done much yet and is one for the autumn and more so for next year."

AKHU NAJLA
20/4 b c Kingman - Galicuix (Galileo)
Owner: KHK Racing Ltd Sales price: 2,700,000gns (Oliver St Lawrence Bloodstock)

Half-brother to 2000 Guineas/St James's Palace Stakes winner Galileo Gold, useful dual 7f winner Eshaasy and 7f 2yo winner Choumicha. Dam a twice-raced maiden half-sister to King's Stand Stakes/Prix de l'Abbaye winner Goldream out of an unraced half-sister to five-time 10/12f Listed winner Mont Rocher; family of top-class middle-distance performer Montjeu.

"An expensive purchase who certainly looks the part. He won't be early but has pleased us so far and will hopefully come to hand around August/September time."

BAYSIDE BOY (IRE)
2/5 b c New Bay - Alava (Anabaa)
Owner: Teme Valley & Ballylinch Stud Sales price: 200,000gns (Richard Ryan)

Half-brother to smart 7-10.5f winner (including at Group 2/3 level) Forest Ranger and Listed-placed 7-8.5f winner Home Cummins. Dam a French 9.5f 3yo Listed winner who was the daughter of a Listed-placed French dual 1m 3yo winning half-sister to French 10.5f 3yo Group 3 winner Tamise (later dam of Australian 12.5f Group 3 winner Motivado) and French 1m 3yo Listed winner Tarzan Cry.

"This is quite a forward colt considering his pedigree doesn't necessarily suggest he should be. He moves nicely and I see him running in June or July over 7f."

BOLD RIBB
15/4 b c Ribchester - Bold Bidder (Indesatchel)
Owner: Teme Valley Sales price: £82,000 (Richard Ryan)

Half-brother to smart 2020 5-7f 2yo winner (including at Group 3/Listed level) Lullaby Moon and useful multiple 5-7f winner Celebration. Dam a useful dual 5f 2yo winner who was a half-sister to Listed-placed 5f 2yo winner Right Answer and once-raced Irish 5f 2yo winner Twenty Questions out of a 7f 3yo winning half-sister to high-class multiple 5f winner (including at Group 2/3 level) Mind Games.

"A sizeable colt, who isn't precocious despite being bred to be. He hasn't done too much yet, but is a likeable sort who shapes as though he will be running over 7f in the middle of summer."

CANNY FETTLE (FR)
7/5 ch c Distorted Humor - Liffey Dancer (Sadler's Wells)
Owner: Merry Fox Stud Limited Sales price: 140,000gns (Vendor)

Full brother to Listed-placed dual 7f 2yo winner Pichola Dance. Dam an unraced sister to Fillies' Mile winner Listen and Moyglare Stud Stakes winner Sequoyah (later dam of 2000 Guineas and Sussex Stakes winner Henrythenavigator and Irish 1m 3yo Group 3 winner/Irish 1000 Guineas and Prix de Diane third Queen Cleopatra, herself grandam of Irish 10f Group 2 winner/Derby runner-up Cliffs of Moher) and half-sister to the grandam of Irish 2000 Guineas/Breeders' Cup Turf winner Magician.

"A late foal, who is still quite weak and immature. He moves nicely but will be one for the autumn."

DUBAI POET
24/2 b c Lope de Vega - Hundi (Fastnet Rock)
Owner: Sheikh Mohammed Obaid Al Maktoum Sales price: 140,000gns (Roger Varian)

Second foal of a useful 6f 3yo winner who was closely related to Group 1-placed triple 7f winner (including at Group 3 level) Air Chief Marshal, smart 6-7f winner (including twice at Listed level) Misu Bond and very useful dual 6f winner/Irish 2000 Guineas runner-up Foxtrot Romeo and a half-sister to Irish St Leger winner Flag of Honour and Group 3-placed 5-8.5f winner (including twice at Listed level) Slip Dance (grandam of Grade 1-placed dual 1m Listed winner Awesometank).

"A nice colt, who moves very naturally and is likeable at this stage. I can see him appearing in June or July over 7f."

FLAG OF TRUTH (FR)
19/1 b c Starspangledbanner - Dalakania (Dalakhani)
Owner: Teme Valley Sales price: £170,000 (Richard Ryan)

First foal of a maiden half-sister to Group 1-placed French 9.5-14f winner (including at Group 2/Listed level) Ziyad, Listed-placed US 7-8.5f winner Machiavelique and the once-raced maiden dam of Listed-placed 9.5-10f winner Victory Bond out of a French 10f 3yo winning half-sister to several smart winners, notably Prix de Diane winner/Prix de l'Arc de Triomphe runner-up Aquarelliste.

"A lovely colt who moves incredibly well. Unfortunately, he has had a setback which has pushed him back, and I can't see him running before the autumn. There's a lot to like about him."

GLAM DE VEGA (IRE)
12/1 ch c Lope de Vega - Glamorous Approach (New Approach)
Owner: Sheikh Mohammed Obaid Al Maktoum Sales price: 160,000gns (Roger P Varian)

First foal of a Group 3-placed Irish 7.5-12f winner (including twice at Listed level) who was a three-parts sister to 2020 Irish 7f 2yo Group 3 winner Poetic Flare out of a once-raced maiden sister to the dam of Irish 1m 1f 2yo Listed winner Dubai Sand; family of Dewhurst Stakes winner Teofilo.

"A big, immature colt who hasn't done much yet. He will probably have one run in the autumn and is going to make a lovely three-year-old. A very good-looking individual."

GOEMON
16/3 gr c Dark Angel - Spangled (Starspangledbanner)
Owner: Mohamed Khalid Abdulrahim Sales price: 125,000gns (Ebonos)

First foal of a 7f Group 3 winner who was the daughter of an unraced sister to Listed-placed 7f 3yo winner Safina (later dam of Fred Darling Stakes winner Marenko) and the dam of 1m 3yo Group 3/Listed winner Zonderland and grandam of Solario Stakes winner Positive out of a four-time 8/10f Group 1 winner (including the 1000 Guineas and Lockinge Stakes).

"The dam was good for us, and this a very natural, athletic type of horse. He should be nice and be running by the middle of the summer."

INDEMNIFY
18/2 gr c Lope de Vega - Karisma (Lawman)
Owner: Miss Yvonne Jacques Sales price: 260,000gns (Yeomanstown Stud)

First foal of a 1m 3yo winner who was a half-sister to Acomb Stakes/Irish 2000 Guineas winner Phoenix of Spain (by Lope de Vega), Listed-placed 5-6f winner Lucky Beggar, very useful triple 10f winner Central Square and useful triple 7f winner Game Player out of a maiden half-sister to French dual 1m Group 2 winner Special Kaldoun.

"A medium-sized colt, who was doing very well until meeting with a setback. He will be fine to appear later in the year and had been pleasing us in all that he was doing until his injury."

INFRAADI
16/3 b/br c Invincible Spirit - Ambivalent (Authorized)
Owner: Ali Saeed Sales price: n/a

Half-brother to smart UK/French 7-12f winner (including at Group 2/Listed level) Al Hilalee and 2020 10f 2yo winner Teona. Dam an Irish 10f Group 1 winner who was a half-sister to Listed-placed 8-14f winner Sunday Symphony, Group 1-placed dual 7f 2yo winner Al Waffi and the dam of Prix de l'Abbaye winner Total Gallery and 5f 2yo winner/Fillies' Mile runner-up Lady Darshaan.

"The dam was smart for us, and we have his year-older half-sister who looks above-average. This is a big, immature colt who we don't know much about at this stage."

KINGMAX (IRE)
13/3 b c Kingman - Baino Hope (Jeremy)
Owner: Amo Racing Limited Sales price: £120,000 (Robson Aguiar)

Second foal of a smart French 10.5-15f winner (including at Group 2/Listed level) who was a half-sister to French 10f 3yo Listed winner Baino Rock out of a French 1m 3yo winning sister to French triple 1m Group 3 winner Take Risks, Listed-placed French 6-7f 2yo winner Lake Baino and the dam of French 7f 2yo Group 3 winner Stella Blue (herself dam of triple 6f-1m Listed winner Sirius Prospect).

"A really nice colt, who is athletic and very natural. He moves nicely and will be one to start with in June or July over 6/7f."

LORD PARAMOUNT
18/3 b c Ribchester - Affluent (Oasis Dream)
Owner: D J Deer Sales price: n/a

Half-brother to Group/Grade 1-placed 6-7f 2yo winner (including at Group 2/3 level) Daahyeh and Group 3-placed 2020 dual 7f 2yo winner (including at Listed level) Saint Lawrence. Dam a useful dual 5f winner who was a half-sister to Group 1-placed 7f-1m winner (including at Group 3/Listed level) So Beloved, smart 5-6f winner (including at Group 2/Listed level) Deportivo and 5f 2yo Listed winner Irish Vale.

"He is a half-brother to a couple of our good two-year-olds in recent seasons, namely Daahyeh and Saint Lawrence. This colt is very natural and looks like he won't let down the family at this stage. He is one to look forward to and should be running in May or June over 6f."

Saint Lawrence

NEGLIGENT
21/3 b f Kodiac - Orpha (New Approach)
Owner: Prince A A Faisal Sales price: n/a

Half-sister to 1m 3yo winner Yimkin. Dam a useful 6f 2yo winner who was a half-sister to Prix Jean Prat winner Olden Times and 6f Listed winner/Cheveley Park Stakes third Festoso (later dam of Italian 7.5f 2yo Listed winner Festive Star) out of a Group 2/3-placed multiple 6f winning half-sister to the dam of high-class miler Dandoun.

"A medium-sized filly who moves nicely. She will be starting sometime in the summer over 6f."

POET
29/3 b c Kodiac - Swiss Diva (Pivotal)
Owner: Lordship Stud Sales price: 100,000gns (Vendor)

Half-brother to French 5f 2yo Listed winner Poetry. Dam a high-class multiple 5-6f winner (including at Group 3/Listed level) who was a half-sister to Group 2-placed 5-6f winner (including at Group 3/Listed level) Swiss Spirit, smart 5-6f winner (including three times at Listed level) Swiss Dream (later dam of 6f 3yo Group 3 winner Yafta), very useful dual 5f winner/Coventry Stakes runner-up Swiss Franc and seven other winners.

"A neat, very strong colt who moves nicely. He met with a setback in the spring and probably won't be in action until July at the earliest."

RUGGLES
1/3 b f Exceed And Excel - Madame Defarge (Motivator)
Owner: The Gredley Family Sales price: n/a

Half-sister to useful 14f-2m 2f winner Land of Oz. Dam a Listed-placed 1m 2yo winner who was a three-parts sister to useful 7f-1m winner Foolin Myself and a half-sister to US 1m 1f Grade 3 winner Gender Agenda and the unraced dam of high-class triple 6f 2yo winner (including at Group 1 level)/Irish 1000 Guineas second Pretty Pollyanna out of an unraced half-sister to Oaks/St Leger winner User Friendly.

"An athletic filly, who will take a little bit of time. She should be running over 7f in July."

SED MAARIB (USA)
30/1 ch c American Pharoah - Sea of Snow (Distorted Humor)
Owner: KHK Racing Ltd Sales price: €320,000 (Oliver St Lawrence)

First foal of a useful dual 5f 2yo winner who was a half-sister to French 10.5f 3yo Group 3 winner Powder Snow and Group 2/3-placed German 7.5f 2yo winner Snow out of a maiden sister to Listed-placed 8-10f winner Abhisheka (later dam of Prix Jean Prat winner Aesop's Fables) and half-sister to Derby/Prix de l'Arc de Triomphe winner Lammtarra and French 1m 2yo Group 3 winner Saytarra.

"An extremely likeable individual, who does everything very naturally at this stage. He looks like he will have the pace to begin over 6f in May or June and is a nice colt."

SHAMPION (IRE)
22/2 b f Shamardal - Nada (Teofilo)
Owner: Sheikh Mohammed Obaid Al Maktoum Sales price: n/a

Second foal of an unraced close relation to Listed-placed 11.5f-2m 3yo winner UAE King and half-sister to very smart 6f-1m winner (three times at Group 1 level, including the Irish 2000 Guineas)/Derby third Dubawi, Lancashire Oaks winner Emirates Queen, Group 2-placed 8-10f 3yo winner (including at Listed level) Princess Nada and the grandam of 2020 1m 3yo Listed winner/1000 Guineas second Cloak of Spirits.

"This filly will take time and is more of an autumn type. She will probably begin over 1m."

SILENCE IS GOLDEN
1/2 b f Golden Horn - Mia Diletta (Selkirk)
Owner: A D Spence, A J Pearson & M B Spence Sales price: 150,000gns
(Vendor)

Full sister to useful 7-7.5f winner Cape Palace and a half-sister to smart Italian
7-9f winner (including at Group 3/Listed level) Poeta Diletto. Dam an Italian
dual 7.5f 2yo Listed winner who was a half-sister to Italian 1m 3yo Group 3
winner Mi Raccomando.

"A medium-sized filly, who is quite light-framed but will fill out as she gets
older. She is by Golden Horn and so won't be doing anything early, but she
moves nicely and will be one for the autumn."

SUBASTAR (IRE)
4/5 b c Sea The Stars - Suba (Seeking The Gold)
Owner: Sheikh Mohammed Obaid Al Maktoum Sales price: n/a

Three-parts brother to once-raced 1m 3yo winner Subaana (by Cape Cross)
and a half-brother to the maiden dam of 2020 1m 3yo Listed winner/1000
Guineas runner-up Cloak of Spirits. Dam an 8.5f 3yo winner who was closely
related to very smart 6f-1m winner (including the Irish 2000 Guineas)/Derby
third Dubawi and a half-sister to Lancashire Oaks winner Emirates Queen and
10f 3yo Listed winner Princess Nada.

"A nice colt who will take a bit of time but has the potential to a be nice one
day. Another who should be in action over 1m in the autumn."

SUPER CUB
31/3 b c Invincible Spirit - Soofiah (King's Best)
Owner: Merry Fox Stud Limited Sales price: n/a

First foal of a 6f 2yo winner who was a full sister to high-class multiple 8-10.5f
winner (including twice at Group 1 level) Sajjhaa and a half-sister to useful
11.5-12.5f winner Myseven and useful 13.5f-2m winner Mobbhij out of a 10.5f
3yo winning daughter of a Lancashire Oaks winner/Oaks runner-up.

"This colt is forward in his work and does everything nicely at this stage. He
will begin over 6f in May or June."

TOOPHAN (IRE)
8/4 ch c New Approach - Maoineach (Congaree)
Owner: Amo Racing Limited Sales price: £190,000 (Ebonos)

Full brother to 2020 Irish 6f 2yo Group 3 winner New Treasure. Dam an Irish 6/7f Group 3 winner who was a half-sister to smart US/UAE 7-9f winner (including at Listed level) Tiz Now Tiz Then and useful 7-10f winner Intrepidly; family of 2020 French 1m 2yo Group 1 winner Gear Up and Irish 1m 1f 2yo Group 3 winner Guaranteed.

"A lovely colt with plenty of quality about him. He moves easily and will debut over 7f in July. There is a lot to like about him."

VOODOO QUEEN
11/3 b f Frankel - Cursory Glance (Distorted Humor)
Owner: Merry Fox Stud Limited Sales price: n/a

Half-sister to 2020 useful dual 7f 3yo winner Tinker Toy. Dam a Moyglare Stud Stakes winner who was a half-sister to the unraced dam of 2020 US 1m 1f Grade 1 winner Digital Age out of a 10.5f 3yo winning sister to French 12f 3yo Group 3 winner Time On (later dam of 7f 2yo Group 3 winner Mot Juste) and half-sister to 2020 1m Listed winner Posted.

"Not overly big but she goes along nicely and does little wrong at present. She should be in action over 7f in midsummer."

UNNAMED (IRE)
9/3 b c Dark Angel - Golden Rosie (Exceed And Excel)
Owner: King Power Racing Co Ltd Sales price: 260,000gns (SackvilleDonald)

Full brother to Group 2-placed UK/UAE 7f-1m winner Golden Goal and a half-brother to Listed-placed 5-6f winner Rosie's Premiere. Dam a 6f 2yo winner who was a half-sister to Group 1-placed prolific 6-8.5f winner (including at Group 2/3 level) Sovereign Debt (by Dark Angel) and Fred Darling Stakes winner/Cheveley Park Stakes fourth Puff.

"A strong, very likeable colt with a good attitude. He should be running in May or June over 6f."

UNNAMED (IRE)
23/3 ch c Iffraaj - Goleta (Royal Applause)
Owner: Sheikh Ahmed Al Maktoum Sales price: 65,000gns (Shadwell Estate
Company)

Full brother to French 5-6.5f winner (including at Group 3/Listed level) Dibajj
and a half-brother to French 10.5f 3yo Listed winner Black Sea. Dam a twice-
raced maiden half-sister to smart multiple 5-6f winner (including at Group 2/3
level) Chineur and the dams of French 5.5f Listed winner Iffranesia (by Iffraaj)
and 2020 French 1m 3yo Group 3 winner/Prix du Jockey Club runner-up The
Summit.

*"A tall colt, who will take a bit of time and likely won't be seen out until the
autumn at the earliest."*

UNNAMED (IRE)
23/3 b c Galileo - Homecoming Queen (Holy Roman Emperor)
Owner: Northern Farm Sales price: n/a

Full brother to 2020 Moyglare Stud Stakes winner Shale and three other
winners. Dam a 1000 Guineas winner who was closely related to six-time 10-
12f Group 1 winner (including the Irish Derby and Prix de l'Arc de Triomphe)
Dylan Thomas and Oaks runner-up Remember When (dam of 2020 Derby
winner Serpentine (by Galileo)) and a half-sister to Cheveley Park Stakes
winner Queen's Logic (later dam of Lowther Stakes winner Lady of The
Desert).

*"A lovely colt, who would have been a midsummer two-year-old but met with
a setback and that will probably mean he will now appear in the autumn. He
obviously has an excellent pedigree and is a very likeable individual."*

UNNAMED
24/4 b c Invincible Spirit - Lanansaak (Zamindar)
Owner: Shadwell Estate Co Sales price: n/a

Half-brother to useful dual 1m winner Montather and once-raced 2020 7f 2yo
winner Zaajirah. Dam a Listed-placed 7f-1m winner who was the daughter of a
Group 3/Listed-placed 1m 2yo winning half-sister to very useful 7f 2yo winner
Maghanim; family of 1000 Guineas winner Shadayid.

*"A very athletic colt who moves nicely. He should be out over 7f in midsummer
and is one I like."*

UNNAMED (IRE)
22/2 b f Kingman - Miss Katie Mae (Dark Angel)
Owner: Bill Crager Sales price: n/a

First foal of a Group 3-placed Irish/Canadian 6-6.5f winner (including at stakes level) who was a half-sister to Group 1-placed 5-6f winner (including at Group 3/Listed level) Eastern Impact and Group 3/Listed-placed multiple 6f winner Summerghand out of a 5f 2yo winning close relation to Irish 5f 2yo winner Liberating and half-sister to Group 3/Listed-placed triple 6f winner/2000 Guineas fourth Bossy Guest and the dam of 1m Listed winner Another Touch.

"This filly won't be as early as some in the family have been. She will take a bit of time to reach full maturity but is a nice sort."

UNNAMED
3/3 b f Dubawi - Nahrain (Selkirk)
Owner: Sheikh Ahmed Al Maktoum Sales price: n/a

Full sister to very smart multiple 7-10f winner (including three times at Group 1 level) Benbatl and Listed-placed 7f-1m winner Fooraat. Dam a high-class 8-10f winner (including at Group/Grade 1 level) who was a half-sister to dual 1m Listed winner Baharah and the grandam of 2020 6f Group 3 winner Far Above out of a Ribblesdale Stakes winner/Oaks runner-up.

"This is a lovely, big filly from a good family well known to us. She will take time and is one for the autumn and next year."

UNNAMED (FR)
1/3 ch c Almanzor - Nehalennia (Giant's Causeway)
Owner: King Power Racing Co Ltd Sales price: 210,000gns (SackvilleDonald)

Half-brother to stakes-placed US 5.5-6.5f winner Navy Hymn. Dam a US 1m winner who was closely related to Irish 5f 2yo Listed winner/Queen Mary Stakes runner-up Meow (later dam of Dewhurst Stakes and 2000 Guineas winner Churchill and Cheveley Park Stakes winner Clemmie) and a half-sister to Irish 9.5f 3yo Group 3 winner Aloof, 2020 Irish 1m 3yo Listed winner Keats and French 1m Listed winner Orator out of a very smart 5f-1m winner (including the Cheveley Park Stakes).

"A big, scopey horse, who has plenty of quality about him. He isn't an early type and won't be appearing until the late summer or autumn but we like what we see."

UNNAMED (IRE)
16/3 br f Oasis Dream - Princess de Lune (Shamardal)
Owner: Shadwell Estate Co Sales price: £450,000 (Shadwell)

First foal of a 7f 3yo winner who was a full sister to Australian 7f/1m Group 2 winner Puissance de Lune and 10f 3yo Listed winner Queen Power and a half-sister to French 1m 1f Group 1 winner Zabeel Prince and the dam of high-class 5f-1m winner (including twice at Group 1 level) Rizeena and smart 6-9f winner (including at Group 2/3 level) Summer Romance.

"A lovely filly who moves nicely. She is forward in her work and should debut over 6f in May or June."

UNNAMED (IRE)
9/2 b c Starspangledbanner - Princess Desire (Danehill)
Owner: Syndicate Sales price: 200,000gns (Sam Sangster Bloodstock)

Half-brother to Listed-placed 6f 2yo winner Mappa Mundi, Listed-placed Italian 6-7.5f winner Bloody Love, dual 6f 2yo winner Lady Desire and 2020 6f 2yo winner Science. Dam a Japanese 7f 3yo winner who was the daughter of an unraced half-sister to 1m 2yo Group 3 winner Intimate Guest and the dam of US 11f Grade 1 winner Prince Arch and Irish 7f 2yo Group 1 winner Kingsfort.

"A good-looking colt who goes nicely at this stage. He won't be out particularly early and will want 6/7f."

UNNAMED
12/4 ch f Dubawi - Starlet's Sister (Galileo)
Owner: KHK Racing Ltd Sales price: €2,500,000 (Oliver St Lawrence)

Half-sister to high-class French/US multiple 8.5-11f winner (seven times at Grade 1 level, including the Breeders' Cup Filly & Mare Turf) Sistercharlie, Prix du Jockey Club/2020 Prix de l'Arc de Triomphe winner Sottsass and French 1m 3yo Group 3 winner My Sister Nat. Dam a maiden sister to French 10.5f 3yo Group 3 winner Leo's Starlet and half-sister to Grade 1-placed French 8-9f 2yo winner (including at Group 3 level) Anabaa's Creation (later dam of US 1m 2yo Listed winner/Albany Stakes fourth Create A Dream).

"Very expensive filly with a lovely pedigree. She is quite forward in her work and has a lot of quality about her. I wouldn't think she will take too long in coming to hand, and she might make her debut over 7f in July. Very pleased with her."

ED WALKER

AMERICAN STAR (IRE)
12/1 b c Starspangledbanner - Signora Valentina (Henrythenavigator)
Owner: David Ward Sales price: 170,000gns (SackvilleDonald)

First foal of an unraced half-sister to Group 1-placed 5-6f 2yo winner (including at Group 2/Listed level) Lilbourne Lad, Group 3-placed 7-10f winner Bobbyscot, useful Irish 7f 2yo winner Bluebell and four other winners out of an Irish 1m 1f 3yo winning half-sister to Irish 10/14f Listed winner/Irish St Leger runner-up Pugin and Irish 12f Listed winner Chartres (later dam of UAE 2m Group 2 winner Certerach).

"He isn't overly big but very strong. He would be as exciting a two-year-old as we have at this stage, and he will begin over 6f in May or June, though will definitely stay another furlong at least."

CAP DRAMONT
9/5 ch c Iffraaj - Miss Cap Estel (Hernando)
Owner: John Pearce Racing Ltd Sales price: n/a

Fourth foal of a 10f Listed winner who was a half-sister to Listed-placed triple 1m winner Cap Francais, Swedish 1m 1f Listed winner St Jean Cap Ferrat and useful 2020 dual 6f 3yo winner Juan Les Pins out of a twice-raced maiden half-sister to 3yo Listed winners Miss Corniche (10f) and Miss Riviera Golf (1m).

"A late foal, who is big and backward but extremely good-looking. I hope to have him out in the autumn and build towards a three-year-old campaign with him. He should be a nice horse in time."

KINDNESS
14/2 b f No Nay Never - Nancy Hart (Sepoy)
Owner: David Ward Sales price: n/a

First foal of a maiden sister to 2020 7f winner Bertog and half-sister to 2021 1m 3yo winner Lightning Lou out of an 8.5f 3yo winning half-sister to high-class 6f-1m winner (four times at Group 1 level, including the 1000 Guineas) Sky Lantern, Irish 6f 2yo Group 3 winner Arctic, Queen's Vase winner Shanty Star and 6/7f Listed winner Hinton Admiral.

"A nice filly, who has strengthened up a lot recently. She goes well and would be one of our sharper youngsters who we'll look to get started in May."

KING OF JUNGLE (IRE)
28/4 ch c Bungle Inthejungle - Ayr Missile (Cadeaux Genereux)
Owner: P K Siu Sales price: £100,000 (SackvilleDonald)

Full brother to Lowther Stakes winner Living In The Past. Dam a maiden half-sister to Group 3-placed multiple 5-7f winner Outer Space and the dam of 2020 Mill Reef Stakes winner Alkumait and Irish 5.5f 3yo Listed winner The Broghie Man out of an unraced half-sister to 12f Group 3 winner Moment In Time.

"This is a good-looking colt, who has grown a huge amount since he was purchased. I thought he would be more of a two-year-old type than he's shaping up to be, though he is quite a late foal. He moves well and will hopefully see the track towards the end of the summer."

KINGOFHELL (IRE)
18/2 b c Dark Angel - Hay Chewed (Camacho)
Owner: P K Siu Sales price: 130,000gns (SackvilleDonald)

First foal of a 5f 3yo Listed winner who was a half-sister to 2020 5f 2yo Group 3/Listed winner Winter Power and Listed-placed 5-7f winner Flying Sparkle out of a 6f 2yo winning half-sister to seven winners including the dam of Irish 1m Group 2 winner/Irish 1000 Guineas third Devonshire and 5f 2yo Listed winner Hurryupharriet (herself the dam of 2021 6f Listed winner Exalted Angel (by Dark Angel)).

"This colt has got more scope than probably quite a few of Dark Angel's progeny possess. His dam was quick and related to several talented speedsters. For all he will be a two-year-old runner, this colt is the type of sprinter who will do better still at three and four. We will aim to get him started in the latter part of the summer, and he could be an exciting horse in time."

MIDNIGHT MOLL (IRE)
27/3 b f Dark Angel - Serena's Storm (Statue of Liberty)
Owner: Rockcliffe Stud Sales price: 210,000gns (SackvilleDonald)

Half-sister to high-class 5f-1m winner (including twice at Group 1 level) Rizeena, smart UK/UAE 6-9f winner (including at Group 2/3 level) Summer Romance, useful 11.5-12f Flat/bumper winner Walpole and 2020 1m 2yo winner Serena's Queen. Dam a 7f 2yo winner who was a half-sister to French 1m 1f Group 1 winner Zabeel Prince and Australian 7f/1m Group 2 winner Puissance de Lune.

"She has only just finished the breaking in process and has gone out for some spring grass. It's fantastic to be sent a horse by Rockcliffe Stud, and she's a beautiful filly with a pedigree to match. I can't see her being out earlier than the latter stages of the summer, but she's a tremendously exciting horse to have been sent to train. It's all about next year with her."

MOSTLY SUNNY (IRE)
27/1 ch c Zarak - Belle Above All (New Approach)
Owner: Ahmad Al Shaikh Sales price: €55,000 (Private Sale)

First foal of an unraced full sister to Listed-placed 7f-1m winner Pretzel and a half-sister to US 12f 3yo Grade 3 winner Dalvina (later dam of 12/14f Listed winner Dal Harraild), 10f 3yo Listed winner Soft Centre (later dam of Nassau Stakes winner Sultanina) and 10.5f 3yo Listed winner French Dressing.

"He is still immature and looks the type to have a run or two at the backend with an eye towards his three-year-old career."

MR ZERO (IRE)
5/4 b c Dark Angel - Choose Me (Choisir)
Owner: P K Siu Sales price: 100,000gns (SackvilleDonald)

Full brother to high-class multiple 1m winner (including the Queen Elizabeth II Stakes) Persuasive and a half-brother to Group 3-placed multiple 1m winner (including at Listed level) Tisbutadream, very useful 6-7f winner Amazour, useful 7-11.5f winner Songkran and 2020 6f 2yo winner Creative Force. Dam a Group 2/3-placed Irish 6-10f winner (including at Listed level) who was a half-sister to Irish 6f 3yo Listed winner Shanghai Glory.

"A strong, stocky colt, who looks sharp and does it all very well at this stage. He is a proper sprinting type, who should kick off in June or July over 6f."

PIFFLE (IRE)
24/3 b f Camacho - Siphon Melody (Siphon)
Owner: Mrs T Walker Sales price: 10,000gns (Ed Walker Racing)

Half-sister to very useful UK/US 7f-1m winner Hotsy Totsy, useful 5.5-7f winner Stationdale Lass, useful 8-10.5f winner Shamdarley, useful Irish 10-12f winner Nimitz and three other winners. Dam a US 5-8.5f winner who was a half-sister to US 12f Grade 2 winner Talloires.

"We know this family well and she looks a speedy, pretty well-set two-year-old. She is sharper than most of the other two-year-olds here and should have a busy year. I imagine she will start off in May. She is pleasing us in all that she does so far."

SPIRIT OF UAE
2/3 b c Postponed - Classic Code (Galileo)
Owner: Ahmad Al Shaikh Sales price: 38,000gns (Federico Barberini/Ahmad Al Shaikh)

Second foal of an unraced half-sister to Irish 7f 3yo Listed winner Requisition out of an Irish 1000 Guineas-winning sister to 5f 2yo winner Take Flight (later dam of Irish 6f 2yo Group 3 winner Smash Williams) and three-parts sister to Listed-placed 6-7f winner Awinnersgame.

"A really nice horse and I am amazed that he didn't make more at the sales. He is a good-looking colt who moves well and isn't quite as backward as I once thought he might be. There is a lot of Dubawi about him, and he is an exciting colt who I hope can be aimed at some proper middle-distance races next year. He will begin over 7f at some point this summer and we'll build from there."

V TWELVE (IRE)
19/3 br c Slade Power - Black Mascara (Authorized)
Owner: P K Siu Sales price: 50,000gns (SackvilleDonald)

Half-brother to Listed-placed dual 6f 2yo winner Lampang and useful 7-9.5f winner Athmad. Dam a maiden half-sister to Group 3/Listed-placed 7-8.5f winner Golden Stunner; family of five-time 1m Group 1 winner (including the Irish 2000 Guineas and Queen Anne Stakes) Canford Cliffs.

"This is an enormous colt who is by an unfashionable stallion but has done everything right to this point. He will be one to start off in the late summer and won't be busy this year. He should be a sprinter with his pedigree."

UNNAMED
30/5 b f Kingman - Stage Presence (Selkirk)
Owner: Lady Bamford Sales price: n/a

Full sister to Group 1-placed 7f-1m winner (including at Listed level) King of Comedy and a half-sister to Prix de Diane winner Star of Seville, 7f 2yo Group 3 winner English Ballet and very useful winners Sacred Act (8-8.5f) and Star of Bengal (9.5-10f). Dam a useful 7f-1m winner who was a half-sister to Irish 7f 3yo Group 3/Listed winner Rum Charger (later dam of US four-time 10/12f Grade 1 winner Winchester) and Irish 6f 2yo winner/Coventry Stakes runner-up Pakhoes.

"She isn't with us yet but I have seen her and she looks really nice. I highly doubt we'll see much of her this year, but it is fantastic to be sent a filly with a pedigree of this calibre by Lady Bamford."

UNNAMED
3/3 b f Acclamation - Vesnina (Sea The Stars)
Owner: Brightwalton Bloodstock Ltd Sales price: n/a

Half-sister to Group 3-placed 6f 2yo winner Nina Ballerina. Dam a useful 6f
2yo winner who was a half-sister to Fred Darling Stakes winner/May Hill Stakes
runner-up Marenko, very useful 8-10f winner Davydenko, useful 6f 2yo winner
Panova and 7f 2yo winners Melnikova and Potapova out of a Listed-placed
7f 3yo winning daughter of 1000 Guineas/Lockinge Stakes winner Russian
Rhythm.

*"An entirely different model to Nina Ballerina who was a sharp two-year-old,
whereas this filly is a more scopey individual. She might go out for some spring
grass and come back to be trained for a late summer/early autumn campaign
with half an eye on next year."*

TOM WARD

BLENHEIM BELLE (IRE)
17/4 b f Churchill - Adja (Rock of Gibraltar)
Owner: The Lockdown Syndicate Sales price: n/a

Half-sister to Grade 3-placed French/US dual 1m winner Amboseli, very useful
French/Hong Kong 6f-1m winner Raging Blitzkrieg and three other winners.
Dam a maiden close relation to French 10.5f Group 2 winner Actrice and a
half-sister to US 1m 1f Grade 1 winner Angara, French 12.5f 3yo Listed winner
Arlesienne (later dam of 10f Group 3 winner Affaire Solitaire) and the dam of
10.5f Group 3 winner Teodoro.

*"A lovely big filly, who has only just arrived but certainly looks a nice type of
horse. She is out of a good mare, who has produced a black type performer
already. This filly looks to be a mid-season type of two-year-old."*

BRAVE LILY (IRE)
20/4 ch f Camacho - Song of Sixpence (Among Men)
Owner: Keep Kicking Racing Sales price: 5,500gns (Keep Kicking Racing)

Half-sister to Irish 7f-1m winner William Ashford. Dam a twice-raced maiden
half-sister to useful Irish 5-7f 3yo winner Ilanga and Irish 8.5-9f 3yo winner
Privatize out of a maiden half-sister to Group 3-placed Irish 1m 3yo winner
Home Bound.

"A nice filly, who looks like being a fairly early type. We haven't pushed any buttons yet, but she has been showing all the right signs. I would hope for her to be running in early May, and she should provide her owners with plenty of sport this year."

BROWN OWL (IRE)
22/4 b f Footstepsinthesand - Serabrina (Iffraaj)
Owner: The Scout Syndicate Sales price: n/a

First foal of a maiden daughter of a once-raced French 5.5f 2yo winner who was a half-sister to 2020 Irish 6f 3yo Group 3 winner Art Power, Irish 6f Group 3 winner Penny Pepper, French 6.5f 3yo Listed winner Morning Frost and very useful UK/US 7-10f winner Shaan.

"This filly has a good way of going and is pretty quick. She certainly has enough speed to begin over 5f and should be one of our first two-year-old runners as things stand."

DARK FLYER
4/2 b c Gutaifan - Light of Love (Dylan Thomas)
Owner: Matthew Webber Sales price: £15,000 (Stroud Coleman BS/Tom Ward)

Second foal of a maiden close relation to smart multiple 6f winner (including at Group 3 level) Bygone Days and half-sister to very useful prolific 5-7f winner Dungannon and useful 10-12f winner Green Light; family of Prix du Jockey Club winner Lawman and Prix de Diane winner Latice.

"A very nice horse who is progressing all the time. He hasn't done much yet, but all the signs have been good so far. I imagine he will wait for the 6f races to begin in earnest."

LADY DOLLARS
15/4 b f Havana Gold - Shozita (Showcasing)
Owner: O J W Pawle Sales price: 6,500gns (Vendor)

First foal of a 6f 2yo winner who was the daughter of an unraced half-sister to smart 10-10.5f winner (including at Group 3/Listed level) Danadana, useful 10-14f winner Semeen and useful 2020 dual 14f 3yo winner Zeeband; family of French 10f Group 1 winner Ajman Princess and 1m Group 2/3 winner Afsare.

"This filly is probably the most precocious of the bunch at present. She has done two bits of work - one on grass and the other on the all-weather - and easily has the speed to kick off over 5f."

UNNAMED
27/1 b f Twilight Son - The Dukkerer (Footstepsinthesand)
Owner: A Syndicate Sales price: 18,000gns (Vendor)

First foal of a 7-10f winner who was a half-sister to US 12f Grade 2 winner
Boule d'Or, US 12f Listed winner Saffron Dancer, useful 12f-2m winner
Knockholt and useful Irish 6f 2yo winner Catoffle out of an Irish 12-13f 3yo
winner.

*"Like most by her sire, she will take a little bit of time. She is a solid, well put
together filly, who won't do much before the middle of the season but certainly
gives off all the right signs."*

UNNAMED (IRE)
23/3 b c Awtaad - Wake Up (Soldier of Fortune)
Owner: Mrs A G Kavanagh Sales price: n/a

Third foal of a French dual 11f 3yo winner who was a half-sister to German 11f
Listed winner Path Wind out a German dual 11f 3yo winning sister to German
12f 3yo Group 2 winner Wild Side (later dam of Park Hill Stakes winner Wild
Coco and German triple 11/14f Listed winner Weltmacht) and half-sister to
French 7f 2yo Group 3 winner White Rose (later dam of Listed winners Elite
Army (12f) and Pure Diamond (7f)).

*"This is a big, scopey colt, who is still rather backward and will likely take some
time. He is a very nice horse, who has shown ability without us having done
much with him yet. I imagine he will be running at the end of the summer or
during the early autumn."*

SEAN WOODS

BORGI (IRE)
3/3 b c Anjaal - One Time (Olden Times)
Owner: S P C Woods Sales price: £3,500 (Dwayne Woods)

Second foal of an unraced half-sister to useful 6f 2yo winner Maccus and Italian 6f-1m winner Fastandelegant out of a maiden sister to German 1m Group 2 winner Sehrezad; family of good jumper Roman Flight and Listed bumper winner Burn Out.

"We picked him up exceptionally cheaply as a yearling and would happily have paid ten times as much for him. He has got a rounded action and should be running over 7f/1m later this year."

ELSAAB
24/2 gr f El Kabeir - Miss Mediator (Consolidator)
Owner: The Storm Again Syndicate Sales price: 29,000gns (Dwayne Woods)

Half-sister to 11.5-12f Flat/2m hurdle winner Peace Prevails and 1m 2yo winner Galahad. Dam an Irish 1m winner who was a half-sister to Irish 6f 2yo Group 3 winner Great White Eagle, very useful 6f 2yo winner Quarrel and very useful UK/Hong Kong 7f-1m winner Kings Shield.

"This filly is owned by people who were owners with us the first time around. Everyone that has one by El Kabeir seems to like them, and this is a sizeable filly who is ready to step up her workload very soon."

LITE AND AIRY
23/2 b c Twilight Son - Spin Doctor (Mayson)
Owner: N O'Keeffe Sales price: £62,000 (Dwayne Woods)

First foal of a useful 5-6f 2yo winner who was a half-sister to smart 7-8.5f winner (including at Group 3/Listed level) Clinical, 7f 2yo Group 3 winner Cupid's Glory, 8/10f 3yo Listed winner Courting (later dam of 1m Listed winner Fury) and 6f Listed winner Prescription.

"A really nice colt who won't be out until July or July but is doing everything right at this stage. He is owned by some lovely people and should be a fun two-year-old for them."

SHAKENOTSTIRRED
19/3 b f Havana Gold - So Funny (Distorted Humor)
Owner: Mrs Melba Bryce Sales price: n/a

Second foal of a French 10-11.5f 3yo winner who was a full sister to US 8.5f 3yo Grade 3 winner Colizeo and a half-sister to useful French 9.5-10.5f 3yo winner Tambourin out of a French 1m 1f 3yo Listed winner; family of Queen Anne Stakes/Sussex Stakes winner Solow.

"She is a homebred from Colin Bryce's Laundry Cottage Stud. I imagine she will come to hand very quickly once we press the button with her."

UDABERRI (IRE)
13/3 gr c Mastercraftsman - Eccellente Idea (Excellent Art)
Owner: S P C Woods Sales price: 55,000gns (Dwayne Woods)

Half-brother to 2020 Norwegian 7f 2yo winner Prince of Fjords. Dam an Italian 10-11f winner who was a full sister to fairly useful multiple 7-12f winner Swift Cedar and a half-sister to US 1m Grade 1 winner Off Limits (by Mastercraftsman) and Listed-placed Italian 5-10f winner Seinellanima.

"This colt wouldn't be your typical Mastercraftsman, and he should be ready to get underway by the early summer. He is progressing all the time and is about to move into fast work."

UNNAMED
21/3 ch c The Last Lion - Blue Crest (Verglas)
Owner: S P C Woods Sales price: 27,000gns (Dwayne Woods)

Half-brother to very useful multiple 5f winner (including at Listed level) Dave Dexter, useful dual 6f winner Silver Machine and fairly useful 5.5-6f winner My Amigo. Dam a useful French dual 7.5f winner who was a half-sister to Listed-placed Italian 5.5-7.5f winner Ideal Coco and useful French 6-9f winner Private Dancer.

"He is growing all the time, and I would hope to see him running sometime in June or July. He will let us know when he's ready."

Dave Dexter

UNNAMED
14/4 b c Pivotal - Celeste (Green Desert)
Owner: S P C Woods Sales price: 100,000gns (Dwayne Woods)

Full brother to Grade 3-placed UK/Canadian dual 7f winner (including at stakes level) Endless Light and a half-brother to very useful Irish/UAE 6-7f winner Van Der Decken. Dam an unraced half-sister to US triple 9/10f Grade 1 winner Megahertz, Group 1-placed 7-9f winner (including at Group 3/Listed level) Heaven Sent, Listed-placed dual 1m winner Heavenly Dawn and very useful multiple 5-7f winner Orion's Bow (all by Pivotal).

"A big horse who will need plenty of time, but he has done everything right to this point and is a very likeable individual with a solid pedigree."

UNNAMED
9/3 b c Pride of Dubai - Cephalonie (Kris S)
Owner: S P C Woods Sales price: 60,000gns (Armando Duarte)

Half-brother to French 1m 3yo Listed winner Arctic Gyr, Group 3-placed 6f-1m winner (including at Listed level) Festivale, Group 3/Listed-placed 6f-1m winner Tell and useful 6f 2yo winner Simple Magic. Dam a French 12f 3yo winner who was a half-sister to Japanese 9/10f Listed winner Fifty Oner out of an unraced half-sister to French 7f Listed winner Esperero and Japanese 11f 3yo Listed winner Shinko Calido.

"I particularly like Pride of Dubai, who has done exceptionally well in Australia. He has been stuck down there for the past couple of years, so there aren't many of them around in this part of the world. This colt will need a fair bit of time as he is a sizeable sort. One for the autumn."

UNNAMED (IRE)
15/3 b c Exceed And Excel - Cottonmouth (Noverre)
Owner: S P C Woods Sales price: £170,000 (Dwayne Woods)

Closely related to Italian triple 10/12f Group 1 winner Dylan Mouth (by Dylan Thomas) and Italian 1m 1f Listed winner Per Un Dixir (by Holy Roman Emperor) and a half-brother to Italian 12f 3yo Listed winner/Derby Italiano runner-up Henry Mouth. Dam an Italian 10f Group 3 winner who was a half-sister to Irish 2m Grade 1 hurdle winner Jumbo Rio.

"He comes from a hugely successful Italian family, which Exceed And Excel should inject some speed into. He is upsides cantering at present and doing everything right."

UNNAMED (IRE)
23/4 b c Holy Roman Emperor - Dame Lucy (Refuse To Bend)
Owner: Ignited Sales price: £50,000 (Dwayne Woods)

Half-brother to Irish 8-10.5f winner Will Be King. Dam a UK/Irish 10-12f winner who was a half-sister to very useful dual 1m winner Mothers Finest out of a maiden half-sister to US 1m 1f Grade 3 winner Coney Kitten and the dam of Dante Stakes winner/Derby runner-up Libertarian and 10f Group 3/Listed winner Prince Siegfried.

"A nice, well-grown colt, who is nearly ready to start working. He has done everything right so far. We've had horses for these owners before, and it's lovely to have been able to put them back together again."

UNNAMED (IRE)
28/4 b c Profitable - Deora De (Night Shift)
Owner: Ignited Sales price: £37,000 (Dwayne Woods)

Half-brother to 2020 5f 2yo winner Risque and five other winners. Dam a once-raced maiden sister to US 1m stakes winner Deal Breaker and half-sister to Richmond Stakes winner Prolific and 6f 2yo winner Scintillating out of a 1m 3yo winning half-sister to Royal Lodge Stakes winner Atlantis Prince.

"This colt isn't overly big but is a well-made type. He comes from the family of our 2000 Royal Lodge Stakes winner, Atlantis Prince, and should start work within the next month or so."

UNNAMED
25/3 b c New Bay - Highlands Queen (Mount Nelson)
Owner: J C H Hui Sales price: £240,000 (Dwayne Woods)

Second foal of a smart French 10-12.5f 3yo winner (including at Group 2/3 level) who was the granddaughter of a Group 3/Listed-placed French 9.5-10.5f winning half-sister to 2m Grade 1 chase winner/Champion Chase third Kalahari King.

"This is the best two-year-old we have got here, both in terms of pedigree and just as an individual. He cost a lot of money but rightly so as he's a lovely colt. I wouldn't swap him for anything."

UNNAMED (IRE)
6/2 ch c Cityscape - Paradise Way (Elusive Quality)
Owner: S P C Woods Sales price: 23,000gns (Dwayne Woods)

Half-brother to useful French 5.5-6f winner Lostinparadise and 7-8.5f winner Bring Us Paradise. Dam an unraced half-sister to useful triple 10f winner Haalan out of a US 1m 1f Listed-winning half-sister to 10f 3yo Listed winner Bonne Etoile.

"A sizeable colt with plenty of scope. He won't be overly early but is a very nice horse in the making."

UNNAMED (IRE)
21/4 b c Caravaggio - Seagull (Sea The Stars)
Owner: J C H Hui Sales price: 105,000gns (Dwayne Woods)

Half-brother to useful 7f 2yo winner Wasaayef and 10f 3yo winner Whimbrel. Dam a useful 12f 3yo winner who was a half-sister to Irish 1000 Guineas winner Nightime (later dam of four-time 10-12f Group 1 winner Ghaiyyath and US 11f Grade 1 winner Zhukova), Listed-placed Irish 1m 2yo winner Mermaid Island and six other winners out of an Irish 1m Listed winner.

"A lovely big colt who is a quality individual. He is maturing at present, and we will look to increase his workload over the next month or so. He will be one for later on but is an exciting prospect."

UNNAMED (IRE)
23/2 b c Holy Roman Emperor - Vibe Queen (Invincible Spirit)
Owner: J C H Hui Sales price: £70,000 (Dwayne Woods)

Third foal of a 7f 3yo winner who was a half-sister to useful triple 12f Flat/2m 3f hurdle winner Batts Rock and Irish 7f 2yo winner Pablo Diablo out of a Listed-placed Irish 1m 3yo winning close relation to Prix de l'Abbaye winner Imperial Beauty and Grade 3-placed French/US 8-10f winner Gulsary.

"A nice colt who has done one piece of work so far which pleased us plenty."

SECTION TWO

JOHN WARREN (THE QUEEN)

Mr Warren reported the following trio of two-year-olds, owned by Her Majesty The Queen, to be *"forward types who are pleasing their trainers at this early stage."*

DUKEDOM (IRE)
27/1 b c Dubawi - Nathra (Iffraaj)
Trainer: John & Thady Gosden Sales price: n/a

First foal of a Group 1-placed triple 7f winner (including at Group 3 level)/Poule d'Essai des Pouliches runner-up who was the daughter of a maiden sister to the dam of Irish 6f 2yo Group 1 winner Dick Whittington and close relation to July Cup winner Owington.

IMPROVISE (FR)
3/4 b f Iffraaj - Set To Music (Danehill Dancer)
Trainer: Michael Bell Sales price: n/a

Full sister to Listed-placed 8.5-10f winner Eightsome Reel. Dam a Group 2/3-placed 10-12f winner (including twice at Listed level) who was a half-sister to Listed-placed Irish 10f 3yo winner Zarafsha, useful UK/Australian 8.5-11f winner Mr Reckless and the unraced dam of Group 3-placed 2020 French 7f 2yo winner La Gioiosa.

PERFECT ALIBI
23/2 b f Le Havre - Daphne (Duke of Marmalade)
Trainer: William Haggas Sales price: n/a

First foal of a 13f Listed winner who was closely related to 7f 2yo winner Queen's Prize (dam of Listed-placed 2020 10-10.5f 3yo winner Award Scheme) and a half-sister to Listed-placed UK/Australian 10-12f winner Bold Sniper and very useful UK/UAE 10-12f winner Highland Glen out of a 12f 3yo winning half-sister to dual 7f Listed winner Golden Stream and 7f 2yo winner/Oaks runner-up Flight of Fancy.

JACK CANTILLON (TINNAKILL HOUSE STUD)

LADY BEAR (IRE)
10/3 b f Kodi Bear - Always The Lady (Cape Cross)
Trainer: Johnny Murtagh Owner: Syndicates.Racing Sales price: £7,000
(Syndicates Racing/Kelly Equine)

Half-sister to useful Irish 1m 3yo winner Claim The Lady and 7f 2yo winner Ray
Donovan. Dam a useful 10f 3yo winner who was closely related to useful 11-
12.5f winner Magellan and a half-sister to smart 8-10.5f winner (including at
Group 3/Listed level) Class Is Class and useful 10f 3yo winner Ascot Lime out of
a Group 3-placed 6f 2yo winner.

*"While not raised at Tinnakill, this filly was well found by John Bourke at the
Tattersalls Ireland September Sale. She is showing all the right signs for Johnny
Murtagh, and she should give her owners a lot of fun. I think she'll prove a
bargain at £7,000."*

LOVE DE VEGA (IRE)
9/2 b c Lope de Vega - Ribble (Motivator)
Trainer: Mark Johnston Owner: Crone Stud Farms Sales price: 92,000gns
(Johnston Racing)

First foal of a maiden three-parts sister to Listed-placed 9.5f 3yo winner Three
Moons (later dam of 12f 3yo Listed winner Tashaar) and useful 12f-2m winner
Steve Rogers and a half-sister to UAE 6f Group 1 winner The Right Man (by
Lope de Vega) and Listed-placed 6f 2yo winner Black Velvet.

*"This colt was bred to be sharp as he's out of a half-sister to Group 1-winning
sprinter, The Right Man (also by Lope de Vega). He took things very easily as a
foal, and I'm delighted to see early entries for him as I didn't expect him to be
appearing quite so soon."*

NEW YORK CITY (IRE)
12/2 b/br c Invincible Spirit - Rajeem (Diktat)
Trainer: Aidan O'Brien Owner: Mrs John Magnier Sales price: 600,000gns (M
V Magnier)

Full brother to Group 1-placed multiple 6f winner (including at Group 2/3
level) Invincible Army. Dam a Falmouth Stakes winner who was a half-sister to
the unraced dam of Fred Darling Stakes winner Dandhu out of a maiden sister
to Prix Morny winner Hoh Magic.

"We've heard some very strong whispers from Tipperary about this colt, and they've certainly backed that up with quite the name! He was the most magnificent foal when he sold to Mimi Wadham and Violet Hesketh for 375,000gns. They did a terrific job with him to build him up into a 600,000gns yearling. He's the horse we are most looking forward to seeing on a racetrack this season. It wouldn't surprise me if I'm sending a mare or two to him in a few years!"

TRANQUIL LADY (IRE)
30/4 ch f Australia - Repose (Quiet American)
Trainer: Joseph O'Brien Owner: Teme Valley 2 Sales price: £160,000 (Richard Ryan)

Half-sister to 2020 Irish 7f 2yo winner/Champagne Stakes third State of Rest. Dam an unraced half-sister to Group 2-placed 8.5-10f winner (including at Listed level) Prince Alzain and 7f 2yo Listed winner/May Hill Stakes runner-up Echo River; family of Champion Stakes/US dual 10f Grade 1 winner Storming Home and Poule d'Essai des Pouliches winner Musical Chimes.

"This filly was all class and we sold her to a great judge in Richard Ryan at the Goffs Orby Yearling Sale at Doncaster for £160,000. The reports from 'the Hill' have all been positive, and we'd love it if she could make up into an Oaks filly for her owners."

ALASTAIR DONALD (BLOODSTOCK AGENT)

KINGOFHELL (IRE)
18/2 b c Dark Angel - Hay Chewed (Camacho)
Trainer: Ed Walker Owner: P K Siu Sales price: 130,000gns (SackvilleDonald)

First foal of a 5f 3yo Listed winner who was a half-sister to 2020 5f 2yo Group 3/Listed winner Winter Power and Listed-placed 5-7f winner Flying Sparkle out of a 6f 2yo winning half-sister to seven winners including the dam of Irish 1m Group 2 winner/Irish 1000 Guineas third Devonshire and 5f 2yo Listed winner Hurryupharriet (herself the dam of 2021 6f Listed winner Exalted Angel (by Dark Angel)).

"First foal from a very fast family. He's an excellent mover who's shaping up well and may well be ready in time for Royal Ascot."

MR ZERO (IRE)
5/4 b c Dark Angel - Choose Me (Choisir)
Trainer: Ed Walker Owner: P K Siu Sales price: 100,000gns (SackvilleDonald)

Full brother to high-class multiple 1m winner (including the Queen Elizabeth II Stakes) Persuasive and a half-brother to Group 3-placed multiple 1m winner (including at Listed level) Tisbutadream, very useful 6-7f winner Amazour, useful 7-11.5f winner Songkran and 2020 6f 2yo winner Creative Force. Dam a Group 2/3-placed Irish 6-10f winner (including at Listed level) who was a half-sister to Irish 6f 3yo Listed winner Shanghai Glory.

"A full brother to Persuasive, who was a bargain at 100k from Book 1 of the Tattersalls October Yearling Sale. He does everything really well and should be ready in the summer for the 6f races."

UNNAMED (IRE)
9/3 b c Dark Angel - Golden Rosie (Exceed And Excel)
Trainer: Roger Varian Owner: King Power Racing Co Ltd Sales price: 260,000gns (SackvilleDonald)

Full brother to Group 2-placed UK/UAE 7f-1m winner Golden Goal and a half-brother to Listed-placed 5-6f winner Rosie's Premiere. Dam a 6f 2yo winner who was a half-sister to Group 1-placed prolific 6-8.5f winner (including at Group 2/3 level) Sovereign Debt (by Dark Angel) and Fred Darling Stakes winner/Cheveley Park Stakes fourth Puff.

"A tough, solid horse who takes things well and looks like being ready in May for the 6f races. His full brother, Golden Goal, is a good horse in Dubai."

UNNAMED
3/4 b c Aclaim - Itsinthestars (Zoffany)
Trainer: Richard Hannon Owner: King Power Racing Co Ltd Sales price: 75,000gns (SackvilleDonald)

Half-brother to useful dual 7f winner Gravity Force. Dam a maiden daughter of a Group 3/Listed-placed Irish 7f 2yo winner who was a half-sister to Listed-placed dual 1m winner Caughnawaga, Listed-placed Irish triple 12f winner Gemini Diamond and Listed-placed French 10f 3yo winner Vellankria.

"This colt looks very professional and should be ready for when the first 6f races are here."

UNNAMED
23/1 ch c Frankel - Mix And Mingle (Exceed And Excel)
Trainer: Andrew Balding Owner: King Power Racing Co Ltd Sales price:
300,000gns (SackvilleDonald)

First foal of a 7f Group 3 winner who was a full sister to useful 2020 dual 7f
3yo winner Double Or Bubble and a half-sister to UK/Qatari 9-10f winner May
Queen out of a 12f 3yo winning close relation to Group 1-placed 7-12f winner
(including at Group 2/3 level)/St Leger runner-up High Accolade.

*"A most impressive individual. The mare was very good, and this is her first
foal. He reminds me of Fivethousandtoone, who was second for us in last
year's Mill Reef Stakes. This colt does everything very well and should be a
midsummer 7f type of horse."*

UNNAMED (FR)
1/3 ch c Almanzor - Nehalennia (Giant's Causeway)
Trainer: Roger Varian Owner: King Power Racing Co Ltd Sales price:
210,000gns (SackvilleDonald)

Half-brother to stakes-placed US 5.5-6.5f winner Navy Hymn. Dam a US 1m
winner who was closely related to Irish 5f 2yo Listed winner/Queen Mary
Stakes runner-up Meow (later dam of Dewhurst Stakes and 2000 Guineas
winner Churchill and Cheveley Park Stakes winner Clemmie) and a half-sister
to Irish 9.5f 3yo Group 3 winner Aloof, 2020 Irish 1m 3yo Listed winner
Keats and French 1m Listed winner Orator out of a very smart 5f-1m winner
(including the Cheveley Park Stakes).

*"A lovely, scopey horse who has a lot of quality. The best of him probably won't
be seen until next year, however, and I doubt he'll be in action until September/
October time."*

UNNAMED
21/3 b c Nathaniel - Robema (Cadeaux Genereux)
Trainer: Andrew Balding Owner: King Power Racing Co Ltd Sales price:
200,000gns (SackvilleDonald)

Closely related to 1m 2yo Listed winner Connect and Listed-placed 7-8.5f
winner Atlantic Sun (both by Roderic O'Connor) and a half-brother to useful
dual 6f 2yo winner Leontes. Dam a 7.5f-1m winner who was a full sister to
Listed-placed 8-8.5f winner Granted (later dam of 10f Listed winner Rewarded
and 1m 3yo Listed winner Perfect Star (herself dam of 7f 2yo Group 3 winner
Kilmah)).

"A very athletic horse, who looks quite an early type for the sire. The mare has done very well, boasting a 5/5 record and producing useful horses who were all by lesser sires than Nathaniel. We hope that this could be a Chesham horse."

ALEX ELLIOTT (BLOODSTOCK AGENT)

ALWAYS LOVE YOU
5/4 b f Siyouni - True Match (Cape Cross)
Trainer: Roger Varian Owner: Amo Racing Limited Sales price: €220,000
(Elliott Bloodstock Services Ltd)

Half-sister to 2020 French 11f 3yo winner Lady Lilnoi. Dam a once-raced maiden who was closely related to useful 7f 2yo winner Zephuros and a half-sister to Group 3-placed 10-12f winner Setting Sail and dual 6f 2yo winner New Winds out of a Prix de Diane-winning half-sister to the dam of high-class performers Thunder Snow, Ihtimal and Always Smile.

"This filly is bred on the same cross as Siyouni's best filly to date, Laurens. She was something of a 'must buy' given that, and the fact she is very well put together. She was pretty strong and forward when purchased, and I look forward to seeing what she can do in the early part of the summer."

CARDINAL ROUGE (IRE)
19/3 br c Holy Roman Emperor - Flawless Pink (More Than Ready)
Trainer: Ralph Beckett Owner: The Audax Partnership Sales price: 70,000gns
(A C Elliott, Agent/R Beckett)

Closely related to dual 6f winner Champagne Supanova (by Camacho). Dam a maiden half-sister to 2021 French 1m 3yo Listed winner Sweet Lady and Lingfield Oaks Trial winner Toujours L'Amour out of a 13f 3yo Listed winner/May Hill Stakes runner-up.

"A cracking colt who is a brother to a two-year-old winner. I loved everything about this horse from the moment I set eyes on him, and he continues to shape up well at home. He is out of a mare by More Than Ready, who is a renowned broodmare sire, while the progeny of the sire, Holy Roman Emperor, show up consistently every season. We are really looking forward to getting him started, and as a mid-March foal should be ready to run in the first part of the season."

DELOREAN (IRE)
7/2 b c Time Test - Dawn of Empire (Empire Maker)
Trainer: Ralph Beckett Owner: The Lucra Partnership II Sales price: 50,000gns
(A C Elliott, Agent/R Beckett)

Half-brother to 2020 6f 3yo winner Crispina. Dam a thrice-raced maiden half-sister to dual 7f 3yo Listed winner Tantina (later dam of UAE 1m 1f Group 1 winner Cityscape and high-class sprinter Bated Breath and grandam of St Leger winner Logician), Grade 2-placed UK/US 9-10f winner Trekking and the unraced dam of Gimcrack Stakes winner Ajaya and 2020 dual 10f Group 3 winner Extra Elusive.

"Probably the best-named horse of all the yearlings I bought in 2020. Delorean in one of five horses owned by The Lucra Partnership that owned New Mandate last season. The premise of the syndicate is to buy staying yearlings that are to be sold on at the end of their three-year-old career. This is a beautiful colt by first-season sire, Time Test. As a son of Dubawi, I give Time Test every chance of making it as a sire. New Bay was in the same shoes last season and produced New Mandate for us so we are hoping lightning can strike twice."

POSTMARK
20/4 b c Postponed - Dream Wild (Oasis Dream)
Trainer: Ralph Beckett Owner: The Audax Partnership Sales price: 52,000gns
(A C Elliott, Agent/R Beckett)

Half-brother to 13.5f-2m winner Swordbill. Dam a 1m 3yo winner who was a half-sister to Yorkshire Oaks winner/St Leger runner-up Quiff, 10f 3yo winner/Chester Vase runner-up Arabian Gulf and 12f 3yo winner/Queen's Vase third Total Command out of a 1000 Guineas-winning half-sister to 10f Listed Flat/2m Grade 2 hurdle winner Ulundi and the dam of May Hill Stakes winner Half Glance.

"Bred by trainer Roger Varian, this colt is the son of first-season sire, Postponed, who although renowned for his exploits as an older horse, made up into a smart two-year-old, starting out in July and finishing his season with a second in a valuable sales race over seven furlongs. I expect this colt to begin his career at a similar stage, and he is showing up well at home."

UNSPOKEN (IRE)
19/2 b c Territories - Silent Secret (Dubai Destination)
Trainer: Ralph Beckett Owner: The Audax Partnership Sales price: 65,000gns
(Vendor)

Half-brother to Irish 7f 2yo Listed winner Sparkle'n'joy and four other winners.

Dam a 7.5f 2yo winner who was a half-sister to Irish 7f/1m Group 3 winner Cheyenne Star (grandam of four-time 8-10f Group 1 winner Barney Roy) and the unraced dam of high-class prolific 6f-1m winner (including at Group 1 level) Gordon Lord Byron.

"Having pointed out New Mandate from early on last year, Unspoken seems to have been the horse that Ralph has nominated each time we have spoken this year. He trained the 98-rated William Bligh last year, so we were keen to get another son of Territories. So far, we have not been disappointed. There are some really hard-knocking performers in this colt's pedigree, such as Barney Roy and Gordon Lord Byron. The stallion's progeny seem best with some cut in this ground, so watch out for this guy when we get some rain."

JOE FOLEY (CLIPPER LOGISTICS)

FRENCH ROMANCE
15/1 b f Le Havre - Soho Susie (Montjeu)
Trainer: Richard Hannon Sales price: £55,000 (Peter & Ross Doyle Bloodstock)

Fourth foal of an unraced close relation to useful 12f 3yo winner Parvana and a half-sister to Group 1-placed 5-6f 2yo winner (including twice at Group 2 level) Mehmas and three other winners out of an unraced half-sister to triple 10/11f Group 3 winner Blue Monday, Australian 7f Listed winner Rugged Cross and the grandam of Poule d'Essai des Pouliches/Prix de Diane winner Avenir Certain (by Le Havre).

"This filly was purchased from Rathasker Stud at the Goffs Orby Sale. She is closely related to Avenir Certain (also by Le Havre) who won two Classics in France, while the dam is a Montjeu half-sister to Mehmas. She is a lovely, big-striding filly who should make a nice autumn two-year-old."

ILLUSTRATING
28/3 b f Showcasing - Maids Causeway (Giant's Causeway)
Trainer: Karl Burke Sales price: n/a

Half-sister to 2020 Canadian 1m Grade 2/US 9.5f Grade 3 winner Elizabeth Way, 6f 2yo winner Gmaash and three other winners. Dam a Coronation Stakes winner/1000 Guineas runner-up who was a half-sister to Group 3-placed Irish 7f 2yo winner Uimhir A Haon; family of Hong Kong Vase winner Vallee Enchantee and French 9/10f 3yo Group 1 winner Vespone.

"Maids Causeway was one of the top fillies of her generation, while her five-year-old daughter, Elizabeth Way, won a couple of graded events in North America last year. This is an athletic filly with a good action, who has pleased all that have ridden her this spring. Karl Burke has done so well with the progeny of Showcasing, and hopefully that proves to be the case once again."

SUPERIOR COUNCIL (IRE)
21/2 b c Kodiac - Odyssee (Teofilo)
Trainer: Richard Fahey Sales price: 185,000gns (Joe Foley)

Half-brother to 2020 6f 2yo winner Sandhoe. Dam a French 1m 1f 3yo winner who was a half-sister to Grade 2/3-placed French/US 7-9f winner Urban King, Listed-placed French 7.5f 3yo winner Victoria College and French 12f 3yo winner Uruguay (later dam of French 7f 2yo Group 3 winner Dame Du Roi) out of an Italian 6f 3yo Group 3 winner.

"This colt cost 185,000gns from Book 1 of the Tattersalls October Yearling Sale. He is a big, good-moving colt, who hasn't long been with Richard at Musley Bank."

UNNAMED (IRE)
11/4 b c Wootton Bassett - Dazzling Rose (Raven's Pass)
Trainer: William Haggas Sales price: 135,000gns (Joe Foley)

Second foal of a 1m 3yo winner who was the daughter of a French 11.5f 3yo winner who was a half-sister to the dams of Prix du Jockey Club/Champion Stakes winner Almanzor and 2020 US 6.5f 3yo Grade 3 winner Guildsman (both by Wootton Bassett); family of very smart miler Darjina.

"This colt was bought for 125,000gns as a foal and is bred along the same lines as Almanzor. He is a good-looking, strong colt, who moves well and has a great attitude. A nice prospect for the autumn."

UNNAMED
14/4 gr f Dark Angel - Katie's Diamond (Turtle Bowl)
Trainer: William Haggas Sales price: 100,000gns (Vendor)

Second foal of a 6f 2yo Listed winner who was the daughter of a French 8.5f winner who was a half-sister to French 7f 2yo Group 3 winner Aquatinta, Swiss 10f Listed winner Armand and German 11f 3yo Listed winner Amazonit.

"The dam was a fast two-year-old for Karl Burke, and this is a nice, athletic filly with plenty of quality about her. She has been showing up nicely at home and has recently joined William Haggas."

UNNAMED (IRE)
24/3 b c Mehmas - La Cuvee (Mark of Esteem)
Trainer: Johnny Murtagh Sales price: £190,000 (Joe Foley)

Half-brother to 2020 Matron Stakes winner Champers Elysees and useful
5-8.5f winner Daddies Girl. Dam a maiden half-sister to Italian 1m 3yo Group 3
winner She Bat (later dam of Italian Listed winners She Breeze (7f) and She Is
Great (10f) and US 8.5f 3yo stakes winner She Spirit di Su) and 1m 3yo Listed
winner Cask; family of Premio Parioli winner Al Rep.

*"This colt is a half-brother to last year's Group 1-winning filly, Champers
Elysees. He has recently joined her in the Curragh yard of Johnny Murtagh, and
is a tough, strong colt who has shown up nicely in his early work."*

UNNAMED
30/1 ch f Night of Thunder - Operettist (Singspiel)
Trainer: Roger Varian Sales price: 44,000gns (Joe Foley)

Half-sister to 2020 5f 2yo winner Toplight. Dam a 7f 2yo winner who was
a half-sister to multiple 7-9.5f winner Admirable Art and 6f 2yo winners
Admirable Spirit and Alpine Affair; family of seven-time 6/7f Listed winner
Quito.

*"This filly shares the same broodmare sire as one of our favourites, Suedois,
and she's by the rapidly-emerging Night of Thunder. She is a flashy individual
who shows plenty of ability."*

UNNAMED (IRE)
25/4 b c Dandy Man - Paddy Again (Moss Vale)
Trainer: Richard Hannon Sales price: £45,000 (Joe Foley)

Full brother to very useful multiple 5f winner Leodis Dream. Dam a 5f 2yo
winner who was a half-sister to very useful multiple 7-12f winner Original
Choice out of a maiden half-sister to Group 2/3-placed dual 10f 3yo winner
(including at Listed level) Asawer and French 6/7f Listed winner Chercheuse
(later dam of US 9/10f Grade 1 winner Questing).

*"This is a good-looking colt and he's all about speed, which isn't a surprise
given he's a brother to the fast and talented Leodis Dream. He should be a
nice, early two-year-old runner over the minimum distance."*

UNNAMED
29/3 br c Siyouni - Patronising (Galileo)
Trainer: William Haggas Sales price: 150,000gns (Joe Foley)

Third foal of an unraced half-sister to high-class 6f-1m winner (including twice at Group 1 level) Lillie Langtry (later dam of very smart multiple 6-12f winner (seven times at Group 1 level, including the 1000 Guineas and Oaks) Minding and Irish 1m 3yo Group 3 winner Kissed By Angels) and Irish 1m 3yo Listed winner Count of Limonade.

"This is a lovely big colt out of a Galileo half-sister to the very smart Lillie Langtry, who herself produced the top-class Minding. He possesses plenty of class but is very much one for the autumn."

UNNAMED (IRE)
11/2 ch f Bated Breath - Queen Andorra (Finsceal Fior)
Trainer: James Fanshawe Sales price: £48,000 (Joe Foley)

First foal of a twice-raced maiden half-sister to Irish 9.5f Group 3 winner Duchess Andorra and Irish 8.5f 3yo winner Expected out of an unraced sister to Cheveley Park Stakes winner Embassy (grandam of Prix Maurice de Gheest winner King's Apostle) and half-sister to Irish 10f Group 2 winner Tarfshi (grandam of 6f 2yo Listed winner Vital Statistics, herself the dam of French 7f 2yo Group 3 winner/Breeders' Cup Juvenile Fillies Turf runner-up/Poule d'Essai des Pouliches third East).

"We have been lucky with progeny of Bated Breath, and this filly is bred on a similar cross to that of our Group 2/3 winner, Space Traveller. This is a nice, good-moving daughter of the Juddmonte stallion, and we've recently sent her to James Fanshawe."

RICHIE GALWAY (ALPHA RACING)

BEGINISH (IRE)
20/2 ch c New Approach - La Superba (Medicean)
Trainer: Jessica Harrington Sales price: 105,000gns (BBA Ireland)

Second foal of a useful 8-8.5f 3yo winner who was a half-sister to Doncaster Cup winner/high-class hurdler Thomas Hobson out of a Listed-placed 8.5f 3yo winning half-sister to 1m Listed winner Brindisi (later dam of 12f Listed winner Livia's Dream) and useful dual 10f Flat/2m Listed hurdle winner Torphichen; family of Oaks winner Talent (by New Approach).

"He is obviously bred to take a bit of time and will make a better three-year-old, but he is a nice colt with a lovely pedigree. Hopefully he can do something in the autumn."

COWBOY JUSTICE
28/2 b c Lope de Vega - Starflower (Champs Elysees)
Trainer: Jessica Harrington Sales price: 50,000gns (BBA Ireland)

Third foal of a French dual 1m 3yo winner who was closely related to Prix Jean Prat winner Mutual Trust and very useful 7.5-9.5f winner Kryptos out of a 10f 3yo Listed-winning half-sister to useful dual 7f 2yo winner Apex Star and the unraced dam of US 1m Grade 1 winner Antanoe.

"A big, strong colt who is by a stallion we obviously like. He is still a bit backward at the moment, though that's perhaps to be expected given his dam's side. That said, he's shown a bit already and will hopefully make an appearance in the middle of the summer."

DUVET DAY (IRE)
3/5 b f Starspangledbanner - Je T'Adore (Montjeu)
Trainer: Jessica Harrington Sales price: £45,000 (BBA Ireland)

Half-sister to Irish dual 10f 3yo Flat/2m Grade 1 hurdle winner A Wave Of The Sea. Dam a twice-raced maiden daughter of a maiden half-sister to US 1m 1f Grade 1 winner Tuscan Evening and 12/14f 3yo Listed winner Barbican.

"This filly looks to be one of our earlier two-year-old runners. Her pedigree doesn't really suggest she should be overly early but she looks it at home. She has got a nice attitude and should make a nice two-year-old."

EUROCRAT
20/4 b g Holy Roman Emperor - Apparatchika (Archipenko)
Trainer: Jessica Harrington Sales price: 26,000gns (BBA Ireland)

Half-brother to useful 7f 2yo winner Arriviste. Dam a 10-12f winner who was a half-sister to Group 2-placed 8-9f winner (including at Group 3/Listed level) Zaaki and useful 10-12f Flat/2m 1f hurdle winner Night of Glory out of a French 7f-1m winning half-sister to French 9/9.5f Listed winner Persona Grata.

"He comes from a good Kirsten Rausing family so will naturally improve with time. I imagine he will be starting off over 7f during the second half of the season."

KANGAROO COURT (IRE)
2/2 b f Australia - True Verdict (Danehill Dancer)
Trainer: Jessica Harrington Sales price: £40,000 (BBA Ireland)

Half-sister to useful 7f-1m winner Vitamin. Dam a Group 3/Listed-placed
Irish 6f 2yo winner who was a full sister to Listed-placed Irish 6.5f 2yo winner
Foolish Ambition out of an unraced sister to Listed-placed Irish 1m 2yo winner
Faint Heart and half-sister to 7f 2yo Group 3 winner Circle of Gold and 6f 2yo
Listed winner Crystal Crossing (later dam of St Leger winner/Derby runner-up
Rule of Law).

*"This is a nice big filly who, being by Australia, is going to be one for the middle
of the season onwards. The bottom half of her page isn't short of speed so she
should make a two-year-old."*

NECTARIS
2/5 b f Sea The Moon - Angelic Air (Oasis Dream)
Trainer: Jessica Harrington Sales price: 58,000gns (BBA Ireland)

Half-sister to useful dual 7f winner Amazing News. Dam a 7f 3yo winner who
was the daughter of a 7/10f Listed-winning half-sister to Grade 1-placed
French/US 10-12f winner (including twice at Listed level) Skipping, Group 3/
Listed-placed French 10.5f 3yo winner Minority (later dam of Prix Marcel
Boussac winner Proportional and Irish 1m 3yo Group 3 winner Vote Often) and
the maiden dam of Canadian 10f Grade 1 winner Folk Opera.

*"We bought this filly from Book 2 of the Tattersalls October Yearling Sale. She
is a nice type who shows promise at this early stage and should make a nice
horse during the second half of the season."*

PAPA K (IRE)
28/2 b c Kodiac - Alonsoa (Raven's Pass)
Trainer: Jessica Harrington Sales price: 78,000gns (BBA Ireland)

Third foal of a 7f 2yo Listed winner who was a half-sister to Group 2-placed
6.5f-1m winner (including at Group 3/Listed level) Alanza out of a 1m 3yo
Listed winner/1000 Guineas third who was closely related to Irish 8.5f 3yo
Listed winner Alaiyma and a half-sister to the dam of 2020 Australian 10f
Listed winner Shared Ambition.

*"A fine big individual who looks to be the most forward of our colts. For all he
has plenty of size about him, he should be capable of doing something of note
from the early summer onwards over 6/7f. Jessica has a pretty high opinion of
him."*

VIAREGGIO (IRE)
25/2 b f Caravaggio - Just Joan (Pour Moi)
Trainer: Jessica Harrington Sales price: 65,000gns (BBA Ireland)

Second foal of an Irish 1m 3yo winner who was closely related to useful French 10.5-14f winner Waheebah and a half-sister to very useful UK/Qatari 7-10f winner Tannaaf and useful 12-13.5f 3yo winner Great Sound out of an Irish 12f 3yo winning sister to Irish 7f 3yo Listed winner Pirateer, close relation to Cheveley Park Stakes winner/1000 Guineas runner-up Wannabe Grand and 7f Group 3 winner Wannabe Better and half-sister to 12f Listed winner Wannabe Posh.

"Another who should be out relatively early, though she won't be one for the 5f races. She has a really good pedigree, being by one of the most exciting first-season sires and coming from a prolific black type family. We like what we've seen of her so far."

ANGUS GOLD (SHADWELL ESTATE COMPANY)

ARYAAH (IRE)
21/3 gr c Dandy Man - Angel Grace (Dark Angel)
Trainer: Kevin Prendergast Sales price: 70,000gns (Shadwell Estate Company)

Half-brother to Group 3/Listed-placed 2020 dual 7f 2yo winner Mystery Angel. Dam an 8.5f 3yo winner who was a half-sister to Listed-placed 5-7f winner Squats (by Dandy Man) and 2020 6f 3yo winner Island Warrior out of a maiden half-sister to Group 1-placed 5f-1m winner (including at Group 3/Listed level) Hurricane Alan.

"This was a very athletic yearling sold by Joe Foley. He has gone to Kevin Prendergast who likes the look of him so far."

ESHKAAL (IRE)
18/2 ch c Exceed And Excel - Falling Petals (Raven's Pass)
Trainer: Richard Hannon Sales price: 120,000gns (Shadwell Estate Company)

Half-brother to 2020 7f 2yo Group 3 winner Saffron Beach. Dam a 7f 2yo winner who was a three-parts sister to 6f 2yo winner/Middle Park Stakes third Huntdown and useful dual 6f 2yo winner Wingbeat and a half-sister to the unraced dam of Group 1-placed multiple 5f winner (including at Group 3/Listed level) Cotai Glory (by Exceed And Excel) and 10f Listed winner Permission.

"He looked a good, solid running colt from the family of Cotai Glory, while his half-sister, Saffron Beach, won the Oh So Sharp Stakes last year."

LAAKHOF (IRE)
28/2 b c Profitable - Ihtifal (Dansili)
Trainer: Dermot Weld Sales price: 160,000gns (Shadwell Estate Company)

Half-brother to useful 2020 dual 6f 2yo winner Seven Brothers and useful French 5f 2yo winner Stratton Street. Dam a useful 6f 3yo winner who was a full sister to smart 7f-1m winner (including at Group 3/Listed level) Zibelina (dam of 2020 French 6f 3yo Group 3 winner Royal Crusade) and a half-sister to 6f 2yo Listed winner Floristry (dam of 2020 5f 3yo Group 3/Listed winner Lazuli).

"I was very impressed with the Profitable yearlings I saw last year, and this colt looks every inch a two-year-old type. Dermot Weld seems pleased with him thus far."

UNNAMED (IRE)
24/2 ch f Profitable - Bold Assumption (Observatory)
Trainer: Owen Burrows Sales price: 150,000gns (Shadwell Estate Company)

Half-sister to 1m 2yo Listed winner/Poule d'Essai des Pouliches runner-up Irish Rookie and three other winners. Dam an unraced half-sister to Listed-placed French 11f 3yo winner Well Dressed and Listed-placed French 12f 3yo winner Tsar's Pride (later dam of Italian 10/12f Group 3 winner Exhibit One and 3yo Listed winners Pavlosk (1m) and Rostova (1m 1f)).

"Another solid individual by Profitable. This filly is a half-sister to Irish Rookie who was second in the Poule d'Essai des Pouliches. It's a good Juddmonte family further back, and she has always looked like a very nice filly to me."

UNNAMED
7/4 b f New Approach - Craighall (Dubawi)
Trainer: Roger Varian Sales price: 80,000gns (Shadwell Estate Company)

Half-sister to useful UK/North American 7-8.5f winner Kylla Instinct and four other winners. Dam a maiden half-sister to smart 10-12f winner (including at Group 2/Listed level) Connecticut (by New Approach), German 11f Listed winner Fleurie Domaine and 1m 3yo winner/Vintage Stakes fourth Castleton.

"This looked a very good-natured New Approach filly from Book 2 of the Tattersalls October Yearling Sale. I would hope she will prove capable of winning as a two-year-old."

UNNAMED (IRE)
28/3 b/br c Aclaim - Kendal Mint (Kyllachy)
Trainer: Owen Burrows Sales price: 145,000gns (Shadwell Estate Company)

Half-brother to useful 2020 6f 3yo winner Fresh. Dam a 6f 2yo winner who was a half-sister to Listed-placed Italian 5f 2yo winner Lady Ro and useful 12f-2m winner Monsieur Lambrays out of a dual 7f 3yo winning sister to Listed-placed 5-6f winner Woodnook and half-sister to 6f 2yo Group 2 winner Nevisian Lad.

"This colt is from the first crop of Aclaim and hails from a solid running family. He cost plenty at Book 2 of the Tattersalls October Yearling Sale but looked a racehorse."

UNNAMED (IRE)
24/4 b c Kodiac - Nations Alexander (Dark Angel)
Trainer: William Haggas Sales price: 300,000gns (Shadwell Estate Company)

Second foal of a 7f 2yo Group 3 winner who was the daughter of a once-raced maiden half-sister to Richmond Stakes winner/Middle Park Stakes third Always Hopeful, Listed-placed 6-7f winner Nacho Libre, very useful multiple 6f-1m winner Extraterrestrial and useful dual 6f 2yo winner Enford Princess.

"This is a really sharp-looking Kodiac colt out of Group-winning Dark Angel mare. He looks all about speed and precocity, and William Haggas seems to like him a lot."

UNNAMED
10/2 ch c Ulysses - Troarn (Wootton Bassett)
Trainer: Roger Varian Sales price: 320,000gns (Shadwell Estate Company)

First foal of a Listed-placed French 9.5f 3yo winner who was a full sister to top-class 7-10.5f winner (including the Prix du Jockey Club and Champion Stakes) Almanzor out of an unraced daughter of a French 12f 3yo Listed-winning half-sister to Group 3/Listed-placed French 12f 3yo winner Darinska (later dam of Poule d'Essai des Pouliches winner Darjina).

"I have been particularly taken by the Ulysses offspring I have seen, both as foals two years ago and again by his yearlings last year. This colt was the most expensive of them, out of a full sister to Almanzor, and he looked a very good sort of horse with plenty of scope. I certainly wouldn't see him running before September/October, but I am sure he will improve dramatically, especially as a three-year-old. I would be disappointed if he didn't have a bit of class to him."

UNNAMED
14/4 b c Sea The Stars - Umniyah (Shamardal)
Trainer: Marcus Tregoning Sales price: 625,000gns (Shadwell Estate Company)

Full brother to once-raced US 8.5f 2yo winner The Path Not Taken. Dam a
once-raced maiden sister to 7/9f Group 3 winner Dubai Prince and half-sister
to Listed-placed Irish 8-12f 3yo winner Jakarta Jade, useful 8-10f 2yo winner
Mojave Moon and the unraced dam of US 1m 1f Grade 2 winner Tuttipaesi
out of an 11-13f 3yo winning half-sister to triple 10f Group/Grade 1 winner
Storming Home.

*"A very powerful colt, who looked all Shamardal as a yearling. He seems to
have a very good temperament and was probably the best horse we bought
last year. Marcus Tregoning seems pleased with him so far."*

UNNAMED
25/2 b c Le Havre - Waldnah (New Approach)
Trainer: Charlie Hills Sales price: 325,000gns (Shadwell Estate Company)

Second foal of a German 1m 3yo Listed winner who was a half-sister to St
Leger winner Masked Marvel and French 10.5f 3yo Group 3 winner Waldlerche
(later dam of Prix de l'Arc de Triomphe winner Waldgeist and French 12f 3yo
Group 2 winner Waldlied) out a Group 2/Listed-placed 7f 2yo winning half-
sister to Deutsches Derby winner Waldpark.

*"This was a very nice individual out of a New Approach half-sister to Masked
Marvel from the family of Waldgeist. Obviously he is more of a three-year-old
on paper, but hopefully he can make up into a nice staying two-year-old at the
end of the season. I know Charles Hills and his team like what they have seen
of him so far."*

TEDDY GRIMTHORPE (JUDDMONTE)

Thanks to Teddy for passing on the following ten two-year-olds from
Juddmonte Farms. He explained: *"Because of all the restrictions I haven't
been around the horses nearly enough to give an accurate description of
them. Aquiano, Deodar and Juncture should be more precocious whereas the
remainder will likely be second-half-of-the-season two-year-olds."*

AQUIANO
21/3 b f Equiano - Abated (Dansili)
Trainer: Ger Lyons Sales price: n/a

Third foal of a 6f 3yo winner who was a full sister to Group 1-placed 5-6f winner (including at Group 2/Listed level) Bated Breath and a half-sister to high-class 8-9f winner (including at Group 1 level) Cityscape, Listed-placed 8-8.5f 3yo winner Scuffle (later dam of St Leger winner Logician and US triple 9.5-12f Grade 3 winner Suffused) and the unraced dam of 2021 UAE 5f Group 2 winner Equilateral (by Equiano).

BLUE BOAT
27/2 b c Frankel - Blue Waltz (Pivotal)
Trainer: Francis-Henri Graffard Sales price: 450,000gns (Juddmonte Farms)

Second foal of a useful triple 10f winner who was a half-sister Group 1-placed UK/US 6-9.5f winner (including at Group/Grade 3 level)/Poule d'Essai des Pouliches third Fantasia (dam of 2020 10f 3yo Group 3 winner Berlin Tango), Irish 12f Group 3 winner Pink Symphony and the dam of French 10f 3yo Group 2 winner Western Hymn.

CHIMED
6/3 ch c Frankel - Timepiece (Zamindar)
Trainer: Sir Michael Stoute Sales price: n/a

Half-brother to 2020 7f 3yo winner Tacitly. Dam a Falmouth Stakes winner who was a half-sister to high-class 7-10.5f winner (including at Group 1 level) Passage of Time (later dam of 8/10.5f Group 2 winner Time Test), King Edward VII Stakes winner/St Leger fourth Father Time and 14f Listed winner Continuum.

CRENELLE
14/2 gr f Kingman - Battlement (Dansili)
Trainer: John & Thady Gosden Sales price: n/a

First foal of a Listed-placed 7f-1m winner who was closely related to US triple 9.5-12f Grade 3 winner Suffused and a half-sister to St Leger winner Logician, 2020 French 12.5f Listed winner Collide and 2020 1m 2yo winner Monsoon Moon (by Kingman) out of a Listed-placed 8-8.5f winning half-sister to UAE 1m 1f Group 1 winner Cityscape and high-class sprinter Bated Breath.

Monsoon Moon

DEODAR
27/2 br c Bated Breath - Tested (Selkirk)
Trainer: Ralph Beckett Sales price: n/a

Third foal of a smart Irish 7-7.5f winner (including at Group 3/Listed level) who was closely related to 7f 2yo winner Escape Proof out of a French 10f 3yo Group 3-winning sister to smart prolific 7-8.5f winner (including at Group 3/Listed level) Vortex and French 12f 3yo Group 3 winner Danefair (later dam of four-time 7f Group 3/Listed winner Trade Fair) and a half-sister to Listed-placed French 1m 1f 2yo winner Estala (later dam of four-time 7f/1m Grade 1 winner Ventura).

JUNCTURE
19/3 gr f Dark Angel - Occurrence (Frankel)
Trainer: Ger Lyons Sales price: n/a

First foal of an unraced half-sister to Irish 10f Group 1 winner Promising Lead, 6/7f Group 3 winner Visit and 7f 2yo winner Revered (later dam of 1m 2yo Group 3 winner Commemorative) out of a 15f 3yo Listed-winning sister to Listed-placed French 5f-1m winner Hasili (later dam of Banks Hill, Cacique, Champs Elysees, Dansili, Intercontinental etc.).

LA BREA
16/1 b f Dubawi - Big Break (Dansili)
Trainer: Francis-Henri Graffard Sales price: n/a

Half-sister to very useful Irish 8.5-10f 3yo winner Georgeville. Dam a smart Irish 7-7.5f winner (including twice at Group 3 level)/Irish 1000 Guineas fourth who was a sister to Group 1-placed Irish prolific 6-10f winner (including at Group 2/3 level) Famous Name and Irish 10f 3yo Listed winner Discipline, closely related to US 12f Grade 3 winner Renown and a half-sister to Group 3-placed Irish 7-10f winner (including at Listed level) Zaminast.

NIKOVO
17/3 b c Kingman - Rostova (Arch)
Trainer: Andre Fabre Sales price: n/a

Second foal of a French 1m 3yo Listed winner who was a sister to 1m 3yo Listed winner Pavlosk and half-sister to Italian 10/12f Group 3 winner Exbibit One out of a Listed-placed French 12f 3yo winning half-sister to the unraced dam of 1m 2yo Listed winner/Poule d'Essai des Pouliches runner-up Irish Rookie; family of 2000 Guineas winner Zafonic.

SPECIAL ENVOY
23/2 b c Frankel - Marlinka (Marju)
Trainer: John & Thady Gosden Sales price: 850,000gns (Private Sale)

Half-brother to high-class multiple 5-6f winner (including the Nunthorpe Stakes and Prix de l'Abbaye) Marsha and high-class prolific 5-6f winner (including at Group 3/Listed level) Judicial. Dam a French 5f 2yo Listed-winning daughter of a dual 6f 3yo winner who was a half-sister to five-time 1m Group 1 winner/1000 Guineas fourth Soviet Song and the dam of French 10f Group 1 winner Ribbons.

THESIS
2/5 b c Kingman - Nimble Thimble (Mizzen Mast)
Trainer: Roger Charlton Sales price: n/a

Full brother to French 1m 2yo winner Boardman and a half-brother to Fillies' Mile winner/1000 Guineas third Quadrilateral. Dam a 9.5f 3yo winner who was a half-sister to Group/Grade 1-placed UK/US 6-8.5f winner (including at Grade 2/Group 3 level) Three Valleys and six other winners; exceptional family of Banks Hill, Cacique, Intercontinental, Champs Elysees, Dansili etc.

HARRY HERBERT
(HIGHCLERE THOROUGHBRED RACING)

AMMOLITE (IRE)
2/3 ch f Profitable - Romie's Kastett (Halling)
Trainer: Simon & Ed Crisford Sales price: 95,000gns (John & Jake Warren)

Half-sister to useful 7f-1m 3yo winner Morning Has Broken, useful 8-10f 3yo winner Global Hunter and useful Irish 8-10f winner Eagle Spirit. Dam an Irish 9.5f 3yo winner who was a full sister to Group 1-placed 7-9f winner (including twice at Group 3 level)/2000 Guineas third/Derby fourth Norse Dancer.

"Bought by John and Jake Warren at Book 2 of the Tattersalls October Yearling Sale, this filly was very typical of her sire's offspring, being strong and precocious and with plenty of class about her too. She is out of a full sister to Norse Dancer, and at this stage looks like being a May starter over 6f. A really lovely filly who is well liked by the father and son trainer duo!"

ATRIUM
21/4 b c Holy Roman Emperor - Hail Shower (Red Clubs)
Trainer: Charlie Fellowes Sales price: 60,000gns (John & Jake Warren)

Half-brother to very useful 6-7f 2yo winner (including at Listed level) Milltown Star. Dam an Irish 6.5-7f winner who was the daughter of a maiden close relation to Group 2/3-placed 7-12f winner Raincoat and half-sister to 12f 3yo Listed winner Quenched (later dam of Australian 7.5/12.5f Group 3 winner Excess Knowledge).

"This colt looks very strong and could be ready to make his debut over 5f towards the end of April or beginning of May. He is a half-brother to a Listed winner and Charlie really likes him. I suspect that he will be better over 6f, but he certainly looks to have ability and could be decent."

BOTANIST
22/3 b c Bated Breath - Sunflower (Dutch Art)
Trainer: George Baker Sales price: 48,000gns (Durcan Bloodstock/G Baker Racing)

Second foal of a 6f 2yo winner who was a half-sister to Group 3/Listed-placed 5f 2yo winner Life of Riley and useful 6-7f winner Battered out of a 5f 2yo winning three-parts sister to Listed-placed prolific 5-6f winner Texas Gold; family of 6/7f Group 3 winner Scarlet Runner.

"Bought by former jockey, Ted Durcan, this colt has turned inside out over the last few months and now looks as though he will be a late May/June starter. George loves him and a fun summer campaign looks likely with this handsome son of Bated Breath."

BROADSPEAR
29/3 b c Le Havre - Flower of Life (Galileo)
Trainer: Roger Varian Sales price: 105,000gns (Karl Burke)

First foal of a maiden half-sister to Group 2-placed UK/Hong Kong 6-7.5f winner (including at Group 3/Listed level) Dundonnell out of an unraced sister to 6f 3yo Group 1 winner/2000 Guineas third Danehill, US 1m 1f Grade 2 winner Eagle Eyed, dual 7f Group 3 winner Shibboleth and US 7f Grade 3 winner Harpia.

"This is an outstanding colt who could be anything. He has grown and changed but has always come back to shape. He has a lovely pedigree, being the first foal out of a Galileo mare who is a half-sister to Dundonnell, the Acomb Stakes winner, who went on to win over £1,000,000 in prize money over in Hong Kong. The grandam is a full sister to Danehill so this colt is really bred to something special! So far he has really pleased Roger and is one to follow for the second half of the season. He moves beautifully and has the look of a horse who could be something special."

CORSINI (IRE)
26/2 ch f Mastercraftsman - Il Palazzo (Giant's Causeway)
Trainer: Martyn Meade Sales price: 140,000gns (D Farrington/John and Jake Warren)

Full sister to Irish 10f Listed winner Still Standing and a half-sister to dual 7f winner Mutahamisa. Dam a maiden half-sister to Group 3-placed Irish 6f 2yo winner Divine Night out of a maiden close relation to French 1m Listed winner Dexterity and half-sister to US 10/11f Grade 1 winner Senure and US 6.5f Grade 3 winner Speak In Passing; family of Irish 2000 Guineas winner Siskin, St Leger winner Logician, UAE 1m 1f Group 1 winner Cityscape etc.

"This is our first horse with Martyn, and we are extremely excited to be 50/50 partners with him in this stunning filly. She cost 120,000gns and is an absolute queen. She is a full sister to the Listed winner, Still Standing, and hails from the Juddmonte family of Cityscape and Bated Breath. This is a big, scopey filly who probably won't be running until the backend, but she could be very good. She moves like a panther and holds herself in the manner of something a bit special."

HARROW (IRE)
19/3 gr c El Kabeir - School Run (Invincible Spirit)
Trainer: Andrew Balding Sales price: 85,000gns (John & Jake Warren)

Second foal of a 5f 3yo winner who was a half-sister to French 1m 3yo Listed winner Noor Sahara out of a 6f 3yo winning half-sister to Flying Childers Stakes winner Land of Dreams (later dam of five-time 6/7f Group 1 winner Dream Ahead and grandam of Cheveley Park Stakes winner Fairyland) and the maiden dam of 6f 2yo Group 3 winner/Cheveley Park Stakes runner-up Princess Noor.

"I love this colt, who looks very athletic. He is really pleasing Andrew and looks the type to be out in May/June over 6f. Certainly one for the shortlist in my opinion!"

HERETIC (IRE)
20/2 ch c Galileo Gold - Al Jawza (Nathaniel)
Trainer: Hugo Palmer Sales price: £25,000 (Avenue Bloodstock)

First foal of a maiden sister to useful 2020 dual 10f 3yo winner Papa Power and half-sister to Listed-placed 6f-1m winner Rufus King and 2020 5f 2yo winner Madreselva out of a Listed-placed 1m 3yo winning daughter of a German dual 1m 3yo Listed winner.

"I first saw this cracking son of first-season sire, Galileo Gold, on Hugo's website! I was lucky enough to be with Al Shaqab when Sheikh Joaan raced Galileo Gold and was part of the team who bought him before he won the Vintage Stakes at Goodwood. He went on at three to win the 2000 Guineas and the St James's Palace Stakes. This colt is the spitting image of his sire, which is what persuaded me to pick up the phone to Hugo to find out more about him! He looks like being precocious enough to start over 6f towards the end of May or early June, just like his father did. Can lightning strike twice? Here's hoping as Hugo reports that this colt is doing everything right so far!"

LYSANSDER
4/2 br c New Approach - Darting (Shamardal)
Trainer: William Haggas Sales price: 120,000gns (John & Jake Warren)

Second foal of a maiden half-sister to Group 1-placed 12f-2m winner (including at Group 2/3 level) Darasim out of a once-raced French 12.5f 3yo winning half-sister to triple 10/12f Group 1 winner Dar Re Mi (later dam of triple 7f/1m Group 1 winner/Irish 2000 Guineas runner-up Too Darn Hot and 10.5f Group 2 winner/St Leger runner-up Lah Ti Dar) and Prince of Wales's Stakes winner/Derby third Rewilding.

"I love this colt, who was bred at Highclere and who ticks all the right boxes in looks and pedigree. He is the first foal out of the Shamardal mare, Darting, who is a half-sister to the Goodwood Cup winner, Darasim. This is the great Lloyd-Webber family of Dar Re Mi, Too Darn Hot and Rewilding. He is only going steadily at the moment as you would expect, but he moves really well and appears to have a great temperament. I suspect that he will be ready to start in August/September, and he is most definitely on my shortlist as one to follow!"

ROYAL PATRONAGE (FR)
13/4 b c Wootton Bassett - Shaloushka (Dalakhani)
Trainer: Mark Johnston Sales price: 62,000gns (John & Jake Warren)

First foal of a French 10-12f winner who was closely related to Irish 10-12f 3yo winner/Irish Derby third Shalapour and a half-sister to useful Irish 10.5-12f winner Shalaman and useful Irish 10-12f 3yo winner Shibina (later dam of French 11f 3yo winner/Tercentenary Stakes runner-up Shikarpour) out of a maiden half-sister to Derby winner Shahrastani.

"John and Jake Warren bought us this very handsome son of leading young sire, Wootton Bassett, for only 62,000gns. He comes from the Aga Khan's family of Derby winner, Shahrastani, and is the first foal out of the three-time winning Dalakhani mare, Shaloushka. This colt oozes class and is already showing Mark and Charlie that he is not short of speed. He will probably start over 7f, but as Charlie told me this week, they might well be tempted to go shorter as he is coming to hand very quickly. I really like this colt and he could be one for those early 7f black type races if good enough."

STROMBOLI (IRE)
11/4 b c Acclamation - Shanooan (English Channel)
Trainer: David O'Meara Sales price: £30,000 (Jason Kelly Bloodstock)

Third foal of a useful Irish 7f-1m 3yo winner who was a full sister to the maiden dam of Coventry Stakes winner/Dewhurst Stakes runner-up Arizona and US 8.5f 2yo Grade 2 winner Nay Lady Nay and a half-sister to Italian 1m 1f 2yo Group 3 winner Fathayer and the maiden dam of Prix Morny/Prix Jean-Luc Lagardere winner Dabirsim.

"This is a cracking son of Acclamation from a very good family. I bought 75% of him when visiting David's yard for the first time and he was the only yearling shown with David retaining a leg! He is strong and powerful and has found it all very easy so far. David will probably start him over 6f in early May, and we hope that he may develop into a Royal Ascot contender. I think he just might be a very exciting prospect."

TUDOR QUEEN (IRE)
7/3 b f Starspangledbanner - Queen Elsa (Frozen Power)
Trainer: Kevin Ryan Sales price: £30,000 (Hillen/Ryan)

Second foal of a once-raced maiden close relation to Mill Reef Stakes winner Toocoolforschool and the dam of Brocklesby Stakes winner/Molecomb Stakes third Show Me Show Me out of a 7f 2yo winning half-sister to Listed-placed 6f-1m Flat/2m hurdle winner Tucker and 2m Grade 2/3 hurdle winner Beau Michael.

"Each year in late December or early January, I head up to Yorkshire to see our horses there and ask the trainers if they have any unsold yearlings/two-year-olds they would like to show me. When Kevin showed me this filly, I was blown away by her wonderful physique and gorgeous head. She is so athletic and looks as though she will be an early starter over 5f or 6f. She is about to head out to do some faster exercise on the grass so we will know more soon, but I would definitely have her on my (long) shortlist!"

TYSON (IRE)
26/2 gr c Starspangledbanner - Ach Alannah (Marju)
Trainer: Richard Hannon Sales price: 75,000gns (John & Jake Warren)

Half-brother to Italian 7f 3yo Listed winner Greach. Dam a twice-raced maiden half-sister to Italian 1m 3yo Listed winner Carioca (later dam of triple 6f-1m Listed winner/Prix Maurice de Gheest third Tupi), Group 2/3-placed multiple 5f-1m winner (including the Windsor Castle Stakes) Irony and the dam of French 6.5f 2yo Listed winner Happy Odyssey.

"This is a very powerful and precocious two-year-old with Richard Hannon, who hopefully will make his debut at Newbury's Greenham meeting in a race we sponsor. He was bought to be an early type and, so far, his work has shown him to be just that! He certainly caught the trainer's eye when working on the grass for the first time recently."

SAM HOSKINS (SYNDICATE MANAGER)

ATTACHE (IRE)
26/2 b c Declaration of War - Go Kart (Intense Focus)
Trainer: Andrew Balding Owner: Kennet Valley Thoroughbreds VII Sales price: £42,000 (Kern/Lillingston Association)

First foal of a Listed-placed triple Irish 5f winner who was a half-sister to useful

Irish dual 5f 2yo winner Dream Kart and fairly useful Irish 8-12f winner Muzbid out of an unraced daughter of a French 1m 3yo Listed winner.

"A forward-going son of Declaration of War out of the very tough stakes-placed mare Go Kart. He is showing up nicely at home and could debut over 6f from the summer onwards. He could be one to target at various sales races in August and September."

BUNKER BAY (IRE)
25/4 b g Australia - Alf Guineas (Sea The Stars)
Trainer: William Knight Owner: Kennet Valley Thoroughbreds X Sales price: 47,000gns (Kern/Lillingston Association)

First foal of a useful 9.5-10f winner who was a full sister to 12f 3yo Group 3 winner Star Storm and useful 2020 1m 3yo winner Sargasso Sea out of a maiden half-sister to Champagne Stakes winner Almushahar, 6f 2yo winner Lonely Ahead and the maiden dam of Group 1-placed 8-12f winner (including at Group 2/Listed level) Mehdaayih.

"A beautifully-bred son of Australia out of a Sea The Stars mare. This is a lovely-moving horse who William has always liked ever since we bought him in December. Anything he does as a 2-y-o will be a bonus, but hopefully he will run a couple of times this autumn."

CABINET MAKER (IRE)
20/2 gr c Mastercraftsman - Elegant Peace (Intense Focus)
Trainer: Mark Johnston Owner: Kennet Valley Thoroughbreds XII Sales price: £48,000 (Kern/Lillingston Association)

Half-brother to 2020 US 5.5f 3yo winner Rakassah. Dam a useful Irish 7-8.5f winner who was a half-sister to Group 2-placed 5-6f winner (including at Group 3/Listed level) Hoh Mike, Listed-placed 6-7f winner Tamayuz Star, Listed-placed Irish 6-7.5f winner Intapeace, Listed-placed 5-6f 2yo winner Dario Gee Gee and very useful 5-6f winner Hogmaneigh.

"This son of Mastercraftsman is out of a half-sister to the fast and precocious Hoh Mike. He is moving nicely at home and is impressing the Johnstons so far."

DOROTHEE
3/5 b f Equiano - Persario (Bishop of Cashel)
Trainer: Charlie Fellowes Owner: Hot to Trot Racing 2 and Mrs E Grundy Sales price: n/a

Full sister to very smart multiple 6f winner (including three times at Group 1 level) The Tin Man and a half-sister to very smart multiple 5-6f winner (including at Group 2/3 level) Deacon Blues, Listed-placed multiple 5f winner Holley Shiftwell and four other winners out of a 6-7f winning half-sister to triple 7f Group 3 winner/Lockinge Stakes runner-up Warningford.

"She is a full-sister to the Group 1-winning The Tin Man, as well as a half-sister to Deacon Blues. Charlie knows the family from his time as assistant to James Fanshawe, and whilst it's not a precocious family, this filly has shown signs of speed early on. She is a late foal who could be one for August time."

EMILY POST
6/3 b f Charming Thought - Mary Read (Bahamian Bounty)
Trainer: Ed Bethell Owner: Hot To Trot Racing 2 & Mrs F Denniff Sales price: n/a

Half-sister to 6-7f winner Jacquotte Delahaye and 8.5-12.5f winner Dubai Bounty (later dam of smart sprinter Kachy). Dam a Group 3/Listed-placed dual 5f 2yo winner who was a half-sister to Listed-placed 6f-1m winner Above N Beyond and Listed-placed 6f 2yo winner Tiana (later dam of five-time 1m Group 2 winner Beat The Bank and smart sprinter Salt Island).

"This filly is a half-sister to the dam of Kachy. She is out of the Molecomb-placed mare, Mary Read, and whilst not whizz-bang early, she's a very nice filly."

GET AHEAD
27/4 ch f Showcasing - Suelita (Dutch Art)
Trainer: Clive Cox Owner: Hot To Trot Racing V Sales price: 200,000gns (C/S Bloodstock)

Full sister to 2020 Mill Reef Stakes winner Alkumait and a half-sister to Irish 5.5f 3yo Listed winner The Broghie Man and Listed-placed 6f 2yo winner Gloves Lynch. Dam an Italian 5-6f winner who was a half-sister to Group 3-placed multiple 5-7f winner Outer Space and the dam of Lowther Stakes winner Living In The Past.

"This is a very nice filly who could be anything. She is a full-sister to last year's Mill Reef winner, Alkumait, and appears fast and straightforward. Clive absolutely loves her."

Alkumait

PLAGIARISE
19/3 b f Showcasing - Copy-Cat (Lion Cavern)
Trainer: Hughie Morrison Owner: Hot To Trot Racing VI Sales price: 40,000gns (Vendor)

Half-sister to Group 2-placed multiple 6f-1m winner (including at Group 3 level) Pastoral Player, Group 2-placed 7f-1m winner (including at Listed level) Chil The Kite, Group 1-placed UK/Hong Kong triple 7f winner Kings Falcon and five other winners including the dam of Group 3-placed 5-7f winner Lincoln. Dam a maiden half-sister to 5f Group 3 winner/Prix de l'Abbaye runner-up Averti.

"This filly is a half-sister to Chil The Kite and Pastoral Player, so it is a family Hughie knows extremely well. She is by a top sire in Showcasing, and Hughie has liked what he has seen of her seen so far."

REGAL ENVOY (IRE)
1/4 b c Ardad - Regina (Green Desert)
Trainer: Clive Cox Owner: Kennet Valley Thoroughbreds I Sales price: £55,000 (Kern/Lillingston Association)

Half-brother to useful 5f 2yo winner Survived, fairly useful 5-6f winner Garsman, fairly useful multiple 5f winner Nibras Again and four other winners. Dam a useful dual 5f 2yo winner who was the daughter of a Cherry Hinton

Stakes winner/1000 Guineas third; family of Cheveley Park Stakes winner Hooray.

"He was the top-priced Ardad at the autumn yearling sales and is a gorgeous specimen who shows up nicely at home."

ROSEBERRY TOPPING
30/3 b f Mayson - Our Poppet (Warning)
Trainer: Andrew Balding Owner: Hot To Trot Racing Sales price: n/a

Half-sister to high-class sprinter Overdose, French 7.5f Listed winner Majestic Mount, Listed-placed French 6-6.5f winner Poppet's Treasure and six other winners. Dam a once-raced maiden half-sister to nine winners, notably 1m Listed winner Musicanna (later dam of UAE 1m Group 2 winner One Man Band) and the great-grandam of 5/6f 2yo Group 2 winner/Cheveley Park Stakes runner-up Raffle Prize.

"This filly is a half-sister to the 'Budapest Bullet,' Overdose, and has impressed both Andrew and her pre-trainer, Hetta Stevens, with all that she has done so far."

UWONTBELIEVEIT (IRE)
9/4 b f Galileo Gold - Ladylishandra (Mujadil)
Trainer: Nigel Tinkler Owner: Hot to Trot Racing 1 - Uwontbelieveit Sales price: £65,000 (Vendor)

Half-sister to high-class 2020 triple 5f 2yo winner (including at Group 2/Listed level) Ubettabelieveit, dual 7f Group 3 winner Tropical Paradise, Italian 5f Group 3 winner Harlem Shake and 1m Listed winner Shenanigans. Dam an Irish 6f 2yo winner who was the daughter of a French 11-12f 3yo winning sister to Irish 12f 3yo Group 3 winner Dancing Sunset (later dam of Irish 6f 2yo Listed winner Lady of Kildare).

"This daughter of the 2000 Guineas-winning first-season sire, Galileo Gold, is a half-sister to Nigel's high class 2yo of 2020, Ubettabelieveit. She moves nicely and should be a lovely filly for midsummer onwards."

UNNAMED (IRE)
14/3 b f Acclamation - Buying Trouble (Hat Trick)
Trainer: Roger Charlton Owner: Hot To Trot Racing Sales price: 35,000gns (Vendor)

First foal of a 6f Listed winner who was a half-sister to French 7f 2yo Listed winner Nucifera out of an unraced half-sister to Preakness Stakes winner War of Will, National Stakes winner Pathfork and US 14f Listed winner Tacticus.

"This filly is the first foal of the Listed-winning Buying Trouble, by the top class sire Acclamation. She is a good-moving filly who is one for the midsummer over 6f."

KIRSTEN RAUSING (LANWADES STUD)

ALIGHIERI
21/3 b c Muhaarar - Alvarita (Selkirk)
Trainer: Jim Bolger Owner: Miss K Rausing & Mrs J Bolger Sales price: n/a

Half-brother to Irish 10f 3yo Group 3 winner Alla Speranza and Irish 12f Listed winner Altesse. Dam a French 10.5f 3yo Group 3 winner who was a half-sister to Group 2-placed Irish/Australian 7-10f winner (including at Group 3/Listed level) My Nordic Hero and Group 2/3-placed French 10-10.5f winner Albion out of a dual Champion Stakes winner.

"A half-brother to no less than eight winners, two of which, Alla Speranza and Altesse, were trained to gain Stakes/Group wins for this colt's handler. His second dam is the dual Champion Stakes winner Alborada."

CHING SHIH
24/3 b f Lope de Vega - Madame Chiang (Archipenko)
Trainer: David Simcock Owner: Miss K Rausing Sales price: n/a

Half-sister to Group 2-placed 1m 2yo winner Oriental Mystique. Dam a smart 8-12f winner (including at Group 1 level) who was a full sister to useful 1m-2m winner Mister Chiang and 1m 2yo winner Chinoiseries and a half-sister to useful 8-8.5f winner Oriental Scot out of a 10-11.5f 3yo winning half-sister to German 14f Listed winner Kiswahili (later dam of 7f 2yo Listed winner Kinetica).

"A filly bred to excel as a three-year-old, she might yet emulate her Group 1-winning dam by winning at two in the latter part of the year."

FINE CHINA
24/1 b f Mastercraftsman - Chinoiseries (Archipenko)
Trainer: Sir Michael Stoute Owner: Miss K Rausing Sales price: n/a

First foal of a 1m 2yo winner who was a full sister to smart 8-12f winner (including at Group 1 level) Madame Chiang who was a full sister to useful 1m-2m winner Mister Chiang out of a 10-11.5f 3yo winning half-sister to German 14f Listed winner Kiswahili (later dam of 7f 2yo Listed winner Kinetica).

"An attractive, strong filly; a first foal. Her dam is a winning own-sister to Group 1 winner Madame Chiang - both sisters won on their debuts in late autumn of their 2yo seasons. This filly is not expected to appear in public until early autumn."

HELVETIQUE
30/3 b f Bobby's Kitten - Helvetia (Blame)
Trainer: Ralph Beckett Owner: Miss K Rausing Sales price: n/a

Half-sister to useful 2020 1m 2yo winner Orgetorix. Dam a 5f 3yo winner who was a half-sister to French triple 5f Listed winner Stern Opinion and Puerto Rican 8.5f Listed winner Dr Arbatach out of a US 6f 3yo winning half-sister to US 6f Listed winner Stormy Atlantic and the dam of US 1m 1f 3yo Grade 1 winner Bandini and 7f 2yo Group 3 winner Discourse.

"The Juddmonte-bred dam won over 5f for Rae Guest at three; her first foal to race was last year's useful 2yo, Orgetorix, also trained by this filly's trainer. The filly is well forward and should be seen out at least by May, all being well."

MADAME AMBASSADOR
5/2 ch f Churchill - Lady Jane Digby (Oasis Dream)
Trainer: Mark Johnston Owner: Miss K Rausing Sales price: n/a

Closely related to very useful French/UK triple 12f winner Galapiat (by Galileo) and 11.5-12.5f winner Francophilia (by Frankel) and a half-sister to four winners. Dam a high-class multiple 7-11f winner (including at Group 1 level) who was a half-sister to Group 1-placed multiple 6-9f winner (including at Group 3/Listed level) Gateman and very useful 7f-1m winner Surprise Encounter.

"The seventh foal of her Group 1-winning dam (she was also trained by this filly's trainer) - the mare's six previous foals have all won. Lady Jane Digby herself won on her debut in September as a 2yo at Doncaster - expect her daughter to appear in public at an earlier date!"

SABLONNE
15/4 b f Dark Angel - Starlit Sands (Oasis Dream)
Trainer: Jessica Harrington Owner: Miss K Rausing Sales price: n/a

Half-sister to useful 6-7f winner Seychelloise, 2020 5f 2yo winner Sands of Time and three other winners. Dam a Group 2-placed 5-5.5f 2yo winner (including at Group 3 level) who was a half-sister to four-time 6f Listed winner Sea Dane, 6f 3yo winner Summer Night (later dam of French 1m 2yo Group

3 winner Songerie and Listed winners Soft Morning (9.5f), Sourire (8.5f) and Souvenance (12f)) and the unraced dam of 1m Group 3 winner Chigun.

"A fourth generation homebred, this filly represents the speedier branch of Lanwades's "S" family. Her dam won the Group 3 5f Prix d'Arenberg and was only beaten a whisker in the Group 2 Queen Mary Stakes at Royal Ascot. She is the dam of five winners from her first six foals and is also the grandam of this year's useful-looking 3yo colt Sea The Shells. Sablonne belies her relatively late foaling date and is quite forward, earning positive comments from her trainer."

SAHARA SPEAR
27/4 b c Oasis Dream - Alumna (Mr Greeley)
Trainer: Richard Fahey Owner: Hamad Ebrahim Sales price: £28,000 (Derek Iceton)

Half-brother to useful dual 12f winner Alpha Theta. Dam a Listed-placed French 8-10f 3yo winner who was a half-sister to very useful triple 10f winner Harrovian out of a French 12.5f Listed-winning half-sister to dual Champion Stakes winner Alborada (grandam of 7f 3yo Group 3 winner Shine So Bright (by Oasis Dream)), German triple 12f Group 1 winner Albanova (later dam of dual 11f 3yo Group 3 winner Algometer) and the dam of 11.5f Listed winner/Derby runner-up Dragon Dancer.

"A tidy and pretty forward colt, with a very laid-back temperament. His dam won twice and was Group-placed in France (Timeform 110); she is also the dam of the useful 4yo filly Alpha Theta. The next dam was a Listed winner in France and a half-sister to Champions Alborada and Albanova."

SPECTATRICE
22/4 b f Fast Company - Songerie (Hernando)
Trainer: Sir Mark Prescott Owner: Miss K Rausing Sales price: n/a

Half-sister to very useful 11.5f-2m winner Summer Moon, useful 12-13f winner Hardstone and 1m 2yo winner Valitop. Dam a French 1m 2yo Group 3 winner who was a full sister to German 12f Listed winner Souvenance and a half-sister to French 9.5f 3yo Listed winner Soft Morning and Swedish 8.5f 3yo Listed winner Sourire out of a 6f 3yo winning half-sister to French 5.5f 2yo Group 3 winner/Queen Mary Stakes runner-up Starlit Sands.

"This filly's dam had Timeform ratings of 105 (at two) and 115 (at three); she won the Group 3 Prix des Reservoirs at Deauville as a 2yo for the filly's handler. The dam has already produced four winners including the useful Summer Moon (Timeform rating 117) last year. Unlikely to be an early type but should be seen to advantage in the autumn."

DAVID REDVERS (BLOODSTOCK AGENT)

CRIOLLO
5/2 gr f Dark Angel - La Rioja (Hellvelyn)
Trainer: William Haggas Owner: Qatar Racing Limited Sales price: n/a

First foal of a 6f 2yo Group 3 winner who was a half-sister to Group 3/Listed-placed 6f 2yo winner Pastoral Girl (dam of 2020 6f 2yo winner/Prix Morny third Rhythm Master (by Dark Angel)), Listed-placed triple 5f 2yo winner Lilbourne Lass and the dam of Group 1-placed multiple 5-6f winner (including at Group 3/Listed level) Liberty Beach.

"A gorgeous filly with a very fast pedigree. Her dam won the Dick Poole Stakes at two and was fourth in the Commonwealth Cup at three. This filly looks the type to make up into a nice two-year-old performer."

FRANKLIN WILLIAM
24/4 b c Frankel - Kiyoshi (Dubawi)
Trainer: Andrew Balding Owner: Sheikha Melissa Al Fahad Sales price: n/a

Half-brother to 8-12f Flat/2m hurdle winner Iron Heart. Dam a smart 6-7f winner (including twice at Group 3 level) who was the daughter of a Listed-placed 8-10f winning half-sister to useful 6f 2yo winner Cosmo.

"A nice, strong colt out of Qatar Racing's Albany Stakes winner, Kiyoshi. He has been very straightforward so far and is an exciting horse for this season."

SUNSTRIKE (IRE)
16/2 b f Dark Angel - Extricate (Exceed And Excel)
Trainer: John & Thady Gosden Owner: Qatar Racing Limited Sales price: 390,000gns (David Redvers Bloodstock)

Full sister to German 7f 2yo Listed winner Dark Liberty and a half-sister to 2020 French 1m 3yo Listed winner Queen of Love. Dam a Norwegian 5.5-7f winner who was a half-sister to smart Swedish prolific 8-9f winner (including at Group 3/Listed level) Entangle and the dam of 5f 2yo Listed winner Miss Work of Art (herself later dam of 7f 3yo Listed winner Tapisserie).

"She is a full sister to the stakes winner, Dark Liberty, and a half-sister to another stakes winner, Queen of Love. A lovely filly, who is going nicely at this stage and looks a precocious two-year-old type, as you would hope with her pedigree."

UNNAMED (FR)
22/2 b f Dabirsim - Twilight Tear (Rock of Gibraltar)
Trainer: Karl Burke Owner: Cornthrop Bloodstock & Partners Sales price:
€182,000 (David Redvers/Cornthrop Racing)

Full sister to smart French 5.5-7f winner (including at Group 3/Listed level)/
Poule d'Essai des Pouliches runner-up Coeur de Beaute and 2020 French 1m
1f 3yo winner Shariq and a half-sister to Group 3-placed French 5.5-7f winner
Coeur de Pierre. Dam a once-raced maiden daughter of a 7f 2yo winning sister
to Fillies' Mile winner Listen and Moyglare Stud Stakes winner Sequoyah (later
dam of 2000 Guineas winner Henrythenavigator).

*"A very attractive, athletic filly, who is a full sister to Group 3 winner and
French 1000 Guineas second Coeur de Beaute. She looks the type to make her
mark as a two-year-old."*

CHRIS RICHARDSON (CHEVELEY PARK STUD)

ANATOMIC
10/4 gr c Ulysses - Diagnostic (Dutch Art)
Trainer: Sir Mark Prescott Sales price: n/a

First foal of a useful 6-7f winner who was a half-sister to useful dual 7f
winner Homeopathic out of an unraced sister to 6f Listed winner Prescription
and half-sister to 7f 2yo Group 3 winner Cupid's Glory, smart 7-8.5f winner
(including at Group 3/Listed level) Clinical (later dam of 7f 2yo winner/Mehl-
Mulhens Rennen runner-up Lockheed) and 8/10f Listed winner Courting (later
dam of 1m Listed winner Fury).

*"A lovely, easy-moving, balanced colt. He looks quite forward at this stage,
which isn't always the case with this family."*

ANIMATO
23/3 ch c Ulysses - Blithe (Pivotal)
Trainer: David O'Meara Sales price: n/a

Half-brother to very useful 6-7f winner Sainted and very useful triple 6f 3yo
winner Telmeyd. Dam a 7f 2yo winner who was a three-parts sister to Group
1-placed multiple 7-8.5f winner (including at Group 2/3 level) Penitent and
smart 5-6f 2yo winner (including at Group 2/Listed level) Supplicant.

*"He comes from a prolific family that produced the Group 2-winning two-year-
old Supplicant. A neat, balanced individual, who looks a potentially sharp sort
at this stage."*

ENSHRINE
3/4 b f Ulysses - Sacre Caroline (Blame)
Trainer: William Haggas Sales price: n/a

Half-sister to Group 2-placed 2020 5f 2yo winner Sacred. Dam an unraced half-sister to five-time US 8-10f Grade 1 winner (including the Breeders' Cup Juvenile Fillies Turf) Lady Eli, US 8.5/9f Grade 3 winner Bizzy Caroline and Grade 3-placed US 8.5f 2yo winner Princesa Caroline out of a US 8.5f 2yo winner; family of Racing Post Trophy winner Palace Episode and Canadian 8.5f 2yo Grade 1 winner Spring In The Air.

"She is related to our Queen Mary, Lowther and Flying Childers runner-up of last season, Sacred. This filly looks more of a backend prospect but is full of potential."

IMPLORE
25/2 ch c Ulysses - Plead (Dutch Art)
Trainer: John & Thady Gosden Sales price: 70,000gns (Norris Bloodstock)

First foal of a 10f 2yo winner who was a full sister to 6f Listed winner Exhort and a half-sister to 2020 Commonwealth Cup winner Golden Horde and very useful 2020 6-6.5f 2yo winner Line of Departure out of a 9.5f 3yo winning half-sister to smart multiple 7f-1m winner (including at Group 2/3 level) Producer.

"It is a family that has enjoyed plenty of recent success and goes back to prolific Grade 1 winner, Serena's Song. This colt looks sharp and could prove an early sort."

PERSIST
18/1 b f Frankel - Persuasive (Dark Angel)
Trainer: William Haggas Sales price: n/a

First foal of a high-class multiple 1m winner (including the Queen Elizabeth II Stakes) who was a half-sister to Group 3-placed multiple 1m winner (including at Listed level) Tisbutadream, very useful 6-7f winner Amazour and 2020 6f 2yo winner Creative Force out a Group 2/3-placed Irish 6-10f winner (including at Listed level).

"The first foal out of our Queen Elizabeth II Stakes winner, Persuasive. While not overly big, she looks sharp and will no doubt improve as she matures with age."

RICHARD RYAN (TEME VALLEY)

BAYSIDE BOY (IRE)
2/5 b c New Bay - Alava (Anabaa)
Trainer: Roger Varian Sales price: 200,000gns (Richard Ryan)

Half-brother to smart 7-10.5f winner (including at Group 2/3 level) Forest Ranger and Listed-placed 7-8.5f winner Home Cummins. Dam a French 9.5f 3yo Listed winner who was the daughter of a Listed-placed French dual 1m 3yo winning half-sister to French 10.5f 3yo Group 3 winner Tamise (later dam of Australian 12.5f Group 3 winner Motivado) and French 1m 3yo Listed winner Tarzan Cry.

"He is a compact, neater and more natural type than you might expect from the mare. He seems to go nicely at this stage and will be out in the middle of the year over 7f."

BOLD RIBB
15/4 b c Ribchester - Bold Bidder (Indesatchel)
Trainer: Roger Varian Sales price: £82,000 (Richard Ryan)

Half-brother to smart 2020 5-7f 2yo winner (including at Group 3/Listed level) Lullaby Moon and useful multiple 5-7f winner Celebration. Dam a useful dual 5f 2yo winner who was a half-sister to Listed-placed 5f 2yo winner Right Answer and once-raced Irish 5f 2yo winner Twenty Questions out of a 7f 3yo winning half-sister to high-class multiple 5f winner (including at Group 2/3 level) Mind Games.

"This colt is a half-brother to last year's good two-year-old, Lullaby Moon, but I don't know whether he's as naturally forward as that filly. He is a grand, big individual who is very strong and does all his canters nicely. There are no negatives at this stage, and he's in the 'could be anything' category."

CLAIM THE CROWN (IRE)
1/3 b c Acclamation - Crown Light (Zamindar)
Trainer: Roger Varian Sales price: £115,000 (Richard Ryan)

Three-parts brother to Italian 8.5f 2yo winner Valore Speciale (by Lilbourne Lad). Dam an unraced half-sister to high-class UK/French 10-12.5f winner (including at Group 1 level) Bateel, French 10f 3yo Listed winner Basemah and useful dual 10f winner Feathered Crown out of a Group 2/Listed-placed Irish 6f-1m winner.

"This colt rather lost his way after the breaking in process, but he's positively thriving now and resembling the horse we liked at auction. He is a good-

actioned horse who is a slower-burning, rangier type than you'd usually associate with those by Acclamation. While he won't be early, I can see him getting underway during the middle of the season."

CLAIM THE STARS (IRE)
2/3 b c Starspangledbanner - Ponty Acclaim (Acclamation)
Trainer: Mark Johnston Sales price: £32,000 (Johnston Racing)

Half-brother to useful 10f 3yo Flat/2m hurdle winner Fraser Island. Dam a 5f 2yo Group 3 winner who was a half-sister to the maiden dam of French 10.5f 3yo Group 3 winner Talk Or Listen out of a maiden sister to four-time 5f Listed winner Astonished and a half-sister to French 5f Group 3 winner Bishops Court and the dam of Listed winners Dazed And Amazed (5/6f) and Stunned (1m).

"A very forward colt, who everyone is pleased with at this stage. He has plenty of size but is out of a Cornwallis Stakes winner, and it's a fast family right the way through. All the signs have been positive so far."

DARK NOTE
10/5 ch c Night of Thunder - Rosa Grace (Lomitas)
Trainer: Joseph O'Brien Sales price: 70,000gns (Richard Ryan)

Half-brother to fairly useful 2020 8-10f 3yo winner Rosa Gold. Dam a Grade 2-placed 7-10f winner (including at Listed level) who was a half-sister to Listed-placed 5-7f winner Secret Night, useful 6-10f winner Eastern Destiny (later dam of Listed-placed winners Montatham (7f-1m) and Troubador (6f, four times)); family of Middle Park Stakes winner Dark Angel.

"We purchased him from Book 1 of the Tattersalls October Yearling Sale for quite reasonable money, considering the sire's continued success. He seems to do things nicely at this stage and will be a lovely 7f type for the midsummer."

DEVOTED POET
31/3 b c Iffraaj - Devotion (Dylan Thomas)
Trainer: Roger Varian Sales price: 65,000gns (Richard Ryan)

Half-brother to Group 2/3-placed UK/UAE 8-8.5f winner (including the 2020 UAE 1000 Guineas) Dubai Love and useful multiple 6f-1m winner Nick Vedder. Dam a Group 3-placed Irish 7f 2yo winner who was the daughter of an unraced close relation to very useful 10f 3yo Flat/Champion Hurdle winner Celestial Halo and half-sister to 6/7f Listed winner/Irish 1000 Guineas third My Branch (later dam of 6f Group 1 winner Tante Rose and grandam of Poule d'Essai des Poulains winner Make Believe).

"This is a big horse who has an awful lot of quality. He is more of a three-year-old type but moves easily and will hopefully be a nice horse one day."

FLAG OF TRUTH (FR)
19/1 b c Starspangledbanner - Dalakania (Dalakhani)
Trainer: Roger Varian Sales price: £170,000 (Richard Ryan)

First foal of a maiden half-sister to Group 1-placed French 9.5-14f winner (including at Group 2/Listed level) Ziyad, Listed-placed US 7-8.5f winner Machiavelique and the once-raced maiden dam of Listed-placed 9.5-10f winner Victory Bond out of a French 10f 3yo winning half-sister to several smart winners, notably Prix de Diane winner/Prix de l'Arc de Triomphe runner-up Aquarelliste.

"He is a horse I love to bits, but he has unfortunately suffered a setback. He is an unusually good mover for such a big horse and has an awful lot of quality. Hopefully, we aren't held up for too long and can still make it out for a mid-late season two-year-old campaign over 7f. He actually reminds me of our nice three-year-old, Legion of Honour, as a type."

MUSIC MAGIC (IRE)
8/3 b c Fastnet Rock - Start The Music (King's Best)
Trainer: Ger Lyons Sales price: £110,000 (Richard Ryan)

Half-brother to Group 3/Listed-placed 6-7f winner Mubtasim, useful 2020 Irish 1m 3yo winner Edward Hopper and useful 7f-1m 2yo winner Stec. Dam a French 11.5f 3yo winner who was a half-sister to Group 1-placed 6f-1m winner Big Time and Listed-placed 10f 3yo winner Liss Ard out of a maiden half-sister to Dewhurst Stakes/St James's Palace Stakes winner/2000 Guineas runner-up Grand Lodge.

"A sizeable colt with a lot a quality about him. Ger trained his half-brother to some effect and was keen to get back involved with the mare's produce. Fastnet Rock is a good international sire, and Ger likes this colt a lot. He will be a 7f+ type who will thrive with time."

TRANQUIL LADY (IRE)
30/4 ch f Australia - Repose (Quiet American)
Trainer: Joseph O'Brien Sales price: £160,000 (Richard Ryan)

Half-sister to 2020 Irish 7f 2yo winner/Champagne Stakes third State of Rest. Dam an unraced half-sister to Group 2-placed 8.5-10f winner (including at Listed level) Prince Alzain and 7f 2yo Listed winner/May Hill Stakes runner-up Echo River; family of Champion Stakes/US dual 10f Grade 1 winner Storming Home and Poule d'Essai des Pouliches winner Musical Chimes.

"I like this filly a lot. She is obviously a half-sister to our good 2020 two-year-old, State of Rest, who is hopefully going to contest one of the Guineas this spring. This filly was a 'must have' based on her pedigree. She does everything willingly at home and shows as much as she can at this stage given her pedigree. I imagine 7f/1m will be her thing later in the year."

MARK WEINFELD (MEON VALLEY STUD)

CLIPPER CLASS
17/3 b f Frankel - Speedy Boarding (Shamardal)
Trainer: James Fanshawe Owner: Helena Springfield Ltd Sales price: n/a

Second foal of a high-class 10-10.5f winner (including twice at Group 1 level) who was a half-sister to very useful dual 10f 3yo winner Elwazir (by Frankel), useful dual 1m winner Next Stage and three other winners including the dam of Queen's Vase winner Dashing Willoughby out of an 11f Listed-winning half-sister to Group 1-placed 8-10f winner (including at Listed level) Dash To The Top (later dam of Oaks winner Anapurna (by Frankel)).

"A very classy-looking filly who will need time. Speedy Boarding's dam is a half-sister to the dam of Anapurna (by Frankel). Unsurprisingly, she will be going to James Fanshawe."

MR ZIPPI
28/4 b c Intello - Izzi Top (Pivotal)
Trainer: Andrew Balding Owner: Castle Down Racing Sales price: 100,000gns (Vendor)

Half-brother to Group 3-placed 7f 2yo winner Prince Eiji, Listed-placed 7-10f winner Willie John, very useful 6-7f winner Dreamfield and 2020 8-8.5f 3yo winner Bizzi Lizzi. Dam a dual 10f Group 1 winner who was a half-sister to Group 1-placed 8-10f winner (including at Group 2/Listed level) Jazzi Top.

"This is a colt that didn't sell at Book 1 of the Tattersalls October Yearling Sale last autumn, but subsequently joined Castle Down Racing, who also had Telecaster. This colt is in pre-training with Ben De Haan and will be going into training with Andrew Balding. Recent reports and videos show this colt to be turning into a very powerful-looking horse."

TANGO TONIGHT
14/2 ch f Pivotal - Last Tango Inparis (Aqlaam)
Trainer: Hughie Morrison Owner: Helena Springfield Ltd Sales price: n/a

Second foal of a Listed-placed 1m 2yo winner who was a half-sister to four winners out of a maiden half-sister to dual 10f Listed winner Marsh Daisy (by Pivotal), Listed-placed dual 6f 2yo winner Fontana Amorosa, Group 3/Listed-placed Irish 11.5f 3yo winner Yankee Doodle and the dam of Group 2/3-placed 7f-2m winner (including twice at Listed level) Mildenberger.

"Her dam was a winner at two and later placed at Listed level in France. A strong, good-moving filly, she will be going to Hughie Morrison who trained Last Tango Inparis."

ULTRA CHIC
4/2 b f Lope de Vega - Very Dashing (Dansili)
Trainer: John & Thady Gosden Owner: Helena Springfield Ltd Sales price: n/a

First foal of a very useful 10f 3yo winner who was closely related to Group 3-placed Irish 6f 2yo winner Dynasty and a half-sister to Oaks winner Anapurna out of a 10f 3yo Listed winner/Yorkshire Oaks runner-up who was a half-sister to 11f Listed winner Dash To The Front (later dam of French dual 10f Group 1 winner Speedy Boarding).

"A nice, racy sort of filly. She is out of a Listed-placed mare and half-sister to Anapurna. Her grandam is a half-sister to the dam of Speedy Boarding who's by Shamardal, the grandsire of this filly. Ultra Chic will be joining John & Thady Gosden."

SECTION THREE

CHARLIE APPLEBY

ALBAHR
7/2 ch c Dubawi - Falls of Lora (Street Cry)
Owner: Godolphin Sales price: n/a

Full brother to UK/UAE 7f-1m winner Imperial Empire and a half-brother to 2021 Australian 1m Group 1 winner Cascadian and useful Irish 11.5-13f 3yo winner Trossachs. Dam a smart 6.5-9.5f winner (including at Group 3/Listed level) who was a half-sister to 2020 7f 2yo Group 2 winner Master of The Seas (by Dubawi) and Group 1-placed triple 7f winner (including at Listed level) Latharnach.

BEFORE DAWN (IRE)
18/3 gr f Dark Angel - Mistrusting (Shamardal)
Owner: Godolphin Sales price: n/a

Full sister to smart 5f-1m winner (including at Group 2/Listed level) Althiqa. Dam a 6f 3yo Listed-winning daughter of a Cherry Hinton Stakes winner/ Cheveley Park Stakes runner-up who was a full sister to 7f 2yo winner Night Song; family of Middle Park Stakes winner First Trump.

JAAH (IRE)
16/3 ch c Night of Thunder - Good Place (Street Cry)
Owner: Abdullah Menahi Sales price: n/a

Third foal of a Listed-placed 7f-1m 2yo winner who was a half-sister to useful 6f 2yo winner Folk Tale, 7f 2yo winner Bint Al Reem and the dam of Listed-placed Irish dual 5f 3yo winner Snowstar out of an Australian 5f Listed winner; family of very smart Australian pair Guelph and Sepoy.

SACRED JEWEL
31/1 ch f Dubawi - Priceless (Exceed And Excel)
Owner: Godolphin Sales price: 420,000gns (Godolphin)

First foal of a smart 5-6f winner (including at Group 2/Listed level) who was a half-sister to Group 2-placed dual 6f 2yo winner Doctor Brown, useful UK/ UAE multiple 6f winner Brazen, useful 6-8.5f winner Insaaf and useful 5-6f 2yo winner Bright Moll (later dam of 6f Group 3 winner Aeolus).

SECRET STATE (IRE)
9/4 ch c Dubawi - Jacqueline Quest (Rock of Gibraltar)
Owner: Godolphin Sales price: 525,000gns (Godolphin)

Full brother to 2020 7f/1m 3yo Listed winner Onassis and a half-brother to four winners, notably Breeders' Cup Juvenile Turf winner Line of Duty and Listed-placed Irish 10f 3yo winner Hibiscus. Dam a disqualified 1000 Guineas winner out of a 12f-2m 1f winning half-sister to dual 10f Group 3 winner Regime and Group 2/3-placed dual 5f 2yo winner (including at Listed level) Salut d'Amour.

WITH THE MOONLIGHT (IRE)
17/2 b f Frankel - Sand Vixen (Dubawi)
Owner: Godolphin Sales price: n/a

Full sister to high-class 7-9f winner (including at Group 1 level) Dream Castle and a half-sister to 2020 7f 2yo winner Inveigle. Dam a smart 5-6f 2yo winner (including at Group 2/Listed level) who was a half-sister to Group 3-placed 6-6.5f winner So Will I.

UNNAMED (IRE)
13/5 b/gr f Invincible Spirit - Antiquities (Kaldounevees)
Owner: Godolphin Sales price: n/a

Half-sister to 2020 Poule d'Essai des Poulains winner/Prix du Jockey Club third Victor Ludorum and Irish 10f 3yo Listed winner/Irish Oaks third Mary Tudor. Dam a Group 3/Listed-placed French 10-10.5f 3yo winner who was the daughter of a French 10.5f 3yo Listed-winning half-sister to US 1m 1f Grade 1/UAE 10f Group 1 winner Street Cry, the dam of four-time 7-10.5f Group 1 winner (including the Poule d'Essai des Poulains and Prix du Jockey Club) Shamardal and the great-grandam of Prix Jean Prat winner/2000 Guineas runner-up Territories (by Invincible Spirit).

UNNAMED
13/4 b c Frankel - Attraction (Efisio)
Owner: Godolphin Sales price: 1,100,000gns (Godolphin)

Full brother to Group 1-placed 7-11f winner (including at Group 2/3 level) Elarqam, a three-parts brother to Grade 3/Listed-placed UK/US 9-10f winner Cushion (by Galileo) and a half-brother to six winners, notably Irish 5f 3yo Group 3 winner Fountain of Youth. Dam a five-time 6f-1m Group 1 winner (including the English and Irish 1000 Guineas).

UNNAMED (IRE)
4/4 b c Invincible Spirit - Autumn Lily (Street Cry)
Owner: Godolphin Sales price: n/a

Half-brother to Group 1-placed 2020 French 1m 2yo winner Botanik. Dam a
very useful 6-7f 2yo winner who was a half-sister to Group 1-placed multiple
6-9f winner (including at Group 3/Listed level) Alexandros out of a French 8.5-
9.5f winning close relation to high-class middle-distance performers In The
Wings and Morozov.

UNNAMED
16/2 b c Dubawi - Black Cherry (Mount Nelson)
Owner: Godolphin Sales price: 480,000gns (Godolphin)

Half-brother to Listed-placed 2020 7.5f 2yo winner Little Rollright. Dam a
Group 3/Listed-placed 7f-1m 3yo winner who was the daughter of a 7f Listed-
winning half-sister to 7f 3yo Group 2 winner Last Resort, German 6f Group 2
winner Barrow Creek, 5f 2yo Listed winner Heard A Whisper and the dam of
smart milers Trans Island and Welsh Diva (herself later dam of UAE 5f Group 3
winner Fityaan).

Little Rollright

UNNAMED (IRE)
14/5 b c Galileo - Eastern Joy (Dubai Destination)
Owner: Godolphin Sales price: n/a

Three-parts brother to 7f 2yo Group 3 winner Easy Victory (by Teofilo) and a half-brother to very smart multiple 7-10f winner (including four times at Group 1 level) Thunder Snow, high-class 7-9.5f winner (including at Group 2/3 level) Ihtimal, Group 1-placed 6-8.5f winner (including at Listed level) Always Smile and UAE 1m 3yo Listed winner Winter Lightning. Dam a French 1m 1f 3yo winner who was a half-sister to Prix de Diane winner West Wind.

UNNAMED (IRE)
8/3 b f Ribchester - Firth of Lorne (Danehill)
Owner: Godolphin Sales price: n/a

Three-parts sister to Group 1-placed triple 7f winner (including at Listed level) Latharnach (by Iffraaj) and a half-sister to 2020 7f 2yo Group 2 winner Master of The Seas, smart 6.5-9.5f winner (including at Group 3/Listed level) Falls of Lora (dam of 2021 Australian 1m Group 1 winner Cascadian) and German 7f 3yo Listed winner Etive. Dam a French 1m 2yo winner/Poule d'Essai des Pouliches runner-up who was out of a Cherry Hinton Stakes winner/1000 Guineas runner-up.

UNNAMED
12/4 ch c Night of Thunder - Indian Petal (Singspiel)
Owner: Godolphin Sales price: n/a

Closely related to high-class multiple 8-12f winner (including at Group/Grade 1 level) Old Persian, 2021 12f 3yo winner Bandinelli (both by Dubawi) and Listed-placed dual 5f 2yo winner Chapelli (by Poet's Voice). Dam a maiden sister to Ribblesdale Stakes winner Silkwood and half-sister to Cherry Hinton Stakes winner Silent Honor and Listed-placed Irish dual 5f 2yo winner Shrill.

UNNAMED (IRE)
5/5 ch c Dubawi - Inner Secret (Singspiel)
Owner: Godolphin Sales price: n/a

Full brother to French 1m 1f 3yo Listed winner Crystal River and a half-brother to French 1m 2yo Group 1 winner Royal Marine and 2021 UAE 1m Group 2 winner Secret Ambition. Dam a once-raced maiden half-sister to Queen Anne Stakes winner Dubai Destination, Prix Jacques Le Marois/Prix du Moulin winner Librettist and high-class middle-distance performer Secret Number.

UNNAMED
24/3 b f New Approach - Kenspeckle (Dubawi)
Owner: Godolphin Sales price: n/a

First foal of an unraced half-sister to high-class 2yo/Derby winner Masar (by New Approach) out of a UAE Oaks/UAE Derby-winning daughter of a 10-11f winner who was a half-sister to Irish 9/10f Group 3 winner Moonlight Magic, French 12.5f 3yo Group 3 winner/Prix de l'Arc de Triomphe third Masterstroke and 12f Group 3 winner Royal Line; outstanding family of Galileo and Sea The Stars.

UNNAMED (IRE)
1/4 b c Kingman - Lombatina (King's Best)
Owner: Godolphin Sales price: 475,000gns (Godolphin)

Half-brother to smart triple 1m winner (including at Listed level) Agrotera and three other winners including once-raced 2020 1m 2yo winner Star Caliber. Dam a French 6f 2yo winner who was a half-sister to Italian 10f Group 1 winner Sortilege, French 10f 3yo Group 3 winner Soudania and five other winners including the dam of 2021 UAE 10f Group 3 winner Star Safari; family of Deutsches Derby winners Samum, Schiaparelli and Sea The Moon.

UNNAMED (IRE)
17/4 ch c Dubawi - Modern Ideals (New Approach)
Owner: Godolphin Sales price: n/a

Half-brother to 2020 6f 2yo winner Modern News. Dam a twice-raced maiden half-sister to French 1m 2yo Group 1 winner Ultra, French 12.5f 3yo Group 3 winner Synopsis, Listed-placed French 12f 3yo winner Epic Simile (later dam of Group 2/3-placed 6f 2yo winner Figure of Speech) and 2020 7f 2yo winner Quintillus (by Dubawi).

UNNAMED
10/2 b c Lope de Vega - Moi Meme (Teofilo)
Owner: Godolphin Sales price: 900,000gns (Godolphin)

Full brother to 2020 US 8.5f 2yo winner Capital Structure and 2020 Solario Stakes runner-up King Vega. Dam a French 10.5f 3yo Listed winner who was a three-parts sister to Group 3-placed French 10-12f winner (including at Listed level) Toi Et Moi and a half-sister to Italian 10f 3yo winner/Oaks d'Italia runner-up Moi Non Plus and French 1m 2yo winner Parle Moi (dam of Grade 2-placed 2020 US 8.5f 2yo winner Public Sector).

UNNAMED (IRE)
11/2 b c Kodiac - Montefino (Shamardal)
Owner: Godolphin Sales price: 255,000gns (Godolphin)

Half-brother to high-class Italian multiple 8-10f winner (including at Group 2/3 level) Anda Muchacho, Group 3/Listed-placed 5-6f 2yo winner Parsley, useful triple 6f winner Love Powerful and useful 6f 2yo winner Aim Power. Dam an unraced daughter of an Irish 10f Group 2 winner who was a half-sister to 6/7f Listed winner Monnavanna and 14f 3yo Listed winner Mill Springs.

UNNAMED
11/4 b c Iffraaj - Mujarah (Marju)
Owner: Godolphin Sales price: n/a

Full brother to very smart 6f-1m winner (four times at Group 1 level, including the Lockinge Stakes and Queen Anne Stakes) Ribchester. Dam a maiden half-sister to high-class multiple 8-10f winner (including at Group 1 level) Matterhorn, Group 2-placed multiple 10f winner (including at Group 3/Listed level) Bangkok, Irish 14f Group 3 winner Tactic, French 12f 3yo Listed winner Yaazy and Listed-placed 8-12f winner Zahoo (later dam of Irish 7f 3yo Group 3 winner Convergence).

UNNAMED (IRE)
3/3 b f Invincible Spirit - Policoro (Pivotal)
Owner: Godolphin Sales price: n/a

Full sister to German 1m 3yo Listed winner Firebird Song and a half-sister to 2020 6-7f 2yo winner Basilicata. Dam a French 11f 3yo winner who was a half-sister to Listed-placed French 8-9f winner Taranto (later dam of Prix Jean Prat winner/2000 Guineas runner-up Territories (by Invincible Spirit)) out of a French 15.5f Group 3-winning half-sister to French 1m 1f 2yo Group 3 winner Graikos.

UNNAMED
27/2 ch f Dubawi - Really Special (Shamardal)
Owner: Godolphin Sales price: n/a

First foal of a 1m 2yo Listed winner who was a half-sister to high-class 8-10f winner (including three times at Group 1 level)/Oaks runner-up Wild Illusion, Group 3-placed 7f 2yo winner Ceratonia and useful 2020 7f-1m 2yo winner Yibir out of a 10f 3yo Listed winner.

UNNAMED
14/4 b c Dubawi - Rumh (Monsun)
Owner: Godolphin Sales price: n/a

Full brother to useful 2020 7f-1m 2yo winner Yibir and a half-brother to
Nassau Stakes/Prix de l'Opera winner Wild Illusion, 1m 2yo Listed winner
Really Special and Group 3-placed 7f 2yo winner Ceratonia. Dam a 10f 3yo
Listed winner who was a three-parts sister to German 10f 3yo Listed winner
Realeza out of a German 1m 2yo Group 3-winning half-sister to US 9.5f Grade
1 winner Royal Highness (later dam of French 10/11f Group 2 winner Free Port
Lux).

UNNAMED (IRE)
5/3 b f Kingman - Sante (Dream Ahead)
Owner: Godolphin Sales price: 1,450,000gns (Godolphin)

First foal of a Listed-placed 7f 3yo winner who was a half-sister to German
1m Group 2 winner Combat Zone, Group 1-placed 9-10f winner (including at
Group 3/Listed level) Scottish, smart 8-13.5f winner (including at Group 3/
Listed level) Royal Empire, Group 3/Listed-placed 7f 2yo winner Bikini Babe
(dam of 2020 7f 2yo Group 3 winner La Barrosa) and Listed-placed French
7f 2yo winner Zut Alors (later dam of Poule d'Essai des Pouliches winner
Precieuse).

UNNAMED
13/4 b c Invincible Spirit - Serene Beauty (Street Cry)
Owner: Godolphin Sales price: n/a

Half-brother to 2020 10f 3yo winner Lightness. Dam a useful 8.5-10.5f 3yo
winner who was a full sister to 7f 2yo Group 3 winner Discourse (later dam
of 2021 UAE 1m Group 3 winner Blown By Wind (by Invincible Spirit) and 1m
Listed winners and Discursus and Hadith) and a half-sister to US 1m 1f Grade
1 winner Bandini and the dam of 2020 Prince of Wales's Stakes winner Lord
North.

UNNAMED
16/2 b c Shamardal - Switching (Street Cry)
Owner: Godolphin Sales price: n/a

First foal of a Group 3/Listed-placed French 1m 1f 3yo winner who was a full
sister to very useful French 8-9.5f 3yo winner Rueing and very useful French
1m 3yo winner Flowrider out of a Prix Saint-Alary-winning half-sister to French
10f 2yo Group 1 winner Mandaean and very useful 7f 2yo winner Winters
Moon (later dam of Prix Morny/Middle Park Stakes winner Earthlight (by
Shamardal)).

UNNAMED (IRE)
8/2 ch f Dubawi - Very Special (Lope de Vega)
Owner: Godolphin Sales price: n/a

First foal of a Group 1-placed 6-9f winner (including three times at Group 2 level) who was a full sister to useful 8.5-11f Flat/2m Grade 1 hurdle winner Mengli Khan and a half-sister to Fillies' Mile/Breeders' Cup Juvenile Fillies Turf winner Chriselliam and Listed-placed UK/US 7-8.5f winner Janicellaine.

UNNAMED (IRE)
16/5 b c Exceed And Excel - Windsor County (Elusive Quality)
Owner: Godolphin Sales price: n/a

Half-brother to Poule d'Essai des Pouliches winner Castle Lady, smart UK/UAE 6-7f winner (including at Listed level) Top Score and useful 6-7f winner Eton College. Dam an unraced sister to top-class 7-10f winner (including the Queen Elizabeth II Stakes and Breeders' Cup Classic) Raven's Pass and a half-sister to US 1m Grade 3 winner Gigawatt; family of Fillies' Mile winner Rainbow View.

UNNAMED
26/3 ch f Shamardal - Winters Moon (New Approach)
Owner: Godolphin Sales price: n/a

Full sister to very smart 5.5-7f winner (including twice at Group 1 level) Earthlight. Dam a very useful 7f 2yo winner who was a half-sister to French 10f Group 1 winners Mandaean (2yo) and Wavering (3yo) and five other winners out of a French 1m 2yo Group 3 winner/Prix Saint-Alary third.

UNNAMED (IRE)
6/5 b c Dubawi - Zibelina (Dansili)
Owner: Godolphin Sales price: n/a

Full brother to useful 7f-1m winner Severnaya and once-raced 2020 7f 2yo winner Royal Fleet and a half-brother to 2020 French 6f 3yo Group 3 winner Royal Crusade. Dam a smart 7f-1m winner (including at Group 3/Listed level) who was a half-sister to 6f 2yo Listed winner Floristry (dam of 2020 5f 3yo Group 3/Listed winner Lazuli (by Dubawi).

SAEED BIN SUROOR

UNNAMED (IRE)
25/3 b c Profitable - Betimes (New Approach)
Owner: Godolphin Sales price: n/a

Half-brother to useful UK/French 6-6.5f winner Theory of Time. Dam a Listed-placed 7f 2yo winner who was a half-sister to smart multiple 5-6f winners (including at Listed level) Aahayson and Take Ten and very useful multiple 6-7f winner Thebes out of a Listed-placed dual 5f winning half-sister to 7f 2yo Group 3 winner Peak To Creek and dual 6f Listed winner Ripples Maid.

UNNAMED
18/2 br c Cable Bay - Bonhomie (Shamardal)
Owner: Godolphin Sales price: 150,000gns (Stroud Coleman Bloodstock)

Full brother to Listed-placed 2020 7f 2yo winner Laneqash. Dam an 8.5f 3yo winner who was the daughter of an unraced half-sister to smart French/US 8-9f winner (including at Grade 2/Listed level) Calista, the dam of French 1m 2yo Group 1 winner Ultra and the grandams of French 8/10.5f Group 1 winner/Prix du Jockey Club runner-up Act One and 10f 3yo Listed winners Cosmodrome and Splashdown (later dam of Solario Stakes winner Aktabantay).

UNNAMED (IRE)
15/5 ch f Ribchester - Kalaatah (Dynaformer)
Owner: Godolphin Sales price: n/a

Half-sister to Listed-placed 6-7f 2yo winner Raeeb. Dam a useful dual 12f 3yo winner who was a half-sister to Group 2-placed Irish/UAE multiple 7f-1m winner (including at Listed level) Ghaamer and 5f 2yo winner Seize The Time out of a Listed-placed 1m 3yo winning close relation to 10/10.5f Listed winner Imtiyaz and half-sister to 7f 2yo Group 3 winner/1000 Guineas third Bint Shadayid and 6f 2yo Listed winner Alshadiyah (later dam of smart performers Farhaan, Haatheq and Wid).

UNNAMED (IRE)
22/4 b c Invincible Spirit - Long Lashes (Rock Hard Ten)
Owner: Godolphin Sales price: n/a

Half-brother to 2020 8-9.5f 3yo winner Beautiful Illusion. Dam a Group 2-placed 6f-1m winner (including at Group 3/Listed level) who was a half-sister to 2020 US 10f Grade 1 winner Combatant and Group 2-placed 5f 2yo winner Mythical Border out of an unraced sister to Grade 3-placed US 8-8.5f winner Plenty and half-sister to Grade 1-placed US 6-8.5f winner Just A Coincidence.

UNNAMED (IRE)
8/4 b c Profitable - Nafura (Dubawi)
Owner: Godolphin Sales price: n/a

Half-brother to Group 2/3-placed 2020 dual 7f 2yo winner Dubai Fountain,
Listed-placed 2020 10f 3yo winner Real World and 12f-2m Flat/2m Listed
hurdle winner Leoncavallo. Dam a dual 8.5f 2yo winner who was a half-sister
to very smart milers Dubai Destination and Librettist, high-class middle-
distance performer Secret Number and the dam of French 1m 2yo Group 1
winner Royal Marine.

UNNAMED (IRE)
25/1 b f Mehmas - Turuqaat (Fantastic Light)
Owner: Godolphin Sales price: 180,000gns (Stroud Coleman Bloodstock)

Half-sister to Listed-placed Italian 7.5f 2yo winner Aisa Dream. Dam an
unraced half-sister to smart Irish 6-7f winner (including at Group 3 level)
Rawaaq out of a maiden half-sister to smart UK/US 7-10f winner (including at
Group 3/Listed level) Muqbil and Group 2-placed 6-7f 2yo winner Mostaqeleh
(later dam of Japanese 7f Grade 3 winner Matera Sky, UAE 7f/1m Listed
winner Nawwaar and Irish 5f 2yo winner/Coventry Stakes third Murillo).

UNNAMED (IRE)
27/2 ch c Iffraaj - Voice of Truth (Dubawi)
Owner: Godolphin Sales price: n/a

First foal of a 7f 2yo winner who was a half-sister to high-class multiple 7-10f
winner (including three times at Group 1 level) Rio de La Plata, useful UK/
French 8-10f winner Beautiful Memory, useful UAE 9.5-10f winner Street of
Dreams, 10-12f 3yo winner Arabian Beauty, 1m 3yo winner Expressly and 7f
2yo winner Ihsas.

UNNAMED
6/5 b f Night of Thunder - Wedding March (Dalakhani)
Owner: Godolphin Sales price: n/a

Three-parts sister to useful French 8-10f winner Ahesta Bero and 2021 dual 6f
winner Declaring Love (both by Dubawi). Dam a useful French 1m 2yo winner
who was a full sister to 10f 3yo Listed winner Elik and a half-sister to Group
1-placed UK/Australian 7.5-14.5f winner (including at Group 3/Listed level)
Mugatoo out of a Group 1-placed German/French 10-11f winner (including at
Group 2/3 level).

CLIVE COX

ALTAI
16/1 ch c Territories - Analytical (Lethal Force)
Owner: AlMohamediya Racing Sales price: 35,000gns (Clive Cox Racing)

First foal of an unraced half-sister to Prix Robert Papin winner Tis Marvellous, Listed-placed multiple 6f winner Mythmaker and three other winners out of a 6f 2yo winning daughter of a Queen Mary Stakes winner who was herself a half-sister to Queen Mary Stakes winner Romantic Liaison.

BENEFIT
8/2 b f Acclamation - Boost (Pivotal)
Owner: Cheveley Park Stud Sales price: n/a

First foal of a 6-7f 3yo winner who was a half-sister to useful dual 1m 3yo winner Restive Spirit out of a Cheveley Park Stakes-winning sister to 6f 2yo winner Hip and half-sister to French 1m 2yo Listed winner Hypnotic and Listed-placed 6f-1m winner Mazyoun; family of smart sprinter Danehurst.

BERMUDA
1/2 b f Kodiac - Poana (New Approach)
Owner: Cheveley Park Stud Sales price: n/a

First foal of a once-raced maiden half-sister to French 6f 2yo Group 3 winner/Prix Morny third Pontenuovo and Listed-placed French 6f 2yo winner Ponte Vespucci out of a Prix Maurice de Gheest winner; family of Doomben Cup winner/Poule d'Essai des Poulains third Pornichet.

CAMBAY SCOUT (IRE)
17/2 b c Profitable - Throne (Royal Applause)
Owner: AlMohamediya Racing Sales price: £52,000 (Clive Cox Racing Ltd)

Half-brother to 2020 6f 2yo winner Kraken Power. Dam a twice-raced maiden half-sister to very smart multiple 5f winner (including at Group 1 level) Kyllachy, Listed-placed multiple 5f winner Borders and nine other winners including the grandam of Irish 5f 2yo Listed winner Yulong Baobei.

CATURRA (IRE)
11/4 b c Mehmas - Shoshoni Wind (Sleeping Indian)
Owner: Saeed Bin Mohammed Al Qassimi Sales price: 110,000gns (Blandford Bloodstock)

Half-brother to Listed-placed UK/Qatari 7f-1m winner Sir Arthur Dayne. Dam a Listed-placed 5-6f winner who was a half-sister to Group 3-placed 6-7f winner

Burnwynd Boy and three other winners; family of Cheveley Park Stakes winner Lightening Pearl and smart stayers Classic Cliche and Mizzou.

CODIFY (IRE)
30/4 b c Lawman - Bayja (Giant's Causeway)
Owner: J Goddard Sales price: 95,000gns (Clive Cox Racing)

Half-brother to Group 2-placed 5-6f winner (including twice at Group 3 level) New Providence, Group 3-placed UK/UAE multiple 6f winner Ekhtiyaar, 6f 2yo winner Ahdaf and 2020 7f 2yo winner Jacinth. Dam a maiden half-sister to Listed-placed French 1m 3yo winner Myrica.

CRAZYLAND (IRE)
8/5 b f Kodiac - Imperialistic Diva (Haafhd)
Owner: P Stokes & S Krase Sales price: 57,000gns (Badgers Bloodstock)

Closely related to Group 2-placed 5-6f 2yo winner (including at Group 3/Listed level) Queen of Bermuda and 5f 2yo winner Mia Diva (both by Exceed And Excel). Dam a very useful UK/US 5-9f winner who was a half-sister to German 1000 Guineas winner Electrelane.

DARK SWANSONG (IRE)
27/2 b c Dark Angel - Pixeleen (Pastoral Pursuits)
Owner: Alan G Craddock Sales price: 100,000gns (Clive Cox Racing)

First foal of a Listed-placed 5-6f winner who was a half-sister to 6f 2yo winner The Mums out of a 6f 2yo winning sister to useful 5-6f 2yo winner Bright Moll (later dam of 6f Group 3 winner Aeolus) and half-sister to eight winners, notably smart 5-6f winner (including at Group 2/Listed level) Priceless.

LET'S FLY AGAIN
6/4 b c Kodiac - Kinnaird (Dr Devious)
Owner: Simon Munir & Isaac Souede Sales price: 125,000gns (Highflyer Bloodstock)

Closely related to Group 3-placed UK/Australian 8-10.5f winner (including at Listed level) Abdon (by Cacique) and a half-brother to smart 7-11.5f winner (including at Group 2/3 level) Berkshire and the dam of Group 1-placed 5-6f 2yo winner (including twice at Group 2 level)/2000 Guineas third Ivawood. Dam a Prix de l'Opera winner who was a half-sister to Chester Vase winner Mickdaam.

MAMBO BEAT (IRE)
10/3 ch c Red Jazz - Bulrushes (Byron)
Owner: Middleham Park Racing CXIV Sales price: £75,000 (Clive Cox Racing)

Full brother to smart multiple 6-6.5f winner (including at Group 3/Listed level) Snazzy Jazzy and a half-brother to French 5.5f Group 3 winner Ross Castle and Irish 7f 3yo Listed winner Ten Year Ticket. Dam an unraced half-sister to Group 1-placed 6-7f winner (including at Group 2/3 level) Tariq and the dam of Irish 6f Group 2 winner Mobsta out of an unraced half-sister to the dam of Flying Childers Stakes winner/Middle Park Stakes runner-up Wi Dud.

MIDNIGHT TRAIN
28/3 b c Iffraaj - Amarysia (Medicean)
Owner: A D Spence & A J Pearson Sales price: 50,000gns (Clive Cox Racing)

Half-brother to useful French 10-10.5f 3yo winner Sejo. Dam a French 9-9.5f 3yo winner who was a half-sister to French 10.5f Group 3 winner Skia (later dam of 2020 Japanese 1m Grade 2 winner Vin de Garde) and 8/11f Listed winner Tropaios out of a French 9-10f winning half-sister to triple 7f Group 2 winner Arabian Gleam, dual 6f Listed winner Kimberella and the dam of 2020 1000 Guineas/Oaks winner Love and dual 6f 2yo Group 2 winner Lucky Kristale.

MOHI
3/2 b c Acclamation - Minalisa (Oasis Dream)
Owner: AlMohamediya Racing Sales price: 60,000gns (Clive Cox Racing)

Third foal of a smart multiple 6f winner (including at Listed level) who was the daughter of a 6f winning half-sister to Irish 5f Group 3/Listed winner Miss Anabaa (grandam of 6f 2yo Listed winner Enjazaat (by Acclamation)), very useful multiple 5-6f winners Move It and Out After Dark and the maiden dam of 2020 Prix Robert Papin winner Ventura Tormenta (by Acclamation).

RUM COCKTAIL
30/4 b f Muhaarar - Tropical Treat (Bahamian Bounty)
Owner: J C Smith Sales price: n/a

Half-sister to dual 6f 2yo winner Tropical Rock. Dam a Group 3-placed dual 5f winner (including at Listed level) who was out of a Listed-placed 5f 2yo winning daughter of a US dual 8.5f winner who was a half-sister to Coventry Stakes/Champagne Stakes winner Sri Pekan and Irish 6f 2yo Group 3 winner Daylight In Dubai.

SAFETY FIRST
13/4 b f New Bay - Soteria (Acclamation)
Owner: China Horse Club International Limited Sales price: £100,000 (Clive Cox Racing Ltd)

Full sister to Listed-placed 2020 6f 2yo winner Imperial Yellow. Dam a maiden sister to 5f 2yo winner Tschierschen and a half-sister to Group 1-placed 6-7f winner Gallagher, Listed-placed UK/UAE 7-10f winner Quick Wit, Listed-placed 7f 3yo winner New Day Dawn and Listed-placed 5-7f winner Roodeye (later dam of 2020 Sussex Stakes winner Mohaather and US 6.5f/1m Grade 2 winner Prize Exhibit and grandam of Queen Anne Stakes winner Accidental Agent).

Imperial Yellow

SHIMMERING SKY (IRE)
1/3 b c Galileo Gold - Oh Simple Thing (Compton Place)
Owner: Miss J Deadman & S Barrow Sales price: £16,000 (Clive Cox Racing Ltd)

Second foal of a maiden half-sister to German 6f Group 2/3 winner Donnerschlag, French 7f 2yo Listed winner Izzy Bizu and Group 3-placed Irish 6f 2yo winner Da Boss Man out of a useful Irish 8-9.5f winning half-sister to Group 2-placed 5-6f winner Funny Valentine, the dam of smart 5-6f winner (including at Group 3/Listed level) Resplendent Glory and the grandam of Norfolk Stakes winner Prince of Lir.

UBERRIMA FIDES
9/4 b c Exceed And Excel - Baileys Showgirl (Sepoy)
Owner: Simon Munir & Isaac Souede Sales price: 62,000gns (Highflyer Bloodstock)

First foal of a Group 3-placed 6-7f 2yo winner (including at Listed level) who was a half-sister to French 6.5f 3yo Listed winner Tribune (later dam of French 1m 3yo Listed winner Deemster) out of a Listed-placed French/US triple 1m winner; family of Zetland Stakes winner Max Vega.

WINGS OF WAR (IRE)
4/3 gr c Dark Angel - Futoon (Kodiac)
Owner: Isa Salman Al Khalifa Sales price: £140,000 (John & Jake Warren)

First foal of a Listed-placed dual 5f 3yo winner who was the daughter of a useful dual 5f 2yo winning sister to Group 1-placed multiple 5-7f winner (including at Group 2/Listed level) Galeota and half-sister to 13f 3yo Listed winner Loulwa (later dam of dual 5f Listed winner Justineo), useful 5-6f winner Lady Livius (later dam of smart sprinters Brown Sugar and Burnt Sugar) and the grandam of 6f 2yo Listed winner Darkanna (by Dark Angel).

UNNAMED
29/3 ch c Profitable - Frabjous (Pivotal)
Owner: Paul & Clare Rooney Sales price: £72,000 (Kevin Ross Bloodstock)

Half-brother to Irish 6f 2yo Listed winner Argentero, useful 7f 2yo winner Titan Rock and two other winners. Dam an unraced half-sister to Prix Maurice de Gheest winner May Ball, UAE 10f Listed winner Rampallion and very useful dual 12f winner Taunt.

UNNAMED
13/4 b c Frankel - One Last Dance (Encosta de Lago)
Owner: J Camilleri Sales price: n/a

Third foal of an Australian 5.5f 2yo Group 3 winner who was the daughter of an Australian 6f 2yo Group 3-winning sister to Australian 5f 2yo Group 2 winner Langoustine and the dam of Japanese 1m 2yo Grade 1 winner Satono Ares and half-sister to Irish 7.5f 2yo winner/Royal Lodge Stakes runner-up Achill Island and Listed-placed Irish dual 5f 2yo winner Marigot Bay.

UNNAMED (IRE)
13/2 b f Zoffany - Savannah Belle (Green Desert)
Owner: Mrs Patricia J Burns Sales price: n/a

Half-sister to Group 1-placed 6f-1m winner (including at Group 2/Listed level)/2000 Guineas runner-up Dubawi Gold, high-class multiple 7f-1m winner (including at Group 2/3 level) D'Bai, Irish 1m 3yo Listed winner Fort Knox, Listed-placed Irish 10f 3yo winner Savannah Storm and six other winners. Dam a 5f 2yo winner who was the daughter of a Ribblesdale Stakes winner.

SIMON & ED CRISFORD

AL AGAILA (IRE)
12/2 b f Lope de Vega - L'Amour de Ma Vie (Dansili)
Owner: KHK Racing Ltd Sales price: €240,000 (Stroud Coleman Bloodstock Limited)

Second foal of a UAE 1m 1f Group 2 winner who was a half-sister to smart US 8.5-14f winner (including at Grade 2/3 level) Scuba out of a Grade 2/3-placed 6-8.5f winning daughter of a US 8.5f Listed winner.

ANTHEM NATIONAL (IRE)
27/3 b c Dark Angel - Anthem Alexander (Starspangledbanner)
Owner: Noel O'Callaghan Sales price: 95,000gns (Vendor)

Full brother to 2020 6f 2yo winner Darvel and a half-brother to 6.5f 2yo winner Full Verse. Dam a Group 1-placed 5-6f winner (including at Group 2/3 level) who was a half-sister to Group 1-placed 5-6f winner (including at Group 3/Listed level) Dandy Man and the maiden dam of 6f Group 3 winner/Prix de l'Abbaye third Hamza.

CROUPIER (IRE)
14/4 b c Invincible Spirit - Aaraamm (Street Cry)
Owner: Edward J Ware Sales price: 100,000gns (Richard Frisby Bloodstock)

Second foal of an unraced sister to Champagne Stakes winner Saamidd and a half-sister to Grade 1-placed 10-12f winner (including at Listed level) Talmada, smart triple 1m winner (including at Listed level) Masaarr and useful 7-10.5f winner Yarroom out of a 12f 3yo winning half-sister to Irish 7f 2yo winner/Irish 2000 Guineas third Oracle.

DESERT TEAM (IRE)
16/4 b f Invincible Spirit - Kilmah (Sepoy)
Owner: Sultan Ali Sales price: n/a

First foal of a 7f 2yo Group 3 winner who was a half-sister to Listed-placed 8-12f winner Tears of The Sun out of a very useful 7f-1m winner (including at Listed level) who was a half-sister to Group 3-placed 7-10f winner (including at Listed level) Rewarded.

DUKEMAN (IRE)
6/5 b c Kingman - She's Mine (Sea The Stars)
Owner: Sheikh Mohammed Obaid Al Maktoum Sales price: 500,000gns (Gainsborough Thoroughbreds)

Full brother to useful 2020 8.5f 3yo winner Imrahor. Dam a thrice-raced maiden half-sister to dual 6f 2yo Group 3 winner/1000 Guineas runner-up Cuis Ghaire, Irish 1m 1f 3yo Group 3 winner/Moyglare Stud Stakes runner-up Scintillula, Irish 12f 3yo Listed winner The Major General, Irish 7f 2yo winner/1000 Guineas third Gile Na Greine and Irish 1m 3yo winner/Irish 1000 Guineas fourth Claiomh Solais.

NIBRAS DRIFT
24/4 gr f Caravaggio - Atlantic Drift (Oasis Dream)
Owner: Saeed H Altayer Sales price: 150,000gns (Gainsborough Thoroughbreds)

Half-sister to 2020 Irish 6f 2yo Group 2 third/Group 3 runner-up Arctician. Dam an unraced half-sister to very smart multiple 1m winner (including the Sussex Stakes) Lightning Spear, 10f 3yo Listed winner Ocean War and 10f 3yo winner/ Chesham Stakes runner-up Seaway out of a 6f 2yo Listed winner.

QUEEN OF CHANGE (IRE)
9/3 b f Sea The Stars - Salacia (Echo of Light)
Owner: Abdulla Belhabb Sales price: n/a

Three-parts sister to Group 1-placed multiple 8-10f winner (including at Group 2/3 level) Century Dream (by Cape Cross) and a half-sister to Queen Elizabeth II Stakes winner/2000 Guineas runner-up King of Change. Dam a 6f 3yo winner who was a half-sister to Listed-placed French dual 1m 3yo winner Melicertes, Listed-placed UK/UAE 9-12f winner Submariner and very useful 8-8.5f winner G K Chesterton.

Century Dream

SPRINGTIME
10/3 b c Postponed - Frangipanni (Dansili)
Owner: Sheikh Mohammed Obaid Al Maktoum Sales price: 280,000gns
(Stroud Coleman Bloodstock)

Half-brother to Group 1-placed 7f-1m winner (including at Group 2/3 level)
Tropbeau and useful 2020 6f 2yo winner Toussarok. Dam a 6-7f 3yo winner
who was the daughter of a July Cup-winning sister to Group 2-placed multiple
6f winner (including twice at Listed level) Firenze (dam of 2020 Irish 6f Listed
winner Harry's Bar) and half-sister to 6f Listed winner Zidane.

UNNAMED (IRE)
22/3 b c Shamardal - Dark Liberty (Dark Angel)
Owner: Sheikh Rashid Dalmook Al Maktoum Sales price: n/a

First foal of a German 7f 2yo Listed winner who was a half-sister to 2020
French 1m 3yo Listed winner Queen of Love out of a Norwegian 5.5-7f winner
who was a half-sister to smart Swedish prolific 8-9f winner (including at Group
3/Listed level) Entangle and the dam of 5f 2yo Listed winner Miss Work of Art
(herself later dam of 7f 3yo Listed winner Tapisserie).

UNNAMED (IRE)
5/4 b c Tamayuz - Dheyaa (Dream Ahead)
Owner: Shadwell Estate Co Sales price: n/a

Second foal of a maiden half-sister to 5/6f 2yo Group 3 winner Brown Sugar (by Tamayuz) and smart 5-7f winner (including at Group 3 level) Burnt Sugar out of a very useful 5-6f winning half-sister to Group 1-placed multiple 5-7f winner (including at Group 2/Listed level) Galeota and 13f 3yo Listed winner Loulwa (later dam of dual 5f Listed winner Justineo).

UNNAMED
25/2 b c Iffraaj - Feedyah (Street Cry)
Owner: Sheikh Ahmed Al Maktoum Sales price: n/a

Half-brother to 7f 3yo winner Nabeyla and 2020 10f 3yo winner Aaddeey. Dam a Group 3/Listed-placed 7f-1m 2yo winner who was a half-sister to Listed-placed 7f-1m winner Red Mist out of a Listed-placed 7f-1m 3yo winning half-sister to Japanese 1m Listed winner Hyblon and the unraced dam of Melbourne Cup winner Fiorente.

UNNAMED (IRE)
21/2 b f Exceed And Excel - Hushing (Pivotal)
Owner: Godolphin Sales price: n/a

First foal of an Irish 5f 3yo winner who was a half-sister to smart 5-6f 2yo winner (including at Group 3/Listed level) Sound And Silence, very useful dual 7f 2yo winner Silent Bullet and useful 2020 dual 5f 2yo winner Miss Jingles (all by Exceed And Excel) out of an unraced half-sister to Racing Post Trophy winner Ibn Khaldun.

UNNAMED (IRE)
11/5 br/gr c Dark Angel - Majeyda (Street Cry)
Owner: Sheikh Ahmed Al Maktoum Sales price: n/a

Second foal of a Group 2/3-placed 6f-1m winner (including twice at Listed level) who was a half-sister to very useful 6f-1m winner Yattwee out of a 5f 2yo Group 3/Listed-winning half-sister to the unraced dam of Group 2-placed multiple 5f-1m winner (including at Group 3/Listed level) Gifted Master.

UNNAMED
8/2 b f Kodiac - Pizzarra (Shamardal)
Owner: Shadwell Estate Co Sales price: 100,000gns (Shadwell Estate Company)

Half-sister to Group 3-placed dual 5f winner (including at Listed level) Fashion Queen, 2020 dual 6f 3yo winner Intrepid Italian and two other winners. Dam a maiden half-sister to Flying Childers Stakes winner Wunders Dream (later dam of 6f 3yo Listed winner Inyordreams) and Group 2-placed 5f-1m winner (including at Group 3/Listed level) Grecian Dancer (later dam of 1m 1f Group 3 winner Muffri'Ha).

UNNAMED
14/2 b f Dubawi - Rizeena (Iffraaj)
Owner: Sheikh Rashid Dalmook Al Maktoum Sales price: n/a

Half-sister to useful 2020 1m 2yo winner Latest Generation. Dam a high-class 5f-1m winner (including twice at Group 1 level) who was a half-sister to smart 6-9f winner (including at Group 2/3 level) Summer Romance out of a 7f 2yo winning half-sister to French 1m 1f Group 1 winner Zabeel Prince, Australian 7f/1m Group 2 winner Puissance de Lune and 10f 3yo Listed winner Queen Power.

ANDRE FABRE

ALENTAR (IRE)
31/3 b c Teofilo - Inspiriter (Invincible Spirit)
Owner: Godolphin SNC Sales price: n/a

Half-brother to Group 3/Listed-placed UK/UAE 5-6f winner Leading Spirit. Dam a French 6f 3yo Listed winner who was a half-sister to 2020 5f 3yo Group 3/Listed winner Lazuli, Listed-placed French 5.5f 3yo winner Bouquet de Flores and 7f 2yo winner Efflorescence out of a 6f 2yo Listed-winning half-sister to 1m 3yo Group 3/Listed winner Zibelina (dam of 2020 French 6f 3yo Group 3 winner Royal Crusade).

ANTELOPE CANYON (USA)
26/2 ch c Kitten's Joy - Hoop of Colour (Distorted Humour)
Owner: Flaxman Stables Ireland Ltd Sales price: n/a

Half-brother to 2020 French 6f 2yo winner Step Beyond. Dam a US 1m 1f Grade 2 winner who was a half-sister to US 1m 1f Grade 1 winner Aruna and once-raced 7f 2yo winner Spy Eye out of a US 8.5f Grade 2 winner who was closely related to the dam of 1m 3yo Listed winner Consort and a half-sister to the dam of Irish 7f 3yo Listed winner/Poule d'Essai des Poulains third Honoured Guest.

ATHABASCAN (FR)
5/5 b c Almanzor - Alzubra (Dansili)
Owner: Mme Andre Fabre Sales price: n/a

Half-brother to 2020 French 7f 3yo Listed winner Arapaho. Dam a French 10f Listed winner who was the daughter of a French 1m 3yo Listed-winning sister to 6-7f winner Balance.

BADGE
17/3 b c Galileo - Joyeuse (Oasis Dream)
Owner: Juddmonte Sales price: n/a

Full brother to 2020 1m 2yo winner Maximal and a half-brother to Group 1-placed 6-7f 3yo winner Jubiloso and Listed-placed triple 6f winner Jovial. Dam a Group 3-placed triple 6f winner (including twice at Listed level) who was a full sister to useful 8-8.5f winner Morpheus and a half-sister to outstanding ten-time 7-10.5f Group 1 winner Frankel, triple 10-12f Group 1 winner Noble Mission (both by Galileo) and Lingfield Derby Trial winner Bullet Train.

Maximal

CASTLE BOLTON
16/4 b c Dubawi - Romantica (Galileo)
Owner: Juddmonte Sales price: n/a

Third foal of a French 10f Group 1 winner who was a half-sister to Group 2-placed French 10-12.5f winner (including twice at Listed level) Ideal World and the dam of 10f 3yo Group 3 winner Sangarius out of a Breeders' Cup Filly & Mare Turf-winning sister to Group/Grade 1 winners Cacique (10/11f), Champs Elysees (12f, three times) and Intercontinental (8/10f) and very smart miler Dansili and half-sister to US 8/9.5f Grade 1 winner Heat Haze (dam of 2020 Australian 12f Group 1 winner Mirage Dancer).

FAI FAI
30/3 b c Acclamation - Sabratah (Oasis Dream)
Owner: Abu Khadra Stables SC Sales price: €160,000 (Charles Gordon Watson Bloodstock)

Half-brother to Group 3/Listed-placed French triple 1m winner Syrtis and useful 2020 dual 10f 3yo winner Valyrian Steel. Dam a French dual 5.5f Listed winner who was a half-sister to smart UK/Swedish multiple 8-9f winner (including at Group 3/Listed level) Kick On and Australian 1m 1f Listed winner Raw Impulse.

GAIDAR (IRE)
31/5 gr c Churchill - Grey Lilas (Danehill)
Owner: Gestut Ammerland Sales price: n/a

Three-parts brother to Poule d'Essai des Pouliches/Prix de Diane winner Golden Lilac and Australian 10f Group 3 winner Grey Lion (both by Galileo) and a half-brother to French 12f 3yo Listed winner Golden Guepard. Dam a Prix du Moulin winner/Poule d'Essai des Pouliches runner-up who was closely related to 10f 3yo Listed winner Kandahar Run.

GALASHIELS (IRE)
13/2 ch c Australia - Glenmayne (Duke of Marmalade)
Owner: Godolphin SNC Sales price: 115,000gns (Stroud Coleman Bloodstock)

Closely related to 2020 1m 2yo winner Sabousi (by New Approach). Dam a useful Irish 1m 3yo winner who was a half-sister to Cheveley Park Stakes winner Millisle, 12f Listed winner Ithoughtitwasover and Listed-placed 7f-1m winner Greenisland (later dam of French 5f 2yo Listed winner Shamson and 2020 UAE 1m Listed winner Boerhan).

GIZALA (IRE)
17/2 b f Invincible Spirit - Golden Gazelle (Galileo)
Owner: Gestut Ammerland Sales price: n/a

First foal of a French 10f 3yo winner who was a full sister to Poule d'Essai des Pouliches/Prix de Diane winner Golden Lilac and Australian 10f Group 3 winner Grey Lion and a half-sister to French 12f 3yo Listed winner Golden Guepard out of a Prix du Moulin winner/Poule d'Essai des Pouliches runner-up.

HAMNET
21/2 b c Siyouni - Havant (Halling)
Owner: Godolphin SNC Sales price: 300,000gns (Godolphin)

Half-brother to 7-12f winner Jamil and 6f 2yo winner Exmouth. Dam a 7f 2yo Group 3 winner who was a half-sister to high-class 7-12f winner (including at Group 1 level) Leadership, five other winners and the unraced dam of Geoffrey Freer Stakes winner Census.

HIGNESS (FR)
12/5 b c Galileo - Queen's Jewel (Pivotal)
Owner: Wertheimer & Frere Sales price: n/a

Third foal of a Prix Saint-Alary winner/Breeders Cup Filly & Mare Turf third who was a half-sister to smart French 7.5-9f winner (including twice at Listed level) Royalmania out of an Argentinian Champion 2yo/US 12f Grade 2-winning half-sister to Argentinian 1000 Guineas winner Safari Miss.

HUYGENS
25/2 b c Le Havre - Amuser (Galileo)
Owner: Niarchos Family Sales price: n/a

Half-brother to Listed-placed Irish 7f 2yo winner Free Solo. Dam an unraced sister to Group 1-placed Irish/Australian 8-12f winner (including at Group 2/3 level) Yucatan, US 9.5f Grade 3 winner Faufiler and Irish 10f 3yo Listed winner Mount Everest and half-sister to French 5f Group 2 winner Planet Five out of a triple 1m Group/Grade 1 winner/1000 Guineas runner-up.

IMPERIOUS MAN
26/2 b c Invincible Spirit - Vicugna (Pivotal)
Owner: Haras Voltaire Sales price: n/a

First foal of a French 8.5f 3yo winner who was a half-sister to French 7f 2yo Group 3 winner Sofast, French 5.5f Listed winner Spiritfix (by Invincible Spirit) and French 3yo Listed winners Eyeful (1m) and Spaday (6.5f) out of a French 5f 2yo Listed winner.

INGRES (IRE)
14/3 b c Galileo - Esoterique (Danehill Dancer)
Owner: Baron Edouard de Rothschild, Michael Tabor & Mrs John Magnier
Sales price: n/a

First foal of a very smart multiple 8-9f winner (including three times at Group 1 level)/Poule d'Essai des Pouliches runner-up who was closely related to French 10f 3yo Group 2 winner Archange d'Or and a half-sister to French 10f 3yo Group 2 winner Russian Cross, French 12.5f Group 2 winner Russian Hope and French 10f Listed winners Russian Desert and Russian Hill (later dam of dual 6f Group 3 winner Russian Soul).

LA GLOIRE
5/4 b f Churchill - Date With Destiny (George Washington)
Owner: Godolphin SNC Sales price: 350,000gns (Stroud Coleman Bloodstock)

Three-parts sister to Group 2-placed UK/Irish 7-10f winner (including at Group 3/Listed level) Beautiful Morning (by Galileo). Dam a Listed-placed 7f 2yo winner who was a half-sister to French 10.5f 3yo Group 3 winner Ombre Legere and Grade 1-placed French/US 10-12f winner Flawly (later dam of French 10f 3yo Group 3 winner/Prix du Jockey Club runner-up Best Name).

LA MONTESPAN
8/3 b f Camelot - Terrienne (Henny Hughes)
Owner: Baron Edouard de Rothschild Sales price: n/a

Closely related to French 1m 2yo winner Connivence (by Motivator). Dam an unraced half-sister to high-class multiple 7f-1m winner (including four times at Group 1 level) Elusive Kate out of an unraced half-sister to Breeders' Cup Classic/Dubai World Cup winner Pleasantly Perfect and French 6.5f 2yo Group 3 winner Hurricane State.

LAKE MANZALEH
9/4 b c Ribchester - Suez (Green Desert)
Owner: Godolphin SNC Sales price: n/a

Half-brother to Fillies' Mile winner Lyric of Light and 2yo winners Bitter Lake (6f), Alfurat River (7f) and Andrassy Avenue (9.5f). Dam a 6f 2yo Listed winner/Cheveley Park Stakes runner-up who was a half-sister to New Zealand 7f Listed winner Polish Princess (later dam of Australian dual 1m 1f Group 2 winner Leebaz, Australian 10f Group 2 winner Polish Knight, Australian 1m Group 3 winner Euro Angel and Australian Derby runner-up Zebrowski).

MARTEL (IRE)
8/3 ch c Frankel - Lady of Shamrock (Scat Daddy)
Owner: Wertheimer & Frere Sales price: n/a

Half-brother to French 7f 2yo winners Oxalis and Silent War. Dam a US 9/10f Grade 1 winner who was a half-sister to US 7f Grade 2 winner Smooth Jazz and US triple 8/8.5f Listed winner She's Sensational (later dam of US 8/8.5f Listed winner Our Way) out of a maiden half-sister to US 12f Grade 1 winner Royal Chariot.

MATHLETIC (FR)
10/2 gr c Kingman - Manerbe (Unbridled's Song)
Owner: Ecurie Ama Zingteam Sales price: €220,000 (BBA Ireland)

Half-brother to Canadian 7f Grade 3 winner Marbre Rose, Grade 3-placed US 5f-1m winner (including twice at Listed level) Gidu and French 7f 3yo Listed winner Aviatress. Dam a US 7.5f 3yo winner who was a half-sister to US 8.5f 3yo Grade 1 winner Zoftig (later dam of US 3yo Grade 1 winners Zaftig (1m) and Zo Impressive (8.5f) and grandam of Racing Post Trophy second Zip Top).

MIRAKOVA
10/3 b f Lope de Vega - Terrakova (Galileo)
Owner: Wertheimer & Frere Sales price: n/a

First foal of a French 10.5f 3yo Group 3 winner/Prix de Diane third who was the daughter of 14-time 7-9f Group/Grade 1 winner Goldikova, herself a full sister to Group/Grade 1-placed French dual 1m 3yo winner (including at Group 3 level) Anodin and a half-sister to French 12f Group 1 winner/Prix de Diane runner-up Galikova, French 1m 1f 3yo Group 3 winner Gold Luck and French 10.5f 3yo Group 3 winner Gold Round (later dam of smart pair Golden Valentine and Goldwaki).

MONEYMAN
2/3 gr c Kingman - Mizz Money (Mizzen Mast)
Owner: Wertheimer & Frere Sales price: n/a

First foal of a US 8.5/9f Grade 3 winner who was a full sister to US 1m 1f 3yo Grade 3 winner One Mean Man out of an unraced half-sister to Listed-placed US 8-8.5f winner More of The Best, US 6f 2yo winner/Grade 1 third Unbridled Express and the dam of Breeders' Cup Mile winner Tourist.

PIZ GLORIA (FR)
26/3 ch f Lope de Vega - Astroglia (Montjeu)
Owner: Niarchos Family Sales price: n/a

Half-sister to useful 8-8.5f winner Astro King. Dam a French 9.5f winner who was a half-sister to the dam of Emollient out of a French 7f/US 1m Listed-winning half-sister to French 1m 2yo Group 1 winner Denebola (grandam of Prix de Diane winner Senga), French 6f 2yo Group 3 winner Loving Kindness and the dam of Prix de l'Arc de Triomphe winner Bago and French 8/9f Group 1 winner Maxios.

QUEENMANIA (FR)
24/3 ch f Frankel - Safari Queen (Lode)
Owner: Wertheimer & Frere Sales price: n/a

Half-sister to Prix Saint-Alary winner/Breeders Cup Filly & Mare Turf third Queen's Jewel and smart French 7.5-9f winner (including twice at Listed level) Royalmania. Dam an Argentinian Champion 2yo/US 12f Grade 2 winner who was a full sister to the dams of Brazilian 10f 3yo Group 2 winner/Brazilian Oaks third Escaramuza and Argentinian triple 7f Listed winner Safe At Home and a half-sister to Argentinian 1000 Guineas winner Safari Miss.

RACLETTE
12/4 b f Frankel - Emollient (Empire Maker)
Owner: Juddmonte Sales price: n/a

Half-sister to Group 2/3-placed Irish 6f 2yo winner Peace Charter. Dam a four-time US 8.5-10f Grade 1 winner who was a half-sister to US 1m 1f 3yo Listed winner/Belmont Stakes third Hofburg and US 1m 3yo Listed winner Courtier out of a French 7f/US 1m Listed-winning half-sister to French 1m 2yo Group 1 winner Denebola (grandam of Prix de Diane winner Senga), French 6f 2yo Group 3 winner Loving Kindness and the unraced dam of Prix de l'Arc de Triomphe winner Bago.

SOBER (FR)
29/4 b c Camelot - Burma Sea (Lope de Vega)
Owner: Wertheimer & Frere Sales price: n/a

Half-brother to Group 2-placed French 6-7f winner (including at Group 3 level) Devil. Dam a Listed-placed French 7.5f 2yo winner who was a half-sister to St Leger Italiano winner Burma Gold and the dam and Irish 7f 2yo Group 3 winner Blue de Vega out of a twice-raced maiden sister to Deutsches Derby winner Borgia (grandam of Prix Vermeille winner Baltic Baroness) and half-sister to Deutsches Derby/Coronation Cup winner Boreal and the dam of May Hill Stakes winner Rich Legacy.

TRIBALIST
10/2 ch c Farhh - Fair Daughter (Nathaniel)
Owner: Godolphin SNC Sales price: 130,000gns (Stroud Coleman Bloodstock)

First foal of an unraced half-sister to Racing Post Trophy winner Crowded House, French 10.5f Listed winner On Reflection, Grade 3/Listed-placed 7f 2yo winner Wiener Valkyrie, Listed-placed dual 6f winner Riotous Applause (later dam of 6f 2yo Listed winner Invincible Warrior), Listed-placed 6-8.5f winner Forest Crown (dam of 2021 10f Group 3 winner Forest of Dean) and the dam of Prix Maurice de Gheest winner Brando and grandam of Prix Morny/Middle Park Stakes winner Reckless Abandon.

WALDSTAR
16/4 ch c Sea The Stars - Waldmark (Mark of Esteem)
Owner: Dietrich von Boetticher/Andreas Jacobs Sales price: 200,000gns (Vendor)

Half-brother to St Leger winner Masked Marvel, French 10.5f 3yo Group 3 winner Waldlerche (later dam of Prix de l'Arc de Triomphe winner Waldgeist and French 12f 3yo Group 2 winner Waldlied), German 1m 3yo Listed winner Waldnah and the dam of 7f 2yo Listed winner Al Dabaran. Dam a Group 2/Listed-placed 7f 2yo winner who was a half-sister to Deutsches Derby winner Waldpark.

UNNAMED (USA)
23/1 b/br c War Front - Gagnoa (Sadler's Wells)
Owner: Mrs John Magnier & Michael Tabor & Derrick Smith Sales price: n/a

Full brother to Irish 6f 2yo Group 3 winner Etoile and very useful Irish 6-7f 3yo winner Most Gifted and a half-brother to Listed-placed French 7f 3yo winner Galateia. Dam a French 8/10.5f Group 3 winner/Prix de Diane runner-up/Irish Oaks third who was closely related to Derby winner Pour Moi, 2020 Irish 2m 3yo Group 3 winner/Irish Derby third Dawn Patrol and Irish 10f 3yo Listed winner Kissed.

UNNAMED (FR)
29/1 b f Wootton Bassett - Green Diamond Lady (Johannesburg)
Owner: Lady Bamford Sales price: 600,000gns (C Gordon Watson Bloodstock)

Three-parts sister to French/Italian 7.5-9.5f 2yo winner Next Factor (by Iffraaj) and a half-sister to French 5f 2yo Listed winner Lady Galore. Dam a US dual 1m 3yo winner who was a half-sister to Irish 1m 1f 3yo Group 3 winner/Secretariat Stakes runner-up Plan and Irish 1m 2yo Listed winner/Fillies' Mile third Dreamtheimpossible out of a Breeders' Cup Distaff winner.

UNNAMED (IRE)
16/2 b c Siyouni - To Eternity (Galileo)
Owner: Lady Bamford Sales price: n/a

First foal of a 12f 3yo Listed winner who was a full sister to 13f 3yo Group 3 winner Shantaram, 14f 3yo Listed winner Forever Now and Irish 7f 2yo winner/2000 Guineas third Gan Amhras out of an Irish 8.5f 3yo winning half-sister to UAE 1m Listed winner Parole Board.

JOHN & THADY GOSDEN

A E HOUSMAN
12/1 b c Oasis Dream - Astronomy's Choice (Redoute's Choice)
Owner: R J H Geffen Sales price: n/a

First foal of a useful 7f 2yo winner who was out of a once-raced maiden half-sister to French 15f 3yo Group 3 winner Pacifique, 2020 Lingfield Derby Trial winner English King and French 11f 3yo Listed winner Prudenzia (later dam of Irish Oaks winner Chicquita and Australian 10f Group 1 winner Magic Wand); family of Oaks winner Alexandrova and Melbourne Cup winner Rekindling.

ABASHOVA
21/3 b f Ulysses - Osipova (Makfi)
Owner: Cheveley Park Stud Sales price: n/a

Half-sister to Group 2-placed dual 7f 2yo winner (including at Group 3 level) Positive. Dam a useful dual 12f 3yo winner who was a half-sister to Group 2-placed 7f-1m winner (including at Group 3/Listed level) Zonderland and three other winners out of a maiden daughter of Russian Rhythm.

Positive (right)

AEROSPACE (IRE)
15/4 b c Sea The Stars - Talent (New Approach)
Owner: Godolphin Sales price: 300,000gns (Stroud Coleman Bloodstock)

Half-brother to Group 1-placed French 10.5-12f winner (including at Group 2/3 level) Ambition. Dam an Oaks winner/St Leger runner-up who was a full sister to useful 1m 2yo winner Forte and a half-sister to Listed-placed 7f-1m winner Skilful out of a Listed-placed 12f 3yo winning half-sister to Listed-placed 11.5f 3yo winner Genoa (later dam of 1m Listed winner Brindisi).

AL AWIR (IRE)
21/1 b f Siyouni - Drumfad Bay (Acclamation)
Owner: Ms Hissa Hamdan Al Maktoum Sales price: 280,000gns (Shadwell Estate Company)

First foal of a Group 3-placed Irish 6f-1m winner (including at Listed level) who was the daughter of an Irish 10f 3yo Group 2-winning half-sister to Listed-placed 6f-1m winner Solid Rock, Listed-placed 10f 3yo winner Bold Choice and useful 6-7f winner River Bravo; family of six-time 10-12f Group/Grade 1 winner Snow Fairy and Derby winner Oath.

ALKAID (IRE)
22/1 b c Sea The Stars - Mubhirah (Raven's Pass)
Owner: Ms Hissa Hamdan Al Maktoum Sales price: n/a

First foal of a once-raced maiden half-sister to Oaks/King George VI And Queen Elizabeth Stakes winner Taghrooda (by Sea The Stars) and 12f 3yo winner/ Queen's Vase fourth Almoghared out of a Group 2-placed Irish 8-14f winner (including three times at Listed level).

ALTRAIF
14/3 b c Kodiac - Redemption (Olden Times)
Owner: Prince A A Faisal Sales price: n/a

Second foal of an unraced half-sister to 7f 3yo Listed winner Solomon's Bay, French 1m 2yo Listed winner Tammani and Group 3/Listed-placed French 10f 3yo winner Meadow Creek out of an Irish 12f 3yo winning sister to Group 2-placed 8-14f winner (including three times at Listed level) Ezima (later dam of Oaks/King George VI And Queen Elizabeth Stakes winner Taghrooda).

AUDIENCE
17/3 b c Iffraaj - Ladyship (Oasis Dream)
Owner: Cheveley Park Stud Sales price: n/a

Half-brother to 6f 2yo Group 3 winner Dark Lady and two other winners. Dam a 7f Listed winner who was a half-sister to useful 1m 3yo winners Enobled and Spanish Point and 7f 2yo winner Kinsman out of a high-class multiple 7f-1m winner (including twice at Group 1 level).

BIRDIE NUM NUM
19/4 b f Siyouni - Mischief Making (Lemon Drop Kid)
Owner: Westerberg Sales price: 680,000gns (Westerberg)

Half-sister to Lancashire Oaks winner/Oaks fourth Horseplay, 10f Listed winner More Mischief and three other winners. Dam a Group 3-placed 9.5-13f winner (including at Listed level) who was a half-sister to dual 7f Listed winner That Is The Spirit and Irish 6f 3yo Listed winner Khukri out of a Canadian 10f Grade 1 winner.

BOUQUET
1/2 gr f Dark Angel - Bound (Galileo)
Owner: Lordship Stud Sales price: n/a

First foal of an Irish 10f 3yo Listed winner who was a sister to 2020 Derby winner Serpentine, Irish 1m 1f 3yo Group 2 winner/Nassau Stakes runner-up Wedding Vow, smart 7-10f winner (including at Group 3/Listed level)/Oaks third Bye Bye Baby and Group 2-placed Irish 8-10f winner (including at Group 3 level) Beacon Rock out of an Oaks runner-up who was closely related to Prix de l'Arc de Triomphe winner Dylan Thomas and 1000 Guineas winner Homecoming Queen (dam of 2020 Moyglare Stud Stakes winner Shale) and a half-sister to Cheveley Park Stakes winner Queen's Logic.

COURAGE MON AMI
11/3 b c Frankel - Crimson Ribbon (Lemon Drop Kid)
Owner: A E Oppenheimer Sales price: n/a

Closely related to Group 3-placed 8-12f winner (including at Listed level) Crimson Rosette (by Teofilo) and Australian 10f Listed winner Astronomos (by New Approach). Dam a 12f 3yo winner who was a full sister to dual 12f Group 2 winner Bronze Cannon and US 1m 1f Grade 3 winner Valiant Girl and a half-sister to King Edward VII Stakes winner Across The Stars.

DIGNIFIED
14/2 b f Galileo - Jack Naylor (Champs Elysees)
Owner: Denford Stud Sales price: n/a

Second foal of a Group 1-placed Irish 7-9.5f winner (including at Group 3/Listed level)/Irish Oaks runner-up who was a half-sister to useful 7-10f winner Hollydaze out of a 10f 3yo Listed winner; family of Group/Grade 1-placed 6-7f 2yo winner (including at Group 2/3 level) Daahyeh and Group 1-placed 7-10f winner (including at Group 2/3 level) Armory (by Galileo).

EXPOUND
30/4 ch c Ulysses - Entity (Shamardal)
Owner: Cheveley Park Stud Sales price: n/a

Half-brother to useful 2020 7f 2yo winner Existent. Dam a dual 10f 3yo winner who was a half-sister to high-class multiple 1m winner (including twice at Group 1 level) Integral and Listed-placed 7f-1m winner Provenance out of a smart multiple 6-9f winner (including at Group 1 level); family of 2000 Guineas winner Entrepreneur and Lockinge Stakes winner Virtual.

FIND
1/4 b c Frankel - Spring In The Air (Spring At Last)
Owner: Prince A A Faisal Sales price: n/a

Half-brother to 2020 7f 2yo winner Third Kingdom. Dam a US 8.5f 2yo Grade 1 winner who was a half-sister to US 6f 2yo winner Ithinkisawapudycat (later dam of US 7f 2yo Grade 1 winner Sweet Loretta) out of a maiden half-sister to US 8.5f 2yo Grade 2 winner/Kentucky Derby runner-up Tejano Run, US 8.5f Grade 2 winner More Royal and the dam of Racing Post Trophy winner Palace

Episode and great-grandam of Irish 7f 2yo Group 2 winner/1000 Guineas third Laughing Lashes.

FRANTASTIC
12/4 b c Frankel - Rhadegunda (Pivotal)
Owner: A E Oppenheimer Sales price: n/a

Full brother to top-class 8-12f winner (including four times at Group 1 level)/ Derby third Cracksman and a half-brother to Solario Stakes winner Fantastic Moon. Dam a French 1m 1f 3yo Listed-winning granddaughter of 1000 Guineas winner On The House.

HIGH MOOR (USA)
20/4 b c War Front - Midday (Oasis Dream)
Owner: Juddmonte Sales price: n/a

Half-brother to Group 2-placed UK/Australian 8-12f winner (including twice at Group 3 level) Midterm, Group 2-placed dual 10f 3yo winner (including at Listed level) Mori and 2020 8.5f 2yo winner Noon Star. Dam a six-time 10-12f Group/Grade 1 winner/Oaks runner-up who was a half-sister to Nell Gwyn Stakes winner Hot Snap and 10f Group 3 winner Sun Maiden.

IDEE FIXEE
22/2 ch c Dubawi - Our Obsession (Shamardal)
Owner: A E Oppenheimer Sales price: n/a

Half-brother to Group 3-placed 1m 2yo winner Frankellina. Dam a 12f 3yo Listed winner who was a half-sister to 2020 Ribblesdale Stakes winner/Oaks third Frankly Darling and Listed-placed 10-14f winner First In Line out of a Cheshire Oaks-winning half-sister to Coronation Stakes winner Rebecca Sharp and the unraced dam of Derby/Prix de l'Arc de Triomphe winner Golden Horn.

INSPIRAL
14/3 b f Frankel - Starscope (Selkirk)
Owner: Cheveley Park Stud Sales price: n/a

Closely related to useful 7-7.5f winner Astrologer (by Intello) and a half-sister to useful 9.5-10f winner Celestran. Dam a Group 1-placed 7f 2yo winner/1000 Guineas runner-up who was a half-sister to 1m Listed winner Solar Magic out of a 1m 3yo winning half-sister to Lockinge Stakes/Eclipse Stakes winner Medicean.

ISRAR
30/3 b c Muhaarar - Taghrooda (Sea The Stars)
Owner: Shadwell Estate Co Sales price: n/a

Half-brother to useful 2020 dual 12f 3yo winner Almighwar. Dam an Oaks/
King George VI And Queen Elizabeth Stakes winner who was a half-sister to
12f 3yo winner/Queen's Vase fourth Almoghared out of a Group 2-placed Irish
8-14f winner (including three times at Listed level); family of Irish Oaks winner
Ebadiyla and Ascot Gold Cup winners Enzeli and Estimate.

KABAYIL
14/2 b c Kodiac - Illaunglass (Red Clubs)
Owner: Ms Hissa Hamdan Al Maktoum Sales price: 280,000gns (Shadwell
Estate Company)

Half-brother to Listed-placed UK/French 1m winner Illaunmore and useful
7f-1m winner Papa Stour. Dam a Group 3-placed 6f 2yo winner who was a
half-sister to Group 3-placed 7f-1m winner (including at Listed level) Redolent,
7f Listed winner Pepita, Listed-placed 6f 2yo winner Ursulina and the dam of
smart sprinter Son of Rest; family of 2000 Guineas winner Night of Thunder.

MATOURY
2/4 b c Kingman - Sinnamary (Galileo)
Owner: A E Oppenheimer Sales price: n/a

Half-brother to 2020 13.5f 3yo winner Golden Rules. Dam a French 1m 1f 2yo
winner who was a full sister to Australian 10f Group 1 winner Magic Wand and
Group 3-placed French 12-14f 3yo winner Je Ne Regretterien and a half-sister
to Irish Oaks winner Chicquita out of a French 11f 3yo Listed-winning half-
sister to French 15f 3yo Group 3 winner Pacifique and 2020 Lingfield Derby
Trial winner English King.

MILLENNIAL MOON
6/2 ch c Dubawi - Wekeela (Hurricane Run)
Owner: Qatar Racing Limited Sales price: n/a

First foal of a Group/Grade 1-placed French/US 8-9f winner (including at
Group/Grade 3 level) who was a full sister to Norsk 1000 Guineas winner
Matauri Pearl (dam of 2020 Breeders' Cup Juvenile Fillies Turf winner Aunt
Pearl) out of a French/Swiss 8-11.5f winning half-sister to the unraced dam of
Prix du Cadran winner Molly Malone (herself later dam of French 10f Group 2
winner Morgan Le Faye); family of Poule d'Essai des Pouliches/Prix du Jockey
Club winner Brametot.

MIMIKYU
6/5 b f Dubawi - Montare (Montjeu)
Owner: George Strawbridge Sales price: n/a

Full sister to high-class multiple 10-12f winner (including at Group 1 level)
Journey and 2020 May Hill Stakes winner/Fillies' Mile runner-up Indigo
Girl and a half-sister to Group 3/Listed-placed French dual 12f 3yo winner
Travelling Man. Dam a French 15.5f Group 1 winner who was closely related to
the dam of 1m 1f Group 2 winner Worth Waiting.

NASHWA
9/5 b f Frankel - Princess Loulou (Pivotal)
Owner: Imad Al Sagar Sales price: n/a

Half-sister to useful 7-10f winner Louganini. Dam a Group 1-placed 8-10f
winner (including at Listed level) who was a full sister to very useful 10-11f
winner Forbidden Planet and a half-sister to very useful UK/French 6-9f winner
Easy Target; family of Middle Park Stakes winner Awzaan.

NATASHA
15/3 ch f Frankel - Darkova (Maria's Mon)
Owner: George Strawbridge Sales price: n/a

Half-sister to top-class 7-10.5f winner (including the Prix du Jockey Club and
Champion Stakes) Almanzor, Listed-placed French 9.5f 3yo winner Troarn
and very useful 2020 French 9.5f 3yo winner Another Sky. Dam an unraced
daughter of a French 12f 3yo Listed winner who was a half-sister to Group 3/
Listed-placed French 12f 3yo winner Darinska (later dam of Poule d'Essai des
Pouliches winner Darjina).

PARK STREET
4/5 b c New Approach - City Chic (Street Cry)
Owner: The Queen Sales price: n/a

Half-brother to 6-7f winner Desert Boots. Dam a 7f 2yo winner who was a
full sister to 7f 2yo Group 3 winner Discourse (dam of 2021 UAE 1m Group 3
winner Blown By Wind and 1m Listed winners Discursus and Hadith (by New
Approach)) and a half-sister to US 1m 1f Grade 1 winner Bandini and the dam
of 2020 Prince of Wales's Stakes winner Lord North.

RAKURAI
21/2 b/br f Deep Impact - Lightening Pearl (Marju)
Owner: Qatar Racing Limited Sales price: n/a

Half-sister to Irish 7f 3yo Group 3 winner Lightening Quick and useful Irish dual 1m 3yo winner Lightening Fast. Dam a Cheveley Park Stakes winner who was a full sister to Japanese 11/12f Grade 1 winner Satono Crown and a half-sister to Grade 2/3-placed Japanese 10-12.5f winner Figlio Allegro (by Deep Impact).

REACH FOR THE MOON
15/2 b c Sea The Stars - Golden Stream (Sadler's Wells)
Owner: The Queen Sales price: n/a

Half-brother to Group 1-placed 8.5-10f winner Invictus Prince. Dam a Group 3-placed triple 7f winner (including twice at Listed level) who was a full sister to 7f 2yo winner/Oaks runner-up Flight of Fancy (later dam of dual 10f Group 3 winner Fabricate) and the dam of 12.5f Listed winner Sextant (by Sea The Stars).

ROYAL VERSE
31/1 b c Frankel - Simple Verse (Duke of Marmalade)
Owner: Qatar Racing Limited Sales price: 600,000gns (David Redvers Bloodstock)

First foal of a St Leger winner who was closely related to Group 2-placed 6-7f 2yo winner Maxentius and a half-sister to Ribblesdale Stakes winner Even Song out of an unraced half-sister to Listed-placed Irish 12f winner Really and useful Irish 11-14f Flat/very useful Irish dual 2m hurdle winner Magen's Star (later dam of Irish 11.5/12f Listed winner Red Stars).

SAGA
25/3 b/gr c Invincible Spirit - Emily Bronte (Machiavellian)
Owner: The Queen Sales price: n/a

Full brother to Group 2-placed 6-7f winner (including twice at Group 3 level) Lockwood and a half-brother to French 1m 2yo Group 3 winner Earnshaw. Dam a French 1m 2yo Group 3 winner who was a half-sister to 6f 3yo Listed winner Zelanda (later dam of French 6f Group 3 winner Time Prisoner and 6f 2yo Listed winner Pearl Grey).

SALANDER (IRE)
21/3 b f Sea The Stars - Diamond Tango (Acatenango)
Owner: Westerberg Sales price: 500,000gns (Westerberg)

Half-sister to Doncaster Cup winner Desert Skyline, Listed-placed French 12.5-14f 3yo winner Doumaran and three other winners. Dam a French 12.5f Group 2 winner who was a half-sister to French 12.5f 3yo Listed winner Crystal Diamond; family of Irish Derby/St Leger winner Capri.

SAMBURU
1/2 b c Kingman - Tempera (Dansili)
Owner: Juddmonte Sales price: n/a

First foal of an Irish 7f 2yo winner who was a full sister to 1m 3yo Listed winner Set Piece and a half-sister to French 6/6.5f Listed winner Alocasia (by Kingman) and very useful multiple 7f winner Peril out of a 7f 3yo winner; family of Elmaamul, Reams of Verse, Midday etc.

SHADOWFAX
21/3 gr c Galileo - Golden Valentine (Dalakhani)
Owner: Qatar Racing Limited Sales price: €450,000 (David Redvers)

First foal of a smart French 9-12.5f winner (including at Group 3/Listed level) who was a full sister to smart French 11-12f 3yo winner (including at Group 3/Listed level) Goldwaki out of a French 10.5f 3yo Group 3-winning half-sister to 14-time 7-9f Group 1 winner Goldikova (later dam of French 10.5f 3yo Group 3 winner/Prix de Diane third Terrakova (by Galileo)) and French 12f Group 1 winner/Prix de Diane runner-up Galikova (by Galileo).

SIR ALEX J (IRE)
5/2 b c Mehmas - Ashtown Girl (Exceed And Excel)
Owner: Amo Racing Limited Sales price: 320,000gns (Blandford Bloodstock)

Half-brother to 7f 3yo winner Ziarah. Dam an unraced half-sister to Group 1-placed 5-6f winner (including at Group 2/3 level) Hot Streak and Listed-placed Irish 5f 2yo winner New Design out of an unraced half-sister to US 10/12f Grade 3 winner Mustanfar and dual 1m Listed winner Tadris; family of Queen Mary Stakes winner Maqaasid.

SOBEGRAND
24/4 b c Decorated Knight - Nouriya (Danehill Dancer)
Owner: Imad Al Sagar Sales price: n/a

Closely related to 2020 10f 3yo Listed winner Majestic Noor (by Frankel) and a
half-brother to high-class 7f-1m winner (including at Group 2/3 level) Aljazzi.
Dam a 10/10.5f 3yo Listed winner who was a half-sister to Listed-placed
multiple 6.5f-1m winner Yuften and Listed-placed 7f 2yo winner Lady Nouf;
family of St James's Palace Stakes winner/2000 Guineas runner-up Zafeen.

STORM CASTLE
21/1 b c Invincible Spirit - Journey (Dubawi)
Owner: George Strawbridge Sales price: n/a

First foal of a high-class multiple 10-12f winner (including at Group 1 level)
who was a full sister to 2020 May Hill Stakes winner/Fillies' Mile runner-up
Indigo Girl and a half-sister to Group 3/Listed-placed French dual 12f 3yo
winner Travelling Man out of a French 15.5f Group 1 winner.

SYLVIA BEACH
14/3 b f Ulysses - Furbelow (Pivotal)
Owner: Cheveley Park Stud Sales price: n/a

Half-sister to high-class multiple 6-6.5f winner (including three times at Group
1 level) Advertise and very useful 6-7f winner Flavius Titus. Dam a 6f 3yo
winner who was a full sister to US 5f Listed winner Red Diadem and closely
related to 6f 2yo winner/Cheveley Park Stakes fourth Adorn (later dam of 6f
2yo Group 2 winner Sayyerr and smart sprinter Ornate).

THE NOTORIOUS RBG
13/2 ch f Iffraaj - Mainstay (Elmaamul)
Owner: Ms Rachel D S Hood Sales price: n/a

Half-sister to smart triple 7f winner (including at Group 2/Listed level) Richard
Pankhurst and 7f 2yo Group 3 winner Crazy Horse. Dam a 1m winner who was
a full sister to smart 8-10.5f winner (including at Group 3/Listed level) Lateen
Sails out of a 6f 2yo winning sister to the grandam of Irish 5f 3yo Group 1
winner Havana Grey.

TOLSTOY (IRE)
23/2 b c Kingman - War And Peace (Frankel)
Owner: Sir Robert Ogden Sales price: n/a

First foal of an unraced half-sister to useful 7f-1m winner Desirous (by
Kingman) and useful 2020 7-8.5f 2yo winner Pomelo out of a Matron Stakes-

winning sister to smart 9-11.5f winner (including at Group 3/Listed level) First Sitting and French 5f 2yo Listed winner Daring Diva (later dam of Irish 1m Group 2 winner Brooch, herself the dam of 2021 US 1m 1f 3yo Grade 2 winner Mandaloun).

YUMMYLICIOUS
1/5 b f Dubawi - Yummy Mummy (Montjeu)
Owner: Newsells Park Stud Sales price: n/a

Full sister to useful 2020 8.5-9.5f 3yo winner Never Alone and 2021 US 1m 3yo winner Sifting Sands and a half-sister to five winners, notably 1000 Guineas winner/Oaks runner-up Legatissimo. Dam an Irish 10f 3yo winner who was a full sister to five-time 10f-2m 4f Group 1 winner (including the Irish Derby and Ascot Gold Cup)/Derby runner-up Fame And Glory and the unraced dam of Musidora Stakes winner Give And Take.

UNNAMED
20/2 b f Dubawi - Aneen (Lawman)
Owner: Shadwell Estate Co Sales price: n/a

First foal of a Listed-placed Irish 7f 2yo winner who was a half-sister to Irish 2000 Guineas winner Awtaad, Group 3-placed Irish 7f 3yo winner Alghabrah, Group 3-placed 2020 Irish 7f 2yo winner Mehnah and very useful 10-12f winner Al Zaraqaan out of a Listed-placed Irish 7f 3yo winning half-sister to the dam of Irish 1m 2yo Group 2 winner/Derby runner-up Madhmoon.

UNNAMED
11/4 b f Dubawi - Dar Re Mi (Singspiel)
Owner: Lord Lloyd-Webber Sales price: n/a

Full sister to very smart multiple 7f-1m winner (including the Dewhurst Stakes and Sussex Stakes)/Irish 2000 Guineas runner-up Too Darn Hot, 10.5f Group 2 winner/St Leger runner-up Lah Ti Dar, Musidora Stakes winner So Mi Dar and very useful UK/US 8.5-10f winner Darain and a half-sister to Group 3-placed French 7-10f winner De Treville. Dam a triple 10/12f Group 1 winner who was a half-sister to Prince of Wales's Stakes winner/Derby third Rewilding.

UNNAMED (IRE)
12/4 b c Sea The Stars - Ezima (Sadler's Wells)
Owner: Shadwell Estate Co Sales price: n/a

Full brother to Oaks/King George VI And Queen Elizabeth Stakes winner Taghrooda and 12f 3yo winner Taqaareed and a half-brother to 12f 3yo winner/Queen's Vase fourth Almoghared. Dam a Group 2-placed Irish 8-14f winner (including three times at Listed level) who was a full sister to Irish 12f

3yo winner Gentle On My Mind (later dam of Listed winners Solomon's Bay (7f) and Tammani (1m)) and a half-sister to Listed-placed Irish 10f 3yo winner Ezalli.

UNNAMED (IRE)
6/4 b f Tamayuz - Holda (Docksider)
Owner: Shadwell Estate Co Sales price: 170,000gns (Shadwell Estate Company)

Full sister to smart 8-10.5f winner (including at Grade 1 level) Blond Me and a half-sister to dual 6f winner Red Larkspur (later dam of Californian Oaks winner Consolida). Dam a once-raced 7f 2yo winner who was a half-sister to Australian 10f Group 1 winner Glass Harmonium and dual 12f Group 3 winner Arab Spring out of a 12f 3yo winning half-sister to St Leger/dual Breeders' Cup Turf winner Conduit.

UNNAMED (IRE)
21/2 b c Dubawi - Intisaar (War Front)
Owner: Shadwell Estate Co Sales price: n/a

First foal of an unraced daughter of a Group 3/Listed-placed Irish 10.5f 3yo winner who was a three-parts sister to Irish 1000 Guineas winner/Oaks runner-up Yesterday, Moyglare Stud Stakes winner/Irish 1000 Guineas, Oaks and Irish Oaks runner-up Quarter Moon (later dam of Irish 10f 3yo Group 1 winner Diamondsandrubies) and Irish 10f 3yo winner/Oaks third All My Loving (later dam of dual 12f Group 2 winner Thomas Chippendale).

UNNAMED
24/3 ch f Galileo - Seta (Pivotal)
Owner: Lady Bamford Sales price: n/a

Half-sister to once-raced 2020 1m 2yo winner Random Harvest and three other winners. Dam a smart 7f-1m winner (including three times at Listed level) who was a half-sister to French 12.5f Group 2 winner Armure and Listed winners Affirmative Action (15.5f), Berlin Berlin (11f) and Gravitas (10.5/12f) out of a Listed-placed 10f 3yo winning half-sister to Irish 2000 Guineas/Breeders' Cup Mile winner Barathea and Fillies' Mile/Irish 1000 Guineas winner Gossamer.

UNNAMED (IRE)
18/3 ch c Frankel - Snow Moon (Oasis Dream)
Owner: Lady Bamford Sales price: n/a

First foal of a useful 8.5f 3yo winner who was a half-sister to useful 12.5-14f winner Surya (by Frankel) out of an Oaks/Irish Oaks-winning half-sister to 14f

Listed winner Gull Wing (later dam of King Edward VII Stakes winner/King George VI And Queen Elizabeth Stakes runner-up Eagle Top, Dante Stakes winner/Derby fourth Wings of Desire and Park Hill Stakes winner/Oaks third The Lark).

UNNAMED
5/2 b f Galileo - So Mi Dar (Dubawi)
Owner: Lord Lloyd-Webber Sales price: n/a

First foal of a smart 8-10.5f winner (including at Group 3/Listed level) who was a full sister to very smart multiple 7f-1m winner (including the Dewhurst Stakes and Sussex Stakes)/Irish 2000 Guineas runner-up Too Darn Hot and 10.5f Group 2 winner/St Leger runner-up Lah Ti Dar and a half-sister to Group 3-placed French 7-10f winner De Treville out of a triple 10/12f Group 1 winner.

UNNAMED (IRE)
20/3 b f Kingman - Taqaareed (Sea The Stars)
Owner: Shadwell Estate Co Sales price: n/a

Second foal of a 12f 3yo winner who was a full sister to Oaks/King George VI & Queen Elizabeth Stakes winner/Prix de l'Arc de Triomphe third Taghrooda and a half-sister to 12f 3yo winner/Queen's Vase fourth Almoghared out of a Group 2-placed Irish 8-14f winner (including three times at Listed level) who was a full sister to Irish 12f 3yo winner Gentle On My Mind (later dam of 7f 3yo Listed winner Solomon's Bay and French 1m 2yo Listed winner Tammani).

UNNAMED (IRE)
15/4 b c Sea The Stars - Wo de Xin (Shamardal)
Owner: Shadwell Estate Co Sales price: 200,000gns (Shadwell Estate Company)

Second foal of an unraced daughter of a maiden sister to Oaks winner Love Divine (later dam of St Leger winner Sixties Icon) and half-sister to 12f 3yo Listed winner/Park Hill Stakes runner-up Floreeda, 1m Listed winner Dark Promise, 12f 3yo winner/Queen's Vase runner-up Solar Sky and the once-raced maiden dam of Hong Kong triple 8/10f Group 1 winner Dan Excel.

UNNAMED
7/5 b f Shamardal - Yasmeen (Sea The Stars)
Owner: Shadwell Estate Co Sales price: n/a

Half-sister to 2020 7f 3yo winner Alkhat. Dam a Listed-placed 7f 3yo winner who was closely related to 7f 2yo Listed winner Mudaaraah and a half-sister to Group 3/Listed-placed dual 7f winner/Poule d'Essai des Poulains fourth Muwaary, 6f 3yo Listed winner Ethaara (later dam of 1m 3yo Listed winner

Etaab) and 7f 2yo Listed winner Sudoor (later dam of French 10.5f 3yo Group 3 winner Raseed) out of an unraced half-sister to very smart miler Bahri.

RICHARD HANNON

AMERICAN KESTREL (IRE)
25/3 b f Starspangledbanner - Marsh Hawk (Invincible Spirit)
Owner: Rockcliffe Stud Sales price: n/a

Half-sister to useful 2020 dual 6f 2yo winner Mohawk King. Dam a Group 3/ Listed-placed dual 7f 2yo winner who was a half-sister to dual 5f 2yo winner/ Queen Mary Stakes third Hairy Rocket out of a Listed-placed dual 6f 2yo winning half-sister to French 10.5f 3yo Listed winner Trinity Joy (later dam of French dual 7f Listed winner Vaniloquio).

BETSHOOF
5/5 b c Night of Thunder - Surprise (Anabaa Blue)
Owner: Shadwell Estate Co Sales price: 250,000gns (Shadwell Estate Company)

Half-brother to 2021 dual 5f winner Cahors. Dam a maiden half-sister to smart multiple 5-6f winner (including at Group 3/Listed level) Triple Aspect and French 6.5f 2yo Listed winner Wonderfilly out of a 6f 2yo winning half-sister to the dam of French 7f 2yo Group 3 winner Guys And Dolls and triple 8-11f Listed winner Pawn Broker.

DARK TULIP
31/3 b f Dark Angel - Rimth (Oasis Dream)
Owner: Denford Stud Sales price: n/a

Half-sister to useful 7f-1m winner Bullingdon, useful 6-7f winner Ginger Fox and two other winners. Dam a 7f 3yo Group 3 winner/Cheveley Park Stakes runner-up who was the daughter of a 1m 3yo winning half-sister to King's Stand Stakes winner Dominica.

DAWN OF LIBERATION (IRE)
6/2 b c Churchill - Danetime Out (Danetime)
Owner: Mrs Susan Roy Sales price: 145,000gns (Michael Roy)

Half-brother to very smart multiple 6f-1m winner (including at Group 1 level) Toormore, smart 6.5f-1m winner (including at Group 2/Listed level) Estidhkaar, useful 5.5-7f winner Try The Chance, two other winners and the unraced dam of 5f 2yo Listed winner Orlaith. Dam an unraced half-sister to Group 3-placed 7-8.5f winner Easaar.

DUELIST
13/2 b c Dubawi - Coplow (Manduro)
Owner: Mrs R J McCreery and Richard Hannon Snr Sales price: n/a

Half-brother to high-class multiple 7f-1m winner (including the 1000 Guineas) Billesdon Brook and 10f 3yo Listed winner Billesdon Bess. Dam a maiden half-sister to 7/8.5f Group 3 winner Anna Nerium, 7f 2yo Group 3 winner Piping Rock (both by Dubawi) and French 1m 2yo Group 3 winner Middle Club.

EVERYDAY
29/4 b c Cable Bay - Humdrum (Dr Fong)
Owner: The Queen Sales price: n/a

Half-brother to UK/Australian 8-12f winner Humbolt Current, 6f 2yo winner Husbandry and three other winners. Dam a very useful UK/French 7f-1m winner who was a half-sister to 6f 3yo Listed winner Musical Comedy, 5.5f 2yo winner Kinematic (dam of 2020 Italian 7.5f 2yo Listed winner Collinsbay and useful 6.5f 2yo winner King's Lynn (both by Cable Bay)) and 6f 2yo winners Otago (by Cable Bay) and Ring of Truth.

GAIUS
13/2 b c Havana Gold - Gemina (Holy Roman Emperor)
Owner: Gillian, Lady Howard de Walden Sales price: n/a

First foal of a Listed-placed 7f 2yo winner who was a full sister to 2020 1m 2yo winner Genuflex, a close relation to useful 11.5f 3yo winner Girling and a half-sister to Listed-placed 7-10f winner Gibeon and useful 2020 10-11.5f 3yo winner Grinling out of a 14f 3yo Group 3 winner; family of Fame And Glory, Legatissimo and Farhh.

GISBURN (IRE)
15/1 ch c Ribchester - Disclose (Dansili)
Owner: Michael Kerr-Dineen & Martin Hughes Sales price: £88,000 (Peter & Ross Doyle Bloodstock)

Half-brother to smart 5-6f winner (including at Listed level) Encrypted. Dam a Listed-placed French 1m 3yo winner who was a full sister to Listed-placed French 7f-1m winner World Ruler and useful French 6f-1m winner Concealing, a three-parts sister to Listed-placed French 5.5-6f winner Grand Vista and a half-sister to the unraced dam of Group 2/3-placed 6-7f 2yo winner Gavota.

INDIAN GURU (IRE)
2/4 ch f Ribchester - Transcendence (Arcano)
Owner: Michael Kerr-Dineen & Martin Hughes Sales price: £60,000 (Peter & Ross Doyle Bloodstock)

First foal of an unraced half-sister to Group 2/3-placed multiple 5-6f winner (including twice at Listed level) Mister Manannan, Group 3-placed UK/US 5-8.5f winner Shermeen (later dam of Irish 6f 2yo Group 1 winner Sudirman) and 7f 2yo winner Angel Bright (later dam of 6f Listed winner Castle Hill Cassie); family of high-class sprinters Anthem Alexander, Dandy Man and Hamza.

KINTBURY
3/4 b f Nathaniel - Promising (Invincible Spirit)
Owner: Denford Stud Sales price: n/a

First foal of a Group 3/Listed-placed 6f winner who was a full sister to Irish 5.5/6f Listed winner Lethal Promise and very useful multiple 8.5-10.5f winner Kaser and a half-sister to 2021 Bahraini King's Cup winner Glen Force out of a useful US 5.5-6f winner.

KODIAS SANGARIUS (IRE)
20/4 b f Kodiac - Oui Say Oui (Royal Applause)
Owner: Middleham Park Racing CIII Sales price: £68,000 (Peter & Ross Doyle Bloodstock)

Half-sister to 2020 Irish 12f 3yo winner Golddragon Reef. Dam a Group 2-placed Irish/US 6-8.5f winner who was a half-sister to Group 2-placed 6f-1m winner (including at Group 3/Listed level) Satchem, smart 8.5f-2m winner (including at Group 3/Listed level) Eye of The Storm, 1m 2yo Listed winner Mohican Heights and Listed-placed 11.5-14.5f winner Curbyourenthusiasm.

MARITIME RULES (IRE)
3/3 b c Mehmas - Beauty of The Sea (Elusive Quality)
Owner: Ziad A Galadari Sales price: £95,000 (Peter & Ross Doyle Bloodstock)

Full brother to useful 6-7f winner Fayathaan. Dam a maiden half-sister to Listed-placed 6f 2yo winner Make Fast (dam of 2020 Windsor Castle Stakes/ July Stakes winner Tactical) out of a smart 5-7f winner (including at Group 3/ Listed level) who was a half-sister to useful 8.5f 2yo winner Big Challenge and useful Irish 11.5f 3yo winner Hikari (later dam of 10f 3yo Listed winner Raise You).

MOUNT SNOWDON (IRE)
18/3 b c War Front - Christmas Joy (Galileo)
Owner: Sun Bloodstock SARL Sales price: n/a

First foal of an unraced close relation to very smart 6.5f-1m winner (including twice at Group 1 level) Toronado and half-sister to the unraced dam of Listed-placed 5f 2yo winner Kemble out of a French 6.5f-1m winning half-sister to Racing Post Trophy winner Casamento and very useful 6f-1m winner Inler.

OH HERBERTS REIGN (IRE)
7/2 b c Acclamation - Western Safari (High Chaparral)
Owner: Team Wallop Sales price: £105,000 (Peter & Ross Doyle Bloodstock)

First foal of a maiden half-sister to Group 2/3-placed prolific 7f-1m winner (including twice at Listed level) Oh This Is Us (by Acclamation) out of a smart multiple 6f-1m winner (including at Group 3/Listed level) who was a half-sister to Irish 7f 3yo Listed winner Imperial Rome.

PETRILA (IRE)
3/4 b c Acclamation - Simply Awesome (Awesome Again)
Owner: Merriebelle Irish Farm Limited Sales price: 92,000gns (Peter & Ross Doyle Bloodstock)

First foal of an unraced half-sister to 5f 2yo Listed winner Sweepstake (later dam of Irish dual 10f 3yo Group 3 winner/Derby fourth Broome) and useful 8-10.5f winner Eurystheus (both by Acclamation) out of a maiden sister to French 10f 3yo Group 3 winner Dust Dancer (grandam of Irish 6f 2yo Group 1 winner Zoffany and 6f Group 3 winner Projection (by Acclamation)) and half-sister to Fred Darling Stakes winner Bulaxie (later dam of Italian 10f Group 2 winner/good producer Claxon).

SIAMSA (IRE)
21/2 b f Starspangledbanner - Sliabh Luachra (High Chaparral)
Owner: Mrs Joan Brosnan Sales price: £240,000 (Vendor)

Half-sister to very useful 7-10f winner Strait Of Hormuz. Dam a thrice-raced maiden close relation to useful 12f 3yo winner Parvana and a half-sister to Group 1-placed 5-6f 2yo winner (including twice at Group 2 level) Mehmas out of an unraced half-sister to triple 10/11f Group 3 winner Blue Monday and the grandam of Poule d'Essai des Pouliches/Prix de Diane winner Avenir Certain.

SOWS (IRE)
9/2 b f Kodiac - Zvarkhova (Makfi)
Owner: Martin Hughes Sales price: £100,000 (Peter & Ross Doyle Bloodstock)

Second foal of a Listed-placed French/US 8-9f winner who was a three-parts sister to smart UK/UAE multiple 8-11f winner (including at Group 3/Listed level) Gm Hopkins out of a Listed-placed French/Irish 10-12f winner; family of 2000 Guineas winner Mark Of Esteem.

SPACE ODYSSEY (IRE)
4/3 b c Sea The Stars - Lady Of Dubai (Dubawi)
Owner: Sheikh Mohammed Obaid Al Maktoum Sales price: n/a

Second foal of a 10f 3yo Listed winner/Oaks third who was a sister to useful French 10-10.5f 3yo winner Indian Skies and a half-sister to two winners out of an unraced close relation to Irish 13f 3yo Listed winner/Irish Oaks runner-up Roses For The Lady and the maiden dam of Irish 1m 1f 2yo Listed winner Call To Battle; family of French 10f 3yo Group 2 winner Knight To Behold (by Sea The Stars).

SPEED DIAL (IRE)
15/3 b f Fast Company - Fairy Lights (Shamardal)
Owner: Sheikh Mohammed Obaid Al Maktoum Sales price: n/a

First foal of a maiden half-sister to once-raced 1m 3yo winner Subaana and the maiden dam of 2020 1m 3yo Group 3 winner/1000 Guineas runner-up Cloak of Spirits out of an 8.5f 3yo winner who was closely related to very smart 6f-1m winner (including the Irish 2000 Guineas)/Derby third Dubawi and a half-sister to Lancashire Oaks winner Emirates Queen and 10f 3yo Listed winner Princess Nada.

THUNDER MAX
11/2 ch c Night of Thunder - Tuolumne Meadows (High Chaparral)
Owner: Amo Racing Limited Sales price: £155,000 (Peter & Ross Doyle Bloodstock)

First foal of a maiden sister to Listed-placed triple 12f winner Tioga Pass and half-sister to French 1m 2yo Group 3 winner Circumvent, Group 2-placed UK/Qatari 7f-1m winner (including at Listed level) Devious Company and Listed-placed 7-7.5f winner Seradim out of an unraced half-sister to Lingfield Derby Trial winner Saddler's Quest and the dam of high-class stayers Marmelo and Vent de Force.

WHIRLWIND
14/2 b c Night of Thunder - Hokkaido (Street Cry)
Owner: Saeed Manana Sales price: 240,000gns (Vendor)

Half-brother to useful dual 1m 3yo winner Mutafani and 2020 dual 5f winner
Sambucca Spirit. Dam an unraced half-sister to Prix Saint-Alary winner Sobetsu
out of a dual 10f Listed winner who was a half-sister to 7f 2yo Listed winner
Sixth Sense and Group 3/Listed-placed 1m 3yo winner Glen Innes.

UNNAMED (IRE)
15/3 b c Acclamation - Colour Blue (Holy Roman Emperor)
Owner: Al Shaqab Racing Sales price: 92,000gns (Peter & Ross Doyle
Bloodstock)

Second foal of a Listed-placed Irish 7-8.5f winner who was a half-sister to six
winners including 7f 2yo winner Blue Mirage and once-raced 6f 3yo winner
Dream The Blues (later dam of Norfolk Stakes/Phoenix Stakes winner Sioux
Nation) and the maiden dam of dual 6f Group 3 winner My Catch, French 6f
2yo Listed winner/Prix Morny third Vladimir and Listed-placed 2yo winners
Pearl Sea (6f) and Natural (6.5f).

UNNAMED
19/3 b c Shamardal - Rayaheen (Nayef)
Owner: Shadwell Estate Co Sales price: n/a

Half-brother to smart 6-7f 2yo winner (including at Group 3/Listed level)
Tajaanus and very useful UK/UAE 5-7.5f winner Motafaawit. Dam a 6f 2yo
winner who was a three-parts sister to 7f Listed winner Mankib and a half-
sister to useful 6.5f 2yo winner Raaqy out of a Cheveley Park Stakes/1000
Guineas winner.

UNNAMED (IRE)
26/3 b c Kodiac - Sodashy (Noverre)
Owner: King Power Racing Co Ltd Sales price: 130,000gns (SackvilleDonald)

Full brother to Listed-placed 5-6f winner Roussel and a half-brother to French
10.5f 3yo Listed winner Talk Or Listen. Dam a maiden half-sister to 5f 2yo
Group 3 winner Ponty Acclaim out of a maiden sister to Group 3-placed
multiple 5-6f winner (including four times at Listed level) Astonished and half-
sister to Group 1-placed prolific 5f winner (including at Group 3/Listed level)
Bishops Court.

CHARLIE HILLS

IBN ALDAR
8/4 br c Twilight Son - Bint Aldar (Zoffany)
Owner: Ziad A Galadari Sales price: £50,000 (Charlie Hills)

Second foal of a fairly useful 5-6f 2yo winner who was a half-sister to Italian 1m 3yo Listed winner Key Master and useful 7f-1m 2yo winner Bremner out of a 5f 2yo winning half-sister to 6f Listed winner One Putra and 7f 3yo Listed winner Teophilip.

LOVES ME LIKEAROCK
7/4 ch f Lethal Force - Love On The Rocks (Exceed And Excel)
Owner: The Chriselliam Partnership Sales price: n/a

First foal of a useful triple 5f winner who was a sister to Listed-placed 5-6f winner Double Up out of a 6f 2yo winning half-sister to 6f Group 1 winner G Force, US 1m 2yo Grade 3 winner Louvain (later dam of Poule d'Essai des Pouliches winner Flotilla and grandam of 2020 Irish 10f 3yo Group 3 winner Crossfirehurricane and 2021 Irish 1m 3yo Listed winner My Generation), 10f 3yo Listed winner Laajooj and Group 3/Listed-placed 5-6f winner Desert Poppy.

ORAZIO (IRE)
29/3 br c Caravaggio - Lady Fashion (Oasis Dream)
Owner: Mrs Susan Roy Sales price: £215,000 (Michael Roy)

Half-brother to Chesham Stakes winner Suits You. Dam a useful Irish dual 7f 3yo winning daughter of a Listed-placed 6f 2yo winner who was a half-sister to Grade 3-placed US 5f-1m winner (including two stakes races) Boat Trip, Group 3/Listed-placed 5-8.5f winner Rallying Cry and Listed-placed Irish 1m 1f 3yo winner Atlantic Swing.

PEACE NEGOTIATION (IRE)
27/2 b c No Nay Never - Madeenaty (Dansili)
Owner: Ziad A Galadari Sales price: 110,000gns (C Gordon Watson Bloodstock)

First foal of an unraced sister to smart 8-10.5f winner (including at Group 3/ Listed level) Mahsoob out of a Listed-placed 1m 2yo winning granddaughter of a 7f 2yo Group 3 winner/1000 Guineas third, herself the daughter of 1000 Guineas winner Shadayid; family of US 6f Grade 1 winner Takaful.

PODEROSO (IRE)
20/3 b c Kodiac - Online Alexander (Acclamation)
Owner: Amo Racing Limited Sales price: 225,000gns (A C Elliott, Agent)

Full brother to Group 2/Listed-placed 2020 5f 2yo winner Yazaman and a half-brother to 2021 6f Listed winner/Commonwealth Cup fourth Royal Commando. Dam a Listed-placed triple 5f winner who was the daughter of a 6f 3yo winning half-sister to 6f Group 1 winner Red Clubs.

POINT LYNAS (IRE)
14/3 b/br c Iffraaj - Initially (Dansili)
Owner: Julie Martin & David R Martin & Partner Sales price: 40,000gns (BBA Ireland/Barry Hills)

Second foal of a maiden sister to French 7f 2yo Group 3 winner/Prix Jean-Luc Lagardere runner-up Early March, smart UK/US 8-10.5f winner (including at Grade 2/Group 3 level) Aviate and very useful dual 7f 2yo winner Wingwalker out of a 1m 3yo winning sister to Grade 1-placed UK/US 8-10f winner Boatman and half-sister to the dam of Hong Kong 1m Group 1 winner Giant Treasure.

SONNY LISTON (IRE)
30/1 b c Lawman - Stars In Your Eyes (Galileo)
Owner: Chelsea Thoroughbreds - Big Bear Sales price: 60,000gns (C Gordon Watson Bloodstock)

Full brother to very useful 7-10f winner Banksea and a half-brother to Group 1-placed 9.5-12.5f winner (including at Group 2/Listed level) Dame Malliot and very useful 8-10f winner Zabeel Champion. Dam a 12f winner who was a half-sister to 1m 2yo Listed winner New Mexican, Listed-placed UK/UAE multiple 10f winner Wild Savannah and very useful 8-10f winner Coordinated Cut.

UNNAMED (USA)
31/3 b c War Front - Aqsaam (Dynaformer)
Owner: Shadwell Estate Co Sales price: n/a

Full brother to useful triple 6f 3yo winner Thafeera and a half-brother to once-raced 2020 7f 3yo winner Badrah. Dam a Grade 3-placed US 7-8.5f winner who was a half-sister to Grade 2/3-placed US triple 6.5f winner Lady Lumberjack out of a US 8.5f 3yo Listed-winning half-sister to US 1m Grade 2 winner Night Patrol.

UNNAMED
18/4 b f Dark Angel - Fadhayyil (Tamayuz)
Owner: Shadwell Estate Co Sales price: n/a

Half-sister to 2020 7f 3yo winner Turaath. Dam a Group 2/3-placed dual
7f winner (including at Listed level) who was a half-sister to Listed winners
Athenian, Cold Stare (both 7f) and Zipzip (10f) and the dam of 2020 French 1m
3yo Listed winner Miss Extra out of a French 5f Group 3/Listed winner; family
of high-class miler Swallow Flight.

UNNAMED (IRE)
26/2 b f Dark Angel - Faraday Light (Rainbow Quest)
Owner: Shadwell Estate Co Sales price: €575,000 (Shadwell Estate Company)

Half-sister to Irish 1000 Guineas winner/1000 Guineas runner-up Just The
Judge, Listed-placed Irish 1m 2yo winner Obliterator and three other winners.
Dam a twice-raced half-sister to Group 1-placed 8-12f winner (including at
Group 3/Listed level)/Oaks third High Heeled (later dam of German 1m 3yo
Listed winner Pabouche) and Irish 1m Listed winner Bella Estrella.

UNNAMED
1/5 b c Muhaarar - Ghanaati (Giant's Causeway)
Owner: Shadwell Estate Co Sales price: n/a

Three-parts brother to very useful multiple 1m winner Afaak (by Oasis Dream)
and a half-brother to 2020 UAE 6f Group 3 winner Wafy, once-raced 2020
7f 2yo winner Mutasaabeq and three other winners. Dam a 1000 Guineas/
Coronation Stakes winner who was a three-parts sister to the dam of Queen
Mary Stakes winner Maqaasid and a half-sister to 12f Group 3 winner/
Champion Stakes runner-up Mawatheeq and 1m 1f 3yo Listed winner/Oaks
third Rumoush (later dam of UAE dual 1m Group 3 winner Muntazah, 7f 3yo
Group 3 winner Talaayeb and 1m 3yo Listed winner Wadilsafa).

UNNAMED (IRE)
2/3 b c Acclamation - Lydia Becker (Sleeping Indian)
Owner: Shadwell Estate Co Sales price: 130,000gns (Shadwell Estate
Company)

Second foal of an unraced sister to 7f 2yo Group 3 winner Crazy Horse and
half-sister to smart triple 7f winner (including at Group 2/Listed level) Richard
Pankhurst out of a 1m winner who was a full sister to smart 8-10.5f winner
(including at Group 3/Listed level) Lateen Sails.

UNNAMED (IRE)
10/4 b f Frankel - Madany (Acclamation)
Owner: Shadwell Estate Co Sales price: n/a

Closely related to 7f Group 2 winner/2000 Guineas runner-up Massaat (by Teofilo) and a half-sister to Commonwealth Cup winner Eqtidaar, 2020 7f 2yo Group 3 winner Mujbar and useful UK/Irish 5-6f winner Hathiq. Dam a useful dual 6f 2yo winner who was a half-sister to French 5f 2yo Group 3 winner Dolled Up and French 6f 2yo Listed winner/good broodmare Zeiting.

Mujbar

UNNAMED (IRE)
19/2 ch f Dubawi - Neshmeya (Lawman)
Owner: Shadwell Estate Co Sales price: n/a

First foal of a useful dual 10f 3yo winner who was a half-sister to German 1m 3yo Listed winner Pabouche and useful dual 10f winner Espadrille (both by Dubawi) out of a 12f 3yo Group 3 winner/Oaks third who was a full sister to Irish 1m Listed winner Bella Estrella and a half-sister to the maiden dam of Irish 1000 Guineas winner Just The Judge.

UNNAMED
3/5 b f Invincible Spirit - Rufoof (Zamindar)
Owner: Shadwell Estate Co Sales price: n/a

Full sister to once-raced 2020 6f 2yo winner Tanmawwy and a half-sister to
two winners. Dam a dual 7f 3yo winner who was a half-sister to top-class
sprinter Muhaarar, 6f 2yo Listed winner Sajwah and Group 3-placed UK/UAE
6-7f winner Tamaathul out of a dual 7f 3yo winning sister to French Listed
winners Green Channel (7f) and Mister Charm (7.5f, twice) and half-sister to
French 1m 2yo Group 3 winner Mister Sacha.

MARK JOHNSTON

AGREEABILITY
2/5 b f Bobby's Kitten - Moi Aussi (Mt. Livermore)
Owner: Miss K Rausing Sales price: n/a

Half-sister to Group 2-placed Irish 8.5f 2yo winner Clonard Street and Group
3-placed 7f 2yo winner Accordance. Dam a dual 1m 2yo winner who was a
half-sister to Listed-placed dual 7f 2yo winner Oblige; family of Dewhurst
Stakes dead-heater Scenic.

AUSTRIAN THEORY (IRE)
16/2 b c Awtaad - Cedar Sea (Persian Bold)
Owner: Dr Jim Walker Sales price: 30,000gns (Johnston Racing)

Three-parts brother to 13f 3yo Group 3 winner/St Leger third Corsica (by Cape
Cross) and a half-brother to 1m Listed winner Tenor and four other winners.
Dam a Listed-placed French 1m 3yo winner who was a half-sister to Coventry
Stakes winner Cd Europe and the unraced dam of Irish 7f Listed winner Iveagh
Gardens.

BOONDOGGLE
1/3 b c Bobby's Kitten - Fresh Strike (Smart Strike)
Owner: Barbara & Alick Richmond Sales price: 20,000gns (Johnston Racing)

Half-brother to useful 2020 French 1m 2yo winner My Kurkum. Dam a useful
French 9.5-10f 3yo winner who was a full sister to French 1m 3yo Listed
winner Green Sweet and a half-sister to Group 1-placed French 7-10f winner
(including at Group 2/3 level)/Poule d'Essai des Poulains runner-up Shaman.

BOY ABOUT TOWN
28/1 b c Frankel - Miss Marjurie (Marju)
Owner: Susan & John Waterworth Sales price: 48,000gns (Johnston Racing)

Second foal of a Group 2-placed 7-12f winner (including at Group 3/Listed level) who was the daughter of a maiden half-sister to five-time 1m Group 1 winner Soviet Song, the dam of French 10f Group 1 winner Ribbons and the grandam of high-class sprinters Judicial and Marsha.

CAPITAL THEORY
22/3 b c Muhaarar - Montalcino (Big Bad Bob)
Owner: Dr Jim Walker Sales price: 26,000gns (Johnston Racing)

Second foal of a Group 3/Listed-placed 1m 2yo winner who was a half-sister to 6f Listed winner Windfast and Irish 7f 2yo winner Windracer out of a maiden half-sister to Italian Derby winner/Prix de l'Arc de Triomphe runner-up White Muzzle and Irish 10f 3yo Listed winner Elfaslah (later dam of Prix Jean Prat/Dubai World Cup winner Almutawakel and 1000 Guineas runner-up Muwakleh).

CAVENDISH
3/4 ch c Iffraaj - Bess of Hardwick (Dansili)
Owner: Kingsley Park 21 Sales price: 15,000gns (Johnston Racing)

Second foal of a 13f Listed winner who was a half-sister to Group/Grade 1-placed 12-15.5f winner (including twice at Group 1 level) Ask and useful dual 12f 3yo winner Require (later dam of French 14f Group 3 winner Monica Sheriff) out of a twice-raced maiden half-sister to 12f Group 2 winner Blueprint and 10f 3yo Listed winner Fairy Godmother (later dam of Australian 10f Group 1 winner My Kingdom of Fife).

CHUFFED TO BITS (IRE)
5/5 b c Churchill - Crystal Valkyrie (Danehill)
Owner: Barbara & Alick Richmond Sales price: 22,000gns (Johnston Racing)

Closely related to Group 3-placed Irish/Australian 10-12.5f winner Granddukeoftuscany (by Galileo), 2020 10f 3yo Listed winner Freyja and 2020 7.5f 2yo winner State of Bliss (both by Gleneagles) and a half-brother to 7f 2yo Group 3 winner/1000 Guineas fourth Sent From Heaven and 10f 3yo Group 3 winner Above Average. Dam a 6f 2yo winner who was the daughter of a maiden half-sister to 6f Group 1 winner Iktamal and the dam of Gimcrack Stakes winner Conquest.

HARB
15/4 b c Muhaarar - Maid For Winning (Gone West)
Owner: Shadwell Estate Co Sales price: 110,000gns (Shadwell Estate
Company)

Half-brother to 6f 2yo Group 3 winner Yourtimeisnow, Group 2/3-placed 7f-1m
winner Hors de Combat, Group 3-placed 6-6.5f winner Stroll Patrol and three
other winners. Dam a thrice-raced maiden half-sister to US 1m 1f Grade 1
winner Stroll and US triple 8.5/9f Listed winner Patrol.

JANOOBI (IRE)
10/2 ch c Night of Thunder - Southern Belle (Aqlaam)
Owner: Shadwell Estate Co Sales price: 155,000gns (Shadwell Estate
Company)

First foal of a useful 5-6f winner who was a half-sister to 1m 2yo Listed winner
Go Angellica, very useful UK/US dual 6f winner Bredenbury (by Night of
Thunder) and four other winners out of a maiden daughter of a US 10f 3yo
winning sister to German 10/12f Group 1 winner Germany.

MACKENZIE ROSE (IRE)
20/2 b f Dark Angel - Kelsey Rose (Most Welcome)
Owner: Mrs S Rowlett Sales price: £62,000 (Johnston Racing)

Full sister to Group 1-placed prolific 6-8.5f winner (including at Group 2/3
level) Sovereign Debt and useful Irish 6-7f winner Sorelle Delle Rose and a half-
sister to Fred Darling Stakes winner/Cheveley Park Stakes fourth Puff. Dam a
Listed-placed triple 5f 2yo winner from the family of 6f 2yo Group 2 winner
Indian Rocket and 6f 2yo Listed winner/Norfolk Stakes runner-up The Bonus
King.

MOON OF REALITY
26/3 b c Sea The Moon - Selenography (Selkirk)
Owner: Teme Valley Sales price: 40,000gns (Johnston Racing)

Full brother to Listed-placed 7.5f-1m 2yo Flat/2021 2m Grade 2 hurdle winner
Tritonic. Dam an unraced half-sister to Irish 1m 2yo winner Luz de La Luna
out of an Argentinian 1m Group 1 winner who was a half-sister to Argentinian
6f/7.5f 2yo Group 1 winner Slew of Reality.

OUTBREAK
20/2 b c Dark Angel - Purr Along (Mount Nelson)
Owner: Qatar Racing Limited Sales price: 67,000gns (David Redvers Bloodstock)

Half-brother to useful 1m 2yo winner Starcat. Dam a Group 2-placed 7f-1m winner (including twice at Group 3 level) who was a half-sister to 5f Listed winner Katawi and Listed-placed UK/US dual 8.5f winner Lady Francesca out of a 7f 3yo winning half-sister to Falmouth Stakes winner Ronda (later dam of US dual 1m Grade 3 winner Istan).

PONS AELIUS (IRE)
28/4 b c Galileo - Laugh Out Loud (Clodovil)
Owner: Susan & John Waterworth Sales price: 95,000gns (Johnston Racing)

Full brother to smart Irish/US 8-10f winner (including at Grade 2/Group 3 level) Platinum Warrior. Dam a Group 1-placed multiple 1m winner (including at Group 2/Listed level) who was a half-sister to dual 12f Listed winner Suzi's Decision, very useful 10-12f winner Baghdad and the dam of 2020 French 6f 2yo Group 2/3 winner Plainchant.

RUBY RUBY
13/3 b f Invincible Spirit - Elas Ruby (Raven's Pass)
Owner: 3 Batterhams and a Reay Sales price: 62,000gns (Johnston Racing)

First foal of a Group 2-placed 8-10f winner (including at Listed level) who was a half-sister to useful 12-14f 3yo winner Elasia out of a Listed-placed 8.5f 2yo winning half-sister to Doncaster Cup winner Pallasator and Listed-placed Irish 7f 2yo winner Alphonsus (by Invincible Spirit).

SHARESA (IRE)
27/3 ch f Mehmas - Najraan (Cadeaux Genereux)
Owner: Mohammed Bin Hamad Khalifa Al Attiya Sales price: 42,000gns (Johnston Racing)

Half-sister to Group 2-placed 2020 6f 2yo winner/Dewhurst Stakes fourth Devilwala. Dam a twice-raced maiden half-sister to 5f 3yo Listed winner Excelette (later dam of dual 5f 2yo Listed winner/Flying Childers Stakes runner-up Well Done Fox) and Group 3-placed 5-6f winner Rapid Applause out of an unraced half-sister to King's Stand Stakes winner Bolshoi.

SPY
19/4 b c Muhaarar - Confidential Lady (Singspiel)
Owner: Kingsley Park 22 Sales price: 15,000gns (Johnston Racing)

Half-brother to 1m 3yo Listed winner Red Box, useful French/UAE 8-10f winner Untold Secret, useful 2020 7f-1m winner Confide, useful 7.5f-1m 2yo winner Tell Me All and the dam of French 6f 2yo Listed winner Private Matter. Dam a high-class 7-10.5f winner (including the Prix de Diane)/1000 Guineas runner-up who was the daughter of a Listed-placed dual 7f 3yo winning half-sister to 7f 2yo Group 3 winner White Crown and Group 3/Listed-placed 6f 2yo winner Wind Cheetah.

STONE AXE (IRE)
8/3 ro c Zoffany - Roystonea (Polish Precedent)
Owner: Susan & John Waterworth Sales price: £36,000 (Johnston Racing)

Full brother to Royal Lodge Stakes winner/Racing Post Trophy third Foundation and a half-brother to very useful UK/UAE 6f-1m winner (including at Listed level) Major Partnership, very useful 6-7f winner Misterioso and very useful Irish multiple 7-10f winner Vastonea. Dam a Listed-placed French 7f-1m winner who was a half-sister to French 1m Listed winners Bermuda Grass (2yo) and Bermuda Rye (3yo).

SUPER STARS (IRE)
4/5 b c Sea The Stars - Valais Girl (Holy Roman Emperor)
Owner: Mr M Doyle Sales price: £34,000 (Johnston Racing)

Full brother to Group 2-placed UK/French 7.5f-1m winner (including at Listed level) Alpen Rose. Dam a useful 6f 2yo winner who was a half-sister to Group 3-placed French 4.5-5.5f 2yo winner Faslen (later dam of triple 8/10f Listed winner Don't Be) out of an unraced half-sister to smart 7-9.5f winner (including at Group 3/Listed level) Hathal, 10f Group 3 winner Gentleman's Deal and several other useful winners.

UNNAMED
3/3 b c Siyouni - Beach Belle (Invincible Spirit)
Owner: Qatar Racing Ltd & Lady O'Reilly Sales price: n/a

Half-brother to smart triple 7f winner (including at Listed level) Surf Dancer. Dam an Irish 6f 2yo Listed winner who was closely related to Group 3-placed 6-7f winner (including twice at Listed level) Naadirr and a half-sister to very useful 7-10.5f winner Marronnier and useful 9-11f winner Aasheq out of a Group 1-placed Irish 8-9f winner (including at Listed level).

UNNAMED
14/4 b c New Approach - Enlace (Shamardal)
Owner: Sheikh Hamdan Bin Mohammed Al Maktoum Sales price: n/a

First foal of a very useful 5-7f winner who was a half-sister to useful 5-7.5f winner Auchterarder and the dam of 2020 Irish 5.5f 3yo Listed winner Lady Penelope out of a French 6f 3yo Listed-winning half-sister to Mill Reef Stakes winner Russian Bond, 5f Group 2 winner Snaadee, the dam of German 10f 3yo Group 1 winner/Deutsches Derby runner-up Ransom O'War and the grandam of Queen Elizabeth II Stakes winner Charm Spirit and 2020 Poule d'Essai des Pouliches winner Dream And Do.

UNNAMED
28/4 b c Iffraaj - Galician (Redoute's Choice)
Owner: Sheikh Hamdan Bin Mohammed Al Maktoum Sales price: n/a

Half-brother to Listed-placed French 8-10f winner Battle of Toro. Dam a Listed-placed multiple 6-8.5f winner who was a half-sister to Australian 12f Group 1 winner Allow out of a 10f 3yo winning half-sister to Grade 1-placed French 8-10.5f winner (including at Group 3 level) Spring Oak and 10f 3yo Listed winner Fragrant Hill (later dam of several smart performers, notably French Group 1 winners Alpine Rose (10f) and Fragrant Mix (12f)).

UNNAMED (IRE)
25/3 br f Muhaarar - Muraaqaba (Dubawi)
Owner: Shadwell Estate Co Sales price: n/a

First foal of a Group 2-placed 6-7f 2yo winner (including at Group 3 level) who was a half-sister to Middle Park Stakes winner Awzaan, Group 3-placed 7f-1m winner (including twice at Listed level) Muteela, Listed-placed 8-10f winner Hajras and very useful 6f-1m winner Khamaary.

UNNAMED
26/3 gr c Dark Angel - Muteela (Dansili)
Owner: Shadwell Estate Co Sales price: n/a

Half-brother to useful 2020 6f 2yo winner Mutazawwed. Dam a 7f/1m 3yo Listed winner who was a half-sister to Middle Park Stakes winner Awzaan, 7f 2yo Group 3 winner Muraaqaba and Listed-placed 8-10f winner Hajras out of a Group 3-placed 6-7f winner (including at Listed level).

UNNAMED
7/4 gr f Iffraaj - Nahoodh (Clodovil)
Owner: Sheikh Hamdan Bin Mohammed Al Maktoum Sales price: n/a

Half-sister to smart UK/UAE 6f-1m winner (including at Listed level)
Hawkesbury and 5f 2yo winner Fire Blaze. Dam a Falmouth Stakes winner who
was a half-sister to useful 5.5-6f 2yo winner Makyon and useful 7f-1m winner
Silver Games (dam of Listed-placed 2020 dual 6f 2yo winner Chocoya).

UNNAMED (IRE)
2/5 ch c Zoffany - Naomh Geileis (Grand Slam)
Owner: Christine Budden & Partners Sales price: n/a

Half-brother to 6f 2yo Listed winner Rebel Assault, Listed-placed 6.5f-1m
winner Assault On Rome and useful 10-10.5f winner Alexander M. Dam a
useful 6f 2yo winner who was the daughter of a US 8.5f winning close relation
to Group 2/3-placed Irish 6f 2yo winner Juniper and half-sister to Irish 12f 3yo
Group 2 winner Andros Bay and the dam of Eclipse Stakes winner/Irish 2000
Guineas runner-up Oratorio.

UNNAMED (IRE)
21/4 b f Iffraaj - Pleasemetoo (Vale of York)
Owner: Sheikh Hamdan Bin Mohammed Al Maktoum Sales price: n/a

Second foal of a Group 3-placed French 7f 2yo winner who was a half-sister
to Group 1-placed French 7f-1m winner (including at Group 3/Listed level)
Siyoushake and smart French 9.5-12.5f winner (including at Group 3/Listed
level) Skyward out of a French 11.5f 3yo winning full sister to US 10f Grade 1
winner Frost Giant.

UNNAMED (IRE)
13/2 b f Dark Angel - Rachelle (Mark of Esteem)
Owner: Sheikh Hamdan Bin Mohammed Al Maktoum Sales price: n/a

Half-sister to Middle Park Stakes winner Amadeus Wolf, 6f 2yo Group 3 winner
Rouleau, Listed-placed 7f 3yo winner Aurum and useful 7f-1m 3yo winner
Always A Rock. Dam an Italian 7f 3yo winner who was the daughter of an
Italian 10.5f 3yo Listed winner/Oaks d'Italia runner-up.

UNNAMED
29/3 ch f Ulysses - Reckoning (Danehill Dancer)
Owner: Mascalls Stud Sales price: 140,000gns (Vendor)

Closely related to 2020 Prix Royal-Oak winner Subjectivist (by Teofilo) and 14f
Group 3/Listed winner/St Leger runner-up Sir Ron Priestley (by Australia) and a

half-sister to useful 2020 7f 2yo winner Alba Rose. Dam a Listed-placed 1m 2yo winner who was a half-sister to Grade 3-placed US 8-8.5f winner Hope Cross.

UNNAMED (IRE)
14/4 ch c Tamayuz - Rocana (Fastnet Rock)
Owner: Shadwell Estate Co Sales price: 125,000gns (Peter & Ross Doyle Bloodstock)

Half-brother to Group 2-placed 2020 7f 2yo winner Youth Spirit. Dam an unraced half-sister to Gimcrack Stakes winner Blaine, 6f 2yo Listed winner Bogart, Group 3-placed 2020 6f 2yo winner Legal Attack and useful UK/ Bahraini 6f-1m winner Byline.

AIDAN O'BRIEN

CONTARELLI CHAPEL (IRE)
27/1 gr f Caravaggio - Chenchikova (Sadler's Wells)
Owner: Michael Tabor Sales price: n/a

Half-sister to 2020 Prix de Diane/Nassau Stakes winner/Irish 1000 Guineas runner-up Fancy Blue, French 12/12.5f Listed winner Casterton and Irish 7f 2yo Listed winner Smuggler's Cove. Dam a useful Irish 7.5f 2yo winner who was a full sister to top-class 7-12f winner (six times at Group/Grade 1 level, including the Derby and Breeders' Cup Turf) High Chaparral and Dante Stakes winner Black Bear Island.

HEART TO HEART
9/4 b f Zoffany - Entreat (Pivotal)
Owner: Westerberg Ireland Sales price: 580,000gns (M V Magnier)

Half-sister to 2020 Commonwealth Cup winner Golden Horde, 6f Listed winner Exhort and very useful 2020 6-6.5f 2yo winner Line Of Departure. Dam a 9.5f 3yo winner who was a half-sister to smart multiple 7f-1m winner (including at Group 2/3 level) Producer; family of smart 2yos/Coronation Stakes winners Rizeena and Sophisticat.

Golden Horde

INSTRUMENTAL
5/2 ch c No Nay Never - Strut (Danehill Dancer)
Owner: Michael Tabor Sales price: 650,000gns (M V Magnier)

Half-brother to smart multiple 6f winner (including at Group 3/Listed level) Mince, useful UK/Hong Kong multiple 6f winner Flying Tourbillon and useful UK/Qatari 5f-1m winner Skate. Dam a Group 3-placed dual 5f 2yo winner (including at Listed level) who was a half-sister to Listed-placed dual 5f 2yo winner Vaunt; family of July Cup winner Mayson.

MADONNADELROSARIO (IRE)
10/3 br/gr f Caravaggio - Muravka (High Chaparral)
Owner: Westerberg Ireland Sales price: n/a

Closely related to useful Japanese 9-10f winner Unicorn Lion (by No Nay Never) and a half-sister to Coventry Stakes/Prix Morny winner The Wow Signal and Group 2/3-placed 6-7f 2yo winner (including at Listed level) Miss Infinity. Dam an unraced half-sister to Irish dual 1m Listed winner Tolpuddle out of a 6f/1m Listed-winning half-sister to Poule d'Essai des Pouliches winner Ta Rib.

MILWAUKEE (USA)
7/3 br c War Front - Ballydoyle (Galileo)
Owner: Westerberg Ireland Sales price: n/a

Half-brother to 2020 Irish 7f 2yo Listed winner Monday. Dam a high-class 7f-1m 2yo winner (including at Group 1 level)/1000 Guineas runner-up who was a full sister to very smart 6-10f winner (four times at Group 1 level, including the Irish 1000 Guineas) Misty For Me (later dam of triple Group 1 winners Roly Poly and U S Navy Flag (both by War Front)) and Irish 9.5f 3yo Listed winner Twirl.

PIMLICO (IRE)
29/3 b/br c No Nay Never - Gems (Haafhd)
Owner: Westerberg Ireland Sales price: €360,000 (Glenvale Stud)

Full brother to 7f 2yo Group 2 winner Mystery Power and a half-brother to Group 3-placed UK/French 6-7f winner Seaella and very useful multiple 6-10f winner Fayez. Dam a 12-13f winner who was a half-sister to triple 12/14f Listed winner Frank Sonata and 7f 2yo Listed winner Peaceful Paradise.

YET (USA)
23/1 br f War Front - Butterflies (Galileo)
Owner: Derrick Smith Sales price: n/a

First foal of a Group 3-placed Irish 1m 2yo winner who was a full sister to Group 3-placed Irish 1m 3yo winner Hanky Panky and a half-sister to top-class 6-10.5f winner (six times at Group 1 level, including the Eclipse Stakes and Juddmonte International Stakes)/2000 Guineas runner-up Giant's Causeway and 6f 2yo Group 2/3 winner You'resothrilling (later dam of 2000 Guineas winner Gleneagles and Irish 1000 Guineas winner Marvellous).

UNNAMED (USA)
1/2 ch f Dubawi - Alice Springs (Galileo)
Owner: Mrs John Magnier Sales price: n/a

First foal of a high-class 7f-1m winner (including three times at Group 1 level)/1000 Guineas third who was a full sister to Group 2/Listed-placed 12f 3yo winner Criteria, Group 3/Listed-placed Irish 1m 3yo winner Hence and Listed-placed Irish/Australian 9.5-12f winner Crocodile Rock.

UNNAMED (IRE)
5/5 b c Galileo - Atlantic Jewel (Fastnet Rock)
Owner: Laurie Macri/Mrs Magnier Et Al Sales price: n/a

Full brother to high-class 8-10f winner (including at Group 3 level) Russian

Emperor. Dam an Australian four-time 7-10f Group 1 winner who was closely related to Australian Thousand Guineas winner Commanding Jewel out of an Australian 7f-1m winning half-sister to the dam of 2020 Australian 5.5f Group 1 winner I Am Excited.

UNNAMED (IRE)
11/1 b f Galileo - Believe'n'Succeed (Exceed And Excel)
Owner: Mrs John Magnier Sales price: n/a

Full sister to Derby winner Anthony Van Dyck and a half-sister to New Zealand 6f Group 1 winner Bounding. Dam an Australian 5.5f 2yo Group 3 winner who was a full sister to high-class Australian 5-5.5f winner (including at Group 2/3 level) Kuroshio and Australian 5f 3yo Listed winner Agulhas.

UNNAMED (USA)
29/3 b f American Pharoah - Cherry Hinton (Green Desert)
Owner: Mrs John Magnier Sales price: n/a

Half-sister to Irish Oaks winner Bracelet, US 10f 3yo Grade 1 winner Athena, 7f 2yo Group 2 winner Wading (later dam of 7f 2yo Group 2 winner Just Wonderful) and Irish 1m 1f 3yo Group 3 winner Goddess. Dam a Group 3/Listed-placed maiden close relation to outstanding 7-12f winner (six times at Group 1 level, including the 2000 Guineas, Derby and Prix de l'Arc de Triomphe) Sea The Stars and Irish 6f 2yo Listed winner Born To Sea and a half-sister to several smart performers, notably Derby/King George VI And Queen Elizabeth Stakes winner Galileo.

UNNAMED (IRE)
21/4 gr f Galileo - Dialafara (Anabaa)
Owner: Michael Tabor Sales price: 850,000gns (McCalmont Bloodstock)

Full sister to Irish Derby/St Leger winner Capri, 2020 Irish 14f 3yo Group 3 winner/Irish Oaks third Passion, Irish 2m 3yo Group 3 winner Cypress Creek, useful Irish 7f 2yo winner Jamaica and 2020 Irish 1m 2yo winner Brazil. Dam a French 12.5f 3yo winner who was a half-sister to Group 3-placed French 7f 2yo winner Diaghan out of a Group 1-placed French 10-12.5f 3yo winner (including at Group 2/3 level).

UNNAMED (IRE)
14/3 b c Galileo - Diamond Fields (Fastnet Rock)
Owner: Mrs John Magnier Sales price: n/a

First foal of a Grade 2-placed Irish 6-7f winner (including at Group 3 level) who was a half-sister to Irish Derby winner Latrobe and Irish 10f 3yo Listed winner/Oaks runner-up Pink Dogwood out of a 6f 3yo winning half-sister to 7f 3yo

Group 3 winner/Cheveley Park Stakes runner-up Sunday Times (later dam of US dual 1m Grade 1 winner Newspaperofrecord).

UNNAMED (USA)
21/3 b f American Pharoah - Imagine (Sadler's Wells)
Owner: Michael Tabor Sales price: n/a

Full sister to 2020 French 1m 2yo Group 1 winner Van Gogh and a half-sister to Prix Jean-Luc Lagardere winner Horatio Nelson, UAE 1m Group 2 winner/ Irish 2000 Guineas third Viscount Nelson and 7f 2yo Group 2 winner Kitty Matcham. Dam an Irish 1000 Guineas/Oaks winner who was a full sister to Irish 8/9f Listed winner/Irish 1000 Guineas runner-up Strawberry Roan and a half-sister to Derby/King George VI And Queen Elizabeth Stakes winner Generous.

UNNAMED (IRE)
12/3 b f Galileo - Inca Princess (Holy Roman Emperor)
Owner: Michael Tabor Sales price: n/a

Full sister to French 7f 2yo Group 1 winner/Melbourne Cup runner-up Johannes Vermeer, Irish 1m 1f 3yo Group 2 winner Elizabeth Browning, 14f 3yo Listed winner Sapa Inca, 2020 Irish 7.5f 2yo winner/Dewhurst Stakes runner-up Wembley and Group 2-placed Irish 7f 2yo winner Petite Mustique. Dam an Irish 6f 2yo winner who was the daughter of a Ribblesdale Stakes-winning half-sister to Geoffrey Freer Stakes winner/St Leger third/Derby fourth Mr Combustible.

UNNAMED (IRE)
27/3 b c Caravaggio - Jigsaw (Galileo)
Owner: Mrs Magnier & M Tabor & D Smith & Mrs A M O'Brien Sales price: n/a

First foal of a maiden sister to Royal Lodge Stakes winner Mohawk out of a smart Irish 6f-1m winner (including at Group 3/Listed level) who was a half-sister to Listed-placed 7f 2yo winner Blue Angel (later dam of Dee Stakes winner Viren's Army).

UNNAMED (IRE)
4/1 b f Galileo - Legatissimo (Danehill Dancer)
Owner: Michael Tabor Sales price: n/a

First foal of a 1000 Guineas winner/Oaks runner-up who was the daughter of an Irish 10f 3yo winning sister to five-time 10f-2m 4f Group 1 winner (including the Irish Derby and Ascot Gold Cup)/Derby runner-up Fame And Glory and the unraced dam of Musidora Stakes winner Give And Take and half-sister to the dams of 14f 3yo Group 3 winner Gravitation (by Galileo) and Australian 9/9.5f

Listed winner Greatwood; family of Lockinge Stakes/Champion Stakes winner Farhh.

UNNAMED (IRE)
3/6 b f Galileo - Lillie Langtry (Danehill Dancer)
Owner: Mrs John Magnier Sales price: n/a

Full sister to very smart multiple 6-12f winner (seven times at Group 1 level, including the 1000 Guineas and Oaks) Minding, Irish 1m 3yo Group 3 winner Kissed By Angels and once-raced 2021 Irish 1m 3yo winner Empress Josephine. Dam a high-class 6f-1m winner (including twice at Group 1 level) who was closely related to Irish 1m 3yo Listed winner Count of Limonade.

UNNAMED (USA)
29/4 b f Quality Road - Marvellous (Galileo)
Owner: Michael Tabor Sales price: n/a

Half-sister to Group 3-placed Irish 6-7f 2yo winner (including at Listed level) Fort Myers. Dam an Irish 1000 Guineas winner who was a sister to four-time 7f/1m Group 1 winner (including the 2000 Guineas) Gleneagles, Group 1-placed 7f-1m winner (including twice at Group 1 level)/1000 Guineas third Happily, Australian dual 12f Group 2 winner Taj Mahal and Irish 7f 2yo winner/ Irish 2000 Guineas runner-up Vatican City.

UNNAMED (IRE)
20/1 b f Galileo - Prize Exhibit (Showcasing)
Owner: Westerberg Ireland Sales price: 2,800,000gns (M V Magnier)

First foal of a smart UK/US 6f-1m winner (including at Grade 2/3 level) who was a full sister to 2020 Sussex Stakes winner Mohaather and a half-sister to six winners including the dam of Queen Anne Stakes winner Accidental Agent out of a Listed-placed 5-7f winning half-sister to 6-7f winner/Prix Morny runner-up Gallagher.

UNNAMED (JPN)
21/1 b c Deep Impact - Promise To Be True (Galileo)
Owner: Mrs John Magnier Sales price: n/a

First foal of a Group 1-placed Irish 7f 2yo Group 3 winner who was a full sister to very smart 6-7f winner (including at Group 1 level)/1000 Guineas third Maybe (later dam of Racing Post Trophy/2000 Guineas winner Saxon Warrior (by Deep Impact)) and Group 2/3-placed Irish 10f 3yo winner Barbados out of a 5f 2yo Listed-winning three-parts sister to Oaks winner Dancing Rain.

UNNAMED
23/1 b f Galileo - Shastye (Danehill)
Owner: Westerberg Ireland Sales price: 3,400,000gns (M V Magnier)

Full sister to Juddmonte International Stakes winner/Derby third Japan, Hong Kong Vase/Grand Prix de Paris winner Mogul, Musidora Stakes/Oaks runner-up Secret Gesture and Irish 10f Group 3 winner Sir Isaac Newton. Dam a Listed-placed 12-13f winner who was a half-sister to Prix de l'Arc de Triomphe winner Sagamix and French 1m 2yo Group 1 winner/Prix de l'Arc de Triomphe third Sagacity.

UNNAMED (IRE)
27/2 b c Caravaggio - Sparrow (Oasis Dream)
Owner: Mrs John Magnier Sales price: n/a

Half-brother to Australian 10/12f Group 1 winner Sir Dragonet and useful 2020 Irish 1m 2yo winner Sir Lucan. Dam a Group 3-placed Irish 6f 2yo winner who was a half-sister to Cheshire Oaks winner/Oaks runner-up Wonder of Wonders (dam of 2020 Irish 7f 3yo Group 3 winner/Irish 1000 Guineas third So Wonderful) out of a 10.5f Group 3 winner/Oaks runner-up who was a full sister to Derby winner Galileo and a half-sister to six-time 8-12f Group 1 winner Sea The Stars.

UNNAMED (IRE)
17/4 ch c Galileo - Stellar Wind (Curlin)
Owner: Michael Tabor Sales price: n/a

First foal of a very smart US multiple 8-8.5f winner (including six times at Grade 1 level) who was the daughter of a US dual 8.5f winning half-sister to US 8/8.5f Listed winner Im Out First (later dam of US 6f 2yo Listed winner Im A Dixie Girl, herself the dam of US 8/8.5f Grade 1 winner Mor Spirit) and US 1m 1f Listed winner Zenith (later dam of US 8.5f 2yo Grade 1 winner/Breeders' Cup Juvenile third Great Hunter).

UNNAMED (IRE)
1/3 b c Australia - Sweepstake (Acclamation)
Owner: Derrick Smith Sales price: 575,000gns (M V Magnier)

Full brother to Irish dual 10f 3yo Group 3 winner/Derby fourth Broome. Dam a 5f 2yo Listed winner who was the daughter of a maiden sister to French 10f 3yo Group 3 winner Dust Dancer (grandam of Irish 6f 2yo Group 1 winner Zoffany and 6f Group 3 winner Projection) and half-sister to Fred Darling Stakes winner Bulaxie (later dam of Italian 10f Group 2 winner Claxon).

UNNAMED (USA)
27/4 b c American Pharoah - Tapestry (Galileo)
Owner: Mrs John Magnier Sales price: n/a

Half-brother to useful 7f 2yo winner New World Tapestry. Dam a Yorkshire Oaks winner/Irish Oaks runner-up who was a full sister to Irish 1m 2yo Group 3 winner John F Kennedy out of a 7f/1m 2yo Group 1 winner; excellent family of Kingmambo, Karakontie, Alpha Centauri, Study of Man etc.

UNNAMED (IRE)
16/2 b c Galileo - Vanzara (Redoute's Choice)
Owner: Derrick Smith Sales price: n/a

First foal of an unraced half-sister to French 10f 3yo Group 1 winners Vazira and Vadawina (later dam of French 12f 3yo Group 2 winner Vadamar and Irish 7f 2yo Group 3 winner/Racing Post Trophy third The Pentagon (by Galileo)) and French 10/10.5f 3yo Group 3 winner Vadapolina (later dam of Poule d'Essai des Pouliches runner-up Veda).

UNNAMED (IRE)
4/3 br/gr f Dark Angel - Wading (Montjeu)
Owner: Michael Tabor Sales price: n/a

Half-sister to Grade 1-placed 6f-1m winner (including at Group 2/3 level) Just Wonderful and Group 3/Listed-placed Irish 5-6f winner Lost Treasure. Dam a 7f 2yo Group 2 winner who was a full sister to Irish Oaks winner Bracelet and a three-parts sister to US 10f 3yo Grade 1 winner Athena and Irish 1m 1f 3yo Group 3 winner Goddess out of a Group 3/Listed-placed maiden three-parts sister to 2000 Guineas, Derby and Prix de l'Arc de Triomphe winner Sea The Stars.

UNNAMED (JPN)
14/1 b f Deep Impact - Winter (Galileo)
Owner: Derrick Smith Sales price: n/a

First foal of a very smart 7-10f winner (four times at Group 1 level, including the 1000 Guineas) who was a full sister to 2020 Irish 1m 3yo Listed winner Lovelier and useful Irish 7f 2yo winner Frosty out of a very useful 6-7f winner who was a half-sister to useful 7f-1m winner Lush Life.

UNNAMED (IRE)
27/4 ch f Galileo - You'resothrilling (Storm Cat)
Owner: Michael Tabor Sales price: n/a

Full sister to very smart 7f-1m winner (four times at Group 1 level, including the 2000 Guineas) Gleneagles, Irish 1000 Guineas winner Marvellous, 7f/1m 2yo Group 1 winner/1000 Guineas third Happily, Australian dual 10f Group 2 winner Taj Mahal, Irish 7f 2yo winner/Irish 2000 Guineas runner-up Vatican City and Grade 1-placed Irish 7f 2yo Group 3 winner Coolmore. Dam a 6f 2yo Group 2/3-winning sister to six-time 7-10.5f Group 1 winner Giant's Causeway.

DONNACHA O'BRIEN

ARTISTIC CHOICE
24/2 br c Caravaggio - Chicago Girl (Azamour)
Owner: Atlantic Thoroughbreds Sales price: 120,000gns (M V Magnier)

Half-brother to 6f 2yo winner Roxy Art. Dam a Group 3/Listed-placed maiden half-sister to smart 6f-1m winner (including at Listed level) Army of Angels, Group 2/Listed-placed 5f 2yo winner Seraphina, Listed-placed 5f 3yo winner Alegranza and the dam of Cheveley Park Stakes winner Serious Attitude out of a 5f 2yo winning half-sister to Prix de la Foret winner Mount Abu.

DON JULIO (IRE)
23/3 b c Caravaggio - Remember Alexander (Teofilo)
Owner: Atlantic Thoroughbreds Sales price: 110,000gns (Donnacha O'Brien)

Third foal of an Irish 7f 2yo Group 3 winner who was a half-sister to 6f 2yo Group 2/3 winner Memory (later dam of US 2m Grade 2 winner Call To Mind and 7f 2yo Group 3 winner Recorder) and six other winners out of a French/US 7f-1m winner.

EL DESPERADO (FR)
26/4 b c Iffraaj - Larceny (Cape Cross)
Owner: Atlantic Thoroughbreds Sales price: €150,000 (Horse France)

Full brother to smart 8-12f winner (including at Group 2/3 level) The Black Princess and a half-brother to useful French 10-12f winner Lucelle (dam of useful 2020 1m 2yo winner Titian (by Iffraaj)). Dam a once-raced maiden close relation to Prix du Jockey Club winner Lawman and a half-sister to Prix de Diane winner Latice (later dam of 7f/1m Listed winner Fencing).

FIRST EMPEROR
6/3 b c Galileo - Sky Lantern (Red Clubs)
Owner: Rockcliffe Stud & Coolmore Sales price: n/a

Half-brother to Irish 10f 3yo winner Gentile Bellini and 2020 12f 3yo winner Noonday Gun. Dam a high-class 6f-1m winner (four times at Group 1 level, including the 1000 Guineas) who was a half-sister to Irish 6f 2yo Group 3 winner Arctic, Queen's Vase winner Shanty Star and 6/7f Listed winner Hinton Admiral.

PIZ BADILE (IRE)
3/2 b/br c Ulysses - That Which Is Not (Elusive Quality)
Owner: Flaxman Stables Ireland Ltd Sales price: n/a

First foal of a Group 2-placed French 9-10.5f winner (including at Listed level) who was a half-sister to the maiden dam of Gimcrack Stakes/Champagne Stakes winner Threat out of an Irish 10.5f Group 1-winning half-sister to Oaks winner Light Shift (later dam of Eclipse Stakes and Juddmonte International Stakes winner Ulysses), French dual 12f Group 2 winner Limnos, French 10f 3yo Listed winner Burning Sunset (grandam of US four-time 11/12f Grade 1 winner/Derby runner-up Main Sequence) and the dam of Prix Ganay winner/ Prix de l'Arc de Triomphe second Cloth of Stars.

RULE SEVENTEEN (IRE)
13/3 b/br c No Nay Never - Sweetasever (Power)
Owner: Mrs A M O'Brien Sales price: n/a

First foal of an Irish 7f-1m winner who was a half-sister to Listed-placed 8-12.5f winner Jumellea out of a twice-raced maiden close relation to the dam of Moyglare Stud Stakes winner Intricately and half-sister to seven-time 7f-1m Group 1 winner (including the 2000 Guineas and Sussex Stakes) Rock of Gibraltar, Group 3-placed Irish 1m 2yo winner Nell Gwyn and very useful Irish 6f 2yo winner Great Pyramid.

SIMPLY GLORIOUS (USA)
18/4 b f War Front - Misty For Me (Galileo)
Owner: Derrick Smith Sales price: n/a

Full sister to high-class 6-7f winner (including the Dewhurst Stakes and July Cup)/Irish 2000 Guineas runner-up U S Navy Flag, high-class 6f-1m winner (including three times at Group 1 level)/Irish 1000 Guineas runner-up Roly Poly and 2020 Irish 6f 2yo winner Elizabethan and a half-sister to US 1m 3yo Grade 3 winner Cover Song. Dam an Irish 1000 Guineas winner who was a half-sister to French 1m 2yo Group 1 winner/1000 Guineas second Ballydoyle.

TEA PARTY (IRE)
17/3 gr f Caravaggio - Airwave (Air Express)
Owner: Derrick Smith Sales price: n/a

Half-sister to Irish 9.5f 3yo Group 3 winner Aloof, Irish 5f 2yo Listed winner/ Queen Mary Stakes runner-up Meow (later dam of Dewhurst Stakes and 2000

Guineas winner Churchill and Cheveley Park Stakes winner Clemmie), 2020 Irish 1m 3yo Listed winner Keats and French 1m Listed winner Orator. Dam a very smart 5f-1m winner (including the Cheveley Park Stakes) who was a half-sister to Nunthorpe Stakes winner Jwala.

UNCONQUERABLE (IRE)
20/3 b c Churchill - Rien Ne Vas Plus (Oasis Dream)
Owner: Atlantic Thoroughbreds Sales price: 210,000gns (M V Magnier)

Fourth foal of a maiden half-sister to Derby winner North Light, dual 2m Group 3 winner Cover Up and 12f Listed winner Researched out of a Prix du Cadran-winning half-sister to the dam of French 12f Group 1 winner Gamut and the grandam of 2000 Guineas winner/Derby runner-up Golan and Dante Stakes winner/Derby runner-up Tartan Bearer.

UNNAMED (IRE)
21/2 br f Caravaggio - All For Glory (Giant's Causeway)
Owner: Mrs John Magnier Sales price: n/a

Half-sister to Irish 9.5f 3yo Listed winner/Oaks third Alluringly and Group 2-placed Irish 6f 2yo winner Toogoodtobetrue (dam of Group 3-placed 2020 Irish 1m 1f 2yo winner Carlisle Bay). Dam an unraced half-sister to Cheshire Oaks winner/Oaks runner-up Wonder of Wonders (dam of 2020 Irish 1m 3yo Group 3 winner/Irish 1000 Guineas third So Wonderful) out of a 10.5f Group 3 winner/Oaks runner-up who was a sister to Derby winner Galileo.

UNNAMED (IRE)
10/5 b f Galileo - Butterfly Cove (Storm Cat)
Owner: Mrs John Magnier Sales price: n/a

Full sister to very smart 6-10f winner (four times at Group 1 level, including the Irish 1000 Guineas) Misty For Me (later dam of triple Group 1 winners Roly Poly and U S Navy Flag), high-class 7f-1m 2yo winner (including at Group 1 level)/1000 Guineas runner-up Ballydoyle and Irish 9.5f 3yo Listed winner Twirl. Dam an unraced half-sister to Prix Morny/Phoenix Stakes winner Fasliyev.

UNNAMED (IRE)
22/3 br c No Nay Never - Instinctively (Cape Cross)
Owner: Mrs John Magnier Sales price: n/a

First foal of an unraced half-sister to the dam of 2020 5f 2yo Listed winner York Express out of a French 12f 3yo winner who was a sister to Greenham Stakes winner Yalaietanee and a half-sister to Molecomb Stakes winner Sahara Star (later dam of Flying Childers Stakes winner Land of Dreams, herself the dam of five-time 6/7f Group 1 winner Dream Ahead and grandam of Cheveley Park Stakes winner Fairyland).

UNNAMED (IRE)
9/4 b f Galileo - Missvinski (Stravinsky)
Owner: Mrs John Magnier Sales price: n/a

Full sister to 2020 Irish 1000 Guineas winner/Prix de Diane third Peaceful, Group 3-placed Irish 7-9.5f winner (including at Listed level) Easter and two other winners. Dam a Group 1-placed French 6-6.5f winner (including twice at Listed level) from the family of very smart middle-distance performer Cacoethes.

UNNAMED (JPN)
1/4 b c Caravaggio - Peeping Fawn (Danehill)
Owner: Derrick Smith Sales price: n/a

Half-brother to Chesham Stakes winner/Fillies' Mile runner-up September, Irish 6f 2yo winner/Coventry Stakes third Sir John Hawkins, 2020 Irish 1m 2yo winner Willow and the maiden dam of French dual 1m Listed winner Alzire. Dam a very smart 8-12f winner (four times at Group 1 level, including the Irish Oaks)/Oaks runner-up who was a half-sister to French 1m 2yo Group 1 winner Thewayyouare.

UNNAMED (USA)
3/2 b c War Front - Together Forever (Galileo)
Owner: Mrs John Magnier Sales price: n/a

Full brother to 2020 Irish 7f 2yo Group 3 winner Military Style and Listed-placed 7f 2yo winner King of Athens. Dam a Fillies' Mile winner who was a full sister to Oaks winner Forever Together and a half-sister to very smart 6f-1m winner (including at Group 1 level) Lord Shanakill.

JOSEPH O'BRIEN

COMET LINE (IRE)
4/4 b f No Nay Never - Honourably (Galileo)
Owner: John C Oxley Sales price: 475,000gns (Canary Bloodstock)

Full sister to Listed-placed 2020 US 5-5.5f 2yo winner Amanzi Yimpilo. Dam a once-raced maiden sister to useful Irish 12-13f winner Botany Bay and half-sister to Listed-placed Irish 7f 2yo winner Coolibah out of an unraced half-sister to Irish 10f 3yo Listed winner Dabtiya (grandam of Listed winners

Di Fede (7f, twice) and Dibayani (11f) and great-grandam of 7f/1m 2yo Listed winner Washaar).

CYNISCA (IRE)
14/3 ch f Footstepsinthesand - Lisfannon (Bahamian Bounty)
Owner: Thoroughbred Racing Syndicate Sales price: £44,000 (Durcan Bloodstock/JP O'Brien)

Half-sister to Irish 5f 2yo winner Mironica (later dam of Irish 5f 2yo Listed winner Sirici), useful 5f 2yo winner Dress Up and three other winners. Dam a maiden half-sister to very useful UK/UAE 5f-1m winner (including at Listed level) Stunned, 5/6f Listed winner Dazed And Amazed and useful 5-6f 2yo winner Quite A Thing (later dam of Irish 7/7.5f Group 3 winner Yulong Gold Fairy).

IN ECSTASY (IRE)
29/3 gr c Caravaggio - Longing (Galileo)
Owner: P M Brant Sales price: £205,000 (White Birch Farm/Demi O'Byrne)

First foal of an Irish 1m 1f 3yo winner who was a full sister to very useful Irish 8.5-12f winner Astronomer and a half-sister to Group 2-placed 6f-1m winner (including at Group 3/Listed level) Ladys First out of a French 10.5f 3yo winning half-sister to the dam of French 10.5/12f Listed winner Golden Wood.

KAPRALOVA (USA)
12/2 b/br f War Front - Lerici (Woodman)
Owner: Mrs M V Magnier & Mrs Paul Shanahan Sales price: $340,000 (Not Sold)

Full sister to US dual 10f Grade 1 winner Avenge and Group 3/Listed-placed dual 5f 2yo winner Pistoletto and a half-sister to US 7.5f 3yo Listed winner Lira. Dam a US 1m 1f 3yo winner who was a half-sister to the unraced dam of US 8.5f Grade 3 winner/Travers Stakes runner-up Grasshopper.

MARIA NOVELLA (IRE)
2/4 gr f Caravaggio - Me And Miss Jones (Smarty Jones)
Owner: Paget Bloodstock Limited Sales price: 130,000gns (BBA Ireland)

Three-parts sister to 6f 2yo winner/Queen Mary Stakes third Take Me With You (by Scat Daddy) and stakes-placed US dual 6f winner Just Ain't Right. Dam an unraced daughter of a US dual 6f 2yo Grade 3 winner who was a full sister to US 6f Grade 1 winner Wildcat Heir.

NATIONAL GALLERY (IRE)
1/4 br/gr c Caravaggio - Dora de Green (Green Tune)
Owner: Mrs A M O'Brien Sales price: 190,000gns (Vendor)

Half-brother to Group 1-placed 5-6f winner (including at Listed level) Forever In Dreams. Dam a maiden half-sister to very smart multiple 5-6.5f winner (including five times at Group 1 level) Marchand d'Or, very useful 2020 French 5.5-6f winner Gold Step and useful French 1m 2yo winner Saga d'Or.

ROSSO CORSA (USA)
22/4 ch f Kitten's Joy - Joya Real (Eddington)
Owner: Scott C Heider Sales price: $800,000 (Heider Family Stables)

First foal of a US triple 5.5f stakes winner who was a half-sister to US 1m 1f Grade 3 winner La Dolce Vita and Grade 3-placed US 8-9f winner Bijou out of a once-raced maiden daughter of a Canadian Oaks-winning half-sister to 1988 Canadian Champion three-year-old colt Regal Intention.

ROYAL STATUS (IRE)
5/2 b c Wootton Bassett - Holy Cat (Kitten's Joy)
Owner: Mrs A M O'Brien Sales price: 140,000gns (John & Jake Warren)

First foal of a Group 3-placed Irish 6f 2yo winner who was a half-sister to stakes-placed US 5f 2yo winner Lucky Lurie out of an unraced sister to four-time US 7-9f Listed winner Uncle T Seven, a close relation to US 1m 1f 3yo Grade 3 winner Wishful Tomcat and a half-sister to the dam of US 7/9f Grade 3 winner Rated R Superstar and the grandam of 2020 US 8.5f 3yo Grade 1 winner Speech.

SANGRIA (IRE)
15/4 b f Gutaifan - Wojha (Pivotal)
Owner: Mrs M V Magnier & Mrs Paul Shanahan Sales price: 180,000gns (Avenue Bloodstock For MV Magnier)

Half-sister to 2020 Irish 5.5f 3yo Listed winner Punita Arora. Dam a 1m 3yo winner who was a half-sister to Fred Darling Stakes winner Muthabara and Group 3/Listed-placed 7f 2yo winner Mustadeem out of a 1m 3yo winning half-sister to Greenham Stakes winner Muqbil and Group 2-placed 6-7f 2yo winner Mostaqeleh (later dam of high-class sprinter Matera Sky and Coventry Stakes third Murillo).

SCARLETT DUBOIS (IRE)
12/2 b f Fastnet Rock - Terrific (Galileo)
Owner: Moyglare Stud Farm Ltd Sales price: n/a

Half-sister to very useful 6f-1m winner Tranchee. Dam a Listed-placed Irish 7f-1m 2yo winner who was a full sister to US 1m 1f 3yo Grade 1 winner/1000 Guineas runner-up Together and a half-sister to French 1m 2yo Group 1 winner/Irish Derby third/Derby fourth Jan Vermeer and the maiden dam of 2020 German 7f 3yo Listed winner Cloud Surfing.

SCHIELE (IRE)
22/4 gr c Dark Angel - The Hermitage (Kheleyf)
Owner: P M Brant Sales price: £355,000 (White Birch Farm/D L O'Byrne)

Full brother to Group 2-placed dual 6f 2yo winner (including at Group 3 level) Angel's Hideaway and Group 2/3-placed 6f 2yo winner Perfect Angel. Dam a Listed-placed 5f 2yo winner who was a half-sister to Group 1-placed 7-11.5f winner (including at Listed level)/Oaks third Crown of Light (later dam of 14f/2m Listed winner Balkan Knight), 1m 2yo Listed winner Alboostan and the maiden dam of 1m 1f Group 3 winner/Racing Post Trophy runner-up Charlie Farnsbarns.

SELADOR (IRE)
3/2 br/gr f Dark Angel - Loreto (Holy Roman Emperor)
Owner: Blue Devil Racing Stable LLC Sales price: 115,000gns (O'Byrne & Grassick/Dan Hayden)

Half-sister to useful Irish 1m 2yo Flat/2m hurdle winner Brutal. Dam a dual 1m 3yo winner who was closely related to 7f 2yo Group 3 winner Drumfire and a half-sister to Irish 7f 2yo Group 3 winner Cabaret (later dam of Vertem Futurity Trophy/2000 Guineas winner Magna Grecia and 2020 Dewhurst Stakes winner St Mark's Basilica) and Group 2-placed UK/Hong Kong 6-7f winner (including at Listed level) Ho Choi.

SNAPIUS (IRE)
30/5 b c Buratino - Snap Alam (Alamshar)
Owner: J P Farrell Sales price: €30,000 (Vendor)

Full brother to Group 2-placed 2020 Irish 7.5f-1m 2yo winner Snapraeterea and a half-brother to Group 3/Listed-placed Irish 1m 3yo winner Snapraeceps. Dam an Irish 6.5-9f winner from the good Aga Khan family of Breeders' Cup Turf/Champion Stakes winner Kalanisi.

SONG SONG BLUE (IRE)
21/4 br f Caravaggio - Runway Dancer (Dansili)
Owner: Justin Carthy Sales price: 55,000gns (Donnacha O'Brien)

Half-sister to Middle Park Stakes winner Astaire and useful Irish 12f 3yo winner Shoshone Warrior. Dam an unraced half-sister to Gimcrack Stakes winner Bannister and Listed-placed 5-6f 2yo winner Roo (later dam of 6-7f winner/Prix Morny second Gallagher, grandam of 2020 Sussex Stakes winner Mohaather and great-grandam of Queen Anne Stakes winner Accidental Agent).

UXMAL (IRE)
23/4 b c Galileo - Only Mine (Pour Moi)
Owner: Flaxman Stables Ireland Ltd Sales price: n/a

First foal of a Group 2-placed multiple 6f winner (including at Group 3/Listed level) who was a half-sister to useful 8-12f Flat/2m hurdle winner Miner's Lamp out of an Irish 10.5f Listed-winning sister to 10f Listed winner True To Form.

WISH FOR ME (IRE)
10/3 b f Mehmas - Big Boned (Street Sense)
Owner: John C Oxley Sales price: £330,000 (Hugo Merry Bloodstock)

Half-sister to 2020 German 6f Group 3 winner K Club and Listed-placed Irish 5-6f winner Back To Brussels. Dam a maiden half-sister to US 6f 3yo Listed winner Cool Bullet and US 7f-1m winner/Chesham Stakes third Caper's Touch out of a US 6f 3yo Listed winner.

UNNAMED (IRE)
14/3 ch f Dubawi - Bracelet (Montjeu)
Owner: Michael Tabor Sales price: n/a

Fourth foal of an Irish Oaks winner who was a full sister to 7f 2yo Group 2 winner Wading and a three-parts sister to US 10f 3yo Grade 1 winner Athena and Irish 1m 1f 3yo Group 3 winner Goddess out of a Group 3/Listed-placed maiden three-parts sister to six-time 8-12f Group 1 winner Sea The Stars and half-sister to Group/Grade 1 winners Galileo, Black Sam Bellamy and My Typhoon.

UNNAMED (IRE)
16/3 b f Galileo - Dawn Wall (Fastnet Rock)
Owner: Magnier/Tabor/Smith/Flaxman Sales price: n/a

First foal of an Australian 1m 3yo Group 3 winner who was closely related to Grade 1-placed 6f-1m winner (including at Group 3/Listed level) Osaila and

Irish 1m 1f 3yo Group 3 winner Obama Rule out of an unraced three-parts sister to Prix de l'Arc de Triomphe winner Carnegie.

UNNAMED (IRE)
4/2 b f Zoffany - Renaissance Rio (Captain Rio)
Owner: Kevin Blake & Dan Hayden Sales price: n/a

Half-sister to useful 6-7f winner Myboyhenry. Dam a once-raced maiden close relation to Group 3-placed multiple 6f winner (including twice at Listed level) Artistic Jewel and a half-sister to 7f 3yo Listed winner Ponty Rossa; family of high-class sprinters Equiano and Encore d'Or.

UNNAMED (IRE)
9/5 b c Caravaggio - Small Sacrifice (Sadler's Wells)
Owner: Mrs Magnier & M Tabor & D Smith & Mrs A M O'Brien Sales price: n/a

Half-brother to 2020 National Stakes winner/Dewhurst Stakes third Thunder Moon, smart 8-10f winner (including at Listed level) Anticipation and very useful 7-12f winner Jaqen H'Ghar. Dam an unraced sister to the dam of 6f 2yo Group 3/Listed winner Love Lockdown and half-sister to Group 3-placed 7f 2yo winner Aahaykid and the dam of French 1m 2yo Group 1 winner Vert de Grece.

BRYAN SMART

BOND CHAIRMAN
2/3 br c Kodiac - Wunders Dream (Averti)
Owner: Bond Thoroughbred Ltd Sales price: 120,000gns (B Smart)

Closely related to Listed-placed 5f 2yo winner Fire Eyes (by Exceed And Excel) and a half-brother to 6f 3yo Listed winner Inyordreams and four other winners. Dam a smart multiple 5f 2yo winner (including at Group 2/3 level) who was a half-sister to Group 2-placed 5f-1m winner (including at Group 3/Listed level) Grecian Dancer (later dam of 1m 1f Group 3 winner Muffri'Ha) and the dam of 5f 3yo Listed winner Fashion Queen.

DRAWDOWN
27/3 b f Profitable - Choisette (Choisir)
Owner: Crossfields Racing Sales price: 23,000gns (Tim Easterby)

Half-sister to very useful multiple 6-7f winner Flying Pursuit, useful triple 6f winner Straightothepoint, fairly useful 5-6f winner Spirited Guest and 2020 7-7.5f 3yo winner Ventura Rascal. Dam a triple 5f winner who was a half-sister to very useful multiple 6f winner Fast Shot out of a useful 5.5f 2yo winning half-sister to 6f 2yo Listed winner Lipstick.

HIGH OPINION
5/4 b c Hellvelyn - Vanity (Thatching)
Owner: The Smart Set Sales price: £18,000 (Bryan Smart Racing)

Half-brother to Group 1-placed 5-6f winner (including at Group 3/Listed level) Lesson In Humility (later dam of 2020 Irish 12f 3yo Group 3 winner/Irish Derby runner-up Tiger Moth and Irish 5f 2yo Listed winner/Norfolk Stakes second Coach House), 7f 2yo Group 3 winner Poet's Vanity and 1m Listed winner Boastful (later dam of 5f 2yo Listed winner Stage Play). Dam a maiden half-sister to 7.5f 2yo Listed winner Ffestiniog (later dam of smart performers Border Patrol, Boston Lodge and Eisteddfod).

INSTINCTION
12/2 b f Brazen Beau - Spontaneity (Holy Roman Emperor)
Owner: Crossfields Racing Sales price: 16,000gns (Bryan Smart Racing)

Half-sister to useful 6f-1m winner Masaru and 2020 5f 2yo winner Equate. Dam a maiden sister to very useful Irish 5-6f winner Nero Emperor, a close relation to very useful UK/UAE 5-7f winner Hajoum and a half-sister to Group 2-placed triple 5f winner (including twice at Listed level) Swiss Lake (later dam of high-class sprinters Swiss Diva, Swiss Dream and Swiss Spirit).

POLITICISM
27/2 b f Churchill - Mythicism (Oasis Dream)
Owner: Crossfields Racing Sales price: 40,000gns (TMB Bloodstock)

Half-sister to Prix Robert Papin winner Tis Marvellous, Listed-placed multiple 6f winner Mythmaker and three other winners. Dam a 6f 2yo winner who was a full sister to useful 5-6f winner Point of Woods out of a Queen Mary Stakes-winning half-sister to Queen Mary Stakes winner Romantic Liaison.

PRINCESS KARINE
11/3 b f Aclaim - Hakuraa (Elnadim)
Owner: N Derbyshire & Partner Sales price: £10,000 (Bryan Smart Racing)

Half-sister to very useful 5-6f winner Green Power and dual 7f 2yo winner Antagonize. Dam an unraced half-sister to useful prolific 6f winner Highly Sprung out of a Listed-placed Irish 6f 3yo winning half-sister to Coventry Stakes winner Hellvelyn, Listed-placed triple 5f winner Golden Bounty and the grandam of 6f 2yo Listed winner/Middle Park Stakes third Summer Sands.

PROJECT DANTE
26/2 ch c Showcasing - Thatsallimsaying (Dandy Man)
Owner: Bond Thoroughbred Ltd Sales price: 115,000gns (B Smart)

Half-brother to 2020 6f 2yo winner/Richmond Stakes third Lauded. Dam a
Listed-placed 6f 2yo winner who was the daughter of an unraced half-sister
to Listed-placed prolific 6.5-7f winner Master Robbie and Listed-placed UK/US
5-8.5f winner Julius Geezer; family of Lockinge Stakes winner Peeress.

SIR MICHAEL STOUTE

ASSESSMENT
4/4 b c Kingman - Clinical (Motivator)
Owner: Cheveley Park Stud Sales price: n/a

Full brother to 2020 7f 3yo winner Clinician, a three-parts brother to useful
5-6f 3yo winner Procedure (by Invincible Spirit) and a half-brother to Group
2-placed UK/Hong Kong 6-7f winner Lockheed. Dam a smart 7-8.5f winner
(including at Group 3/Listed level) who was a half-sister to 7f 2yo Group 3
winner Cupid's Glory, 8/10f 3yo Listed winner Courting (later dam of 1m Listed
winner Fury) and 6f Listed winner Prescription.

BELIEVE IN STARS (IRE)
17/4 b c Make Believe - Cruck Realta (Sixties Icon)
Owner: Saeed Suhail Sales price: 175,000gns (Blandford Bloodstock)

Full brother to Group 2-placed 5-10.5f winner (including three times at Group
3 level) Rose of Kildare. Dam a 10f 3yo Listed winner who was a full sister to
useful 7f-2m winner Davy's Dilemma out of a 10f 3yo winner; family of Fillies'
Mile winner Red Bloom.

CRYSTAL CAPRICE (IRE)
17/3 b f Frankel - Crystal Zvezda (Dubawi)
Owner: Sir Evelyn de Rothschild Sales price: n/a

Second foal of a 10f 3yo Listed winner who was a half-sister to very smart 10-
12f winner (including the Prince of Wales's Stakes) Crystal Ocean, high-class
7-12f winner (including at Grade 1 level) Hillstar and high-class 10-12f winner
(including at Group 2/3 level) Crystal Capella out of a 7f 2yo Listed-winning
half-sister to 12f 3yo Listed winner Waila.

DUNGEON
28/2 b c Dubawi - Dank (Dansili)
Owner: James Wigan & T Hirosaki Sales price: n/a

Third foal of a Breeders' Cup Filly & Mare Turf winner who was closely related to Hong Kong Cup winner/Derby runner-up Eagle Mountain and a half-sister to Prix Marcel Boussac winner Sulk (later dam of UAE 1m 1f Group 1 winner Ibn Battuta), 1m 3yo Listed winner Wallace and the unraced dam of Irish 6f 2yo Group 3 winner Bye Bye Birdie (herself the dam of 2020 Irish 14f 3yo Group 3 winner Delphi).

EVERY BLUE MOON (IRE)
25/2 ch f Lope de Vega - Celestial Lagoon (Sunday Silence)
Owner: Niarchos Family Sales price: n/a

Half-sister to Group 3-placed French 6-9f winner (including at Listed level) Maria Gabriella (later dam of French 1m 3yo Listed winner Mariafoot), Group 3-placed French 7.5f-1m winner (including at Listed level) Night of Light and Group 2-placed 7-10.5f winner Highest Ground. Dam a French 7f 2yo winner who was a half-sister to 2m Listed winner Justice Belle.

IN PLAY
19/1 b c Starspangledbanner - Partitia (Bated Breath)
Owner: Juddmonte Sales price: n/a

First foal of a useful dual 6f 2yo winner who was a half-sister to 2020 Irish 7f 2yo winner Angel Palm out of a 6f 3yo winning sister to Gimcrack Stakes winner Showcasing, Group 3/Listed-placed 6f 2yo winner Tendu and Listed-placed dual 6f 3yo winner Bouvardia and half-sister to 6f 3yo Listed winner/Jersey Stakes runner-up Camacho.

INFINITIVE
15/3 b f Ulysses - Integral (Dalakhani)
Owner: Cheveley Park Stud Sales price: n/a

Half-sister to very useful 7f-1m winner Fundamental and 2020 12f 3yo winner Inherent. Dam a high-class multiple 1m winner (including twice at Group 1 level) who was a half-sister to Listed-placed 7f-1m winner Provenance out of a Matron Stakes-winning half-sister to dual 1m Group 2 winner Chic.

INVIGILATE
5/4 b f Acclamation - Exemplify (Dansili)
Owner: Juddmonte Sales price: n/a

Full sister to high-class 6.5f-1m winner (including the Breeders' Cup Mile) Expert Eye and a half-sister to 2020 7f 2yo winner Duty of Care and 7f 3yo winner Clerisy. Dam a French 1m 2yo winner who was a half-sister to Cheveley Park Stakes/1000 Guineas winner Special Duty out of an unraced sister to US seven-time 7-9f Grade 1 winner Sightseek and half-sister to US 9/10f Grade 1 winner Tates Creek.

KIRILENKO
8/3 b f Ulysses - Marenko (Exceed And Excel)
Owner: Cheveley Park Stud Sales price: n/a

Second foal of a Group 2-placed 7f-1m winner (including at Group 3 level) who was a half-sister to very useful 8-10f 3yo winner Davydenko, 6f 2yo winners Panova and Vesnina and 7f 2yo winners Melnikova and Potapova out of a Listed-placed 7f 3yo winning sister to the dams of Group 3 winners Spangled (7f) and Zonderland (1m).

NEW DIMENSION
1/4 b c Ulysses - Azhar (Exceed And Excel)
Owner: Flaxman Stables Ireland Ltd Sales price: 120,000gns (Flaxman Stables Ireland)

Second foal of a 6f 2yo winner who was the daughter of an unraced sister to Breeders' Cup Mile winner Domedriver and half-sister to French 10f Group 3 winner Tau Ceti and the grandam of Prix Marcel Boussac winner Albigna; family of 2000 Guineas/Irish Derby winner/Derby runner-up El Gran Senor and Dewhurst Stakes winner Try My Best.

RED RAMBLER
5/4 ch c Iffraaj - Blushing Rose (Dalakhani)
Owner: Sir Evelyn de Rothschild Sales price: n/a

First foal of a useful 7-10f winner who was the daughter of a Group 2-placed 6f 2yo winning half-sister to dual 6f winner After John and 7-14f winner Kingarrick out of a maiden half-sister to Eclipse Stakes/Juddmonte International Stakes winner Notnowcato.

SEE (USA)
12/4 br f War Front - Faufiler (Galileo)
Owner: Flaxman Stables Ireland Ltd Sales price: n/a

Second foal of a Grade 2-placed French/US 8-10f winner (including at Grade 3/ Listed level) who was a full sister to Australian 10f Group 2 winner/Racing Post Trophy runner-up Yucatan and Irish 10f 3yo Listed winner Mount Everest and a half-sister to French 5f Group 2 winner Planet Five out of a triple 1m Group/ Grade 1 winner/1000 Guineas runner-up.

TRANSPIRE (FR)
27/2 b c Frankel - Estimate (Monsun)
Owner: The Queen Sales price: n/a

Half-brother to useful 13.5-14.5f 3yo winner Calculation. Dam a high-class 12f-2m 4f winner (including the Ascot Gold Cup) who was a half-sister to Ascot Gold Cup winner Enzeli, Irish Oaks winer Ebadiyla, Irish 7f 2yo Group 1 winner Ebadiya and Listed-placed Irish 9.5-12f 3yo winner Eytarna (later dam of Irish 10f Group 2 winner/Irish Oaks third Eziyra).

UNNAMED (USA)
4/4 b c Kitten's Joy - Uniformly Yours (Grand Slam)
Owner: Shadwell Estate Co Sales price: $500,000 (Shadwell Estate Company)

Half-brother to US 8.5f 2yo Grade 2 winner Selflessly and US 7f 3yo Listed winner Enchanted Ghost. Dam a maiden half-sister to Canadian 8.5f Stakes winner Sans Souci Island (later dam of US/Canadian 8.5f Grade 3 winner River Seven) and Listed-placed US/Canadian 8.5f winner Nomistakeaboutit (later dam of Vintage Stakes runner-up Stentorian).

OTHERS

CITYJET (IRE)
19/2 b c Air Force Blue - Pellucid (Excelebration)
Trainer: Martyn Meade Owner: Mrs Perle O'Rourke & Manton Park Sales price: 105,000gns (D Farrington)

First foal of a Group 3-placed 6f 2yo winner who was a half-sister to high-class 5f-1m winner (including at Group 2/3 level) Space Traveller out of a 12f 3yo winning daughter of a 7f 2yo winner who was a half-sister to Fillies' Mile winner/Irish 1000 Guineas runner-up Crystal Music, May Hill Stakes winner Solar Crystal and Lancashire Oaks winner State Crystal.

FEEL (USA)
4/3 b f Into Mischief - Beta Leo (A.P. Indy)
Trainer: Pascal Bary Owner: Flaxman Stables Ireland Ltd Sales price: n/a

Half-sister to Prix de Diane winner Senga and French 1m 3yo Listed winner Bolting. Dam a French 5.5f 2yo winning daughter of a Prix Marcel Boussac winner who was a half-sister to US triple 8.5-11f Grade 3 winner Snake Mountain, French 6f 2yo Group 3 winner Loving Kindness, French 7f 3yo Listed winner Glia (grandam of four-time US 8.5-10f Grade 1 winner Emollient) and the unraced dam of Prix de l'Arc de Triomphe winner Bago and French 8/9f Group 1 winner Maxios.

GOZAK (FR)
5/4 b c Goken - Cosachope (Soave)
Trainer: Philippe Sogorb Owner: Guy Pariente Sales price: n/a

Second foal of a French 5f 2yo Group 3 winner who was the daughter of a twice-raced maiden half-sister to useful French 5-7f winner Mister Chop and the grandam of 2020 French 5f 2yo Group 3/Listed winner Livachope (by Goken); family of dual 5f 2yo Listed winner/Flying Childers Stakes runner-up Well Done Fox and 2020 6f 2yo winner/Dewhurst Stakes fourth Devilwala.

ILIC (IRE)
4/5 b c Iffraaj - Impressionnante (Danehill)
Trainer: Freddy Head Owner: Wertheimer & Frere Sales price: n/a

Half-brother to Prix du Jockey Club winner/Prix de l'Arc de Triomphe third Intello and useful French 8-9.5f winner No Mood. Dam a French 1m 3yo Group 2 winner/Poule d'Essai des Pouliches runner-up who was closely related to French dual 5f Group 3 winner Only Answer and the dam of 2020 French 5f 2yo Group 3 winner Kalahara and French 6f 2yo Group 3 winner Sasparella and a half-sister to 8/10f Grade 1 winner Mondialiste.

LOCKE (IRE)
31/1 b c Muhaarar - Single (Singspiel)
Trainer: Brian Meehan Sales price: Manton Thoroughbreds VI Sales price: £40,000 (Sam Sangster Bloodstock)

Half-brother to Group 3/Listed-placed French 6.5-7f winner Duhail. Dam a Group 3-placed French dual 1m winner who was a half-sister to Irish 7f 2yo Group 3 winner Kenya, French 1m 2yo Group 3 winner Zantenda and Listed-placed French dual 7f winner Elusif out of a Listed-placed French 5f 2yo winning half-sister to French 5.5f Listed winner Diableneyev.

MANU ET CORDE (IRE)
9/3 b c Teofilo - Tiffilia (Macho Uno)
Trainer: Jim Bolger Owner: Mrs J S Bolger Sales price: n/a

Full brother to useful Irish 9.5-12.5f 3yo winner Change of Velocity. Dam an Irish 7f 2yo winner who was the daughter of an unraced half-sister to the maiden dam of 2020 French 1m 2yo Group 1 winner Gear Up and Irish 1m 1f 2yo Group 3 winner Guaranteed (both by Teofilo).

MOJOMAKER (IRE)
30/1 b c Mehmas - Ajla (Exceed And Excel)
Trainer: David Loughnane Owner: David Lowe Sales price: £40,000 (Compas Equine/Dave Loughnane)

Half-brother to 6f 2yo winner Swift Mover. Dam a twice-raced maiden half-sister to 1m 3yo Group 2/3 winner Independence (later dam of Eclipse Stakes winner Mount Nelson and Great Voltigeur Stakes winner/St Leger third Monitor Closely), very useful 8-10f winner Teslin and the maiden dam of Listed-placed Irish/US 5f-6.5f winner Spy Ring.

NIGHT TRAVELLER
28/2 ch f Night of Thunder - Travelling (Dubai Destination)
Trainer: Chelsea Banham Owner: Longview Stud & Bloodstock Ltd Sales price: 40,000gns (Vendor)

Fourth foal of a 7-9.5f winner who was a half-sister to useful UK/US 7-10f winner Bonfire Knight out of a 7f 3yo Listed-winning sister to useful 10f 3yo winner Adventuress and half-sister to fairly useful 7-10f winner Asharon; family of Royal Hunt Cup winner Teamwork.

PATRICIAN (IRE)
11/4 b f Kodiac - Jane's Memory (Captain Rio)
Trainer: Paddy Twomey Owner: Team Valor Sales price: 35,000gns (Paddy Twomey)

Second foal of a Group 3-placed 5-6f winner (including at Listed level) who was a half-sister to Group 3-placed 6f-1m winner (including twice at Listed level) On Her Toes (by Kodiac) and the dam of Group 3/Listed-placed 2020 dual 6f 2yo winner Internationaldream out of an 8-10f winning half-sister to smart multiple 5-7.5f winner (including at Group 2/3 level) The Kiddykid.

PIRATE JENNY (IRE)
4/2 b f Exceed And Excel - Chica Whopa (Oasis Dream)
Trainer: Ger Lyons Owner: Sean Jones/David Spratt/Mrs Lynne Lyons Sales price: 105,000gns (Gaelic Bloodstock)

Half-sister to Richmond Stakes winner Barraquero. Dam a 7f 3yo winner who was a half-sister to Italian 6f 2yo Listed winner Jezebel (later dam of US 6f 3yo Listed winner Ancient Goddess) out of a French 6f 2yo Listed-winning half-sister to 10f 3yo Listed winner Always On A Sunday and the dam of 5f 2yo Listed winner Signs.

QUEEN VENDOME (FR)
26/2 gr f Kingman - Classe Vendome (Kendargent)
Trainer: Frederic Rossi Owner: Guy Pariente Sales price: n/a

Second foal of a useful French 9-10f 2yo winner who was a half-sister to Poule d'Essai des Pouliches winner Style Vendome and French 1m 2yo Listed winner/Poule d'Essai des Poulains runner-up Prestige Vendome out of a Listed-placed French 5.5-6f 2yo winner; family of 2yo Group 3 winners Bungle Inthejungle (5f, twice) and Dobby Road (5.5f).

ROCKET YOGI (IRE)
7/4 ch c Fast Company - Yogi's Girl (Harbour Watch)
Trainer: Jane Chapple-Hyam Owner: Gordon Li Sales price: 40,000gns (Jane Chapple-Hyam Racing)

First foal of a useful dual 5f 2yo winner who was a half-sister to Lowther Stakes winner Living In The Past out of a maiden half-sister to Group 3-placed multiple 5-7f winner Outer Space and the dam of 2020 Mill Reef Stakes winner Alkumait; family of Queen Elizabeth II Stakes winner Markofdistinction and triple 2m Group 2 winner/Ascot Gold Cup runner-up Opinion Poll.

SHANKO
22/3 b c Oasis Dream - Beach Bunny (High Chaparral)
Trainer: Stuart Williams Owner: Opulence Thoroughbreds Sales price: £50,000 (Opulence Thoroughbreds)

Full brother to Group 3-placed 6-7f winner (including twice at Listed level) Naadirr, a three-parts brother to Irish 6f 2yo Listed winner Beach Belle (by Invincible Spirit; also dam of 2020 7f 3yo Listed winner Surf Dancer) and a half-brother to very useful 7-10.5f winner Marronnier. Dam a Group 1-placed Irish 8-9f winner (including at Listed level) from the family of 1000 Guineas winner Miss France.

TARTAN CHIEF
25/2 br c Dark Angel - Pink Symphony (Montjeu)
Trainer: Paul & Oliver Cole Owner: Mrs Fitri Hay Sales price: n/a

Half-brother to Group 2/3-placed 5-10f winner Highland Chief and two other winners. Dam an Irish 12f Group 3 winner who was closely related to Group 1-placed UK/US 6-9.5f winner (including at Group/Grade 3 level)/Poule d'Essai des Pouliches third Fantasia (dam of 2020 10f 3yo Group 3 winner Berlin Tango) and a half-sister to the dam of French 10f 3yo Group 2 winner Western Hymn.

TOP EXHIBIT
28/1 b c Showcasing - Must Be Me (Trade Fair)
Trainer: Archie Watson Owner: Mohammed Rashid Sales price: 130,000gns (Blandford Bloodstock)

Closely related to 2020 Irish 6f 2yo winner Luminesce (by Muhaarar). Dam a UK/Italian 6f-1m winner who was a three-parts sister to useful 5-7f winner Roodle (later dam of Queen Anne Stakes winner Accidental Agent) and a half-sister to 2020 Sussex Stakes winner Mohaather and US 6.5f/1m Grade 2 winner Prize Exhibit (both by Showcasing).

MARTEN'S FAVOURITES

Here are a few of the two-year-olds that I like from those featured in the book. My views are drawn from personal knowledge of the families, not information, with a preference for horses that are bred with long-term potential.

Broadspear (Roger Varian): As you will perceive from my nominations for this feature I am drawn towards horses that are stoutly bred on the dam's side. I like to see the speed with the sire and the stamina with the dam's sire. I much prefer that to a page showing a staying sire and a sprint-bred mare. Horses that fall into the latter category have what I call an 'upside-down pedigree'. This colt is by 2009 Prix du Jockey Club winner Le Havre, who was retired to stud after his Chantilly success, and the first foal of a maiden half-sister to the Group 3 winner Dundonnell, winner of five races and over £800,000 in prize money. The family traces back to the top-class sprinter and sire Danehill and it is encouraging that the colt is already pleasing his trainer.

Bunker Bay (William Knight): First foal of a dual winner, from just six starts, full sister to Group 3 Cumberland Lodge winner Star Storm and the lightly raced Sargasso Sea, a winner of one from three starts and from the family of Champagne Stakes winner Almushahar. By Australia, who sired two Group 1 winners in 2020, and bred to thrive at three. Watch for backend promise.

Ching Shih (David Simcock): This daughter of Lope De Vega is from one of Miss Kirsten Rausing's most successful families. Her dam Madame Chiang ploughed through the mud to win the Group 1 Qipco British Champions Fillies & Mares Stakes at Ascot in 2014. She is a full sister to the useful Mister Chiang and Chinoiseries so expect this filly to do well when the emphasis is on stamina. The type to show up in an autumn maiden on easy ground.

Cowboy Justice (Jessica Harrington): Another son of Lope De Vega with a pedigree for next year. His dam Starflower won her first two starts as a three-year-old and only raced twice more before retiring to the paddocks. She is a three-parts sister to Prix Jean Prat winner Mutual Trust and middle-distance winner Postcode, from the family of Oaks runner-up All At Sea. The fact that he has already shown his trainer something is most encouraging given the long-term profile of his pedigree. This is a family I like and his trainer is sure to get the best out of him.

Dark Note (Joseph O'Brien): Night Of Thunder colt and a half-brother to three-race winner Rosa Gold, still in training with Rae Guest. Their dam Rosa Grace, by Lomitas, won over 7f at two and a 1m 2f Listed race and is related to winners, from the family of Dark Angel. Looks one for midsummer maidens.

Denning (Sir Mark Prescott): Son of Acomb Stakes winner Recorder, who retired to stud after his two-year-old season, from the family of Oaks winner Casual Look. Home-bred by Brian Haggas, whose son William trained the sire for the Queen, and will stay beyond a mile next season. Has the profile of a slow burner for his patient connections.

Deauville Legend (James Ferguson): A strong middle-distance pedigree, by Sea The Stars out of a German 11f-winning daughter of Hernando. Reported by his trainer to be a "big colt", he looks one to keep on the back burner for the autumn and next season.

Duelist (Richard Hannon): This two-year-old is a half-brother to 1000 Guineas winner Billesdon Brook, a filly close to my heart having nominated her at 66/1 for the Newmarket Classic on the strength of a remarkable performance to win a nursery the previous season at Goodwood. Although that was a relatively modest contest, the way she extricated herself from a pocket and changed gear to get up close home was extraordinary. She retired to stud the winner of seven races including the Group 1 Sun Chariot Stakes. Although the dam Coplow is by staying influence Manduro, Billesdon Brook was never tried over a mile and a half despite being bred for the trip on both sides. It will be interesting to see how this half-brother gets on.

Electress (Ralph Beckett): Bred to stay well, by Galileo and out of Irish 1,000 Guineas winner Just The Judge, a favourite of mine who ran second to Sky Lantern in the Newmarket Guineas before winning in Ireland. Just The Judge went on to win the 1m 2f E. P. Taylor Stakes at Woodbine. This filly could be classy next year over a mile or more. Very nice family.

Elite Etoile (Jonathan Portman): I can't think of any trainer who does as well with bargain basement acquisitions as Jonathan Portman. This former assistant to Luca Cumani trained 1,000gns yearling acquisition Mild Illusion to win four races culminating in the Listed Bosra Sham Stakes at Newmarket. She was subsequently sold for 160,000gns, while the same season he trained Walk On Walter and Ashazuri to win three races each. Three years earlier he sent out Mrs Danvers to win five of her seven starts including the Group 3 Cornwallis Stakes, ending that season the winner of almost £200,000 in prize money. Remarkably she had also cost just £1,000. Elite Etoile was a little more than those two, at £16,000, and out of a Dansili mare he is more stoutly bred, but given the trainer's proven track record you can rest assured he will get the best out of him.

Franklin William (Andrew Balding): This son of Frankel is out of the Dubawi mare Kiyoshi, a winner three times including the Group 3 Albany Stakes and the following season the Group 3 Sceptre Stakes. At stud she has produced dual-purpose performer Iron Heart, a winner twice for this trainer and then over hurdles for David Pipe. Franklin William is expected to be effective this season before stepping up to a mile and a quarter or more next year.

Heatherdown Hero (Michael Bell): As you will soon appreciate, if you haven't already, I am drawn towards horses with middle-distance pedigrees and, consequently, long-term futures. This son of Sea The Moon is the first foal of a dual-winning daughter of Archipenko, so he has stamina on both sides of his pedigree. Had I been at his sale I would certainly have taken a look at 22,000gns.

Honky Tonk Man (Roger Charlton): This 68,000gns son of Tamayuz is a half-brother to a handful of winners including HMS President, a horse that I included in my *Dark Horses Annual* as a handicapper to follow. Unfortunately, despite running well on numerous occasions, HMS President has not won as many times as his ability warrants. This is a good family, though, packed with winners and I'm encouraged that his trainer describes him as being "laid-back".

Lionel (David Menuisier): Philippa Cooper of Normandie Stud likes to spread her horses about and Lionel is the second foal of her smart Group 2 Park Hill Stakes winner Gretchen, who is a half-sister to Irish St Leger winner Duncan, Group 2 Doncaster Cup winner Samuel and the useful Deirdre and Stella Bellissima. This is an extremely successful middle-distance family and Lionel is entitled to enhance the page even further.

Lumberjack (Tom Clover): I've been keeping an eye on Tom Clover, who is one of the country's up-and-coming trainers having spent his earlier days with Charlie Longsdon and David Simcock. Lumberjack is a half-brother to a handful of winners including eight-race winner Sands Chorus from the family of top stayer Franklins Gardens and Group 3 winner Polar Ben. I have a fondness for Mastercraftsman's progeny and this grey could be well bought at 20,000gns.

Mimikyu (John & Thady Gosden): This family will look even better if her full sister Indigo Girl has a good season. Indigo Girl is already useful, having won last season's May Hill Stakes and finished runner-up in the Fillies' Mile. The family name was established with the successful exploits of full sister Journey, winner of six of her 17 starts including the Group 1 Qipco British Champions Fillies & Mares. The dam Montare won the French St Leger, so there is plenty of stamina on the page.

M'Lady Nicole (William Haggas): This daughter of Sea The Stars is a full sister to Knight To Behold, a very useful late developer who was adroitly placed by Harry Dunlop to win a Group 2 at Deauville as a three-year-old. He later ran third in the Group 2 York Stakes over an extended 1m 2f as a four-year-old. Others in this very successful family include 1m 2f Group 3 winner Beauty O'

Gwaun, Japanese 1m 3f to 2m 1f winner Cosmo Meadow and Irish/US winner Angelonmyshoulder. The dam is a full sister to a Derby third and a half-sister to St Leger winner Millenary and middle-distance Group 3 winner Head In The Clouds. This is a family I have monitored for many years and I expect her to enhance the family name.

Nobel (Andrew Balding): Not cheap at 825,000gns but bred to be effective over middle distances next season, by Lope De Vega out of 1m 4f winner Starlet, a daughter of Sea The Stars. He is a half-brother to Group 3 winner Love Locket and dual winner Raakib Alhawa, a son of Kingman, who was trained by David Simcock – a horse that he once told had top-class potential but struggled with injuries.

Novel Legend (Hugo Palmer): A son of Nathaniel and a half-brother to Clive Cox's Group 3 and Group 2 Rockfel Stakes winner Isabella Giles and a German Listed winner. The dam won a Group 3 at two and is from the family of Irish 2,000 Guineas third Lope Y Fernandez. Isabella Giles is by the speedy Belardo but this colt won't be as precocious.

Reach For The Moon (John & Thady Gosden): The dam Golden Stream won three, including twice at Listed level, and was twice placed over 7f in Group 3 company. She is a full sister to Oaks runner-up Flight Of Fancy and three more winners over middle distances. This son of Sea The Stars has a pedigree that is all about next year and a distance of ground.

Sonny Liston (Charles Hills): This one's dam Stars In Your Eyes has produced four winners of 14 races including Group 2 winner and Group 1-placed Dame Malliot, five-race winner Zabeel Champion and Banksea, a full brother to this colt who was rated 104 at his peak. The dam is a half-sister to, among others, four-race winner Wild Savannah. This son of Lawman may need time as he's from a late-developing family.

Space Odyssey (Richard Hannon): The dam Lady Of Dubai ran third in the 2015 Oaks but failed to build on that in her five subsequent runs. Bred by Luca Cumani's Fittocks Stud, she went to Shamardal and produced Royal Harmony, now in training with the Crisfords. The family traces back to St Leger winner Millenary and Knight To Behold, so with Sea The Stars as the sire this colt looks like being one for middle distances next year.

Spirit of UAE (Ed Walker): Son of first-season sire Postponed, winner of the Juddmonte International and Coronation Cup, out of an unraced daughter of Irish 1,000 Guineas winner Saoire. Sire's stock likely to improve with time, as he did, and this colt could look very well bought at 38,000gns once he matures and has a distance of ground to cover. Expect to see him show something this backend.

Springtime (Simon & Ed Crisford): Another from the first crop of Postponed out of the Dansili mare Frangipanni, whose dam is from the family of July Cup winner Firenze and Listed winner Zidane, trained very successfully by James Fanshawe. The distaff side of the family acted very well on soft ground. Bred with the long term in mind.

Surrey Knight (Charlie Fellowes): This son of 2009 Prix du Jockey Club winner Le Havre is a daughter of Prix de Diane runner-up Millionaia, a daughter of Peintre Celebre. This is a strong staying family so it's most encouraging the colt is showing early promise in his work at home.

Sweet William (Roger Charlton): This son of Sea The Stars is a half-brother to Hurricane Lane, a winner of his only start at two and then a winner again of a decent 1m 2f Class 3 contest at Newbury this spring. The dam won a Listed race over two miles and is a half-sister to Seal Of Approval, winner of the Group 1 British Champions Fillies & Mares Stakes at Ascot. This is the pedigree of a horse for the long term.

Transpire (Sir Michael Stoute): Never will I forget the joy on the face of Her Majesty the Queen when Estimate won her the 2013 Ascot Gold Cup, having battled bravely to hold the determined challenge of Simenon by a neck. The following year the mare won the Group 2 Doncaster Cup before retiring to the paddocks after one more run. Sent to Dubawi she produced Calculation, a winner of three staying races but return visits to the sire have not, at the time of writing, borne fruit. The dam is a half-sister to some of the Aga Khan's best stayers, among them Ascot Gold Cup winner Enzeli, Irish Oaks winner Ebadiyla and Group 1 winner Edabiya, and the switch from Dubawi to Frankel may inject more fire into the family.

Waldstar (Andre Fabre): Half-brother to St Leger winner Masked Marvel, German 1m Group 3 Listed winner Waldnah and to French Group 3 winner Waldlerche (the dam of Arc winner Waldgeist and this season's progressive colt Waldkonig). This son of Sea The Stars has the profile of a top middle-distance performer for next season.

SIRES WITH FIRST TWO-YEAR-OLDS 2021

BY MICHELLE KINANE

Every Flat season unleashes some potentially exciting young sires with their first two-year-olds. It also gives an insight into how established European sires will perform as sires of sires. Perennial champion sire Galileo, who has emerged into a solid sire of sires, is represented by some intriguing recruits. They include European champion Churchill, triple Group 1 winner Decorated Knight, globetrotting superstar Highland Reel and the regally bred Ulysses. Leading juvenile sires Scat Daddy and Kodiac are also well represented including Royal Ascot-winning juveniles Caravaggio and Ardad. Irish National stud stalwart Invincible Spirit has two Group 1-winning sons in Profitable and National Defense. Darley's leading sire Dubawi, who is already emerging as a sire of sires, has multiple Group 1 winner Postponed, French-based sire Zarak and Group winner Time Test. Another Darley stalwart and exciting sire of sires Iffraaj has another intriguing recruit in Group 1-winning miler Ribchester. Meanwhile world champion Sea The Stars has French-based Group 1-winning miler Zelzal to represent him.

Aclaim (IRE)
Bay colt by Acclamation out of Aris by Danroad
A paternal half-brother to European record-breaking freshman sire Mehmas, Aclaim could also be in for a successful season with his debut crop. This Group 1 Prix de la Foret winner is from the stallion-making family of Montjeu and is out of a stakes-performing half-sister to Classic heroine Again. His first yearlings made up to 145,000gns. Aclaim stands at the National Stud in Newmarket for a fee of £9,500.

Almanzor (FR)
Bay colt by Wootton Bassett out of Darkova by Maria's Mon
One of the first high-class sons of his sire at stud, he was champion European three-year-old of his year. He is the best performer out of his dam, who also produced the stakes-placed Troarn, a full-sister to Almanzor. This is from the immediate family of the high-class mare Darjina as well as French Derby victor Darsi. Almanzor's first yearlings sold for up to €260,000. He stands at Haras d'Etreham in France for a fee of €30,000.

Al Wukair (IRE)
Bay colt by Dream Ahead out of Macheera by Machiavellian
One of the top French milers of his generation and the only high level-winning son of his sire at stud. Al Wukair is a full brother to the stakes-placed Dream Today. They are out of a daughter of French Oaks heroine Caerlina. This female

line also produced dual Classic-placed La Nuit Rose, multiple Group 1-placed Sri Putra and last season's Group 3 scorer Antonia De Vega. Al Wukair's first crop yearlings sold for up to €95,000. He stands at Haras de Bouquetot for a fee of €6,000.

Ardad (IRE)
Bay colt by Kodiac out of Good Clodora by Red Clubs
A son of leading two-year-old sire Kodiac. Ardad was himself a top juvenile winning the Windsor Castle Stakes at Royal Ascot. He hails from a family synonymous with producing precocious horses including Group 1 winners Maarek and Anita's Prince. He also hails from the same female line of Group winner Swiss Dream. His first yearlings made up to 55,000gns. Ardad stands at Overbury Stud for a fee of £4,000.

Arrogate (USA)
Grey colt by Unbridled's Song out of Bubbler by Distorted Humor
The American stallion ranks was dealt a massive blow with the sudden passing of Arrogate following a neurological issue. His final crop are foals in 2021. He became one of the world's richest ever earners winning the Dubai World Cup and Pegasus World Cup in what turned out to be a glorious racing career. He is the best performer from his female line. His third dam Meadow Star was champion juvenile filly of her year. This is also the line of dual Grade 1 heroine Belle Gallantey. Arrogate's first crop were warmly received with a top price of $750,000.

Attendu (FR)
Bay colt by Acclamation out of Gwenseb by Green Tune
A Group 3-winning son of leading juvenile sire and sire of sires Acclamation. He is a half-brother to stakes horses Foreign Tune, Impassable, Spotify and Gwendola. This is also the female line of Grade 1 winner Seville and Italian champion Will Dancer. Attendu's first crop sold for up to €72,000. He stands at Haras du Quesnay for a fee of €3,000.

Caravaggio (USA)
Grey colt by Scat Daddy out of Mekko Hokte by Holy Bull
A precocious son of leading juvenile sire and sire of sires Scat Daddy. Caravaggio is a half-brother to Grade 2 winner My Jen. She herself is the dam of Japanese Graded placed Satono Gold. Caravaggio's dam line includes a host of Grade/Group 1 winners including Foundry, Spring At Last, Sharp Lisa, Bien Bien and South African champion filly Oh Susanna. His first yearlings went through the American and European sales ring with a top price of $400,000. Caravaggio has since relocated to Coolmore's American-based Ashford Stud where he stands at $25,000.

Churchill (IRE)
Bay colt by Galileo out of Meow by Storm Cat
A regally bred son of Galileo, out of a stakes-winning half-sister to three stakes winners including Aloof. Churchill is a full brother to Group 1 heroine Clemmie and Group 3 winner Blenheim Palace. The second dam is European champion filly Airwave. This is from the same family as Group 1-winning sprinters Jwala and Dream Of Dreams. His first crop yearlings realised up to 340,000gns. Churchill stands at Coolmore for €30,000.

Cotai Glory (GB)
Chesnut colt by Exceed And Excel out of Continua by Elusive Quality
This son of Exceed And Excel was a Group-winning two-year-old and was second in the Group 1 King's Stand Stakes as a four-year-old. His full sister Excel's Beauty was stakes-placed while their half-sister Permission achieved stakes success. They are out of an unraced full sister to Middle Park Stakes-placed Huntdown. Their three parts sister Falling Petals is the dam of last season's Group-winning two-year-old Saffron Beach. His first yearlings realised up to 180,000gns. Cotai Glory stands at Tally Ho Stud for a fee of €5,000.

Decorated Knight (GB)
Chesnut colt by Galileo out of Pearling by Storm Cat
This regally bred son of Galileo hails from an extraordinary female-producing family. He is out of a full sister to champion sire Giant's Causeway and high-class producer You'resothrilling, already the dam of five stakes horses including Group 1 winners Marvellous, Happily and Gleneagles. Another half-sister Love Me Only is the dam of dual Classic-placed Storm The Stars. Decorated Knight's first crop yearlings sold for up to 44,000gns. He stands this year at the Irish National Stud for €7,500.

De Treville (GB)
Bay colt by Oasis Dream out of Dar Re Mi by Singspiel
This lightly raced son of multiple Group 1 heroine Dar Re Mi is equipped with a royal pedigree. He is a half-brother to leading miler and young sire Too Darn Hot as well as Group-winning fillies Lah Ti Dar and So Mi Dar. Dar Re Mi herself is a half-sister to Group 1 winners Rewilding, Diaghilev and Darazari. This is from the female-producing line of leading sire and broodmare sire Darshaan as well as Group 2 heroine Fanny Logan. His first crop yearlings sold at public auction made up to €90,000. De Treville stands at Haras du Mezeray for a fee of €2,500.

Ectot (GB)
Bay colt by Hurricane Run out of Tonnara by Linamix
Ectot is the second high-level winner out of his dam Tonnara. He is a half-brother to Group 1-winning miler and sire Most Improved. Tonnara herself is a half-sister to stakes performers Johnny Barnes, Albisola and Bufera. This

female line also produced Classic-placed Daban. Ectot's first yearlings sold for up to €55,000. He stands at Haras de Bouquetot in France at a fee of €4,000.

El Kabeir (USA)
Grey colt by Scat Daddy out of Great Venue by Unbridled's Song
The latest son of emerging sire of sires to join the stallion ranks. El Kabeir was typical of his sire becoming a Group winner as a juvenile and placing in further Group races. He raced exclusively in America. His dam is a half-sister to stakes horses Too Much Bling, Barnsy, Ready For Roses and Got Bling. The family traces back to German champion sprinter Mister Slippers. His yearlings realised six figures last year including prices of up to 180,000gns. El Kabeir stands at Yeomanstown Stud for a fee of €6,000.

Galileo Gold (IRE)
Chesnut colt by Paco Boy out of Galicuix by Galileo
The only son of Group 1-winning miler Paco Boy at stud, he proved himself one of Europe's top milers winning the Group 1 2000 Guineas and St James's Palace Stakes. His dam is an unraced half-sister to dual Group 1-winning sprinter Goldream. This is from the immediate female line of champion sire Montjeu as well as Classic heroine Again and Group 1-winning miler and fellow freshman sire Aclaim. His first crop yearlings realised up to 82,000gns. Galileo Gold stands at Tally Ho Stud for €5,000.

Highland Reel (IRE)
Bay colt by Galileo out of Hveger by Danehill
A top-class multiple Group 1-winning globetrotter out of a sister to champion Australian older horse Elvstroem and a half-sister to champion Australian miler Haradasun. Highland Reel is a brother to Derby-placed sire Idaho, Australian Group 1 winner Cape Of Good Hope and Group 3 winner Nobel Prize. This is also the immediate family of champion Australian sprinter and leading juvenile sire Starspangledbanner. His first yearlings sold for up to 320,000gns which included a half-brother to Group 1-winning miler Palace Pier. Highland Reel stands at Coolmore Stud for a fee of €10,000.

Jack Hobbs (GB)
Bay colt by Halling out of Swain's Gold by Swain
Jack Hobbs was recognised as one of the leading colts in his Classic generation winning the Group 1 Irish Derby. He followed that up with another victory in the Dubai Sheema Classic. His second dam Golden Pond was a Grade 2 winner. He hails from the same female-producing family as Group 2 winner Pollenator and Australian Derby winner Dance The Day Away. Jack Hobbs' first crop sold for up to 24,000gns and his stock may need time to progress. He stands at Overbury Stud for a fee of £3,000.

Mondialiste (IRE)
Bay colt by Galileo out of Occupandiste by Kaldoun
Mondialiste triumphed in two of America's most recognised Grade 1 turf races. He is the highest level winner out of his dam Occupandiste. She is the dam of three other stakes horses and is best known as the granddam of French Classic winner Intello. Her daughters have also produced Group 3 winners Kalahara and Sasparella. This is the immediate family of leading miler Ribchester as well as Group 1 winners Elnadim and Mehthaaf. Mondialiste has since relocated from Elwick Stud to Haras d'Annebault and stands for a fee of €4,000.

National Defense (GB)
Bay colt by Invincible Spirit out of Angel Falls by Kingmambo
National Defense was the joint top-rated juvenile colt of his year following victory in the Group 1 Prix Jean-Luc Lagardere. He is a half-brother to dual stakes-placed Nordic Defense. Their dam Angel Falls is a half-sister to Classic-placed Anna Salai and stakes horses Advice and Iguazu Falls. This is the female family of Grade 1 heroine Ave and her stakes-winning half-sister Anipa as well as Australian Group 1 winners Helmet and Epaulette. National Defense's first crop yearlings realised up to 75,000gns. He stands alongside his sire at the Irish National Stud at a fee of €5,000.

Postponed (IRE)
Bay colt by Dubawi out of Ever Rigg by Dubai Destination
Postponed developed into a top older horse winning some of Europe's most prestigious Group 1 middle-distance races. He hails from a solid female line. He is a half-brother to Italian Group 1 heroine God Given. Their second dam Bianca Nera was champion juvenile filly in Ireland. She produced three stakes horses at stud and is the granddam of Grade 1-placed Turning Top and Group 3 scorer Robin Hoods Bay. This is also the family of Classic-placed and Group 1-winning Simply Perfect as well as fellow Classic-placed pair Bondi Beach and Gale Force Ten. Postponed's first yearling realised up to 145,000gns. He stands at Dalham Hall Stud for a fee of £7,500.

Profitable (IRE)
Bay colt by Invincible Spirit out of Dani Ridge by Indian Ridge
Profitable was undoubtedly one of the best sprinters of his sire Invincible Spirit. A winner of the Group 1 King's Stand Stakes, he was rated superior to his sire during his racing career. He is the highest rated performer out of his dam who has produced a further four stakes horses. They include Group-placed stakes producers Danidh Dubai and Full Mandate. His other half-siblings include Group 3 winner Ridge Ranger and Group-placed Crafty Madam. Profitable's first yearlings realised up to 160,000gns. He stands at Kildangan Stud for a fee of €10,000.

Recorder (GB)
Chesnut colt by Galileo out of Memory by Danehill Dancer
A Group 2-winning juvenile out of a Group 2-winning juvenile. Recorder is also a full brother to Grade 3 winner Call To Mind. Their three-part sibling Learn By Heart won a Group 3 in Sweden. Their dam Memory is a half-sister to Group 3 winner Remember Alexander. Recorder's first yearlings sold for up to €70,000. He stands at Montfort et Preaux in France for a fee of €4,000.

Ribchester (IRE)
Bay colt by Iffraaj out of Mujarah by Marju
Ribchester proved himself one of Europe's best milers winning four Group 1 mile races. He is the only multiple Group 1-winning miler of his sire at stud. He is the best performer out of his dam who is a half-sister to four stakes horses. These include local Grade 1-winning Matterhorn, Group 3 winner Bangkok, Group 3 winner Tactic and the stakes pair Yaazy and Zahoo, dam of Group 3 winner Convergence. This is from the immediate family of champion filly Mehthaaf, champion Italian filly Najah, champion sprinter Elnadim and French champion Intello. Ribchester stands at Kildangan Stud at a fee of €17,500.

The Grey Gatsby (IRE)
Grey colt by Mastercraftsman out of Marie Vison by Entrepreneur
A top-class French Classic winner and one of the first sons of his sire at stud. The Grey Gatsby is the highest achiever produced by his dam. She in turn is a half-sister to stakes performers Steady As A Rock and Saint Thomas. His second dam is out of Group 1 winner Maximova. She later turned into a successful broodmare producing Group 1 winners Septieme Ciel and Macoumba. This female line also produced leading American sire Temple City. The Grey Gatsby's first yearlings sold for up to €130,000. He resides at Haras du Petit Tellier in France for a fee of €7,000.

Time Test (GB)
Bay colt by Dubawi out of Passage Of Time by Dansili
A multiple Group-winning son of leading sire Dubawi, he is the best performer out of Group 1-winning Passage Of Time. His dam is a half-sister to Group 1-winning Timepiece and a full sister to stakes horses Father Time and Continuum. Time Test hails from a solid female line which includes leading older horse Twice Over and Grade 1-winning Yoshida. This is also the family of Grade 1 winners Antonoe, Hilda's Passion and champion sprinter Banshee Breeze. Time Test's first yearlings sold for up to 150,000gns. He stands at the National Stud for a fee of £8,500.

Ultra (IRE)
Chesnut colt by Manduro out of Epitome by Nashwan
A Group 1-winning two-year-old from the successful Monsun sire line. Ultra is a half-brother to Group 3 heroine Synopsis. They are out of a daughter

of Italian champion sprinter Proskona. She is a half-sister to the dam of champions Bosra Sham, Hector Protector and Group 1 scorer Shanghai. This is from the female family of Group 1 winner and sire Act One. Ultra's first yearlings made up to €30,000. He stands at Darley's French-based Haras du Logis for a fee of €5,000.

Ulysses (IRE)
Chestnut colt by Galileo out of Light Shift by Kingmambo
Ulysses is undoubtedly one of the more regally bred sires among this year's freshman stallions. He is by perennial champion Galileo and Classic heroine Light Shift. Ulysses progressed rapidly from three to four and was subsequently crowned champion European older horse. He is the best performer out of his Classic-winning dam who sadly died prematurely. She is a half-sister to champion older mare Shiva, later the granddam of juvenile Group-winning Threat. Another of Light Shift's half-sisters is the granddam of multiple Grade 1 winner Main Sequence. Her full sister Strawberry Fledge produced champion older French colt Cloth Of Stars. This is also the female line of Brazilian champion Jeune-Turc. Ulysses's first yearlings made up to 320,000gns. He stands at Cheveley Park Stud for a fee of £10,000.

Zarak (IRE)
Bay colt by Dubawi out of Zarkava by Zamindar
This exquisitely bred colt possesses huge sire appeal being by champion sire Dubawi out of unbeaten champion mare Zarkava. Zarak's half-siblings include Group 1 placed Zarkamiya and the stakes-winning Zaykava. Zarkava herself is a half-sister to Group 3-winning Zarshana, dam of the stakes-placed Zawara. Another half-sister is Zarakiysha, dam of Group 3 placed Zarzali. This is also the immediate family of leading hurdler Zarkandar. Zarak's first yearlings sold for up to €112,000. He stands at his breeders' French-based Haras de Bonneval for a fee of €12,000.

Zelzal (FR)
Brown colt by Sea The Stars out of Olga Prekrasa by Kingmambo
The only Group 1-winning miler by his sire at stud, Zelzal is a half-brother to Group 3 winner Ibiza. His dam's half-sisters produced the stakes performing pair of Ice Cave and Zenbennie. The third dam is the multiple Group-winning State Crystal. Her best performer at stud was the stakes performing Crystal Curling. She is the granddam of the Group-winning pair of Libran and Three Rocks. This is from the female line of Group 1 winner Crystal Music and Group winners Dubai Success, Solar Crystal, Tchaikovsky and Ocovango. Zelzal's first yearlings sold for up to €70,000. He stands at Haras de Bouquetot for a fee of €6,000.

THREE GENTLEMEN - A TRIBUTE

Horse racing has lost three of its most prominent owners and breeders in Prince Khalid Abdullah, Sheikh Hamdan Al Maktoum and David Thompson during the past five months.

To list the above trio's achievements, and indeed top-level winners, would provide sufficient material to fill this book.

Since purchasing his first broodmare, **Metair** in 1979, Khalid Abdullah lovingly built up Juddmonte Farms into the world-leading breeding and racing organisation we see today. The likes of **Sookera**, **Razyana**, **Bahamian** and **Slightly Dangerous** soon followed in the 1980s and became the bedrock upon which Juddmonte's breeding operation was built.

Not mentioned above was the acquisition of **Rockfest** from Jock Whitney's dispersal sale in 1983. She enjoyed relatively minor success as a broodmare. However, she did produce the 1993 Lancashire Oaks winner, **Rainbow Lake**, who was subsequently the dam of three Group/Graded winners and a skittish but talented filly called **Kind**. She in turn, of course, produced probably the best racehorse seen in the famous pink, green and white silks and indeed in recent racing history - **Frankel**.

Another notable purchase around that time was Ferrans Stud in County Meath in 1982. One member of the broodmare band that came as part of the deal was an unremarkable dual winner by the name of **Fleet Girl**. She went on to produce the 1987 Oaks runner-up, **Bourbon Girl**, who herself provided Juddmonte with a pair of Group winners, including one by Shirley Heights named **Apogee**, before her untimely death in 1997.

Apogee would in turn go on to produce Prix de Diane runner-up, **Dance Routine**, later dam of multiple Group/Grade 1 winner, **Flintshire**, and a Listed winner by the name of **Concentric**. The latter, of course, proved to be the dam of eleven-time Group/Grade 1 winner, **Enable**.

The fact that both Frankel and Enable were third and fourth generation homebreds respectively encapsulates everything about what Juddmonte has evolved into. With Frankel's dam, Kind, passing away in March, and the very recent retirement of long-standing racing manager, Lord "Teddy" Grimthorpe, it does rather feel like the end of an era. Let's hope Juddmonte is able to continue in one form or another for several years to come and provide us with many more champions.

Hamdan Al Maktoum's entry into British racing came around the same time as that of Khalid Abdulla. He purchased what is now Shadwell Estate in Thetford in 1984.

Perhaps his most important bloodstock purchase came when procuring **Height of Fashion** from The Queen in 1982. A talented filly on the track, she was to become one of the finest broodmares of her generation off it. **Unfuwain**, **Nashwan** and **Nayef** were the headline acts, while Listed winner **Sarayir** went on to produce Shadwell a 1000 Guineas winner in **Ghanaati**.

Al Bahathri, **Salsabil**, **Harayir** and **Shadayid** were other high-class fillies, though they enjoyed rather mixed fortunes as broodmares. The first-named produced subsequent 2000 Guineas and Champion Stakes victor, **Haafhd**, who was also sired by Sheikh Hamdan's Dewhurst Stakes winner, **Alhaarth**.

In more recent years, the likes of **Taghrooda** and **Battaash** have flown the blue and white flag with great distinction, whilst underscoring the skill of Shadwell's team in sourcing stock from elsewhere.

Taghrooda's dam, **Ezima**, hails from one of the Aga Khan's best families and was purchased for 320,000gns soon after her racing days - which had yielded three wins at Listed level - had ended.

Battaash was a 200,000gns purchase as a yearling, and it's notable that the very best of grandam Portelet's descendants were all purchased by the Shadwell team. The aforementioned Battaash, Duke of York Stakes winner/ multiple Group 1 runner-up **Tasleet** (£52,000) and Champagne Stakes winner/ July Cup third **Etlaala** (160,000gns) were all well bought as yearlings at auction by Shadwell.

More than anything, Sheikh Hamdan was a tremendously loyal man to his staff - including riders and trainers - and is another who leaves an enduring legacy. I have barely scratched the surface when it comes to the magnitude of what he achieved in horse racing.

David and Patricia Thompson purchased Cheveley Park back in 1975 and enjoyed early success with the Gimcrack Stakes winner, **Music Boy**.

It was another sprinter, **Pivotal**, who was to shape the movement of Cheveley Park's breeding empire into the 21st century, despite being initially viewed as a source of 'cheap speed' when going to stud in 1997 (stood for a fee of £5/6,000 during his first five seasons as a sire).

However, that soon changed, to the extent that his fee had jumped to £85,000 by 2008, courtesy of the exploits of **Excellent Art**, **Halfway To Heaven**, **Kyllachy** and **Saoire**, alongside Cheveley Park's own **Chorist**, **Heaven Sent**, **Infallible**, **Peeress** and **Virtual**.

More recent success stories include **Addeybb**, **Farhh** and **Sariska**, all of whom proved best at trips above 1m, showcasing both Pivotal's durability and versatility as a stallion. He has also become one of the most prominent sires of broodmares in recent years, perhaps unsurprisingly given he's an easy outcross for breeders looking to mate their mares with stallions from the Sadler's Wells sireline.

It is hard to believe any of the above could have been dreamt of, let alone hoped for, when Pivotal finished ninth of 20 on his racecourse debut at Newbury back in the autumn of 1995.

Medicean was one of the first crop of homebred colts retained by the stud and went on to score three Group 1 victories during the 2001 season. As a stallion, he went on to produce several high-class performers, including Dutch Art and Garswood, both of whom stood as stallions at Cheveley Park Stud.

There are, of course, many other notable horses that have carried the famous red, white and blue silks over the years, such as Medicean's daughter, **Nannina**, **Russian Rhythm**, **Spacious**, **Echelon**, **Integral**, **Queen's Trust**, **Confidential Lady** and **Cesare**.

The last-named appeared once over hurdles, and it's the jumping game where Cheveley Park have invested so heavily and enjoyed such significant success recently via the likes of **Envoi Allen**, **Sir Gerhard**, **Ballyadam** and **A Plus Tard**.

Not that success in the National Hunt sphere was anything new for the Thompsons. Although the silks carried weren't those of Cheveley Park Stud, **Party Politics** was a notable jumper for the pair in the 1990s, winning the 1992 Grand National and finishing second in the race three years later.

Medicean died in 2018, whilst Pivotal was retired from active duty earlier this year. Both they, and more so Thompson, leave an indelible mark, both on the breeding scene and on horse racing in general. I am sure that his wife, Patricia, and all the team at Cheveley Park will continue to try and enhance that legacy for many more years to come.

Racing could ill-afford to lose three gentlemen in such a short space of time. Condolences to all their friends and loved ones.

HURWORTH
BLOODSTOCK

Proud sponsor of the
2020 Group 1 Coronation Cup

COMPETITIVE HORSES AT COMPETITIVE PRICES

KHATM (8,000gns)
6 wins from 11 starts (6 wins in the space of 5 weeks)

THREE C'S (<£10,000)
6 wins from 27 starts

SONGKRAN (16,000gns)
5 wins from 14 starts

PHOLAS (18,000gns)
4 wins from 10 starts (inc. AW Championships Fillies & Mares Final)

ISLAND OF LIFE (€25,000)
4 wins from 19 starts (inc. Gr.3 & Listed-placed)

MIRAGE MAC (22,000gns)
3 wins from 7 starts

INVOLVED (25,000gns)
2 wins from 3 starts

ALBERT CAMUS (40,000gns)
2 wins from 7 starts

FOUR WHEEL DRIVE (90,000gns)
4 wins from 8 starts (inc. Gr.2 & Gr.3)

MISS O CONNOR (<£100,000)
3 wins from 5 starts (inc. Gr.3 & Listed)

Many thanks for the fantastic continued support from trainers and owners.

HORSE INDEX

TRAINER INDEX

DAM INDEX

SIRE INDEX

Muhaarar	9, 21, 23, 38, 41, 59, 76, 103, 106, 117, 132, 135, 163, 240, 263, 283, 299, 302, 303, 305, 306, 330
Mukhadram	162
Nathaniel	12, 17, 64, 147, 215, 293
National Defense	139
Nayef	46
New Approach	49, 60, 74, 108, 116, 194, 221, 225, 233, 255, 284, 306
New Bay	21, 62, 80, 140, 152, 155, 187, 209, 246, 264
Night Of Thunder	52, 62, 150, 167, 220, 247, 251, 254, 260, 291, 295, 296, 303, 331
No Nay Never	8, 67, 198, 297, 309, 310, 317, 318, 319
Norse Dancer	64
Oasis Dream	9, 14, 25, 54, 68, 92, 117, 123, 131, 139, 197, 242, 278, 332, 341
Olympic Glory	109
Outstrip	118, 184
Paco Boy	342
Pearl Secret	158
Pivotal	69, 104, 134, 207, 250
Poet's Voice	142
Postponed	10, 56, 78, 123, 176, 182, 201, 217, 268
Pride Of Dubai	164, 207
Profitable	17, 35, 36, 37, 40, 63, 96, 108, 109, 118, 132, 143, 208, 225, 231, 259, 260, 261, 265, 324
Quality Road	313
Raven's Pass	69
Recorder	125, 161
Red Jazz	263
Reliable Man	141, 153
Ribchester	29, 36, 39, 71, 83, 181, 187, 190, 246, 254, 259, 274, 292, 293
Scat Daddy	340, 342
Sea The Moon	8, 23, 24, 97, 134, 223, 303
Sea The Stars	52, 76, 79, 87, 104, 105, 174, 186, 193, 227, 267, 277, 279, 280, 285, 286, 288, 290, 295, 305, 345
Shalaa	124
Shamardal	176, 177, 192, 257, 258, 268, 290, 296
Showcasing	43, 89, 91, 107, 112, 120, 128, 133, 140, 182, 183, 184, 218, 237, 238, 326, 333
Sixties Icon	10
Siyouni	6, 48, 61, 73, 80, 93, 97, 102, 126, 127, 170, 216, 221, 273, 278, 279, 280, 305
Slade Power	138, 148, 201
Starspangledbanner	21, 34, 66, 100, 107, 150, 174, 188, 197, 198, 222, 235, 247, 248, 291, 294, 327
Swiss Spirit	171
Tamayuz	24, 50, 110, 269, 289, 308
Teofilo	51, 270, 331
Territories	18, 81, 111, 125, 217, 261
The Gurkha	29, 47, 66, 153
The Last Lion	65, 206
Time Test	56, 61, 113, 115, 146 ,157, 158, 217
Twilight Son	45, 46, 47, 129, 204, 205, 297
Ulysses	28, 71, 85, 86, 131, 159, 160, 172, 226, 244, 245, 278, 281, 287, 307, 317, 327, 328
Unbridled's Song	340
Vadamos	154, 156, 170
War Front	277, 282, 294, 298, 310, 317, 319, 320, 329
Wootton Bassett	22, 32, 219, 234, 277, 321, 339
Zarak	65, 152, 200
Zoffany	85, 107, 122, 137, 266, 305, 307, 308, 324